The End and the Beginning:
The Nicaraguan Revolution

Also of Interest

†Available in hardcover and paperback.

Westview Special Studies on Latin America and the Caribbean

The End and the Beginning:
The Nicaraguan Revolution
Second Edition, Revised and Updated
John A. Booth

In this second, revised and updated edition, Dr. Booth assesses the performance of the revolutionary government since 1979. The structure and operation of the regime is closely examined, as well as its policies and their implementation. The author details the difficulties the Sandinistas have encountered with the breakdown of their revolutionary coalition and the emergence of domestic and external opposition. He also discusses the difficulty of achieving economic recovery due to the effects of economic reorganization, private sector fears, and external economic sanctions. Finally, Dr. Booth focuses on the foreign policy of the Sandinistas, in particular their increasingly tense relationship with the United States.

John A. Booth, associate professor of political science at North Texas State University, has written extensively on political violence in Latin America and is acquainted with Nicaraguans on all sides of the conflict. Research for this volume was conducted while he was a Fulbright lecturer in international relations at the National Autonomous University of Costa Rica and during several subsequent trips to the region. He is also coauthor (with Thomas W. Walker) of *Understanding Central America* (forthcoming from Westview Press).

The End and the Beginning:
The Nicaraguan Revolution

John A. Booth

Second Edition, Revised and Updated

Westview Press / Boulder and London

Westview Special Studies on Latin America and the Caribbean

Copyright © 1982, 1985 by Westview Press, Inc.

Published in 1985 in the United States of America by Westview Press, Inc., 5500 Central Avenue, Boulder, Colorado 80301; Frederick A. Praeger, Publisher

First edition published in 1982 by Westview Press, Inc.

Library of Congress Cataloging in Publication Data
Booth, John A.
  The end and the beginning.
  (Westview special studies on Latin America and the
  Caribbean)
  Bibliography: p.
  Includes index.
  1. Nicaragua—History—Revolution, 1979—Causes.
2. Nicaragua—Politics and government—1979–
3. Nicaragua—Politics and government—1937–1979.
I. Title. II. Series.
F1528.B66 1985   972.85'052   85-683
ISBN 0-8133-0108-4
ISBN 0-8133-0109-2 (pbk.)

Printed and bound in the United States of America

10   9   8   7   6   5   4   3   2

Contents

Figures and Tables

Preface to the Second Edition

Revisions to this edition concentrate largely upon expanding and updating material on the evolution of the government and policy of revolutionary Nicaragua (formerly Chapter 9) from 1979 through 1984. Material on government and opposition and on public policy are now divided into two substantially expanded chapters (9 and 10). Although some reviewers have commented that the theoretical material in Chapter 1 seemed too little related to subsequent substantive chapters for scholarly taste, many teachers have praised its inclusion as valuable for their students. The book was written both for scholars and for students, so I have taken the easy way out of the dilemma posed by writing the new material for one focus or the other, but Chapters 1 through 6 and Chapter 8 remain unchanged.

The generally kind reception of the first edition of this book by students, teachers, and reviewers has been most gratifying. To all of you who have been so encouraging I extend my sincere thanks. I am grateful to North Texas State University for travel assistance and other support for preparation of this manuscript, to Cathy Huante for table typing and patience, to Megan Schoeck for her extermination of a thousand gerund clauses, to the Latin American Studies Association for the opportunity to be a part of its observer delegation to the 1984 Nicaraguan elections, and to the Consejo Supremo Electoral for its cooperation and assistance in Managua. In the preparation of this second edition several people have been most helpful with their time, guidance, data, contacts, travel assistance, and goodwill. My heartfelt appreciation goes to Iván García, Carlos Vilas, Tom Walker, Mike Conroy, John Donahue, Laura Enríquez, Ann Henderson, Cris Arcos, and Halima López.

John A. Booth
Managua, 4 November 1984

Acknowledgments

Many people have helped me with this book. Assistance with obtaining data and contacts has come from Enrique Torres, Enrique Torres Rivas, Auxiliadora de Figueroa, Mirna Carmen López de López, Jorge Espinoza Estrada, Terri Shaw, Anthony González, Tom Walker, Mark Rosenberg, Neil Pearson, Fred Morris, Bob Meade, and the staffs of the Biblioteca Centroamericana of the University of Costa Rica and of the Library of the School of International Relations of the National Autonomous University of Costa Rica. John Newhagen graciously gave permission to use his fine photographs, and *Barricada* provided others. Other valuable support has come from Bob Meade and Gordon Murchie of the International Communications Agency in San José, Costa Rica, where I was a Fulbright lecturer during 1979–1980, the period in which much of the fieldwork for the book was done. I also received subsequent assistance in the preparation of the manuscript from the Division of Social Sciences of the University of Texas at San Antonio. Excellent discussions with Central American scholars have helped me understand the Nicaraguan revolution; my thanks to Roberto de la Ossa, Colón Bermúdez, Cristina Eguizábal, Francisco Rojas, Jorge Cáceres, and Enrique Torres Rivas. Typing has been performed conscientiously and graciously by Elisa Jiménez, Carolyn Luna, and Ada Chávez. Susan McRory's copy editing was superb. I am grateful to the proprietors of the Hotel Nuevo Siete Mares, who provided a home in Managua and many valuable favors and excellent meals.

I owe a special debt of gratitude to those who have read parts of the manuscript and shared with me their valuable insights and counsel: Tom Walker, Fred Morris, Mitch Seligson, Bill Carroll, Rob Patch, Karl Schmitt, Carl Leiden, and Julie Booth. My deepest thanks and love go to my wife, Julie, and my daughters, Caroline and Catherine, for their tolerance and love during my absences and grouchiness while working on this book.

J.A.B.

1
Revolutionary Theory and Nicaragua's Sandinista Revolution

Turbulence and disorder mark the frontier of history, where present and past break and blend into future, where vigor and growth are qualities which ultimately must redeem the inconvenience and unrest of an emerging social order.

—H. L. Nieburg[1]

On 17 July 1979, Anastasio Somoza Debayle fled Nicaragua, ending a forty-three-year dynastic dictatorship founded by his father. His flight capped eighteen years of guerrilla struggle and a year and a half of massive civil insurrection. Despite the powerful instruments of the Somoza regime and its broad institutional backing, once considered virtually invulnerable, a coalition of Nicaraguan social forces under the military leadership of the Sandinista National Liberation Front (Frente Sandinista de Liberación Nacional—FSLN) had found the means to shatter the despotic dynasty. This book seeks to explain how and why this rebellion occurred and how it succeeded, why the old regime failed, and what effects the subsequent revolution is having upon Nicaragua.

Several reasons justify studying the Nicaraguan revolution. Rebellion, revolution, and violence have long fascinated students of history[2] and today still constitute major lines of inquiry in history, political science, sociology, and philosophy.[3] This scholarly preoccupation may reflect in part the traditionally insecure status of scholars within rapidly changing societies, but the concern also falls clearly within a more general pattern of human interests. Few things have either been more deplored or attracted more enthusiastic attention than violence. Public altercations, riots, assassinations, and war all rivet our attention. Human beings study turmoil both to protect themselves from violence and to learn how to use it to promote their interests.[4] Violence does indeed mark history's frontiers, and thus it both threatens and teaches, both warns and attracts.

The appearance in Nicaragua of mass violence in the form of a great sociopolitical conflagration signifies great human problems drastically

1

confronted. Nicaragua's conflict can show us much about a complex social structure from observing its collapse and transformation. Moreover, the Nicaraguan revolution can teach us much about repression from its rejection, about the limits of corruption from its repudiation, and about the limits of certain kinds of public policy from its failure.

The Theory of Revolution: Key Aspects

The study of revolution is and has perennially been a favorite of scholars, but some of the discussion of social violence and revolution has generated more acrimony than consensus, while other aspects have simply proved unfruitful. However, certain major themes from the study of revolution and violence will help shed some light upon the Nicaraguan revolution.

Not even the definition of revolution has yet reached the status of scholarly consensus. The intellectual history of the very concept reveals that different historical moments have given the term widely divergent meanings.[5] At least four approaches to revolution compete with each other today: as the reordering of society, as an inevitable stage of historical development, as a permanent attribute of the ideal social order, and as a psychological outlet. The first two of these, of most interest to us here, share the notion that by revolution society becomes radically altered. The role of violence in revolution's definition has also become a sticking point for some.[6] One side insists that violence need not accompany massive change, the other that violence always accompanies extensive social reorganization. Although in theory the first perspective seems quite defensible, the empirical evidence certainly shows that sociopolitical violence serves as the midwife of radical change far more often than not.

We may skirt some of this definitional haggling by noting that the Nicaraguan insurrection was extremely violent, here rendering the issue moot. For this study, and for the sake of convenience and clarity, Greene's summary definition, culled from "the almost unanimous opinion of writers on the subject," serves admirably:

> "Revolution" . . . means an alteration in the personnel, structure, supporting myth, and functions of government by methods which are not sanctioned by prevailing constitutional norms. These methods almost invariably involve violence or the threat of violence against political elites, citizens, or both . . . and a relatively abrupt and significant change in the distribution of wealth and social status.[7]

Other students of revolution have attempted theory building based upon stages and revolutionary typologies. As for stages, all revolutions clearly pass through phases with distinctive characteristics. Nevertheless, efforts to systematize these stages and seek universal models of revolution have not been very successful.[8] Stage theories in particular have failed to explain why revolutions occur. Typological efforts have also proved rather barren as an avenue for theory building.[9] The flaws of typologies range from hopelessly elaborate lists of typifying criteria to purely idiosyncratic categories.[10]

On a brighter horizon, from the extensive descriptive analyses of revolutions have emerged more useful generalizations about important aspects of and commonalities among revolutions. Greene, Schmitt, and Leiden, and others[11] have reviewed this literature and identified several key topics: the nature and roles of leaders and followers, ideology, organization, methodology, external involvement, catalysts or accelerators, and basic causes or preconditions. These concepts will help order the subsequent discussion of the insurrection and revolution in Nicaragua.

Revolutionary *leaders* have tended to come more from the same social strata as the incumbent elite whom they challenge than from among the ranks of the classes in whose name they make revolution. Thus, rebel leaders often have middle- or upper-class origins and have had far more education than the norm for their societies.[12] Indeed, rebel leaders have often represented disaffected factions or elements from within the political elite itself, as well as intellectuals and students. In general, the more leftist the ideology of the revolutionaries, the less access to the extant regime the rebel leaders have had and consequently the more they have developed their organizational resources and skills.[13]

Revolutionary *followers* have historically varied somewhat according to the nature of their movements. According to Greene, leftist revolutions have tended to attract followers from the lower classes, while bourgeois revolutions have attracted middle-strata followers and rightist movements lower-middle-class supporters. Given the extraordinarily severe punishment most entrenched regimes inflict for the use of violent means and for rebellion against the established order, one very rational strategy for most citizens caught up in a rebellion has been to remain uncommitted. Those who have committed themselves have tended to do so not because ideologies have persuaded them, but because events have overtaken them and reduced the risk of taking sides or making a commitment, because belligerents have forced them to take part, or because some other personal experience has involved them. Active revolutionary followers appear to have constituted a minority of the population in most revolutions, and some revolutions have succeeded with very little mass mobilization. Coalitions among diverse social sectors with different grievances and aspirations have been typical of successful revolutionary movements; single-class or single-group movements have commonly failed.[14]

Ideology has served to forge a winning coalition among divergent groups and social forces during most revolutions, on behalf of either the revolutionaries or the regime. Because class interests usually vary enormously and may actually be in conflict on any given program, ideologues have tended to appeal to broad and general ideals, such as nationalism, or to make more specific appeals consonant with cultural traditions or with the immediate needs of large groups.[15]

Revolutionary *organization* has traditionally sought to take advantage of spontaneous popular opposition to the incumbent regime, to mobilize additional support for the insurgent cause, or to neutralize support for the regime. Rebel organization has promoted cohesion, loyalty, and discipline within the insurgent ranks and developed new institutions to replace the old regime after its defeat. A strong and coherent internal structure within insurgent movements has typically minimized internal conflict, maximized the clarity of command structures, regularized recruitment and training of cadres, and permitted flexibility for adaptation to local needs at the operational base.[16]

Studies of revolutionary methodology have examined the role of *violence,* terror, guerrilla warfare, and counterinsurgency in the process and progress of rebellion. Violence, the use of actions that threaten or harm life and property, has occurred at different phases in different revolutions, sometimes preceding the capture of power by the revolutionaries and sometimes coming afterward as they seek to implement their sweeping reforms against opposition. Many revolutions have involved violence at both stages. The intensity and duration of violence have typically been greater the more balanced the strength of the regime and the rebels, as well as the greater the foreign intervention on either side. The successful use of terror by rebels has required great caution in order to embarrass the regime and to provoke it into overreaction while limiting direct hurt to the population by the rebels' own acts. Regime terror and counterinsurgency have also succeeded only through cautious management, because excess has commonly provoked an anti-regime reaction. Strong guerrilla organizations have typically employed less terror than weaker insurgents, as more conventional military challenges are not only more effective against the regime but necessary for eventual victory in an internal war.[17]

External involvement has often played a decisive role in insurrections. Financial, military, and moral backing for either regime or insurgents has tipped the balance one way or the other, or prolonged and intensified conflict by equalizing previously unequal forces. Of particular importance to guerrilla rebels has been sanctuary, whether within the nation or in a friendly foreign territory, permitting them a safe staging, supply, and training base, as well as a refuge.[18]

The Theory of Revolution: Causes

The most fruitful theoretical musings on revolution have concerned causes. This theme has generally divided into two parts, one concerned with the root causes or preconditions that set the stage for revolutionary movements, and the other oriented toward the more proximate causes (accelerators or catalysts) of revolution. This second aspect examines the sparks igniting the final conflagration—those things that transform structural strains or a disaffected populace into an overt movement to overthrow the old regime.

A warehouse full of cardboard does not become a four-alarm fire until flame touches paper. Indeed, many warehouses full of cardboard or even more flammable items never burn at all because nothing sets them off. Likewise, many societies have experienced intensely the preconditions or basic stresses that create great revolutionary potential, but they have not undergone a revolution or even an attempted revolt. In these cases of nonrevolution, nothing has catalyzed the disaffected to focus their hostility upon the state; nothing has significantly debased the regime's supporting myths and brought conflict into the open. Scholars commonly list among the accelerators of revolution such things as military defeat, economic crisis, excessive government violence, elite fragmentation and collapse, and even efforts at reform and political change.[19]

Efforts to identify the fundamental causes or preconditions of revolution have achieved greater progress than any other aspect of the theory of revolution. In this area, explanations for the outbreak of sociopolitical violence, and of revolution as a subset of violence, have taken three basic theoretical tacks. One looks at violence and revolution in structural terms, as the products of stresses and strains within societies. Although helpful in identifying societal features that accompany revolution, such approaches typically receive criticism for mechanistic traits and for ignoring the role of the individual in social processes.[20] Another approach is primarily psychological in nature, seeking the origins of rebellion in the psychological drives of the human organism. Psychological explanations, of varying degrees of sophistication, posit that humans may react to the frustration of their expectations with aggressive behavior. Critics typically fault this approach for failing to explain why frustration does not always produce aggressive social behavior and for overlooking the complex structural realities that condition and constrain individual behavior.[21]

The third theoretical approach to the causes of violence and revolution integrates both psychological and structural features, thus avoiding many of the drawbacks of each. Based upon the motivation theories of the frustration-aggression school, this approach weaves psychological motives into a sophisticated network of structural constraints. The integrated theory thus attempts to predict the circumstances under which frustration in the form of relative deprivation (RD) may occur, under which RD may attain significance as a collective motivation or may be diffused or dampened, and under which resultant aggressive impulses may turn toward political targets. Perhaps the most comprehensive effort along these lines comes from Gurr, whose *Why Men Rebel*[22] and several empirical articles both posit and test a broad array of propositions from an integrated theory of violence.

Perhaps the most important generalization about the causes of political violence involves its linkage to rapid economic change through individual and collective relative deprivation. Rapid economic change, be it growth and development or crisis, tends to produce dramatic short-run dislocations that affect many members of a society. Shifts in land ownership, rapid industrialization or changing investment patterns, collapsing export prices, industrial decline, and rapid and severe inflation all have great potential to damage substantially the interests of individuals and groups. Such phenomena can quickly shift relative status positions among social groups and suddenly alter the degree of control that individuals have over their own well-being. In nations characterized by material scarcity, low levels of industrial development, and low institutional capacity to respond to economic crisis, such rapid changes tend to affect the way many people see their lives, achievements, and chances for attaining their goals.[23]

The integral theory of violence focuses, in particular, upon how the structural strains of rapid economic change affect the way citizens perceive their shifting economic opportunities. At stake is how threatened people perceive their interests to be. Theorists of this school argue that those who see themselves as somehow adversely affected by such changes may experience a frustrating sense of deprivation. This deprivation rarely appears to be absolute, for the truly prostrate have low expectations and tend to be resigned to struggling for mere survival. Rather, the deprivation is relative; it is compared to what people have recently experienced, to what they reasonably expect to receive or achieve, or to other important reference groups. Thus, those whose material achievements suddenly decline, after having steadily increased for some time, experience frustration by being relatively deprived. Witnessing the rapid enrichment of other sectors previously equal or inferior in status while one's own group declines can also generate RD-induced frustration. The frustration of the relatively deprived enhances their potential for engaging in aggressive behavior. In general, the faster the rate of change in the economic positions of social groups, the greater the number of shifts among the different groups' relative status, the greater the proportion of all social groups affected, the smaller the number of alternate economic opportunities, and the smaller the resources of the social groups affected, the greater is the RD in a society and the greater is the potential for collective violence.[24]

Despite their pervasive importance, economic conditions are not the only potential sources of relative deprivation. Scholars have identified numerous other factors that can produce similarly large gaps between what individuals expect and their perceived achievements. The sudden reduction of political repression or the announcement of reforms may generate a rapid elevation of expectations that concrete policy and government practice may then frustratingly fail to match. A rapid increase in the intensity and scope of political repression can cause many people to perceive a relative decline in their political capacities and freedom. In this vein, becoming the object of life-threatening political repression by the regime can not only produce intense RD, but can also so lower the relative costs of aggressive behavior that the regime's purpose in repressing protests or other demands becomes thwarted. In this process, excessive repression — intended to dissuade opposition — may not only generate hostility, but may also convince some that their only hope for survival lies with joining the rebels. Political beliefs, ethnic issues, and even religious values, if sufficiently threatened or harmed, can generate intense RD.[25]

The transformation of relative deprivation, whatever its source, into an effort to overturn the government in power and to remake society depends upon several factors, some environmental and some psychological. The greater the capacity of the regime to cope with the causes of RD among affected groups — whether lowering expectations through persuasion or adjusting achievements through reform or ameliorative policy — and the greater the legitimacy of the government, or the respect that citizens feel for the incumbent regime and for sociopolitical "rules of the game," the less likely citizens will be to attack either regime or rules. Conversely, the greater the tradition of political violence in the society (a model for present behavior), the more likely it is that RD will become channeled into rebellion. The more aggressive the messages circulating within the society through the various media of communication, the greater will be the incitement to political violence. Finally, the more critics of the system voice direct appeals to violence as a means of solving society's ills, the greater becomes the likelihood of political violence.[26]

The magnitude of violence eventually generated by such accumulated

RD and by conditions facilitating the open expression of aggressive impulses depends in turn upon other structural conditions. In particular, the ratios of the institutional support and coercive capability of the regime to those of the dissidents have great bearing on the severity of their clash. For institutions, the number of organized supporters, their degree of loyalty, and the cohesiveness and flexibility of their organizations, as well as the resources of institutions and their capability to act, all materially affect the capacity of each side to carry forward its struggle. The greater the equality of institutional support for both sides, the greater will be the violence. The same applies to coercive control (firepower and military capacity). The proportion of the population controlled, access to a secure base of operations (especially sanctuary for the dissident forces), the size and competency of military organizations, and the loyalty of military forces to their sides all contribute to the coercive power of the competing forces. The more equal the two sides, the greater tends to be the magnitude of the resulting violence. And finally, the more the dissidents have channels to protest the policies and actions of the regime, the lower will be the intensity of conflict.[27]

Gurr argued that different combinations of social conditions lead to different types of political violence. He distinguished three: turmoil, widespread and rather spontaneous mass violence with little leadership; conspiracy, elite efforts to oust the incumbent rulers; and internal war, highly organized violence with broad mass participation. Turmoil is most likely when only a few issues generate RD, when dissidents are dispersed and have little institutional support or organization, and when the regime has a high capacity for coercion. Conspiracy, in contrast, tends to occur when it is mainly the elites (especially those denied political influence) who experience RD, when the dissidents have great resources but a narrow institutional base, and when regime forces are either weak or relatively disloyal. Internal war, involving a much greater degree of both organization and participation of a diverse dissident coalition, tends to develop when intense RD affects many sectors, both mass and elite, when the regime and dissidents have relatively equal institutional and coercive strength, and when dissidents either effectively control territory or enjoy sanctuary and external support.[28]

The Roots of Revolution in Nicaragua

The search for the origins of the contemporary Nicaraguan revolution (in terms of the issues raised by the preceding theoretical material) leads back to the eighteenth century and covers a stage much larger than the national territory of the small Central American nation itself. One must understand the intense political factionalism of Nicaraguan society, a phenomenon traceable to the Spanish colonial era. Even before independence (1823) emergent Liberal and Conservative factions of the socioeconomic elite had fought bitterly over ideology and policy. Independence expanded their conflict to include control of the state and its attendant rewards. This protracted factional struggle engendered a tradition of militarism, *caudillismo,* and political violence that has cost thousands of lives, spawned dictatorships, and reinforced political hatreds still burning in Nicaragua today.

Another factor is Nicaragua's geography. The apparent blessing of a river and a lake system facilitating transit across the Central American isthmus has in fact made external intervention, great power interference, and foreign political and economic adventurism extraordinarily influential in Nicaragua's history. Interference from outside has traditionally played a critical role in the factional conflict among and within Nicaragua's parties and among public institutions, determining the outcome of many key struggles for power.

Another critical set of variables that have long shaped Nicaragua's fate is economic. Nicaragua's relationship to the world economy has traditionally been dependent — as a consumer of imported manufactured goods and as a supplier of commodities. Nicaragua's main exports (coffee, cotton, beef and hides) have suffered dramatic price fluctuations that have, especially since the late nineteenth century, badly buffeted the tiny nation. The internal socioeconomic consequences of such economic fluctuations have often been intense. The efforts of economic elites to protect their wealth and income or to take advantage of momentary opportunities for profit have repeatedly affected the living conditions of the working class in pernicious ways. In the twentieth century, growing working-class efforts to challenge this insecurity have intensified class conflict. Under the stimulation of Central American economic integration in the 1960s and early 1970s, the politico-economic elite factions of Nicaragua converged into an ever more unified bourgeois (or capitalist) class. But in the 1970s, the economic role of the Somoza family itself became so immense that it began to affect profoundly the lives and interests of all Nicaraguans. The economic power of the Somozas and the growing economic and political instability of the 1970s ultimately arrested the unification of the capitalist class. Key elements among the nation's major investors in the end turned against the regime and some became reformers or revolutionaries.

The following narrative, then, traces the roots of the Nicaraguan revolution among both large and impersonal social forces as well as influential personalities with complex motives. These roots go deep into Nicaragua's past and intertwine domestic with international conflicts and institutional development on a global scale with details of the behavior of factions and classes.

2
Factional Strife and Manifest Destiny

The history of Nicaragua is the history of civil war.[1]
— José Coronel Urtecho

The Nicaraguan insurrection of 1977–1979 has roots in the eighteenth century. The social, economic, and political realities of contemporary Nicaragua have direct links to a remote but surprisingly influential past — to the problems of a nation emerging from colonialism into tentative and troubled independence in the 1820s and 1830s. Between its independence and 1909, Nicaragua developed many of the characteristics and processes that not only set the stage for, but shaped the outcome of, the insurrection of 1977–1979 and the ensuing social revolution. Regional and class-factional conflict between groups known by the mid-nineteenth century as Liberals and Conservatives became highly institutionalized and made control of the government a form of booty. Foreign economic and political winds buffeted Nicaragua so that its developmental and political course shifted erratically. Nicaraguan politicians, often without sufficient power of their own to defeat and to rule their opponents, repeatedly sought aid from outsiders that elevated the toll of victims in Nicaragua's civil wars.

Independence and the Central American Federation

What is today the Republic of Nicaragua was until 1821 part of the Spanish colony known as the Captaincy General of Guatemala, which included the Central American isthmus from Mexico's Chiapas state south to Costa Rica.[2] During the eighteenth century, this region experienced intense social change due to administrative and economic reforms under Spain's Bourbon monarchs and to the introduction of the reformist ideology of economic liberalism. Among other things, liberalism advocated the freeing of trade from monarchical controls and thus appealed to interests that sought to circumvent established economic mo-

11

nopolies and concessions. As the Bourbon reforms permitted substantial relaxation of such economic controls in the eighteenth century, throughout the captaincy general parties either favored or injured by such changes began to emerge and to clash.

In Nicaragua, certain landed interests that had not benefited by previously extant royal agricultural and trade concessions raised the banner of free trade liberalism. Among these Liberals were innovative producer, exporter, and related interests that had been encouraged by the economic growth and prosperity of the eighteenth century. On the other side, Conservatism represented vested interests based on earlier crown-controlled production and export arrangements. Conservatives chafed under the new policies, which threatened them with new competition and new taxes. The Liberals, strongest in the city of León, included a faction of the landed creoles (citizens of Spanish extraction born in the New World), plus a tiny nascent urban middle stratum of public employees, artisans, and small businessmen who stood to benefit from increased economic activity. Liberals advocated reducing restrictions on trade and commerce, increasing basic infrastructure development (such as roads and ports), and ending exemption from taxes for the church. The Conservatives came from another creole elite faction, concentrated more heavily in the city of Granada, whose wealth had been built primarily upon previous trade and agricultural production concessions. Conservatives opposed the competition generated by new trade and external markets and advocated retention of the very traditional institutions that the Liberals opposed.

Competition for influence upon colonial government policy sometimes led to violent clashes between León's Liberals and Granada's Conservatives, so that the two cities and their surrounding hinterlands eventually developed an intense mutual hatred that added coals to the ideological fire between the factions. When it came, independence from Spain and Mexico merely altered the arena, but not the nature, of the struggle between these regionally based ideological factions. During the colonial era the two sides had exerted pressure on colonial administrators to favor their position, occasionally resorting to arms. Separation from Spain in 1821 eliminated the powerful referee between the factions represented by the colonial administration and its armed forces; thus the internecine struggle among Nicaraguans greatly intensified after independence.

Nicaraguan independence came in two stages, the first beginning in 1821 when the captaincy general was separated from Spain as an appendage of the Mexican Empire. The armed struggle between Mexico and Spain occurred primarily within Mexico itself, and little fighting touched the Central American isthmus. When Liberals eventually gained the upper hand throughout Central America, they broke with the Conservative-dominated Mexican Empire; on 1 July 1823, the United Provinces of Central America (most of the old Captaincy General of Guatemala) seceded from Mexico. The five Central American provinces (Guatemala, Honduras, Nicaragua, El Salvador, and Costa Rica) had achieved independence without war with either Spain or Mexico, but the new federation erupted into civil war almost immediately upon independence. The long-standing Liberal-Conservative sectarian clash began to intensify once no strong central authority restrained it. Within Nicaragua, as throughout the other provinces, the Liberals sought to consolidate their authority by violently repressing the Conservatives.

Conservative resistance, however, grew steadily in the 1830s, both within Nicaragua and elsewhere in the isthmus. The continuing civil war, marked by widespread atrocities on both sides, eventually destroyed the Central American Federation and completed the second step of Nicaraguan independence. In 1838 Nicaragua, now led by the newly victorious Conservatives, separated itself from the collapsing federation. Unfortunately for Nicaragua, the prosperity and economic growth of the late colonial era had foundered, due in no small part to the lengthy and debilitating civil war. Nicaragua thus began its republican existence in the throes of a depression. Moreover, the partisan-regional hostilities and frequent recourse to political violence had cemented themselves into Nicaraguan political culture.[3]

Early Republican Nicaragua and the Walker Filibuster (1838–1857)

In 1824 Nicaragua had only some one hundred ninety thousand inhabitants, centered mainly in the small urban nuclei of León, Granada, Managua, and Masaya and their hinterlands. By mid-century the population had grown to roughly two hundred ninety thousand, but remained concentrated in the western, or Pacific, third of the national territory (see Figure 2.1). Other important towns and villages were located along transit routes or at harbors and mines. In early nineteenth-century Nicaraguan society, social and economic class membership corresponded roughly to race. Although colonial Nicaragua had experienced more Indian-European racial mixing than Guatemala and Costa Rica, there remained a relatively more European creole class of larger landowners, commercial entrepreneurs, and public leaders. A middle stratum consisted of the racially mixed (Indian-European) *ladinos,* who were normally excluded from the elite. Ladinos concentrated in artisanry, petty commerce, the professions, and small-scale agriculture. At the bottom of the status and economic system were the Indians, whose numbers had

Figure 2.1: Nicaragua (c.1850)

declined markedly from disease, dislocation, and even attempts at extermination during the colonial era. After independence, the Indian's
relative economic position and social systems continued to suffer from
creole and ladino encroachment.

The chronic Liberal-Conservative civil wars, especially after 1823,
tended to keep Nicaragua's population dispersed as men sought to avoid
impressment into military service and to protect their families and farms
from predatory armies. This population dispersal combined with the nation's extreme regionalism and chronic political unrest to retard economic growth and to keep economic activity concentrated along tradi-

tional lines: subsistence agriculture and production of dyes (*añil*) among smallholders, cattle and hide production by the creole largeholders, and mining. Coffee growing, which by the mid-nineteenth century was already revolutionizing neighboring Costa Rica and beginning profoundly to affect Guatemala and El Salvador, did not become well established in Nicaragua until the late nineteenth century.[4]

Within this context of economic depression and political fragmentation, three interrelated political problems plagued the policymakers of Nicaragua: national and international interest in a waterway to permit a quick Atlantic-to-Pacific passage for ocean vessels, the economic and military presence of Britain, and the rapidly expanding interest in Central America on the part of the United States.

Nicaragua's first big problem, to a considerable degree also the source of its difficulties with Britain and the United States, involved the possibility of constructing an interoceanic waterway, utilizing the navigable Río San Juan and the Great Lake of Nicaragua, and a canal to connect the lake with the Pacific. First proposed by the Spanish centuries earlier, the canal idea rapidly gained importance as a Nicaraguan national issue after 1838. Viewed as a source of guaranteed prosperity, the transisthmian waterway became a passion for Nicaraguan leaders. As Nicaragua lacked the capital and technology to undertake such a large project alone, Nicaraguan leaders courted several foreign powers for help. Canal route surveys by both the United States and Britain stirred excitement in Nicaragua in the 1830s; in 1844 France tried but failed to negotiate a canal treaty with Nicaragua.[5] Despite the dreams aroused by such initiatives, however, the canal proposals ultimately brought Nicaragua almost nothing but frustration and trouble.

As its second problem, tiny Nicaragua had to contend with interference by Great Britain, at that time the world's foremost economic and military power. British interest in Nicaragua's Atlantic region dated from the early 1800s, when the British established a protectorate over the Miskito Indian territories (see Figure 2.1). British commercial interests in Nicaragua, defended by overwhelming naval power, grew steadily. Indeed, the British presence eventually encompassed a near-monopoly of all Central American Atlantic shipping, as well as the establishment of mines, colonization schemes, and loans to the new republics of Central America. The British hoped to establish a transisthmian waterway, for which Nicaragua seemed to offer the best route. To further this interest, Britain in 1847 seized the Nicaraguan town of San Juan del Norte on the Río San Juan. San Juan del Norte, redubbed Greytown, was the most likely Atlantic terminus for a Nicaraguan canal and therefore a potential site for a key port.[6]

A third major difficulty for early republican Nicaragua was growing

U.S. interest in Central American commerce and in a canal route, together with the growing tensions that these interests engendered between the United States and Britain. The United States tentatively began to challenge Britain's commercial and strategic superiority in the Caribbean region just as Nicaragua embarked upon its voyage as an independent republic. Britain and the United States could not simultaneously exercise dominion in the Caribbean. Consequently the established naval power and its upstart former colony clashed over the issue as U.S. military and economic power grew steadily throughout the 1840–1860 period. U.S. foreign policy concerns in Central America thus complicated for Nicaragua both the British and the transit route questions. A combination of official and private U.S. initiatives concerning transisthmian transit, at times encouraged by Nicaragua's frequently warring factions, at mid-century provoked a series of crises.[7]

U.S. President James Monroe, responding in 1823 to Russian claims to portions of the American Northwest and to prospects that the Holy Alliance powers might help Spain reconquer its former American colonies, pretentiously but rather unrealistically (and without consulting Latin America) declared the Americas closed to further European colonization or intervention in the affairs of the Latin American republics. Implementation of this bold, if wistful, policy faced great obstacles — the U.S. Navy for several decades lacked the strength to enforce such demands, especially given the overwhelming naval power of the British in the region. Indeed, Britain from the outset roundly ignored the Monroe Doctrine in Central America, although the British presence did tend to keep other powers at bay. Originally intended to promote the freedom of the United States by preventing European meddling in Latin and North America (and to counter Russian claims in the Pacific Northwest), the Monroe Doctrine began to evolve as U.S. military prowess grew and as the nation's economic growth brought expanded commercial interests in Latin America.[8] Americans began to speak of their nation's "manifest destiny" — the goal of expansion across the continent — an idea that had gained great currency in the United States by the late 1830s. This burgeoning expansionist ideology gave U.S. foreign-policy makers territorial designs on Latin America, and they modified the Monroe Doctrine to include the idea that the United States itself might intervene at will in the region. Pursuing its continental expansion, the United States between 1836 and 1846 separated Texas, New Mexico, and California from Mexico and annexed them. The discovery of gold in California in 1848 soon inflamed to a near frenzy U.S. desires to facilitate transportation between the country's eastern and western coasts via the Central American Isthmus.

Central America and the Caribbean region at mid-century also became the object of U.S. interest in the dispute over the abolition of slavery. Proslavery forces in the United States regarded the Caribbean and Central American area as a potential zone for the expansion of slavery by adding new slave states to the union. Central American countries had abolished slavery in 1821, but the proslavery forces in the United States believed that military expeditions could rather easily overthrow local governments, seize these small countries, and convert them to ally slave states. This proslavery expansionism, plus the desire for a quick route across the isthmus, sharply increased the U.S. presence in Nicaragua and raised the curtain on one of the nation's most dramatic and tragic periods.

The United States began to challenge the British in Central America in the 1840s as the California gold rush gathered speed. The new U.S. posture attracted the attention of Nicaragua's Liberals, who were then struggling to recover political ascendancy over the Conservatives. The Conservatives, who had led Nicaragua out of the Central American Federation in 1838, had later become discredited by their embarrassing cooperation with British interventionism on Nicaragua's Atlantic coast. The British capture of San Juan del Norte in 1847 elicited a strong U.S. protest and eventually led to the Clayton-Bulwer Treaty of 1850, which provided (without consulting Nicaragua) for joint U.S.-British control of any transisthmian canal. But U.S.-British tensions did not subside. Fanned by the excesses of the U.S. consul and agents of a U.S.-owned transisthmian transit company, the Anglo-American dispute flamed into violence in 1850. The warship U.S.S. *Cyane,* technically reacting to a British insult to a U.S. representative but in fact simply stepping up pressure upon the British, first bombarded British-held Greytown (San Juan del Norte), then landed a party of marines to burn down what remained of the town. Only British forbearance, required at this time by the Crimean War's drain upon Britain's military strength, prevented a showdown with the increasingly pugnacious United States. The British eventually retreated before U.S. demands in 1859 by returning the Miskito Coast to Nicaragua and by dropping territorial and protectorate claims in Central America, exclusive of Belize (British Honduras).[9] Throughout this episode, neither the United States nor Britain manifested any serious concern for either the sovereignty of Nicaragua or the life and property of its citizens. But such intrusions and arrogance pale when compared to the filibustering invasion of William Walker and the resultant Central American National War.

As mentioned above, when the California gold rush of 1849 began, the now age-old Nicaraguan party factional struggle was heating up again as Liberals sought a way to dislodge the Conservatives from power. This Nicaraguan political dispute dovetailed with financial intrigues, U.S. expansionism, and internal U.S. politics, leading Nicaragua inexorably into war. In 1849 Cornelius Vanderbilt and his associates had obtained concessions from the Conservative regime to establish a transit route across Nicaragua. California-bound fortune seekers would travel by boat up the Río San Juan and across the Great Lake of Nicaragua, then go by stagecoach to the Pacific. The route of this concession, in operation by mid-1851 as the Accessory Transit Company, connected with Vanderbilt's steamship routes to and from New York and San Francisco.

The Nicaraguan route, faster and more comfortable than the competing Panama passage (until 1855 when the Panamanian transisthmian railroad was completed) turned a handsome profit. So profitable was the line that it inspired two of Vanderbilt's associates—Cornelius Garrison, Vanderbilt's California manager, and New York financier Charles Morgan—to try to take over Accessory Transit for themselves. When Vanderbilt foiled their attempt in 1853, Garrison sought Nicaraguan help and soon managed to escalate the conflict from the boardroom to the international battleground. Liberals, continually frustrated by the Conservatives, were also seeking help, and they contacted Cornelius Garrison. Garrison brought into the fray another San Francisco resident, William Walker, who promised to help the Liberals defeat the Conservatives in exchange for land grants. This convenient deal caused a cruel turn in history that was to make manifest destiny and the dispute over slavery in the United States immediately and horribly real to Nicaraguans.[10]

William Walker, a gifted but frustrated Tennessee native, had earned medical and law degrees and had edited the antislavery New Orleans *Crescent* before emigrating to California in the late 1840s following a personal tragedy. From there the young journalist, pursuing his democratic ideals and personal fortune, participated in a doomed filibuster (freebooting invasion attempting to seize territory) into Sonora, Mexico, in 1853. A passionate advocate of manifest destiny, the idealistic but impecunious Walker then met Cornelius Garrison, who convinced him that Nicaragua offered an irresistible combination: an opportunity to expand democracy and to make a fortune through land development.[11]

Under contract with the Nicaraguan Liberals and supporting Garrison and Morgan in the Accessory Transit squabble, Walker invaded Nicaragua in June 1855 with fifty-seven other Americans. Initially defeated, Walker retrenched, regrouped with the Liberals, and received reinforcements from California, permitting him in October to capture Granada, the heart of Conservative territory. The stunned Conservatives quickly capitulated, and the U.S. government recognized Walker's puppet Liberal regime. Walker soon sacrificed his democratic idealism on the altar of expediency; the new strong man quickly resorted to exiling and executing his Conservative opponents. Walker increased his military strength through the support of Morgan and Garrison, who sent money, volunteers, and arms in their effort to undercut Vanderbilt's control of the transit route. Moreover, proslavery Southerners swelled Walker's army to twenty-five hundred. In order to secure this source of support, Walker forsook his own past abolitionism and advocated slavery and Nicaraguan annexation to the United States.[12]

Liberal support for Walker's anti-Conservative measures outraged Conservatives throughout Central America, and the fear of annexation by the United States grew. By early 1856, the Conservative governments of the four other Central American republics had agreed to send troops to help liberate Nicaragua. Britain, still smarting over the Greytown incident, egged them on. Thus, when Costa Rica declared war on Walker in March of 1856, the British began to send that country military supplies. Conservative forces rapidly accumulated in Nicaragua; by November a large united Central American force had engaged Walker.[13] This "national war" had become a struggle for Central American sovereignty and had rekindled hopes for regional reunification.

The war grew more intense and destructive as 1856 wore on. As Walker's army steadily lost ground, the filibuster's efforts became progressively more high-handed. Under pressure, Walker dealt ruthlessly even with his Liberal allies, whom he suspected of flagging support.[14] This ruthlessness, combined with the efforts of Cornelius Vanderbilt's agents to undermine the Liberals, undercut Walker's Nicaraguan base. Walker had himself elected president of Nicaragua in July 1856 as he strove desperately to consolidate and to retain his support among Americans (especially with annexationist U.S. slaveholders). His measures reflected an urgency sometimes tinged with madness: he offered land grants to attract American troops, declared English the official language, legalized slavery, decreed a vagrancy law to ensure forced peasant labor for landowners, appropriated major landholdings, and instituted a general Americanization program. Ineffective in attracting major new recruits to Walker's cholera-ridden army, these measures served mainly to alienate more Nicaraguans. Following a major encounter with a Guatemalan army in April 1857, an exhausted Walker accepted a truce arranged by the U.S. naval commander on the scene, surrendered, and escaped to the United States with his army under navy protection. William Walker pursued his dreams of wealth and power through three more attempts to return to Nicaragua, but this obsession proved his undoing. British marines eventually captured Walker in Honduras in 1860. They turned him over to the Hondurans, who quickly tried and then executed him.[15]

The effects of the filibuster and the National War were varied. For the region as a whole, Central Americans' briefly rekindled dreams of isthmian reunification soon faded, but the power of Conservative parties lingered for years in an era of Liberal disgrace. Nicaragua underwent major changes in addition to the destruction visited by the war. The once-growing Liberal party, thoroughly discredited, languished out of power, and the faction's leaders changed as supporters of Walker lost influence. The Conservatives regained control of the Nicaraguan government and ruled for more than thirty years of unprecedented stability. Ironically, Vanderbilt's Accessory Transit Company, a major cause of the upheaval, declined after the opening of the Trans-Panama railroad—in which Vanderbilt himself became a major shareholder. Nicaragua's Conservative leaders manifested an understandable hostility toward the United States. These destructive U.S. initiatives connected with transit across the isthmus, like all previous and future ones, had left Nicaragua frustrated and still without a canal. U.S. interest, so destructively focused on Nicaragua for a decade, now waned because of the U.S. Civil War. Subsequently, U.S. involvement in Nicaragua long remained at a low ebb due to the completion of the North American transcontinental railway, which largely solved U.S. east-west transport needs. The railroad also opened high investment opportunities for U.S. capital in the American West. Overall, such changes greatly reduced the economic importance to the United States of tiny and war-ravaged Nicaragua.[16]

The Rise of Coffee Production and the Decline of Ideology (1857-1909)

The decades of Conservative predominance following the war were times of political quiescence but considerable social and economic change. The mid-century decline in the European market for Central American natural dyes would have hit Nicaragua very hard had it not been for the appearance of coffee as a substitute export. Introduced in the 1850s, the bean began to attain significance as an export in the 1870s. The rise of Pacific coast shipping facilitated exportation, and Conservative governments, especially under President Pedro Joaquín Chamorro after 1875, encouraged coffee cultivation through a series of economic "reforms": (1) transforming Indian *ejido* (communally owned and farmed) lands into private holdings to facilitate coffee expansion; (2) reduction of the amounts of land in church hands; (3) stimulation of coffee cultivation through prizes, subsidies, technical publications, land grants, and recruitment of immigrants to grow coffee; (4) infrastructural development (telegraphs and railways); and (5) encouragement of a credit system to finance coffee (mainly through British banks). As these measures took effect, coffee became the principal export by 1890.[17] Such stimuli to coffee production, as they had when implemented elsewhere in Central America, started important transformations in Nicaraguan society. These changes would eventually contribute to the formation of the Somoza dynasty through new class and political alignments.

One set of changes affected land tenancy and rural labor relations. In its steps to increase coffee plantings, the government went especially after the land of Indian communities, the church, and small subsistence farmers. This process began a concentration of land in the hands of an emergent coffee producer (*cafetalero*) faction and some expansion of membership within the landed class. The coffee producers included some creole latifundists, some small- and middle-sized farm owners, a segment of middle-class public functionaries who took advantage of government stimuli to attain coffee holdings, and foreign (especially German and British) investors who eventually came to control coffee exporting and credit.[18]

The now pressing need for a reliable labor supply for the coffee planters led to the institution of several systems designed to keep peasants (*campesinos*) handy to cultivate and harvest coffee. Such systems, commonplace through most of Central America and Mexico, set a repressive and sometimes bloody pattern for rural labor relations. Erecting the new prosperity of cafetaleros on the backs of peasants, these systems included debt peonage, forced recruitment of agricultural workers (especially Indians) through "vagrancy laws," prohibition of cultivation of basic subsistence crops to force peasants onto latifundia, and work taxes to be paid to largeholders. Not suprisingly, these vicious measures caused many to flee to the cities, to the sparsely inhabited and rugged northern mountains, or to the Atlantic forests to escape such obligations.[19] Moreover, such exploitation contributed directly to an 1881 rebellion by Matagalpa Indians, whose anger exploded in a seven-month uprising that the Conservatives repressed with extraordinary cruelty.[20]

Another set of changes affected the political realm. Conservatives, despite their political advantages over Liberals, had eventually come to accept much of the heart of classical liberal (capitalist) economic dogma. Thus, the economic policies by which Conservatives were transforming Nicaragua—classically liberal in conception—reflected an ideological realignment within the bosom of Conservatism that, by reducing the policy distance between parties, facilitated a Liberal comeback in 1893.[21] Moreover, the rise of coffee exportation increased the resources, size, and power of the Nicaraguan government and of the export business, nourishing a rising urban middle sector. These elements felt more naturally attuned to Liberal economic thinking as well as the proclaimed (but not yet demonstrated) Liberal preference for political democratization than to Conservative ideology and policies, despite the latter party's performance. The consequence of these trends was a gradual shift in the balance of political support toward the Liberal faction as the last decade of the nineteenth century began.

These changes had whetted Liberal appetites for further growth, especially among the coffee sector and the urban middle class. However, coffee complemented rather than displaced traditional productive sectors (such as beef and hides) and their associated political factions. Unlike in Costa Rica, El Salvador, and Guatemala, the cafetalero sector grew slowly and reinforced both great traditional factions, although the Liberals benefited more than the Conservatives. Nevertheless, the cafetaleros failed to gain full control of the Nicaraguan political system as they did in most of the rest of Central America. Thus the social and political transformations gradually diminished the capacity of the Conservatives to rule while progressively introducing strains into the system that made governing ever more difficult for them.[22]

The United States, for the time being wrapped up in its own internal development and conflicts, left Nicaragua alone, except for comparatively minor canal-related diplomacy. Thus the Nicaragua of 1890, with a population estimated at 423,199, was becoming progressively more integrated into the world economy through coffee production. Other world-market exports included cotton, gold and silver, rubber, leather, sugar, and tobacco; cattle, cheese, and cacao were exported to other Central American countries. What little industry existed was very light, producing products for local consumption.[23] Liberals wished to stimulate economic development and further integrate Nicaragua into the world economy.

In 1893 Liberal desires and social and political strains proved the undoing of the Conservatives. President Roberto Sacasa, a León Conservative, attempted to retain power for another term, precipitating a political crisis. Granada Conservatives, angered, refused to support Sacasa, with the result that a Liberal, José Santos Zelaya, assumed the presidency. Zelaya enjoyed backing among the rising Managua middle sectors that had expanded during the coffee boom, among intellectuals, and among coffee (and to some extent tobacco) producers and exporters. Zelaya immediately accelerated the pace of liberal reforms, beginning with a new constitution. He encouraged foreign investment, established a system of public primary education, speeded up infrastructure development, heavily encouraged export commodity production, and instituted a national labor draft. Zelaya's policies stimulated economic growth by integrating Nicaragua more fully into the world-market economy. However, virtually all the benefits of this process went to the economic elite, and especially to Zelayistas, who began to develop a substantial economic base. Zelaya, a nationalist with anti-U.S. and expansionistic pretensions, also significantly increased the power of the national government. He tamed the recalcitrant cities of León and Granada, reduced the economic power of the church and of certain Conservatives, built a professional national army to replace the ad hoc armies led by *caudillos,* and expanded communication networks, education spending, and the electorate.[24]

Zelaya's upper-class opposition, especially among the old Conservative faction's largeholders, cattle producers, and importers, resented their own displacement from the import-export trade by Zelaya cohorts, especially by the Germans among them; they also resented the rise of ladinos to new influence. As for their impact upon the lower classes, Zelaya's policies were, on balance, rather negative. Although he supported urban labor unions, Zelaya's rural labor policy changes tied more and more peasants to the plantations by means of a labor draft and by the destruction of communal lands. His own businesses speculated in basic commodities and consumer goods and thus increased prices for the poor.[25]

The ultimate result of these policies was growing popular resistance to the regime by the Conservative faction, which led Zelaya to increase repression. Zelaya has been wrongly portrayed as a bloody ruler,[26] but he did rule in a dictatorial manner and sparked the development of a lively clandestine political literature printed abroad and smuggled into the country. Ultimately he alienated many of his original Liberal collaborators through his excesses; some former allies aligned with burgeoning Conservative efforts to dislodge him. The 1903 explosion of a government powder magazine gave Zelaya a pretext for executing alleged plotters from the Conservative band. The Conservative party responded by stepping up its conspiring, and Zelaya in turn arrested still more Conservatives. A Conservative uprising of major proportions followed; it failed, although out of it emerged a new Conservative caudillo—General Emiliano Chamorro Vargas.[27]

Zelaya's foreign and economic policies, combined with a resurgence of U.S. interventionist zeal following the Spanish-American War and the development of "dollar diplomacy," caused his political demise. Nicaragua's Conservatives could not dislodge the firmly entrenched dictator with their resources alone. They required an outside source to augment their power, a need that increasingly corresponded with certain foreign interests, especially after 1900. Foreign hostility to Zelaya stemmed from his zeal to control investments. Zelaya had encouraged Nicaragua's development through foreign investment of capital and technology, but he had often dealt harshly with foreign investors who failed to observe regulations. Such reluctance to give foreign interests a free rein, for example, had led the United States to decide to build the transisthmian canal in Panama, despite its preference for the Nicaraguan route for technical reasons. The Panamanian government was much less protective of its own rights and territory and very cooperative with the United States. Thus, foreigners holding interests in Nicaragua or wishing to invest there had eventually come to resent Zelaya sharply.

Ultimately certain foreign elements, especially British interests that had been allied with the Conservatives, connived to overthrow the Liberal dictator.[28] Zelaya, infuriated by the U.S. decision on the canal, sought a canal treaty with the emergent naval powers of Japan and Germany and so also angered the United States, which now wished to ensure its canal monopoly. One concrete tactical error made by Zelaya was his decision to pick on a U.S. mining concession once represented by U.S. attorney Philander C. Knox. Knox, now President William Howard Taft's secretary of state, took angry exception to Zelaya's ploy and began to seek to oust the feisty Nicaraguan. At this juncture, the U.S. government and private interests joined with the plotting British and Conservatives. The foreign conspirators backed the Conservatives' revolt against the regime in the Atlantic port of Bluefields in 1909. President Taft then landed U.S. Marines "to protect U.S. lives and property" and to support the rebels. Zelaya resigned, ending the Liberal era and ushering in twenty-five years of chaos.[29]

Zelaya's sixteen-year rule had brought much greater economic and political integration of the Nicaraguan nation and had markedly modernized and strengthened the Nicaraguan state. In the process, the economic factions behind the Liberal and Conservative parties had shifted and realigned. The aristocratic Conservative largeholder-importer group's fortunes declined relatively because of the expansion of the coffee producer-exporter sector with its newly rich foreigners and ladinos. Despite such sectarian factionalism and realignments of cliques at the top of the Nicaraguan social pyramid, however, the upper sector's internal differences remained minor compared to the widening gap between rich and poor. Now with few significant ideological differences, the Nicaraguan ruling class—larger landowners, important merchants, holders of government contracts, and high civilian and military officials—remained, in the words of one historian, "highly homogeneous."[30] Conservative and Liberal elites alike prospered overall. The economic and political factions that consolidated during this era would last for decades. Zelaya, backed by a professional military of his own creation, controlled sufficient power to manage purely internal sedition by old opponents and former supporters angered by his progressively more repressive rule. Thus, opponents of the regime, unable to veto Zelaya on their own, sought derivative power by aligning themselves with foreign economic and political interests – by inviting intervention.

Overall, then, the Zelaya period realigned somewhat the traditional economic and political party factions, with coffee cultivation giving the power advantage to the Liberals. To oust the Liberals, the Conservatives conspired with the United States and Britain. In addition to its developmental progress, the regime of José Santos Zelaya also provided a model for the political-economic organization that would come with the Somozas some twenty-five years later. One analyst has argued that during the Zelayista period Nicaragua's socioeconomic elite learned that it could survive more safely and profitably under caudillo rule. The period revealed to the elite "a durable model for developing ever-more centralized and personalist administrations. Subsequently the nation's most powerful clans lent their support to the National Liberty Party, that is, to the inheritors of Zelaya's political tradition."[31]

Summary and Conclusions

Several historical phenomena from the eighteenth and nineteenth centuries help to explain Nicaragua's contemporary social and political processes and problems and, as Chapter 3 will demonstrate, also contribute directly to our understanding of the foundation of the Somoza dynasty: (1) Liberal and Conservative party/economic factions, divided along both regional and ideological lines, continuously confronted each other with arms. Full-scale civil war was frequent between 1824 and 1857, and sporadic factional rebellions punctuated the less violent 1858–1909 era. (2) Many political actors in Nicaragua – public and private, Conservative and Liberal, national and foreign – systematically abused human life, rights, and dignity. Such violent political methods, first used in the colonial era and refined throughout the nineteenth century, established the tone of politics for the twentieth century. (3) Political factionalism, civil war, regionalism, rebellion, and a diversified and very slowly changing agricultural system all combined to keep Nicaragua economically stagnant and institutionally weak until the late nineteenth century. After 1870, however, coffee production and liberal developmental initiatives stimulated the growth and modernization of the state and increased Nicaragua's involvement in the world economic system. The Liberal government of José Santos Zelaya (1893–1909) made considerable strides toward national development and economic growth. (4) Foreign intervention (especially by Great Britain and by the United States) pursued both governmental and private ends in Nicaragua. The amount of intervention rose and fell, with peaks in the decades 1850–1859 and

1900–1909. A relative lull in intervention between 1860 and 1900 permitted Nicaragua considerable institutional and infrastructural development, largely free from the devastating civil strife of the 1824–1857 era.
(5) During interventionist periods, Nicaraguan factional leaders (Liberals
in the 1850s, Conservatives after 1900), too weak to oust their enemies
from power using their own devices, encouraged foreign intervention in a
quest for resources. This foreign intervention markedly intensified and
prolonged factional conflict. Foreign meddling also contributed directly
to major national crises and either impeded or reversed the development
of national political institutions.[32]

3

From Dollar Diplomacy to Sandino

In Nicaragua, the mouse beats the cat.[1]

U.S. military incursions into Nicaragua before 1909 had been sporadic, but with the landing of Marines to help overthrow Zelaya the United States initiated more regular, long-term intervention, now motivated by its recently acquired overseas empire and by new economic and strategic interests in Central America. From 1909 to 1933, at the behest of Roosevelt and Taft's "dollar diplomacy" and Wilson's "missionary diplomacy," U.S. Marines would spend twenty years in Nicaragua, imposing or trying to impose U.S. policies and in the process undermining much of the development achieved under Zelaya.

U.S. Foreign Policy (1898–1920)

In 1898 the United States seized the last vestiges of once-powerful Spain's empire. Of the reawakened expansionism behind this act, the *Washington Post* editorialized in 1898 that

> the policy of isolation is dead. . . . A new consciousness seems to have come upon us — the consciousness of strength, and with it a new appetite, a yearning to show our strength. . . . Ambition, interest, land-hunger, pride, the mere joy of fighting, whatever it may be, we are animated by a new sensation. . . . The taste of empire is in the mouth of the people, even as the taste of blood in the jungle.[2]

By 1900 the United States had become the world's foremost industrial power, had acquired territorial claims stretching from the Caribbean to the Pacific, and wished to expand and protect its new empire.

Articulating and shaping this "taste of empire" was a group of foreign-policy makers of surprising homogeneity. Members of a quasi-aristocracy and devoted to promoting U.S. interests abroad, U.S. presidents and secretaries of state for two decades following the turn of the century were nearly all Northeasterners, wealthy in their own right or represen-

27

tatives of corporate power, intellectuals, professionals, and politicians. The flavor of this foreign policy is evident from their words: Elihu Root, secretary of state from 1905 to 1909, glorified his boss, Theodore Roosevelt, as "the greatest conservative force for the protection of property and capital." Root's successor, Philander C. Knox, President William Howard Taft's secretary of state (1909–1913), invented the term "dollar diplomacy." By this he meant the pursuit of order in such unstable areas as Central America by using U.S. businessmen as agents of foreign policy and by using the Department of State to promote U.S. business interests. These men pursued U.S. economic prosperity, which they hoped to found upon perpetually expanding foreign trade to be secured by an "open door" abroad to U.S. business. In 1901 Theodore Roosevelt summed it up: "America has only just begun to assume that commanding position in the international business world which we believe will more and more be hers."[3]

U.S. naval power reached supremacy in the Western Hemisphere in the 1890s, supplanting that of the British. But despite the growing U.S. fleet, Japan and Germany emerged on the world scene as major naval powers in the early twentieth century, profoundly worrying U.S. military strategists. U.S. investments and trade had expanded all over the world following the Spanish-American War, also increasing the government's concern about its military capability. But to the shapers of U.S. policy there was more: Regarding the nations of Asia and Latin America as peopled by inferior beings with inferior social systems, U.S. decision makers saw themselves as "civilizers," as bearing "the white man's burden" to "elevate" foreigners by Americanizing them. Roosevelt himself supplied many examples of this attitude. He once called Venezuelan dictator Cipriano Castro an "unspeakable villainous monkey" and spoke of punishing — indeed of "spanking" — "misbehaving" Latin American states. Woodrow Wilson added a patronizing missionary zeal to the quest for order. His goal? Merely to "teach the South American Republics to elect good men."[4]

Overall, then, U.S. foreign policy in the early decades of the twentieth century manifested economic and political expansionism, strategic insecurity because of the rise of competing naval powers and the recent extension of U.S. territory, and a chauvinistic bent that bred disrespect for other peoples and their rights. Moved by these spirits, the United States sent gunboats to China, made a protectorate of Cuba, and sent troops to the Dominican Republic, Haiti, Mexico, Panama and Nicaragua.[5]

Wealthy Republican Theodore Roosevelt, who in 1898 had led his Rough Riders into Cuba, set the tone for U.S. relations with the Central American isthmus when he became president in 1901. Roosevelt, a patrician reformer with globalist views, believed that internal stability in the

United States could best be promoted through expanded economic interests abroad. He saw the United States as a "policeman" to the world's "backward" peoples. One Roosevelt adviser, strategist Alfred Thayer Mahan of the Naval War College, had evidently convinced the new president of the wisdom of his argument that "wherever situated, whether at Panama or Nicaragua, the fundamental meaning of the canal will be that it advances by thousands of miles the frontiers of the United States."[6] But the Clayton-Bulwer Treaty of 1850, providing for joint U.S.-British operation of a transisthmian canal, stood between the United States and Roosevelt's dream of a waterway built, operated, and defended solely by the United States. The British, however, had by this time recognized U.S. strategic superiority in the Western Hemisphere and had decided to leave the United States to promote more freely its military and economic interests there. The British thus gave Roosevelt one of his first policy victories by agreeing to replace Clayton-Bulwer with the Hay-Pauncefote Treaty of 1901, which permitted the United States alone to build and fortify a canal.[7]

The next big question became, Where? In November 1901, a study by the Isthmian Canal Commission, headed by Admiral John G. Walker, recommended the Nicaraguan route. Nicaragua held a cost advantage because the French already owned costly canal rights and works in Colombia's Panamanian isthmus. But suddenly, representatives of the French company lowered the asking price to the United States for their assets from $109 million to $40 million and mounted a furious lobbying marathon with Roosevelt, key senators, and members of the Walker Commission. Under the onslaught the commission bowed and found the Panama route both politically and economically more attractive than the northern passage. Upon this reversal, U.S. Secretary of State John Hay quickly pressured Colombian ambassador to the United States Tomás Herrán to sign a canal treaty in 1903. The terms would have provided Colombia $10 million for lease rights and $250,000 annual rent and would have given the United States control over a six-mile (ten-kilometer) zone for a century, renewable for another hundred years at the sole option of the Americans.

The U.S. Senate ratified the treaty in the blink of a diplomatic eye, but the Colombian Senate stalled. Colombia, unhappy with the terms imposed by Hay and Roosevelt and economically stricken by a three-year civil war, tried several ways to renegotiate portions of the deal and to extract additional payments from the Canal Company. Roosevelt and Hay intervened, stepping up pressure, the president in his inimitable way. Enraged by the delay, Roosevelt referred to the Colombian Senate as "those contemptible little creatures in Bogotá."[8] Colombia's congressmen, fearful of the treaty's costs to the country's sovereignty and increasingly worried by the United States's pugnacious attitude, rejected the treaty unanimously in August 1903.

Frustrated on the diplomatic front, the Rough Rider president turned to other, more direct means. All the while flatly denying to Congress that his government had any connection whatever with subsequent events, Roosevelt conspired with Canal Company representatives to foment a "revolution" in Panama and sent gunboats to Colón to discourage the Colombian army from interfering with the U.S.-inspired insurrectionists. In a matter of hours on 3 and 4 November 1903, the Colombian army renounced the fray and departed, the United States recognized the newly "independent" republic, and canal treaty talks began in Washington between Hay and Canal Company executive-cum-lobbyist-cum-diplomat Philippe Bunau-Varilla. On 18 November the Hay–Bunau-Varilla Treaty was signed. It gave the United States a ten-mile (sixteen-kilometer) zone for the canal to govern "as if it were sovereign," and provided the newly seceded Panama rental terms virtually identical to those that Colombia had earlier rejected. Waxing more forthright in 1911 than he had with Congress earlier, Roosevelt crowed: "I took the Canal Zone and let Congress debate."[9]

The U.S. Senate ratified the Hay–Bunau-Varilla pact in 1904, and construction of the canal began almost immediately. It was completed in 1914.[10] This incident had shattered Nicaragua's hopes for a waterway and set in motion in Nicaragua events from which that country has yet to recover.

In Nicaragua, José Santos Zelaya's coolness toward the United States turned into a festering resentment. His subsequent overtures to the Japanese and Germans about a Nicaraguan canal to compete with the U.S. waterway proved the last straw for the United States. Seeking to be rid of Zelaya, the United States supported a rebellion by Conservatives under the leadership of Juan Estrada, then landed four hundred marines at Bluefields to protect the rebels. Secretary of State Knox then strongly reprimanded Zelaya for the execution of two U.S. mercenary terrorists who had dynamited government troop boats, and diplomatic relations were severed. Under such pressure Zelaya resigned.

Far from solving the problem, however, Zelaya's departure made the situation worse. The Nicaraguan Congress named as Zelaya's successor a León Liberal, Dr. José Madriz. The United States refused to recognize Madriz and held to its argument that Estrada's minority Conservative party revolutionaries represented "the great majority of the Nicaraguan people."[11] Negotiations failed to bring peace, and the war resumed. Estrada's muddling forces would have lost to the government in 1909 but for the continued defense of their Bluefields stronghold and supply lines by the U.S. Navy. Eventually Madriz's forces, weakened by the delays, began to fall apart while the well-supplied Conservatives regained strength, nurtured by the U.S. control over the Bluefields customs houses. On 20 August 1910 José Madriz, too, succumbed to the pressure and resigned. Juan Estrada, sponsored in his insurrection by the United States and reportedly financed for nearly $1 million by foreign businessmen, took control of Nicaragua's government.

With this apparent but in fact illusory victory in hand, the U.S. government moved to consolidate its three major objectives in Nicaragua—promoting political stability under Conservative rule, solidifying U.S. business opportunities, and securing the monopoly of the transisthmian canal.

To promote political stability, the Department of State sent Thomas Dawson to help organize the Estrada government and its finances in ways acceptable to the United States. Dawson wielded his influence with the new leader and other Conservative figures to establish a bipartisan coalition government with Estrada as president. Despite the presence of some Liberals in the cabinet, Conservatives like Adolfo Díaz (vice-president), General Emiliano Chamorro Vargas (leader of the Constituent Assembly), and General Luis Mena (minister of war) dominated the government. The Liberal-Conservative coalition soon proved highly unstable, especially because of Liberal ministers' agitation. Estrada's fears about his own party's allies led him to exile Chamorro. Nevertheless, Estrada's position steadily weakened relative to those of both General Mena, who remained in Nicaragua, and the fractious Liberals. In 1911 Mena played his hand, forcing Estrada to resign in favor of Díaz. Mena then persuaded the new Constituent Assembly to name him president to succeed Díaz in 1913. The U.S. Department of State, however, had worked closely with Díaz in the 1909 uprising and preferred his businessman's managerial skills to Mena's military talents. The United States thus refused to recognize Mena's election.

Luis Mena, turning then to time-tested Nicaraguan precedents, revolted against the Díaz government in July 1912. Almost immediately Liberal Benjamín Zeledón seized the day on behalf of the coffee grower-exporter faction and attacked government troops. Díaz, alarmed by this bilateral assault and bereft of any independent power base, requested military assistance from the United States. On 4 August 1912 President Taft sent the first U.S. Marine contingent; the force soon ballooned to twenty-seven hundred men. Mena, overwhelmed, immediately gave up the struggle and abandoned the country, freeing the marines to give chase to Zeledón. When the Liberal rebel refused to surrender, his army was pursued by both the marines and Nicaraguan toops loyal to Díaz. The vastly superior combined forces finally crushed the poorly armed Liberal insurrection in November 1912. The victors, who captured and killed Zeledón in the final act of this short drama, paraded the rebel leader's corpse, lashed to the back of a horse, before the public.

U.S. Ambassador George T. Weitzel then persuaded Emiliano Chamorro, now back from exile, to become the Nicaraguan envoy to Washington. This eliminated the last major challenge to Díaz from within his own party, putting a definitive end to the 1912 insurrections. The United States subsequently reduced the marine contingent in Nicaragua to a token 100 men. However, this small force amply signified which party the United States preferred, as well as the U.S. willingness to use its military power. The reminder discouraged further Liberal uprisings and kept the Conservatives in power until the marines withdrew in 1925.[12]

Promoting U.S. investments, the second major goal of the United States for Nicaragua, came under the heading of "dollar diplomacy." The Department of State's representative, Thomas Dawson, a young attorney from the secretary of state's law firm, negotiated a series of economic pacts and contracts with the highly cooperative Nicaraguan government (which he had just organized). Among these agreements figured the Castillo-Knox Treaty, which provided for U.S. loans of $15 million to Nicaragua in return for the right of the United States to protect its interests there and to arbitrate any dispute in which Nicaragua became involved.[13] In effect, the document would have made Nicaragua a U.S. protectorate. Never ratified, the treaty did not take effect, but for all intents and purposes it outlined the nature of the economic and political relationship between the two countries for years to come. U.S. capital in the form of private bank loans to the government began to flow into marine-stabilized Nicaragua.[14] The rapid transformation of Nicaragua's economy from 1910 to 1920 had generally negative results for the weaker partner. Sergio Ramírez has described the period colorfully and, as the following paragraphs reveal, accurately as one of "government among cousins and relatives who docilely continued turning the nation over to foreign interests, acquiring usurious debts, and giving more goods and resources as collateral."[15]

Under one agreement the Brown Brothers Bank of New York lent the Nicaraguan government $1.5 million, permitting the issuance of stable bonds and currency in the badly disrupted economy. The government secured the loan by ceding control of the Nicaraguan customs operations to a U.S.-appointed customs inspector. Under this arrangement Brown Brothers always got the first cut of one of Nicaragua's principal sources of public revenue in order to ensure the timely repayment of principal and interest. The agreement also provided for the establishment of the National Bank of Nicaragua, of which the Brown Brothers Bank owned 51 percent. The board of directors of the Nicaraguan National Bank met in New York and consisted entirely of Brown Brothers' U.S. representatives, except for a token Nicaraguan.

For more loans the Conservatives signed over to other foreign bankers

(J. and W. Seligman, U.S. Mortgage Trust, and others) the revenue of the national rail and steamship lines. Profit-making opportunities abounded. For instance, Brown Brothers bought up discounted British-owned debts, then easily collected them at face value through the rail and steamship revenues. Another scheme established by the Dawson contracts created a Mixed Claims Commission, chaired by Dawson himself, to evaluate foreign damage claims against the Nicaraguan government. Many of the petitioners made exaggerated or fraudulent claims, which U.S. bankers bought up at a discount. The new claim owners then collected from the government at face value, because the Mixed Claims Commission almost always recognized their validity and the banks' customs and transport revenue concessions assured payment. Overall, the Mixed Commission required Nicaragua to pay out $1.8 million (an amount estimated to exceed the total U.S. investment in the country) for alleged damages from civil disorder.

But the U.S. bankers became so rapacious that they eventually alienated even their government. The bankers demanded that the entire $3 million rent that the United States paid to Nicaragua for canal rights under the Chamorro-Bryan Treaty go directly to them to amortize Nicaragua's huge debts. Woodrow Wilson's government would not consent to this preference without the complete reorganization of Nicaraguan finances. The Nicaraguan government and the bankers thus accepted new financial procedures under the supervision of a joint High Financial Commission. The resulting coordinated control of revenues from customs plus the reduction of debt acquisition eventually permitted Nicaragua to retire most of the debts that it had acquired under pressure before 1916.

U.S. financial intervention and supervision had several effects, mainly negative. First, the Nicaraguan government found itself with a chronic shortfall of income, its major sources of revenue garnisheed by U.S. financial houses. This contributed to a continual inability to supply many basic public services, not to mention the incapacity to continue the infrastructural development programs of the Zelaya era. Public services declined and economic development stagnated. As an economy measure the government reduced the size of the army, thus permitting increased banditry and civil strife. Second, the penetration of the Nicaraguan government's economic policy making by U.S. bankers and the actions of the Mixed Claims Commission produced an extraordinary public indebtedness in the 1911–1915 period. After Woodrow Wilson's government forced the 1917 economic reorganization to control the U.S. bankers and this runaway debt, Nicaragua (or Nicaragua's foreign managers) became financially "responsible." The debt burden began to shrink steadily due to the rigid controls over public income, eventually permitting Nicaragua to regain some financial independence in the mid-1920s. Third, Nicaragua's economic links to the United States strengthened tremendously. U.S. investments rose from $1 million in 1908 to $7.13 million in 1919 to $17.3 million by 1929. U.S. companies became more important in the Nicaraguan economy, and Nicaragua's foreign trade became much more concentrated with the United States. The U.S. share of both imports and exports rose to between 75 and 80 percent.[16]

In sum, U.S. supervision of the Nicaraguan economy diminished the power of the Nicaraguan state, interrupted development programs, and promoted ever greater integration of the Nicaraguan economy into the economic sphere of the United States. The Nicaraguan government almost completely lost control of public debts and finances to U.S. financiers between 1911 and 1916. The U.S. government, however, intervened in 1916–1917 to establish a system of fiscal coordination and control. This system, combined with expanded exports and better prices due to World War I, carried Nicaragua into the 1920s with somewhat improved economic conditions.

The third U.S. interest in Nicaragua was protecting the canal monopoly. The United States now no longer wished to build a canal in Nicaragua. Rather, it desired simply to maintain its monopoly over transit through Panama by preventing construction of any other canal. Such a monopoly would virtually assure U.S. strategic dominance over the Caribbean. It would checkmate a significant potential challenge to U.S. naval superiority by either the Germans or the Japanese. The canal monopoly would also reinforce the economic dominance of the United States in the hemisphere.

The negotiations for exclusive U.S. canal rights (or, more accurately, rights to block canal construction) in Nicaragua aggravated the already heavy U.S. involvement in Nicaraguan internal politics. Conservative General Emiliano Chamorro Vargas, who had been persuaded by the United States in 1912 to accept the ambassadorship in Washington in order to calm things down for President Adolfo Díaz, nominally represented Nicaragua's interests. Many observers, however, believe Chamorro agreed to the quite unfavorable terms of the Chamorro-Bryan Treaty (signed in 1914, ratified in 1916) to obtain U.S. backing to become the next president.[17] The terms of the Chamorro-Bryan Treaty speak for themselves: "The Government of Nicaragua grants in perpetuity to the Government of the United States, forever free from all taxation or other public charge, the exclusive proprietary rights necessary and convenient for the construction, operation, and maintenance of an interoceanic canal."[18] The treaty also gave the United States a ninety-nine-year lease to Nicaragua's Caribbean Corn Islands, as well as a naval base on the Gulf of Fonseca, "subject exclusively to the laws and sovereign authority of the United States."[19] In exchange for these rights the United

States paid $3 million, all of which passed directly to the U.S. banks that held Nicaragua's debts.[20]

The Chamorro-Bryan Treaty had three principal effects. First, it ensured that Nicaragua would *not* have a transisthmian canal, thus satisfying the security concerns of the United States by preventing Japan or Germany from building one there. Second, the treaty torpedoed an incipient Central American unification movement. This occurred when the United States and Nicaragua rejected a judgment by the Central American Court of Justice, which held that the pact violated Honduran rights in the Gulf of Fonseca and Costa Rica's rights over the Río San Juan. Nicaragua's neighbors realized that the United States was disavowing the very court system that it had so strongly advocated for them and disbanded the court in 1918.

Third, the United States continued its intimate meddling in Nicaragua's internal politics, keeping its commitment to Chamorro. In the elections of 1916 Emiliano Chamorro received the mandate of the Nicaraguan people—such as it was, given that the Liberals could not campaign and that U.S. officials had prevailed upon Díaz's candidate, Dr. Carlos Cuadra Pasos, to withdraw before the election. Later, in 1921, Chamorro's uncle, Diego Manuel Chamorro, succeeded the general in the presidency with the backing of the United States. Thus, Conservatives ruled Nicaragua until 1923, albeit solely by means of the power that they derived through collaboration with the U.S. occupation force.

The Slow U.S. Retreat from Interventionism (1921–1933)

In the 1920s the orientation of U.S. foreign-policy makers toward military intervention and toward the Caribbean and Central America where the United States had employed so much naked force, had begun to change. The State Department's Latin American section, quite influential in policy toward the region, had begun to favor the withdrawal of U.S. troops—unless it seemed that chaos might result. Dana Munro, an insider, spelled out the department's view:

> We thought that the first requisite for progress in the Caribbean was the development of orderly republican government. . . . We realized, however, that there were great obstacles to the holding of free elections . . . and we were inclined to support constituted governments against any attempt to overthrow them by force, in the belief that only the maintenance of peace would permit the sort of progress that was necessary for the development of democratic institutions. For the same reasons, we endeavored . . . to persuade the Central American states to replace their graft-ridden, undisciplined armies with police forces trained by foreign instructors.[21]

The State Department regarded economic development as the key to all its other goals but saw no prospects for direct foreign aid from the U.S. government. It thus tried to promote economic development and financial stability by attracting U.S. investment and by favoring and continuing to organize financial administration schemes. The willingness to use U.S. military force to protect U.S. lives and property continued, but the rising domestic and international unpopularity of such intervention, especially in Latin America, had made this option decreasingly satisfactory.

Foreign policy leanings had begun to change at the presidential level as well. The United States took on a generally isolationist mood following the First World War. In the press and in the Senate, criticism of military intervention in the Caribbean and Central America grew steadily throughout the 1920s. Warren Harding, who succeeded Woodrow Wilson as president in 1921, had criticized Wilson's military policy in Central America. Apparently sensitive to the winds of opinion, Harding felt considerably less comfortable with interventionism than his three predecessors, although he did not dramatically reverse U.S. policy. This presidential unease with intervention increased throughout the succeeding Coolidge and Hoover administrations. The complexities and failures of intervention and occupation themselves, together with pressing new international strategic concerns, led eventually to a major redefinition of U.S. Latin American policy. When Franklin Roosevelt became president in 1933, the United States adopted the "Good Neighbor Policy" and largely eschewed overt intervention. Paradoxically, however, throughout the twelve-year passage from Harding's diminishing enthusiasm for the use of force to Roosevelt's policies of "nonintervention" and "pacific protection" of U.S. interests, the United States intervened anew or continued occupations—in Haiti, Santo Domingo, and Cuba. Nicaragua, too, continued to be a stage where U.S. diplomats—often inept and guided by vacillating U.S. policy—scripted, directed, stage-managed, and played major roles in a national tragedy.[22]

Nicaraguan Reaction to the New U.S. Policies (1923-1927)

Nicaragua in the 1920s had about six hundred thousand inhabitants ruled by a U.S.-backed Conservative government unable to control or to recover from a state of general disorganization. The capacity of the government to supply services, to keep the peace, and to promote development had generally declined because of the endemic party warfare, minority rule imposed from the outside, and the customs receivership that kept the state in penury. Dana Munro, who served in the U.S. diplomatic mission in Managua in this period, described life in the capital in an era when the automobile was a novelty and the mule and ox-cart still served as major modes of transport: "Managua, with some

40,000 inhabitants, had few buildings of more than one story, and its un-paved, badly drained streets made it appallingly dusty most of the year. The American legation, which was one of the finest houses, had no glass windows and was dimly lit by unshielded electric bulbs hanging from high ceilings."[23] The León-centered Liberal coffee-producer-exporter faction and its urban middle-sector supporters had prospered with the continued growth of the coffee industry, despite its exclusion from political power. This elite faction, richer yet more politically frustrated than ever, encouraged popular agitation to harass the Conservative regime and hatched scheme after scheme to return to power.[24]

The byzantine complexity of Nicaraguan politics before 1920 seems simple by comparison to developments of the next fifteen years. Nicaragua's politicians were often ruthlessly Machiavellian but also often maladroit. Their failures, however, were due partly to the highly fragmented nature of power and partly to the evolving role of the United States. The following narration omits much of the plotting, maneuvering, calculation, and betrayal that occurred after 1923 in Nicaragua.[25] However, some of what went on requires telling here in order to under-stand the emergence of the National Guard (Guardia Nacional) and the Somoza dynasty. The following account highlights some of the critical events of the 1923–1927 period.

Diego Manuel Chamorro followed his nephew to the presidency in 1921. He ruled with very little autonomy. When the elder Chamorro died in office in 1923 Vice-President Bartolomé Martínez, a representative of the anti-Chamorrista wing of the Conservative faction, took over the of-fice. Martínez bitterly opposed Emiliano Chamorro's desire to return to the presidency. Martínez thus turned to the Liberals to forge a coalition that might thwart the caudillo's fond hopes for a second presidential term.

These developing events meshed with the aims of Department of State policymakers. In 1921 and 1922, a series of ugly events occurred between the U.S. Marine legation guard and the local population and police. The State Department was already predisposed to withdraw the leathernecks, and the guard's morale and discipline problems intensified the U.S. government's desire to end the occupation. The department came to view the development of a coalition government as a hopeful sign. The United States pressed hard, and successfully, for the adoption of a revised elec-toral law and for sufficient electoral supervision to prevent a massive election fraud that would return Chamorro to power.

Martínez's designated candidates, Conservative Carlos Solórzano for president and Liberal Juan Bautista Sacasa for vice-president, won a solid victory. The Department of State, still frustrated in its attempts to establish a nonpartisan and professional military force, told the vic-torious Solórzano that the marines would be withdrawn in August 1925. Extremely conscious of his vulnerability as a coalition leader without the

full support of either of the bitterly antagonistic party factions, Solórzano became distraught at the prospect of the marines' departure. He
reluctantly agreed to create a national constabulary to replace them. In
June 1925 the Nicaraguan government made a contract with retired U.S.
Army major Calvin B. Carter to head the new National Guard and its
training school. Carter arrived in July and the marines left Nicaragua on
4 August 1925.

The highly unstable coalition's seams immediately began to split one
by one. Before the National Guard could develop significant strength to
back up the wobbly government, General Alfredo Rivas took the first
step down the road to civil war. Rivas, who was the president's brother-in-
law, and some troops broke into a party at the Club Internacional in
Managua, seized most of the cabinet and several diplomats as hostages,
and demanded that Solórzano purge the Liberals from the cabinet. The
president complied. In October Emiliano Chamorro, fearing that the
germinal but growing Guard might block his rise to power, seized control
of the Conservative-dominated army. Chamorro then demanded that Solórzano purge the remaining Liberal appointees from the government.
Solórzano complied. Liberal Vice-President Sacasa, reading these events
like tea leaves, saw that sudden travel would be propitious for his health
and fled the country. The now nearly all-Conservative Congress replaced
Sacasa as president-designate with Chamorro. The general then made his
final move. President Solórzano, ever cooperative, resigned in January
1926, and Emiliano Chamorro assumed the presidency. The Department
of State had seen in these events dark auguries for the future. Fearing that
the Liberals would rebel, the United States consistently opposed Chamorro's
moves and then refused to recognize the Chamorro government.

The Department of State's fears proved prescient. The first Liberal
uprising came in May 1926, capturing Bluefields and surprising even
many of the party's principal leaders. Sacasa assumed leadership of the
movement from abroad but did not return. Direct U.S. intervention involved landing marines from the U.S.S. *Cleveland* at Bluefields and
declaring the city a neutral zone. The United States intervened indirectly,
however, via the new constabulary. Major Carter and his aides had
helped Chamorro build up the National Guard to nearly full strength and
armed it well with the support of the State Department. Against this now
rather formidable force, the uprising collapsed almost immediately.

U.S. Embassy Secretary Lawrence Dennis, acting to head off a feared
second Liberal rebellion, began to pressure Chamorro to resign. The
strong-willed Dennis, meddling with a verve that embarrassed even
hardened State Department Nicaragua hands, repeatedly demanded
Chamorro's resignation and even incited other Conservative factions to
oust him. This failed to bring results by August, however, when the
year's second Liberal revolt commenced. This time the insurgents

threatened more convincingly. Sacasa had obtained money and arms from Mexico's President Calles, and thus buttressed, he led a two-pronged rising in both the heavily populated West and in the eastern jungles, the traditional rebels' haven. Although quickly contained in the west, the rebels held on in the Atlantic region. Under the generalship of José María Moncada, the insurgents captured Río Grande, north of Bluefields, and rapidly extended their control over most of the Atlantic area. Once again the United States landed marines in Bluefields to "protect American lives and property." The marines did not interfere seriously with either side in this episode.

Although the much-strengthened (and now no longer neutral) National Guard aided the Conservatives, the Liberals offset this advantage with substantial aid from Mexico. The cost of the war grew onerous for the government, and the insurgents' military progress bogged down. The war stagnated. President Chamorro, harassed by Dennis at the U.S. Embassy and besieged by growing war costs for which no aid was forthcoming, eventually agreed to a conference to seek a negotiated settlement. Under a fifteen-day cease-fire, the parties met aboard the U.S.S. *Denver* in the Corinto harbor to discuss truce terms. Chamorro agreed to quit, to everyone's delight, but the conference then broke up on the shoals of partisan ambition and wrangling about who would succeed him. With Chamorro out of the way, the Conservatives apparently believed that they would receive decisive U.S. aid. The Liberals, with the advantage of considerable popular support, opted to hold out for promised further Mexican help. To break the stalemate Lawrence Dennis engineered the return of Conservative ex-president Adolfo Díaz to power. The United States, still clinging to the minority party as if it were the last hope, recognized the Díaz government. This action prompted Juan Bautista Sacasa to declare himself (correctly so) "Constitutional President" from the Liberal redoubt of Puerto Cabezas. Mexico recognized Sacasa's government.

At this point the Mexican aid might have tipped the scales toward the Liberals had not the United States reinforced its intervention on behalf of the Conservatives. But the U.S. government feared the spread of Mexican "bolshevism" because of the possibility of Mexican nationalization of U.S. oil holdings. In addition, Mexico's anti-Yankee posture and its own foreign intervention aroused primal geopolitical fears among U.S. strategists. Mexico appeared to threaten U.S. political and military sway in the strategic area surrounding the Panama Canal. In light of such fears, the doomed Conservatives still appeared to be the only acceptable choice to the Department of State.

Following the collapse of another peace proposal in December and renewed fighting, the United States permitted additional arms sales to the government and arranged new loans to help finance the war. Díaz then asked for U.S. troops. President Coolidge complied, dispatching a con-

tingent of 160 marines to Managua on 6 January 1927. This step signaled
the beginning of a new wave of mayhem. The massive buildup of U.S.
forces that followed immediately began a six-year nightmare for everyone concerned.

The United States had thus renounced its preference for reduced intervention when it was confronted with a challenge to its geopolitical
goals. U.S. foreign-policy makers sought to prevent a Mexican
"triumph" on the flanks of the U.S. empire by stabilizing Nicaragua and
organizing free elections for 1928. The Nicaraguan parties' aims held
forth little prospect for success—the Conservatives scrambled frantically
to retain power while the Liberals pressed with relentless fury to dislodge
their bitter enemies. In retrospect, the U.S. attempt to stabilize the situation by backing a doomed minority government and promoting power-
sharing seems amazingly out of touch with Nicaraguan reality. In effect,
the United States expected the Liberal and Conservative caudillos and
their followers—despite more than a century of bitter antagonism,
armed conflict, and atrocities against each other, and in the middle of a
terrible civil war—to kiss, make up, and walk hand in hand into the
future in mutual trust and respect.

When Liberals seized Chinandega in early February the government
launched a ferocious campaign to oust them, assisted by National Guard
aircraft flown by Americans. The army and the Guard retook
Chinandega with such violence that most of the city was reduced to rubble. The United States then poured more troops and naval forces into the
area to protect the Corinto-Managua railroad and to shore up the Díaz
government. By late February 1927 eleven U.S. cruisers and destroyers
were in Nicaraguan ports, and more than fifty-four hundred marines
were occupying all the principal cities. Nicaragua was in chaos. The
fighting and forced drafts had driven peasants from the fields, threatening crop loss and potential famine. Banditry had become generalized.
Armies on both sides were committing atrocities against each other and
against civilians. The massive U.S. aid had permitted the Conservative
forces to stalemate the rebels once again.

At this point Calvin Coolidge and Secretary of State Kellogg decided
to seek mediation of the conflict yet again. In April 1927 they sent Henry
Stimson to seek an accord among the warring Nicaraguans so that the
United States might begin to extricate itself. The U.S. negotiator sought
to include two key elements in the hoped-for accord: First, Díaz must
complete his term. If the Liberals accepted this, the United States would
accept the outcome of a free, U.S.-supervised presidential election in
1928. This would mean certain Liberal victory. It also gave Stimson a
wedge to drive between Moncada and Sacasa—presidential ambition.
Second, Stimson demanded that the Nicaraguan government organize a
truly nonpartisan guard to exercise police and military functions. The

force would permit the U.S. forces to withdraw and in theory would serve as the impartial guarantor of public order and electoral probity in the Nicaragua of the future.

Adolfo Díaz, virtually devoid of freedom to differ with his patrons, accepted the terms for a cease-fire. Backed up with a force of marines to prove that the United States would not permit a Liberal military victory, Stimson went to work on the Liberals. In a series of meetings Stimson sought and received Liberal assurances that the party intended no socialist reform under Mexican influence. Stimson then sought out General Moncada at Tipitapa and, it is rumored, promised him U.S. support for the presidency in 1928 in exchange for an end to the fighting. Whether this is true or not, Moncada accepted Stimson's proposal and recommended to his generals that they lay down their arms. Beginning the following day both government and rebel forces began to suspend hostilities and the civil war wound down. On May 12 the Espino Negro Pact, so named for the thorn tree under which Stimson and Moncada met, was signed by all the Liberal generals—all, that is, except one.

Augusto César Sandino and the Anti-Interventionist War (1927–1933)

Two of the men who would mold Nicaragua's future for the next half century played minor and radically different roles in the Tipitapa agreement. Both "generals" in the insurgent band by virtue of raising small forces to fight against the Conservatives, these men followed different lights and, in so doing, profoundly affected the course of Nicaraguan history. Henry Stimson believed as the agreement was signed that he had presided at the funeral of the Liberal-Conservative civil war. He did not realize that he had in truth witnessed both the birth of a war of liberation and the conception of a revolution still a half century in the future. The two minor Liberal generals remained momentarily eclipsed by the truce. Anastasio Somoza García, a glib former used car salesman with fluent colloquial English and a dubious legal record, threw in his lot with the Liberals' new patrons, the Americans. Augusto César Sandino, once a fugitive from Nicaraguan justice and recently returned from laboring in the Mexican oilfields, refused to sign the pact. From this moment forward the destinies of these two men and Nicaragua became inextricably entwined.

Sandino began to play his historic part immediately. Augusto Sandino was the illegitimate son of a smallholder from the mountainous region of Las Segovias. From his birth in 1895 until his adolescence he lived with his mother, who did agricultural day labor under the commonplace debt bondage arrangements of the day. While once imprisoned for unpaid debts to her patron, Sandino's pregnant mother aborted in the presence of the horrified child. In his teens Augusto went to live with his father, an ardent Liberal. His education and political awareness began to develop during these years. Sandino worked as a laborer, merchant, and mechanic's helper in his early manhood. At about twenty-five he wounded a man in a fight and fled Nicaragua to escape prosecution. In Honduras he worked for the United Fruit Company; he moved on to Guatemala and then again to Tampico, Mexico, where he worked for the Hausteca Petroleum Company. In Mexico Sandino joined the Masonic order, reinforcing the strong Liberal leanings he had absorbed in his youth. In the revolutionary effervescence of working-class Mexico in the 1920s, he encountered many ideas that appear to have shaped his later political attitudes. Ultimately Sandino was to express sentiments in favor of improving the lot of the rural poor and ending foreign intervention in Nicaragua, but he never manifested a doctrinaire ideological strain of any sort. Sandino's ideology became populistic and reformist, but not Marxist.[26]

While working in the Tampico oilfields, Sandino grew progressively angrier with reports of U.S intervention in Nicaragua and its blockage of Liberal rule. He later reported an incident that moved him to return to Nicaragua. With the day's newspaper before him on the table while conversing with some stevedore and oilfield-hand friends, Sandino mentioned that he was contemplating returning to take up arms against the U.S. intervention. Referring to the Nicaraguan leaders' tradition of inviting foreign interference, one of his companions scoffed that Nicaraguans would all just as soon sell out their country. Sandino related that this accusation made him toss in his bed that night and many others, thinking that to remain silent before such betrayal was just as bad as the betrayal itself.

His meager savings in his pocket, Sandino returned to Nicaragua a few weeks before the second Liberal uprising of 1926. He took work in a mine in his native region and began to recruit followers to fight for the Liberal cause. When the revolt started he attempted to join Moncada, but the haughty general rejected Sandino as a nobody. Undaunted, Sandino fought anyway, leading his ragtag, peasant-and-miner army under a red and black flag emblazoned "Liberty or Death." After an early defeat, Sandino and his three hundred men adopted guerrilla tactics and became ever more dangerous to the Conservatives. Sandino's strongly committed Liberalism appears to have taken on a steadily more important and intense hostility toward the U.S. intervention, especially after the January 1927 occupation of the whole country. Moncada stunned Sandino by accepting the Espino Negro pact and asking the Liberal generals to surrender. Sandino later recalled feeling his rage mount as he contemplated Moncada's suspected sellout to the Americans. He remembered that sarcastic voice in Tampico saying that he too would sell out his country. He decided that what mattered was not who would become president, but that the United States had no right to invade a small country and humiliate it.[27] Sandino refused to sign the pact and returned to the mountains of Segovia. From there he and his army would continue to battle the invaders.

At first, however, none of the other major actors really regarded Sandino as anything but a nuisance—as a political renegade turned bandit. Nicaraguan party faction leaders busied themselves with jockeying for advantage for the 1928 elections. For their part, members of the U.S. mission bent their energies to refereeing the continual Liberal-Conservative and intraparty disagreements about the application of the truce. Preparations for the 1928 elections and the reorganization of the Nicaraguan government also tied up the Americans. The reconstruction of the National Guard, of course, formed the linchpin of the U.S. effort. The Díaz government agreed to disband the old Guard, and the U.S. Marines agreed to guide training, organization, and operations until the new force could stand on its own feet.

The United States sharply cut back its occupation forces in mid-1927, just after the reorganization of the National Guard. The Americans thought the Guard would soon substitute handsomely for the marines. The optimism proved unfounded, however, and the new constabulary was to suffer through several years of serious problems: the constant and growing harassment by Sandino, language and cultural problems between the U.S. officers and their Nicaraguan troops, partisan political interference, enormous transportation and communications difficulties, inadequate financing, and difficulties adjusting to the performance of police duties. These difficulties notwithstanding, the Guard gradually grew in size and capability. It developed a sound training program, a national radio communication network, a medical and health program, and an air wing for combat and transport. Regular and improved pay and benefits steadily cut desertion rates, despite the stream of casualties produced by the war with Sandino and the frequent minor uprisings against the government.[28]

The government, the Guard, and the Americans began to take the renegade Liberal more seriously as the months wore on. Sandino declared himself in word and deed in May and June 1927. When General Moncada "most affectionately" urged the rebel to accept the peace for the "honor of Liberalism," the leader of the self-styled Army for the Defense of Nicaraguan National Sovereignty (Ejército Defensor de la Soberanía Nacional de Nicaragua) snapped back sarcastically:

> I do not know why you wish to command me now. I remember that you always regarded me badly when you were General-in-Chief of the Liberal armies. You never accepted my requests for troops to fight the enemy

with. . . . You undoubtedly know my temperament and that I am un-
breakable. Now I want you to come disarm me; I await you at my post.
You will not make me cede by any other means. *I am not for sale; I do not
give up:* you will have to defeat me. I believe that I am thus doing my duty,
and for posterity I will write my protest in blood.[29]

Sandino inscribed the first page of his protest on 16 July 1927, when his
army attacked the National Guard garrison at Ocotal. The frontal attack
on a fortified position proved quixotic. Strafing by U.S. planes left
heavy casualties among the attackers; the garrison's losses were very
light. Gamely calling his defeat a victory, Sandino retreated to the hills
once again to meditate on tactics.

From that point forward Sandino's army, never more than one thousand strong and averaging half that number, engaged in a classic rural
guerrilla war. The liberation forces reportedly operated from a cloud-
shrouded (and perhaps mythical) mountain camp known as El Chipote.
Divided into several columns, Sandino's forces moved in sympathetic territory, utilized the local populace for intelligence, and avoided open confrontations with the marines and the Guard. The guerrillas often worked
their fields by day, their weapons buried. Word of an approaching
government or marine patrol worked a terrible magic. The invisible army
suddenly materialized and moved into hidden positions along the trail. A
chilling chorus of cries from the guerrillas' children—known as the
"angels' choir" (*el coro de los ángeles*)—would sound disorientingly all
around the patrol. Within seconds the ambush would begin with a
withering cross fire from the steamy forest, often devastating the government forces. As unexpectedly as they appeared, Sandino's soldiers would
then fade back into the jungle, returning to hidden camps or resuming
their labors.

The war went on steadily from mid-1927 until 1933, waxing and waning, but the government was never in control. The Guard and the
marines, despite the steady increase in their force and capability, turned
more and more to acts of terrorism against those suspected of aiding the
guerrillas. Away from the war, in the urban belt along the west coast,
life went on more or less normally for some time. José María Moncada
won the 1928 presidential election. Supervised by the United States
and refereed by the U.S.-commanded National Guard, this election
was by most reckonings the least fraudulent Nicaragua ever had. Four
years later the Sacasa Liberal faction received its turn, the Liberals
demonstrating their popular base by winning a second supervised election.[30]

Augusto César Sandino continued to press his struggle against the occupation forces—relentlessly, ruthlessly. Nagged by Sandino's persistence, President Herbert Hoover felt compelled to leave about two

thousand Marines in Nicaragua to supplement the Guard. President Moncada became increasingly frustrated by the lack of military progress, not to mention by the Americans' obstinate determination to keep the National Guard politically neutral. Seeking to politicize the force, Moncada twice created a volunteer force of Liberals (some of them foreign mercenaries) to supplement the Guard. In 1929 the volunteer units so widely used terrorist methods against civilians and Moncada's political enemies that the United States emphatically demanded, and received, their demobilization. In 1931, following two unsuccessful antiguerrilla campaigns the previous year, "volunteer" battalions again took the field alongside the Guard. During one of the 1930 campaigns against the insurgents, the National Guard attempted to relocate much of the population of Las Segovias in order to disrupt Sandino's popular base. This tactic aroused such public indignation that the government dropped it as counterproductive.[31]

As time passed, Sandino's war became a bigger and bigger drain upon the Nicaraguan government. New U.S. bank loans and the continued customs receivership kept the state heavily indebted and short of cash for operations. As early as 1929 the National Guard was absorbing a whopping one-fourth of the depression-pinched budget.[32] For all its efforts, the Moncada government did little more than hold its ground against the rebels. Sandino continued to be a threat despite the major antiguerrilla campaigns, the viciousness of the National Guard volunteers, the terrorism against suspected rebel sympathizers, and the steadily growing capabilities of the Guard. His spirit undaunted after five years, Sandino repeatedly excoriated the "North American pirates" and their "criminal international policy." He saved the bitterest invective of his voluminous letters, manifestos, and reports, however, for the Nicaraguan politicians who had betrayed Nicaraguan sovereignty to the Americans. For example, in 1932 Sandino fired the following salvo: "We have declared that Nicaragua will be free only by bullets and at the cost of our own blood. That pack of political mongrels who fight to grovel under the invader's whip will, by their own fault, be wiped out in the not too distant future and the people will take the reins of national power."[33] From 1929 on the effects of the Great Depression upon the Nicaraguan economy seemed to increase support for Sandino. By 1932 the rebel columns had begun to strike into the western zones, which had previously been free of such attacks.

In the United States the inexorable lengthening of the marine casualty lists for Nicaragua aroused popular opposition to the intervention. The most strident criticism came from certain liberal periodicals, labor unions, and members of Congress. The legislators resented unilateral executive decisions to intervene in Nicaragua (and in the Dominican Republic and Haiti) that, it was argued, undercut Congress's constitutional war power. The arguments about containing Mexican "bolshe-vism" in Nicaragua and about establishing free elections prompted con-gressional derision. Senator George Norris, for example, suggested that if the marines could guarantee honest elections they should be sent first to Philadelphia and Pittsburgh.[34] A group of senators repeatedly tried to restrict funds for the occupation forces; they eventually succeeded in 1932. The United States had also begun to fear Japan and the Soviet Union as growing and potentially hostile powers, a perception that made improving dismal U.S. relations with Latin America an increasingly high priority. Confronted with such growing domestic pressure and new strategic worries, President Hoover and his secretary of state, none other than Henry Stimson, viewed the deteriorating military picture in Nicaragua with mounting trepidation. They decided to pull out U.S. forces following Nicaragua's 1932 presidential election.[35]

The U.S. Withdrawal and Its Impact

The United States published its intention to withdraw its expeditionary forces, and U.S. diplomats in Managua stepped up pressure for inter-party cooperation and feverishly tried to prepare the National Guard for its new role. The selection of a Nicaraguan commander for the Guard became a major political event, and another figure of Nicaragua's malign fate, Anastasio Somoza García, made his entrance. At first cautiously feeling his way through the brambles of Nicaragua's political thicket, Somoza began to make his moves. "Tacho," as his friends called him, came from the lower-middle-class ranks of the Liberal faction. In 1926 he had ingloriously led a rebel troop against the Conservative garrison in San Marcos. Defeated, Somoza retained his self-conferred rank of general but wisely eschewed further such armed exploits. He turned in-stead to the cultivation of the powerful. As a nephew of Juan Bautista Sacasa, Somoza easily gained access to Liberal inner circles. In 1927 he had aided and amused the Stimson mission, and favorably impressed Stimson himself, by translating with his excellent colloquial American English. By 1932, when the plan to withdraw the marines became known, Somoza had insinuated himself into the government and had be-friended and impressed the U.S. diplomatic mission. The aging Matthew Hanna, the U.S. ambassador, pushed for Somoza as the best candidate to command the National Guard. Uncharitable tongues in Managua gossiped that the very young and attractive Mrs. Hanna championed Somoza's cause with her husband perhaps with more ardor than cir-cumspection and may have greatly influenced the selection. Whether or not the foreign interests of Mrs. Hanna may have exceeded those of the United States in this matter, the fact remains that when Presi-dent Sacasa won the 1932 election, he designated Somoza to com-

Figure 3.1. (above) Augusto César Sandino (third from left) and his generals; (below) Sandino (right) with General Anastasio Somoza García just before Sandino's 1934 assassination. (Photos from *Barricada* archives)

mand the National Guard—with the enthusiastic blessings of the United States.

The U.S. Marine Corps expeditionary force, after twenty frustrating years of occupation, abandoned Nicaragua in January 1933. Once the occupation forces were no longer present to enforce the policy preferences of the United States on its client government, several natural realignments in the Nicaraguan political system swiftly began. One was the politicization of the National Guard. Anastasio Somoza García and President Sacasa began to name Guard officials to replace the departed U.S. officers. True to Nicaraguan tradition, the majority of the appointees were qualified by Liberal party loyalty rather than by training in the National Guard's academy. Although the politicizing process took some time because Somoza's hold on the Guard was not initially strong—indeed the appointments almost caused his ouster by resentful officers—Somoza had in a few days begun to undo the neutrality of the Guard for which the Americans had so tenaciously and ingenuously struggled. Somoza remained an outsider and politico, not at first trusted by the Guard's veteran officials who had fought the hated Sandino. Somoza had to earn the loyalty of the Guard, now the most powerful element in the wobbly Nicaraguan state. In one of the cruelest ironies of Nicaraguan history, Somoza would purchase the Guard's loyalty through an act of treachery and betrayal—the assassination of Sandino.

As a second consequence of the U.S. withdrawal, intimately related to Anastasio Somoza's gradually growing power, the Guard's new commander became increasingly independent from his uncle, the president. Somoza, a man of enormous political cunning, recognized the potential for power inherent in commanding a well-trained professional army in a chronically weak state. With each gain in his footing and his confidence, Somoza acted with ever greater autonomy from the constitutional government. By mid-1934 President Sacasa's de facto power had so shrunk that Somoza effectively ruled Nicaragua and ignored Sacasa's mandates with impunity.

The U.S. withdrawal also brought the end of the six-year war with Sandino. Sandino immediately entered peace negotiations; his letter announcing his terms for peace reached President Sacasa the very day the marines withdrew. Sacasa had named the educator Sonfonías Salvatierra, a Sandino confidant, as his minister of agriculture and labor. Salvatierra promptly arranged peace talks between the government and the rebel. Despite continued clashes between the Guard and the rebel army, Sandino met Dr. Sacasa in Managua on 2 February 1933. They came to terms that very day, agreeing to an immediate bilateral cease-fire, complete amnesty for the guerrillas, the disarming of all but a hundred of Sandino's men (this small force to act as a guard for

Sandino), and the cession to Sandino and his followers of some land for a cooperative farm in the Río Coco region. The peace began among general public rejoicing as Sandino returned to Las Segovias to supervise his part of the bargain. When some of Sandino's men resisted the truce the general demonstrated his resolve and crushed the incipient revolt by executing the two men he believed responsible.[36]

Nicaragua in 1933 had just traversed one of the bleakest peoriods of its rather grim history, but short-run economic prospects at the time of the truce promised little relief. The spiraling decline of world trade had begun to depress coffee prices, spelling a deep depression for Nicaragua. Coffee dropped from $0.86 per kilogram in 1929 to $0.52 per kilo in 1930, later to bottom out at $0.32 in 1940. This long slide in the value of the nation's main export sent waves of lowered profits, reduced wages, defaulted loans, and unemployment through the Nicaraguan economy. As taxes on exported coffee provided a major income source, the Nicaraguan government's revenues shrank drastically, even further constraining the state's already abysmal capability for confronting the nation's immense problems.[37]

The grim economic picture notwithstanding, some Nicaraguans saw, at least for a while, some promise in the future. Although impoverished, the country had regained some measure of its sovereignty and dignity when the U.S. troops left. The political faction with the majority of electoral support now held power. Peace between Sandino and the Sacasa government had followed hard on the departure of the U.S. occupation forces, raising hopes for a permanent end to civil strife. Sadly, history has shown that Nicaragua did have a period of comparative stability coming, but it was to be a stability enforced by the tyrant's heel.

The year 1933, then, was a time of hope—soon to be disappointed—for most Nicaraguans and a time of brief victory for the campesinos and miners who, as Sandino's soldiers, had worried the occupiers until they left. Some have blamed Sandino for the failure that was soon to come. Many have wondered why Sandino himself did not press on to seize power once and for all. The explanation, however, is simple. Sandino's goal was nothing more than the expulsion of the invaders; he had fulfilled his mission.[38]

The epilogue of the story of Augusto César Sandino—to be presented in the next chapter—entwines the final strands of his destiny with those of the liberation fighter's historical nemesis. Sandino was a truly tragic figure, his achievements fatally flawed. The liberation movement he led remained uninformed and unguided by either an ideology or an organization capable of consolidating its ultimate victory. Lacking these, the movement in its moment of glory succumbed to the imperative traditions of Nicaraguan political history—to ambition, conspiracy, betrayal, and despotism.

Summary and Conclusions

For roughly fifty years following the great National War of 1856–1857, a string of Conservative presidents and then the modernizing Liberal dictator José Santos Zelaya (1893–1909) had achieved for Nicaragua a slow but undeniable process of economic growth and national institutional development. Two main factors accounted for this tentative growth and development. First, Nicaragua had remained relatively free from chronic interfactional warfare; Liberals and Conservatives had fought each other less and had devoted more of their energy to economic growth—especially to expanding coffee cultivation. Second, external intervention by the United States and Great Britain had generally been less than in the 1850s. With less external meddling, Nicaraguan national institutions had stabilized and developed somewhat, growth-oriented economic policies had begun to take effect, and fewer human and productive resources had been consumed or destroyed by war.

With the marked increase of U.S. and British interests in Nicaragua and the escalation of their direct intervention there in the early twentieth century, the process of stabilization and slow progress of the previous half century changed to a process of destabilization and destruction. Much of what Zelaya and his predecessors had accomplished was undone. The minority Conservatives accepted U.S. and British encouragement to try to overthrow Zelaya. This provoked a civil war, following which the United States had to prop up the Conservatives by physically occupying Nicaragua with several thousand men. Despite all this, the Americans still could not achieve in Nicaragua the order they sought to protect their strategic and economic interests. The damage to the economy of this internal conflict combined with the drain on the Nicaraguan treasury by U.S. business interests to erode the economic and political development so slowly won during the previous era.

Then in 1927 the United States finally decided to change sides, from the hapless Conservatives to the stronger Liberals, in pursuit of that elusive stability and political order that might permit it permanently to withdraw its forces from Nicaragua. In so doing it created an unanticipated difficulty—the anti-interventionist rebellion led by Sandino. This six-year war added additional burdens to the reeling nation's woes just as the Great Depression began, thus still further taxing political institutions and the economy. The war also kept U.S. troops fighting on Nicaraguan soil for six more years. When in 1933 the United States finally abandoned its thoroughly unproductive overt intervention in Nicaragua, it left behind a political monster—the National Guard in the hands of Anastasio Somoza García. Within a year Somoza would take the founding step of his family's forty-six-year dynasty by planting his boot on the fresh earth of Augusto César Sandino's shallow grave.

The Foundation of the Dynasty

*The peace of the Republic does not bar the free discussion of public affairs,
the enjoyment of broad freedoms, nor the logical exercise of political activities. . . . I welcome from the Opposition Party or from private citizens
any honest criticism of administrative acts that do not meet the goals of national interest which guide my government.*
                                —Anastasio Somoza García, 19 April 1952[1]

Augusto César Sandino, his father Gregorio, and others dined in the
Presidential Palace in Managua on 23 February 1934. This was the third
meeting between President Sacasa and Sandino to work out difficulties
in the transition to peace. The truce and cease-fire between the rebels and
the government had grown progressively more tense in the early new
year. Sacasa had negotiated in good faith and Congress had cooperated
with the rebels, but the National Guard kept clashing with Sandino's men
in the Río Coco region around Wiwilí, where the Sandinistas had their
cooperative farm.

The productive meeting ended at 10:00 P.M. Sandino, his father, rebel
generals Umanzor and Estrada, and Labor Minister Sonfonías
Salvatierra left the Presidential Palace for the Managua home of
Augusto's brother Sócrates, where they were to spend the night. A few
blocks away their path was blocked by a National Guard vehicle, apparently broken down. But suddenly armed men swarmed around the car
and the party was arrested—under direct orders from Anastasio Somoza
García, head of the National Guard. Sandino requested of his captors a
conference with Somoza, who refused. The squad then straightaway conducted Sandino, Umanzor, and Estrada to an empty field by the old airport north of Managua and murdered them.

In jail not far away Salvatierra and Gregorio Sandino heard the
shooting. The father knew: "Now they are killing them. Those who
would be redeemers will always die crucified."[2] He lost another son that
same night when the Guard arrested Sócrates Sandino and another Sandinista general, Santos López. The victims' bodies were buried unmarked
on the outskirts of Managua; they have yet to be discovered. The same

night, the Guard surrounded Sandino's headquarters in Wiwilí and massacred at least three hundred of Sandino's followers, including women and children.[3]

Somoza García Takes Control

When appointed director in chief of the Guard, Anastasio Somoza was a man on a tightrope. Limited in administrative experience, Somoza's major talents were his personal charm and his ability to extricate himself from scrapes with the law.[4] To one side of the line on which Somoza balanced was President Juan Bautista Sacasa, who sought earnestly to accommodate Sandino and to pacify the nation. Sacasa also hoped to control the National Guard by appointing only Liberal officers. On the other side lurked the Guard's own veteran officers, who resented Somoza's military amateurism, his political meddling with the Guard, and the government's accommodation of Sandino.

Somoza's behavior in these early months was that of a man desperately seeking to keep his footing while buffeted by contradictory pressures. He made conflicting promises to his officers, the president, and the U.S. ambassador; he cajoled, wheedled, and lied. He constantly maneuvered to stay on top of the Guard—he manipulated assignments to placate the disgruntled and thus foiled several coup attempts. Under pressure from the Guard, he sought the approval of U.S. Ambassador Arthur Bliss Lane to arrest Sandino, but promised to leave him alone at Lane's insistence. Shortly before ordering Sandino's murder Somoza made a show of embracing his adversary publicly to allay suspicion of the plot (see Figure 3.1).

Under these circumstances, Somoza recognized the National Guard as a nonpareil resource. Nicaragua was prostrate because of war and the Great Depression. Weakened by twenty years of U.S. interference and by the collapse in coffee prices, both the Liberal and Conservative faction elites lacked resolve. The Guard, three thousand strong, constituted the best-trained and most disciplined fighting and police force in Nicaraguan history. To control the Guard would be to counteract the disdain of old-line Liberals who saw Somoza as a latecomer who had only married into the fold. To dominate the Guard and its power would provide Somoza the means to overcome his lower-middle-class background and his history as a business failure, petty criminal, and sometime inspector of latrines. The murder of Sandino thus became the key to the Guard and the Guard the key to everything that Nicaragua had to offer.

Portrayals of this period commonly present Somoza as an iron-fisted tyrant from his first days as director in chief of the National Guard, plotting Sandino's death cold-bloodedly from the outset. However, Millett's detailed analysis of the events suggests otherwise. Somoza was apparently backed inexorably into the assassination plot in his effort to keep control of the Guard. Senior officers of the Guard had neared the breaking point over Sandino and over political manipulation of Guard appointments, and Somoza's overthrow by the Guard itself seemed imminent. Regardless of whether Somoza himself initiated the plot or was forced into it, the results are indisputable. He gathered the senior staff into the conspiracy by means of a signed document sharing responsibility. Somoza falsely reported to his fellow conspirators that U.S. Ambassador Lane supported the killing — an affirmation denied heatedly by the State Department. With the cynical flamboyance that was to become his trademark, Somoza gathered the officers who were not involved (to preclude their acting to counter the plot) for a poetry reading — the first and probably the last in the history of the Guard — while the assassinations took place. Immediately after the assassination Somoza feigned outrage, denied knowledge of the events, and pledged a thorough investigation to his infuriated uncle, President Sacasa. But later, surer of his footing in the National Guard, Somoza openly admitted his role in the murders.

Other evidence indicated how tentative Anastasio Somoza's position was in early 1934. First, despite widespread expectations to the contrary, he did not overthrow President Sacasa immediately after Sandino's removal. At that time the Guard was momentarily weakened by its internal divisions and lacked a clear monopoly of force. The president had a separate guard, control over a significant munitions dump, and his own armed loyalists in León. Somoza therefore placated the president throughout the first half of 1934. He denounced the Sandino assassination publicly and promised to discover and to punish those responsible. (No one was ever punished for the murders.)[5]

Second, President Sacasa's position even seemed to strengthen for a while as he enacted a decree that enhanced his control over the Guard and replaced several officials close to Somoza with persons loyal to himself (especially blood kin). Third, in July an informant betrayed another band of discontented veteran officers who were plotting to assassinate Somoza. Somoza dismantled this conspiracy with considerable diplomacy in order to avoid further clashes with the group. Meanwhile, Sacasa supporters continually pressed for the director in chief's ouster, but they failed to obtain the support they wished from Ambassador Lane, who adhered firmly to his government's instructions not to intervene on either side (see below).

As 1934 progressed, however, Somoza's confidence grew. He raised his ambitions to include the presidency in 1937 and began to challenge President Sacasa openly. (Blocking his path, however, was a constitutional antinepotism provision that would prohibit him from succeeding his uncle in the presidency for at least six months.) In a showdown with Sacasa in Congress in late 1934, the director in chief won amnesty for all involved in the Sandino assassination. The president and Somoza clashed over several more issues in 1935; Somoza generally won. Only admonitions by U.S. Ambassador Lane kept these arguments from erupting into violence. In September 1935 Somoza publicly announced his presidential candidacy. Despite efforts to dissuade him, Somoza remained in contention and received support from key Conservative party figures who saw him as capable of calming growing labor unrest and perhaps of undermining Liberal unity. In April 1936 the last vestiges of U.S. restraint upon Somoza vanished when the United States replaced Lane and abandoned its policy of not recognizing illegally seized governments. Somoza's machinations immediately picked up speed. He backed a fascist street gang's actions against the government and against his own critics and began to replace key Guard commanders appointed by Sacasa.

In late May came the denouement. Somoza's troops surrounded the Presidential Palace and its guard, as well as the main stronghold of Sacasa loyalists in León. Somoza prevailed with little bloodshed when Sacasa resigned on 6 June 1936. The Guard chief then forced the thoroughly cowed Congress to name his preferred designate as interim president and to postpone the December elections long enough to make his assumption of the presidency "constitutional." He also resigned (for a few months) as director of the Guard to comply with the prohibition against a military officer's running for President. His short-term successor as director was a loyal lieutenant who never held any real power.[6]

Now instead of walking the tightrope, Anastasio Somoza held both ends and was on his way toward owning the entire circus. He had become the dictator of Nicaragua.

Somoza García and the National Guard

The National Guard constituted the core of Somoza's political power in Nicaragua for twenty years. By the elimination of Sacasa's presidential guard and Liberal volunteers in León, Somoza had effectively monopolized public force in the country. This made his position virtually unassailable except from within the Guard itself. In 1933–1934 Somoza had had difficulty maintaining the loyalty of the Guard's officers, and throughout his later reign disgruntled, ambitious, and patriotic Guard elements would revolt against the director in chief.[7] How, then, did he manage to control the organization, to ride this tiger, for so long?

The answer lies in the dictator's considerable political talent and resourcefulness, which permitted him to wield all sorts of means—legal and illegal, positive and negative, humane and cruel—to make the National Guard the extension of his personal will. Under Anastasio Somoza the Guard became efficient yet corrupt, modernized yet paternalistic. Somoza insinuated the Guard into the most intimate crannies of Nicaraguan society, simultaneously isolating it from the population. The Guard became both the instrument and the victim of repression. Many of the military techniques through which Somoza manipulated the National Guard—military modernization, internal spying, and repression—had been used before.[8] Somoza, however, perfected these techniques.[9]

One means of enhancing the loyalty and effectiveness of the National Guard was to cater to its institutional interests. All bureaucracies have goals of their own, such as more institutional responsibility, authority, funding, technological development, and other perquisites. Somoza manipulated the Guard's structure, powers, training, and equipment in order to maximize the institution's morale, esprit, and career attractiveness. Policies along this line benefited not only the Guard as an institution, however, but its director as well.

The National Guard quickly assumed control over an extraordinarily broad range of public functions. It operated the national radio and telegraph networks, the postal service, and the immigration service. It controlled customs, taking special interest in the importation of arms, munitions, and explosives. It conducted all police functions and controlled the National Health Service (Dirección General de Sanidad). The Guard collected taxes and operated the railways. The Office of National Security (Oficina de Seguridad—OSN), organized with U.S. aid, spied on domestic dissidents. This diversity of functions made the Guard virtually omnipresent in Nicaraguan life, enhancing the sense of importance of its functionaries. This all-pervasiveness also extended the dictator's vigilance over citizens' affairs, ranging from business to private correspondence to personal movements.

Morale- and loyalty-building policies included the creation of an air force (Fuerza Aerea Nacional—FAN) and a navy in 1938. Both initiatives began with serious organizational difficulties, technical limitations, and nearly catastrophic equipment problems. The navy's first vessel, bought from the U.S. Coast Guard, was so roach-infested it could not put to sea. Inexpert pilots crashed most of the FAN's first planes within a few months of their acquisition. But the onset of World War II led to vastly increased U.S. assistance. By 1945 the FAN had more than forty aircraft and the navy several patrol vessels. Somoza's enthusiasm for the FAN continued throughout his rule. Even when the United States refused to sell him equipment and planes in the early 1950s, Somoza procured used B-24s from Brazil for possible retaliation against Costa Rica for permitting insurgents to organize there. World War II brought in millions of dollars of war material and helped keep the Guard well equipped. In the 1950s, the United States began a new military aid program that further enhanced the Guard's equipment posture (see next section).

In 1939 Somoza persuaded Franklin Roosevelt to send a U.S. officer to help reestablish the Military Academy; another U.S. adviser followed shortly. By the early 1940s the Academy provided a thorough three-year training program in basic military studies, which notably increased the Guard's capability. U.S. military missions and other training in the Panama Canal Zone further expanded technical assistance to Nicaragua's National Guard in the 1950s.

Both the Guard and Somoza were concerned with the force's responsibilities. The dictator convened a Constituent Assembly in 1939, which resolved the matter by declaring the National Guard "the only armed force of the Republic."[10] Another of Somoza's goals for the Guard was to improve compensation and benefits. Through the compliant Congress Somoza rebuilt the Guard's pay scale, which had deteriorated in previous years. In 1938, for example, officers received a 30 percent raise and enlisted men got 50 percent. Budget increases for the Guard came frequently, often to augment pay and benefits. Such pay policies made an officer's career relatively lucrative compared to most civilian jobs, especially because of special legal privileges and access to the corruption that thoroughly infected the institution's far-flung administrative domain.

The negative face of Anastasio Somoza's control over the National Guard involved management techniques that stimulated servile loyalty through fear but undermined professionalism. Somoza's paternalism involved him personally with his subordinates. He ostentatiously meted out rewards and favors, using personal gifts to ingratiate himself with an officer or soldier momentarily in financial straits. Those fallen from grace occasionally regained it through the benevolence of the commander. But repression lurked on the other side of the director in chief's personal generosity. Spies and informants abounded within the ranks, ferreting out several plots against Somoza before fruition and identifying many potential insubordinates and malcontents. Assignments, retirements, and expulsions were manipulated to disrupt conspiracies and to punish those suspected of disloyalty. Military tribunals (unconstitutional in peacetime) condemned Guard plotters to prison or death. Barbaric torture awaited those considered truly threatening, and prison conditions of themselves were so atrocious as to constitute torture.

Somoza assigned members of his own family to key positions in the Guard. For example, his oldest son, Luis Somoza Debayle, served in the Guard after graduating in engineering from Louisiana State University.

Luis's younger brother Anastasio ("Tachito") graduated from the United States Military Academy directly into a commission and major command responsibilities. By 1956 he commanded the air force and was deputy commander of the entire Guard. The elder Somoza's illegitimate son José rose through the ranks from private to major by the 1950s. Thus nepotism provided the dictator with loyal commanders and trustworthy spies in key places, while establishing the foundations of the dynasty.

Somoza countenanced widespread corruption to help buy Guard loyalty. The immense administrative responsibilities (police, traffic control, auto and driver registration, postal service, tax collection, health and sanitation inspection, customs, and immigration) provided many opportunities for both petty and grand corruption. Nicaraguans had to bribe officials of all sorts merely to have them perform their legal public responsibilities—to obtain licenses and permits, to ensure police "protection," and to receive a thousand other services. Guard officers and local quasi-judicial officials (*jueces de mesta*) often employed fraud and force to steal land from peasants. Guard officials, reportedly including the Somoza family, operated illegal gambling and prostitution rackets. Corruption thoroughly penetrated the Guard, enriching those on the inside but provoking distrust and disgust among the people of Nicaragua.

Somoza García also alienated the Guard from the civilian population. Combined with the flagrant corruption, the ever-present spying and repression carried out by the Guard engendered hate toward the institution and its individual elements. Troops and their families were encouraged to live on base and to socialize among themselves in order to promote internal unity while reducing scruples about repressing civilians. Throughout the Guard's history it became more and more isolated from the populace, a detested and feared occupation army within its own national territory.

Anastasio Somoza García had thus institutionalized most of the negative aspects of Nicaragua's military tradition—corruption, violence, deceit, and repression—in a bizarrely effective fashion. The National Guard became both the extension of the tyrant's own personality and a microcosm of Nicaraguan society—corrupted and repressed, an accomplice in the crimes of the regime.

U.S. Policy

One key variable in the Nicaraguan political equation had long been U.S. involvement, as previous chapters have shown. The U.S. ambassador had often tipped the scales of power among weak power contenders. Although the U.S. Marine Corps could never extinguish Sandino's guerrilla movement, it had easily controlled the cities, the government, and the traditionally splintered partisan factions. However, the inefficacy of such direct imperialism plus growing concern about U.S.–Latin American relations had led Herbert Hoover to withdraw U.S. forces. Ironically, it was this U.S. recognition of the failure of military intervention and the withdrawal of the marines from Nicaragua that gave Anastasio Somoza García control of the National Guard.

Franklin D. Roosevelt, firmly committed to reducing U.S. intervention, succeeded Hoover in 1933. Roosevelt personally preferred multilateral hemispheric cooperation to armed U.S. interference and wished the United States to behave as a "good neighbor." One aspect of this neighborliness was U.S. acceptance of the Convention on the Rights and Duties of States at the Montevideo Inter-American Conference of 1933. Among the convention's key provisions were the principles of equality of states, nonintervention, and the inviolability of territory and a renunciation of force.[11] In essence, then, after decades of heavy-handed intervention in Nicaragua's internal affairs, ostensibly pursuing "order" and "constitutional government," the United States after 1933 officially renounced such meddling. Ambassador Lane thus adopted a neutral stance vis-à-vis the struggle for power. He requested, but did not "order," that Somoza not arrest Sandino; earlier ambassadors might have given such instructions without a qualm. The United States also refused more than once to back efforts by Sacasa sympathizers to contain Somoza's power, despite its obvious threat to constitutional government. In 1936 the United States reversed its policy against diplomatic recognition for governments that had seized power illegally, accelerating Somoza's plans for a coup. When the expected *golpe* came in July 1936, the United States automatically recognized the regime, thus helping Somoza ensconce himself securely. The United States had thus passed from sins of commission to sins of omission, first intervening to engender a monster, then later refusing to abort it.[12]

Subsequent changes in world politics brought the United States and Somoza steadily closer.[13] The Roosevelt administration remained cool toward Somoza for a few years, but the growing threat of the German-Italian-Japanese Axis gradually replaced the U.S. flirtation with vague reformist foreign policy principles with geopolitical realism. In 1939 Somoza conferred with Roosevelt in Washington and pledged loyalty to the antifascist West—despite his own openly fascist episode in the mid-1930s. Somoza wheedled from Roosevelt help to reestablish the Guard's Military Academy, to organize a navy, and to build a highway to Rama in the Atlantic zone, a major infrastructure project.

When the United States declared war upon the Axis powers on 7 December 1941, Nicaragua followed suit two days later. Although no Nicaraguan troops ever entered combat, Nicaragua nevertheless underwent important changes because of its ties to the United States during the war. Nicaragua's wartime Price and Commerce Control Board was headed by an American officer, who helped integrate the Nicaraguan economy into the wartime inter-American economic plan and on at least one occasion assisted in smothering an anti-Somoza general strike. The Nicaraguan armed forces benefited from the hemispheric defense efforts with a U.S.-built naval station, an air base, ships, planes, and training.

In 1944, democratic movements, spawned in part by the Allied pro-democratic propaganda effort, overthrew the dictators of El Salvador and Guatemala. When similar democratic aspirations appeared in Nicaragua in the form of opposition to Somoza's reelection bid for 1947, Somoza sought U.S. endorsement and more arms for the Guard. The U.S. reaction to Somoza's pretensions went through two stages of retreat from Roosevelt's earlier anti-interventionism. First, the United States opposed the dictator with mild policy initiatives, denying the requested arms and frowning upon Somoza's reelection. This U.S. policy intensified opposition to Somoza's continued reign, ultimately persuading him to leave the presidency (although not the directorship of the Guard). Somoza thus engineered the election of Dr. Leonardo Argüello of the Liberal party, whom he expected to be acceptably pliable. Argüello, however, immediately revealed an independent streak that was anathema to Somoza—the fledgling president fired Somoza as director of the Guard and ordered him to leave the country. Incensed, Somoza overthrew Argüello after the latter had served only a few weeks in office. The United States then refused to recognize Somoza's new government and demanded that Nicaragua return certain military equipment. Despite several efforts by Somoza to mollify the United States, including outlawing the Nicaraguan Socialist (Communist) party in the new 1947 constitution, Washington withheld recognition for almost a year and then conceded it only under broader Latin American diplomatic pressure.

In the second stage of its retreat from Franklin D. Roosevelt's noninterventionism, the United States traded its prodemocratic principles for anticommunism. Harry Truman had brought to the presidency an enormously enhanced concern about Soviet expansionist pretensions, so that preference for democracy in the hemisphere became secondary to securing primordial U.S. strategic interests. The United States promoted the Rio Treaty (1947) for mutual defense in the hemisphere and the Organization of American States (1948) and began to support any anticommunist regime regardless of the type of government involved. When Guatemala's democratic government began to include communists, Truman and his successor Dwight Eisenhower backed neighboring conservative regimes in Central America. Eisenhower eventually moved to eliminate communist influence in the U.S. zone of interest by helping overthrow Guatemalan president Jacobo Arbenz in 1954.

Anastasio Somoza sniffed this change in the wind and modified his style accordingly. His rhetoric assumed a radically anticommunist tone. In addition to outlawing the Communist party and repressing the left, Somoza helped the United States overthrow Arbenz. As a consequence, Nicaragua began to receive increased U.S. aid. In the early 1950s the United States established military missions with the Nicaraguan air force and the army (the Guard's infantry) and began a major military assistance program.

Indeed, the links between Somoza and the U.S. government became extraordinarily close after the 1951 appointment of Thomas Whelan as U.S. ambassador in Managua. Whelan became a close friend of the Somozas:

> He reportedly had private business dealings with them . . . , he was photographed with the family on every possible occasion, he helped them govern, dined privately with them . . . always leaning toward the Somozas' side in his attitudes and reports. "Tom" the President called him. Whelan responded with "Tacho." Tom and Tacho joked together, gave each other gifts, and the former defended and justified the latter.[14]

As a final token of support from the United States, Ambassador Whelan persuaded President Eisenhower to fly the dictator to a military hospital in the Canal Zone when he was shot in 1956 and to send top U.S. military medical specialists to attend him in a vain struggle to save his life.

Somoza García and Nicaraguan Political Institutions

Somoza controlled the Nicaraguan government by dominating the National Guard, which supplied him with an extensive network of spies and informants. The police harassed suspects identified by the spy system. Should Somoza's subtler pressures fail to produce conformity or silence, the National Guard provided brute force. It beat up, exiled, imprisoned, tortured, and murdered at the dictator's behest.[15]

Some examples may help convey the flavor of the terror maintained by Somoza. Pedro Hurtado Cárdenas, a member of the Conservative party, and other members of his family were arrested on 27 November 1940. The Office of Investigation (predecessor of the dread Office of National Security) held Hurtado incommunicado for two weeks on trumped-up charges. His office was searched without a warrant. His captors repeatedly threatened to shoot him. Police agents applied electric shocks to his feet and genitals, eliciting a false confession. A military tribunal (unconstitutionally used to try a civilian) then convicted Hurtado of distributing antiregime handbills. But the end of this macabre incident came with the twisted benevolence of General Somoza, who suddenly released Hurtado and his relatives on 24 December 1940.[16]

Another example of how Somoza instilled terror among his opponents and trained his sons in statesmanship comes from Pedro Joaquín Chamorro's recollection of his imprisonment for participating in a 1954 attempt to overthrow the regime: "I remember having once seen Anastasio Somoza Debayle, his right hand taped like a boxer, enter a small room from which soon came the groans of Major Domingo Paladino who, tied hand and foot, stoically received the blows of Somoza's younger son. Later Paladino and many others confirmed that, with Teodoro Picado's son,[17] Anastasio Somoza Debayle had hung Jorge Rivas Montes by his testicles."[18] As for killings, Anastasio Somoza García had chalked up so many by the 1950s—campesinos murdered, prisoners shot or tortured to death, demonstrators gunned down[19]—that it becomes impossible to detail them. His own cruel joke sums it up well: "Bucks for my friends, bullets for my enemies."[20]

The rest of the Nicaraguan government and the law became the personal domain of the dictator. Crooked elections supplied a pliant Congress that legislated and appointed judges according to Somoza's whim. The bureaucracies and courts repressed Somoza's enemies. Nicaragua was under a state of siege (with suspension of all constitutional guarantees) during all of World War II, mainly to control political opposition. Even in normal times, opponents' freedom and livelihood suffered from denials of government permits and licenses and from seizures of their property and imprisonment through the manipulated courts. The opposition press, although never entirely silenced, was periodically harassed with violent acts against newspapers and their personnel.

Somoza expanded the government and its functions and thus increased the resources available for his personal enrichment and for the patronage he used to buy loyalty. Collaborators with the regime received lucrative public contracts, concessions, exemption from taxes, free utilities, public jobs, and access to bribes without threat of punishment. Somoza's advice to one overly ostentatious young government employee was an earthy admonition to be more discreet: "Look, son, when you dine on chicken, you have to hide the feathers—not throw them out in the middle of the road."[21] One classical mode of graft involved "ghosts" (*fantasmas*), persons whose names appeared on the payroll of (sometimes several) government agencies but who appeared only to pick up their paychecks. Somoza himself received salaries, honoraria, and fees from dozens of public institutions and administrative "rights" in the production of certain public concessions such as mines and timber, not to mention direct bribes. Thus, in addition to enriching himself at public expense, Somoza shared the despoilment of public resources in order to co-opt and corrupt many Nicaraguans, who then had a vested interest in his regime. Despite the expansion of government and its functions, corruption weakened the state by reducing income, diverting expenditures from legitimate public ends, and ensuring administrative incompetence.

Under the regime of Somoza García, Nicaragua's old political-economic factions and their parties continued to deteriorate. The León-centered Liberal party, with its connections to the coffee producer-exporter group, and the Granada-centered Conservative party, once tied to the traditional grand latifundist–importer faction, had already lost much of their significant distinctiveness by the 1930s. True ideological differences over economic policy had disappeared in the late nineteenth century. From 1909 to 1933, Liberal-Conservative warring had greatly reduced the cohesion of both parties, as had U.S. intervention and its shifting allegiances. Aggravating this centrifugal trend was the kaleidoscopic splitting and recombining of factions within both camps, motivated by the traditional opportunism of such caudillos as Liberal José María Moncada and Conservative Emiliano Chamorro. By the 1930s, then, the Liberal and Conservative factions had become little more than customary, clan-based cliques with little cohesion.[22]

Investment patterns and agricultural diversification and development had drawn the interests of economic elite factions ever closer throughout the early twentieth century. Moreover, when the depression dropped coffee prices from $0.46 to $0.15 per kilogram between 1929 and 1933 (sugar and banana production also suffered badly) it severely damaged the entire apparatus of the agro-export economy.[23] The agricultural elite responded by rapidly planting more coffee in hopes of recouping lost income by increasing volume. This displaced thousands of subsistence farmers into the swelling ranks of the unemployed agricultural proletariat (including banana and sugar workers) and urban migrants. These increasingly dissatisfied poor became unruly, solidifying the class base for labor unrest and the 1927–1933 Sandinista insurrection. The Nicaraguan Worker party (Partido Trabajador Nicaragüense—PTN) and numerous labor unions materialized in the 1930s.

Such signs of eroding political and economic control terrified the upper classes, regardless of party, and many came to regard Somoza as their main hope for protecting their basic interests. Many leaders of both parties thus backed Somoza as he moved to unseat Dr. Sacasa. The would-be strongman astutely capitalized on this sympathy from Conservatives while he overthrew Sacasa and the president's traditional Liberal backers. Loyal only to himself, however, Somoza soon turned on the Conservatives.[24]

Once in power, Somoza took over the Liberal party and rebuilt it into his own vehicle, the Liberal Nationalist party (Partido Liberal Nacionalista—PLN). The new Liberal organization, dominated by Somoza's cronies and with his son Luis as president, operated the Congress, the courts, and the bureaucracy to satisfy the dictator in exchange for what he would let them embezzle and take in bribes. Many Liberals profited from Somoza's takeover and reorganization of the party and collaborated consistently. Others, however, merely endured the tyrant during the war, finally to balk when he announced his reelection intentions for 1947. Repudiating Somocista continuismo and the dictator's methods and party, reformist Liberals in 1944 formed the Independent Liberal party (Partido Liberal Independiente — PLI).

Somoza kept the Conservatives confused and divided. Certain Conservative leaders backed him at first, viewing the opportunistic upstart Somoza as a weapon against the Sacasa Liberals and against lower-class unrest. With Conservative hopes to regain power through Somoza soon frustrated, Gen. Emiliano Chamorro provoked several abortive uprisings, each followed by a wave of anti-Conservative repression. Conservatives refused to participate in certain elections as a protest. However, when lower-strata unrest in the late 1940s destabilized the regime, Somoza bought off Chamorro and other leading Conservatives in a 1950 deal, known as the "pact of the generals," that gave one-third of congressional seats and public appointments to Chamorrista Conservatives and guaranteed "commercial liberty" in the 1950 constitution.

Throughout his career Somoza constantly varied his treatment of both major parties, mixing repression with cooperation according to his momentary needs. In sum, such abuse and manipulation, always abetted by greedy insiders willing to abandon principle for personal gain, killed the Liberal and Conservative parties as ideological and programmatic organizations. Much of the Nicaraguan citizenry came to regard both as corrupt, opportunistic, and unworthy of public trust.

While the parties declined under Somoza's rule the government in general underwent two main changes. First, as noted above, the Nicaraguan state became more extensive and integrated, but always as a function of the interests of Anastasio Somoza García. Second, the Nicaraguan state became thoroughly corrupt as innumerable petty and grand perversions of its functions served myriad private interests.

Economy and Society Under the Dictatorship (1936–1950)

During the regime of Anastasio Somoza García, the Nicaraguan economy passed through two distinct cycles that vastly affected the distribution of wealth, the class system, and the fortunes of the regime. The 1930s were years of depression; World War II brought a brief remission but recession returned in 1945, not to fade until the early 1950s. These international economic forces and the new political reality of the Somoza regime interacted to change the class structure of Nicaraguan society and to lay the foundations for a modernized and diversified, yet dependent, export economy.

Nicaragua entered the 1930s by sliding into a major economic collapse. Worldwide depression had knocked the bottom out of the coffee market—prices dropped to one-third of their 1929 levels by 1933, not to recover to pre-1929 levels until 1947.[25] Sugar prices and banana exports also fell drastically. This catastrophic decline of the major productive sector, export agriculture, affected different social strata in different ways. The agricultural exporting elite, stung by the decline in income, rapidly expanded land under coffee cultivation and thus raised coffee export volume to double the levels of the previous decade in order to compensate for lost income. Simultaneously, Anastasio Somoza introduced a new member into the national bourgeoisie—himself. His immense income and his domination of the government and the legal system permitted him to acquire vast landholdings and to invest in all the major traditional areas of the economy—coffee and cattle production, exporting, and importing.

Nicaragua's new coffee plantations came mostly from public land and from the land of former middleholders and smallholders, often subsistence cultivators. These smaller farmers lost their land to largeholders by expulsion (for "public utility" or lack of title) and by foreclosures due to indebtedness promoted by coffee processors, merchants, middlemen, and loan sharks. Land thus became concentrated more and more in upper-strata hands. Those who lost their small lots swelled the ranks of agrarian squatters on the nation's frontiers, the salaried (but increasingly unemployed) agricultural proletariat, and the urbanward migrants. Many of these agricultural wage laborers became bound to latifundia through the device of credit extended through company stores (*comisariatos*); peasants could not legally leave jobs if they owed debts acquired to buy food and tools (usually at extortionate prices and usurious interest).

Nicaragua mined and exported more gold and silver than in the 1920s in order partially to counterbalance the agricultural export decline. However, neither capital resources nor initiative existed for significant import-substitution industrialization. Thus, unlike elsewhere in Latin America, Nicaragua's industrial proletariat increased only very slowly during the 1930s and 1940s. Nevertheless, labor organization among peasants and miners grew, as did labor conflict. The processes that had generated lower-stata support for Sandino continued, even though political repression kept them superficially quiescent for many years. Overall, then, the 1930s and early 1940s diminished lower-sector well-being and brought the beginnings of working-class organization.

World War II altered this picture somewhat as Nicaragua supplied raw materials (especially rubber, metals, and wood) to the Allied war effort. Although national income improved, exports declined even further. Economic dependency upon the United States hit a historical peak as European markets vanished—the U.S. market absorbed more than 90 percent of Nicaraguan exports, up from 67 percent in 1938. The end of the war economy caused a sharp recession in the middle and late 1940s. Laborers suffered most, and they became so fractious that Somoza adopted a populist stance in 1944–1945 in order to co-opt the Socialist party (Partido Socialista Nicaragüense—PSN) and the unions. He promised, then implemented in 1945 an apparently progressive labor code to secure working-class support while he confronted simultaneous Conservative rebelliousness. As soon as Somoza succeeded in buying off his upper-sector opponents in the late 1940s, however, he forgot the Labor Code.

Some have viewed Somoza as a populist who enjoyed some popularity among the working class, citing as evidence his labor links and the labor legislation he passed in the mid-1940s.[26] Somoza's personal charm, paternalism, and political skill undoubtedly did win him certain labor support—especially during the period in which he favored organized labor—but this image of him as a populist is quite misleading. He adopted the populist guise during the 1940s, just as he did many other guises (e.g., profascist in 1934–1936 to win the support of an upper-class brown shirt youth group, and rabid anticommunist after 1948 to win U.S. aid). Somoza's populist affectations simply provided him with a useful tool in his struggle to survive the movement for democracy of 1944–1948. His prolabor policies and cultivation of the Socialist (Communist) party and the union movement helped deny proletarian support to the prodemocracy movement of the postwar years. Organized labor refused to join the anti-Somoza coalition. Once Somoza García had quelled and co-opted other major opponents (students, Conservatives), however, he dismantled the new labor reforms, took over and corrupted union leadership, violently purged the former union leaders, and forced many unionists and socialists into exile.

Economy and Society under the Dictatorship (The 1950s)

Steadily recuperating coffee prices and diversification of export agriculture brought economic recovery in the late 1940s and early 1950s.[27] Coffee's preeminent role declined relatively as the government promoted cotton production due to very high world prices. Cotton required extensive, relatively flat land, plus complex machinery and chemical fertilizers and insecticides—in short, heavy capital investments possible only for the government or the wealthy. Somoza and major elements of both factions of the economic elite—now cooperating following the pact of the generals—became the protagonists of the cotton boom.

The populous Pacific coast region, ideal for cotton, underwent a major transformation as the new industry centered there. Production of the fiber increased 120-fold between 1949 and 1955, eventually occupying about 40 percent of the nation's cultivated land. But the expansion of cotton cultivation required the removal of many small farmers from their lands in southern Pacific regions; this land was acquired with the same techniques used to expand coffee plantations in the 1930s. The resultant land concentration expanded the salaried agricultural work force by one hundred eighty thousand seasonal cotton workers and contributed to a new wave of urban migration. However, as these jobs did not nearly absorb the number of peasants displaced, the cotton boom also caused a new wave of agrarian colonization on the northern and eastern frontiers. Overall, these changes considerably accelerated the process of polarization of Nicaragua's bourgeoisie and proletariat, and lowered living conditions among a major segment of the poor.

By mid-twentieth century, five factors had caused great new concentrations of capital in Nicaragua: (1) the greatly increased land concentration in the coffee and cotton industries; (2) the coffee and cotton price increases (and the cotton cultivation boom) beginning in the late 1940s; (3) the expanded ties of Nicaraguan capitalists to U.S. banks and investors; (4) the political peace purchased by Somoza through permitting Conservative faction participation in government; and (5) the growing role of Somoza and his family in the economy. Thus by the early 1950s, three major economic groups had begun to coalesce within the Nicaraguan bourgeoisie. Wheelock has called one such concentration the "Banco de América group," its members coming from the old Granada commercial interests and latifundists producing cattle, sugar, and alcoholic beverages. The "Banco Nicaragüense group" coalesced around powerful cotton interests, together with certain industrialists. The "loaded dice group," the Somoza faction, would develop later, building around the growing nucleus of Somoza García's landholdings and industrial investments (see Chapter 5). The steady growth of the state and of these three bourgeois factions began to expand the technocratic and bureaucratic middle sectors.[28]

Although they were distinct, these capitalist factions developed many links among them, revealing a general convergence of upper-strata interests.

At the beginning of the fifties the Conservative oligarchy joined in an important share of local political power, and the apparent contradiction between Conservatives and Liberals vanished. Under these signs were founded the Banco Nicaragüense and the Banco de América, nuclei of the most important financial coalitions of the Nicaraguan bourgeoisie. At the same time the Somoza family broadened the orbit of its economic power, erecting the largest enterprises ever organized in the country.[29]

Somoza García's Wealth and the Economy

Just how did Anastasio Somoza and his family become so wealthy? By what devices did this once bankrupt grocer, inveterate poker player, inspector of latrines, and petty counterfeiter rise to great economic power? The answer is that virtually absolute political power is the most important economic resource one can possess.

Early in his reign, Somoza developed several means for generating large amounts of income independently of his salaries as president and National Guard chief.[30] One device involved granting concessions (to both foreign and local interests, the latter usually close associates) to exploit gold, rubber, and timber. For such concessions Somoza received "additional contributions," "executive levies," and "presidential commissions." Associates estimated his take from gold mining alone at from $175,000 to $400,000 per year during the 1940s. Second, he extracted bribes from illegal gambling, prostitution, and clandestine alcohol operations. Third, Somoza had laws passed to restrict certain imports (infringing on traditional Conservative interests), then organized a large contraband operation to circumvent these very laws and sold the merchandise through his own stores. Somoza worked a similar deal with restrictions on exporting cattle. He illegally exported livestock to Costa Rica and Panama, earning enormous profits. He also earned "commissions" from some other cattle producers for letting them also break these laws.

During World War II Somoza took advantage of anti-German legislation to acquire large coffee plantations. The government seized various German-owned properties, then sold them to Somoza or his relatives at ridiculous prices. He acquired many other interests the same way, including farms and gold claims in the Segovia mountains, resources that once belonged to Sandino's followers. Somoza soon became the largest landowner in Nicaragua. By 1944 he owned fifty-one cattle ranches, and his forty-six coffee plantations made him the largest coffee producer in Nicaragua.

Somoza exploited the government for personal gain. As Nicaragua lacked strong private financial institutions in the 1930s and 1940s, the government necessarily functioned as a major capital supplier through such institutions as the National Bank, the Mortgage Bank, the Popular

Credit Fund, and others. Somoza and his appointees controlled these funds and lent themselves money not available to others. Moreover, Somoza manipulated public regulations, contracts, and purchasing for the benefit of himself and his cronies. Licenses, import permits, bank credits, and concessions all generated income—by going directly to the Somoza coterie or through cash bribes or stock in new enterprises. Direct theft and graft abounded. For example, Somoza named himself sole director of the Pacific Railroad, receiving a monthly salary of $3,000 for his services. Moreover, the line moved his merchandise and cattle free, built him a palace in Managua, built trunk lines and loading docks on Somoza's Montelimar sugar plantation, and maintained without charge his vehicles and agricultural equipment. Government lake ferries often operated as if they were the property of the dictator. President Somoza regularly paid for personal business acquisitions with public funds and paid his businesses' employees from public institutions' payrolls. "Throughout the war, Somoza was hurriedly absorbing any income-producing resource of the government, as well as multiplying his illegal businesses, blackmailing or eliminating his competitors, until he accumulated a gigantic economic power with which he descended omnipotently over the country's economy, infiltrating all its strategic branches."[31]

Somoza's enormous income made possible widely ranging investments. His early acquisitions included coffee and cattle farms and the massive sugar operation at Montelimar, as well as a tannery, a match factory, a cement factory, the National Insurance Company, the electric power companies of several cities, urban rental properties, the newspaper *Novedades,* and certain textile interests. He also acquired real estate, stock, and ranching interests in the United States, Canada, and Costa Rica. Although accurate figures on his fortune are unavailable, by 1945 he was estimated to have between $10 and $60 million.

This was just the beginning, however. In the early 1950s Somoza García reorganized and rationalized family businesses along modern lines. This facilitated greater expansion and industrial investments, especially with the cooperation of the government. For example, Congress required that milk be purified before sale, thus assuring fabulous profits for the family's La Salud dairy—the only pasteurizing facility in Nicaragua. In the early 1950s Somoza also founded two textile companies, the merchant marine company MAMENIC Lines, and Líneas Aéras de Nicaragua (LANICA). He established a new port on the Pacific, founded freight handling enterprises there, and logically dubbed the facility Puerto Somoza.

Thus, Anastasio Somoza García converted his virtually absolute political dominion into immense economic power. The public purse became his own, government enterprises became lackeys to his personal interests, and regulatory powers stifled his competition. Unchallenged conflict of interests, theft, embezzlement, and graft generated wealth that financed his somewhat more legitimate investments. Somoza thus did not have to be a business genius to make himself rich — anyone could become another Croesus with such advantages.

Antagonism within the traditional economic elite and between these factions and Somoza diminished by mid-century. The growing power and convergence of the bourgeoisie brought with it a proletarization of agriculture, a moderate increase in the industrial proletariat, and the broadening of the middle class. These changes conditioned a progressive inequality of income, with the poor uncushioned by social welfare provisions. From 1928 to 1944, for example, gross national product grew by 145 percent, but mean personal incomes rose only 50 percent. Later changes continued this trend, as rapidly increasing population and land concentration boosted unemployment among the lower classes.[32] Thus, Somoza had sealed the pressure cooker with the National Guard and corruption and had turned up the fire with economic growth and increased inequality. In the period 1955–1975 these economic trends continued and intensified (see Chapter 5).

So Shall Ye Reap

Although Anastasio Somoza García garnered immense rewards for this tyranny, it also cost him dearly. The tiger he rode, the National Guard, never thoroughly accepted his rule or his methods. Plots against him from within the Guard occurred periodically, the most serious coming in 1954. Progressively more fearful of both Guard and popular rebelliousness, Somoza centralized the instruments of his power and protection in a presidential residence (and later in a highly fortified command headquarters known as the Bunker) at the Guard's First Battalion headquarters on the skirts of the Tiscapa volcano in Managua's center.

Within a radius of 500 meters from the head of the dynasty's bed stood an armed company of 45-ton Sherman tanks, the only artillery company in the country, an infantry battalion armed with the latest equipment, a riot control company, the center of all the army's radio and telephone networks, as well as the military's major supply depots, its offices of investigation and security, and all the arsenals of weapons and munitions — controlled by a single master key.

Over his own quarters were anti-aircraft cannons, and in the kitchen of the house slept no fewer than 60 chosen soldiers, all armed with carbines and ready to act as a personal escort, commanded directly by those officers most intimately linked to the family.[33]

The president and director in chief of the Guard traveled with extreme caution — he sent spies out days ahead and his aides organized everything meticulously. Buildings and businesses nearby were closed, and the local Guard contingent was replaced by elements of Somoza's personal guards and the First Battalion. Somoza even took his own liquor and bartenders. This thoroughness and distrust of his own Guard, however, proved fatal. On 21 September 1956 the dictator attended a party in León to celebrate his renomination by the PLN for yet another presidential term. As usual, military intimates of the dictator ejected local Guard elements, including a Corporal Obando, who had been assigned to scrutinize everyone who came near the president. Obando knew nearly everyone in León and probably would have spotted Rigoberto López Pérez, a known opponent of the regime.[34]

López, a poet and printshop worker of twenty-seven, had recently returned to León from five years in El Salvador, where he had worked with an exile group plotting an anti-Somoza invasion. Some dispute exists as to how wide a conspiracy existed to help López to kill Somoza García. López's own words in his last letter to his mother suggest that he acted alone, although some twenty people were eventually convicted of conspiring to assist him: "Although you have never known it, I have been working in opposition to the deadly regime of our country. And because all previous efforts to make Nicaragua again (or perhaps for the first time) a free country without blemishes have been futile, I have decided . . . to try by myself to start the beginning of the end of this tyranny."[35] At the party López slipped past security, which was momentarily relaxed by Somoza's overconfident order. The poet drew near his target and fatally shot him when the crowd separated for a moment. Rigoberto López himself lay dead seconds later at the hands of Somoza's enraged bodyguards. Having reaped the hatred he had sown among his own people, General Anastasio "Tacho" Somoza García died on 29 September 1956 in the Gorgas Hospital of the Panama Canal Zone.

5
Like Father Like Sons

"My program of government is forged by the voices and hands of the people, with the proper deliberation and according to their hopes and needs."
— Anastasio Somoza Debayle[1]

Within days after Rigoberto López Pérez shot Anastasio Somoza García, the National Guard arrested thousands of Nicaraguans. The crazed search for a conspiracy eventually led to the jailing for interrogation or trial of some three thousand people—anyone suspected of even knowing López and virtually every known opponent of the regime. Rigoberto López had rid Nicaragua of Somoza García, but the assassination instituted a dynasty and intensified rather than ended the tyranny. Nevertheless, it catalyzed a new form of opposition. The wave of repression it unleashed steeled the determination of many of its victims—among them those who would bring down the dynasty in 1979.[2]

Pedro Joaquín Chamorro Cardenal, editor of the Conservative opposition daily *La Prensa* and participant in an abortive anti-Somoza invasion in 1954, was one of the first arrested. Twenty-two years later Chamorro's death at the hands of the Somozas would prove the last straw for the fed-up Nicaraguan people. But before we study Chamorro's murder, we must examine a critical phase of his life—his arrest, imprisonment, interrogation, torture, trial, and punishment in 1956.

Agents of the Office of National Security (OSN), some trained by the U.S. Federal Bureau of Investigation and Britain's Scotland Yard, interrogated Pedro Joaquín Chamorro at length on the completely unfounded suspicion that he had assisted Rigoberto López. For months Chamorro, his whereabouts unknown to his family, waited between questioning-torture sessions in a series of filthy cells. One such session, in the sewing room of the Presidential Palace, lasted six sleepless days.

I received thousands of blows all over my body—I especially remember those below the belt. I heard unspeakable insults, was forced to physical exercise to the limits of total exhaustion, had applied to my eyes powerful spotlights that burned my pupils and the skin of my face until my brain seemed to explode.[3]

Anastasio Somoza Debayle, now head of the Guard and of the investigation, frequently took part in these interrogations. Chamorro recalled:

> They stripped me completely . . . they made me squat with a lighted cigarette in my mouth, until I finished it, until I chewed it up and burned my mouth, squatting until I felt intense pains in my knees and fell for the first time. Then I received a hail of blows from bare fists and booted feet. They lifted me up and I fell again to receive another shower of kicks [that] rolled me about on the floor.[4]

But for all that, Chamorro was lucky, for he escaped the even more diabolical tortures suffered by his companions: electrical shocks with an airplane magneto, repeated near-drowning, lifting or dragging by a cord tied around the genitals, imprisonment in a coffin-sized cell, or time in the Somoza family's private zoo. This last method incarcerated prisoners, for months in some cases, in barred cages open to the weather, next to lions and panthers, in the garden of the presidential residence.

> In front of these animal cages often strolled the current president of the dynasty, Luis Somoza, and his brother Anastasio, with their wives, relatives, and children. From the end of the garden where I was being held [in a more ordinary cell] . . . several times I saw their innocent children, carrying their dolls and toys, pass before the cages where men lived together with the beasts, More than once I saw children of the palace servants pass before them, their young faces revealing a mixture of pain and astonishment caused by this spectacle.[5]

Ultimately Anastasio Somoza Debayle and his OSN extracted enough confessions (both false and valid) to stage a farcical show trial before an unconstitutional tribunal. There a chorus of Managua's prostitutes, paid by the regime and led by one Nicolasa Sevilla, humiliated both prisoners and their families with screamed obscenities and shouts to execute the accused. The principal convicted conspirators went to prison, three to be shot in 1961 "trying to escape." Others received sentences to exile. Chamorro, exiled to San Carlos on the southern tip of the Great Lake of Nicaragua, soon escaped with his wife Violeta Barrios across the border to Costa Rica.

The Heirs to the Dynasty

Luis and Anastasio ("Tachito") Somoza Debayle both came to embody and to exaggerate their father's traits. At his knee they had learned corruption, repression, and exploitation of public power for personal purposes. Somoza García trained his sons to follow him in power, to have technical skill greater than his own, yet tempered in the laboratory of practical experience. Both boys attended La Salle Military Academy in New York. Luis (b. 1923) went to Louisiana State University for a degree in civil engineering and returned to a captaincy in the Guard and a leadership role in the PLN. By 1956 Luis had served as president of the PLN and president of the Congress and was first designate for succession to the Nicaraguan presidency. Anastasio (b. 1925) graduated from West Point in 1946 and, according to the wags of the period, received an army for his graduation present. He complemented this formal military training with several key Guard commands and a first-hand study of the techniques of repression, including personal participation in torturing political prisoners.[6]

The personality differences between Luis and Anastasio paralleled the two sides of their father; they complemented each other in their shared rule. Luis, urbane and personable, remained remote from the dirty side of dictatorship. Anastasio, however, took the role of soldier and enforcer, becoming progressively more abusive. Luis gained the reputation of openness and stirred hopes for liberalization. Anastasio meanwhile, kept order. In comparison to his brother, "Luis decidedly deserved to be called Luis 'the Courteous.' . . . His brother killed and he made the excuses. Anastasio witnessed the terrible drama of torture and death, while Luis gave the courteous explanations to the families of the dead and tortured."[7]

The brothers Somoza Debayle, although well trained for tyranny and heirs to their father's malevolent talents, faced increasingly varied and determined opposition. They confronted several major crises and dozens of minor challenges. They thus resorted to a bewildering array of formulas to retain power. From 1956 through 1979, however, Anastasio always held effective command of the National Guard (with only temporary cosmetic resignations for the sake of constitutional appearances when running for or holding the presidency). Luis was president from 1956 to 1963. Unrest in the early 1960s prompted him to pass the presidency to René Schick and Lorenzo Guerrero for the 1963–1967 term and to promote another apparent (although also illusory) liberalization. Following Luis's death from a heart attack in 1967, however, Anastasio exercised progressively greater sway over the government from his posi-

Figure 5.1. Anastasio (left) and Luis Somoza Debayle with their father, Anastasio Somoza García, at LaSalle Military Academy, Oakdale, N.Y., in the early 1940s. (Photo *Barricada* archives)

tion as director of the Guard. He had himself "elected" president in 1967, but scandal and unrest forced him in 1971 to cede executive power to a three-person junta that included Fernando Agüero, head of the Conservative party. The 1972 quake permitted Anastasio Somoza Debayle to seize full executive control once again; he ruled by decree until resuming the presidency in 1974 formally for a term that was to end in 1981.[8]

The transition of government from father to sons exaggerated the traits of rule under Somoza García. But the restraint with which Luis balanced Anastasio's excesses vanished with Luis's death, and the dark side of the Somoza legacy prevailed.

The United States and the Regime

In the years of Somoza García's rule the U.S. position toward the Nicaraguan government twice cycled from a certain distaste and reserve to active support, according to U.S. strategic concerns. When Luis and Anastasio came to power in 1956, U.S. support for the regime was high and would so remain for two decades. The energy the United States injected into the country in the form of moral support, economic aid, and military muscle discouraged opponents of the regime, enriched the brothers Somoza, and increased their capacity to co-opt and to repress their compatriots. Two aspects of the relationship between the United States and the Somoza regime merit attention here—the formal links between governments and the informal social and economic ties.

First, U.S. government assistance to Nicaragua, as to other Third World countries, reflected several assumptions: that aid-stimulated economic development would promote pro-U.S. political stability; that aid should promote democratic institutions; and according to a Cold War doctrine, that aid should promote narrow security concerns. The Cold War approach was always present from the late 1940s on, predominated throughout most of the 1950s and the late 1960s, and continued to influence U.S. policy in the 1970s.[9] "The theory was that aid could promote non-Communism, pro-Americanism, and stability, which were viewed as conducive to American security in the context of the Cold War."[10]

All types of U.S. assistance to Nicaragua grew steadily from 1953 through 1975. Military aid rose from an average of about $200,000 yearly for the 1953–1961 period to $1.8 million per year for 1967–1975. Overall economic assistance for the same periods grew from an annual average of some $1 million to $17.3 million. The biggest shift in both military and economic assistance to the Somoza brothers' regime occurred with the beginnings of the Alliance for Progress programs in 1962, when the average annual rate of economic assistance more than doubled and military assistance rose sevenfold.[11]

This enormous aid increase in the early 1960s betrayed the growing U.S. fear of communism's spread in Latin America following the 1959 Cuban revolution. The aid boost coincided with and helped the Somozas weather a wave of internal unrest from 1959 to 1963 (see Chapters 6–8).[12]

U.S. aid to the National Guard, including military missions to the infantry and to the air force, substantially improved equipment (helicopters, fighter and cargo planes, trucks, and roadbuilding and communication gear) and training (jungle warfare, counterinsurgency, and police). The U.S. government sought to integrate the Nicaraguan armed forces into a hemispheric defense plan. For Nicaragua this meant joining in 1961 the Central American Defense Council (Consejo de Defensa Centroamericano—CONDECA), which included all Central American nations but Costa Rica. CONDECA, a unified international command equipped and trained to coordinate with the U.S. Army's Panama-based Southern Command, was to protect against a possible Cuban invasion, to secure regional supply and communication routes, and to conduct anticommunist counterinsurgency and "civic action" (military civic activities to promote civilian good will).

This aid, equipment, coordination, and training helped the Guard smash early guerrilla efforts of the FSLN in 1963. In return for the U.S. help, the Somoza brothers consistently collaborated with the United States in the United Nations and the Organization of American States. Nicaragua also permitted the Central Intelligence Agency (CIA) to train in and to launch from Nicaragua the Cuban exile invasion of the Bay of Pigs in 1961. In 1965 Nicaragua sent troops to help the United States occupy the Dominican Republic. Nicaraguan and Guatemalan forces helped defeat a reformist coup in El Salvador in 1972.

Perhaps the best official friend Anastasio Somoza Debayle ever had was U.S. Ambassador Turner Shelton, an executive of the Howard Hughes conglomerate. Shelton was appointed to the post by Richard Nixon, who later received a $200,000 contribution from Hughes in the 1972 campaign. Shelton's determination that no criticism of the dictator should leave his embassy for Washington was an obsession with him. He so badly blocked normal communication channels with the Department of State that embassy staffers actually had to smuggle to Washington data on the true state of Nicaraguan affairs.

In 1971, Anastasio Somoza Debayle's regime confronted a crisis stemming from opposition to his reelection intentions and internal strains within the National Guard. Turner Shelton, however, quickly arranged for Somoza to visit President Nixon, whose warm reception gave the dictator some political breathing space at home. Shelton then arranged the negotiations with Conservative party leader Dr. Fernando Agüero. This parlay resolved the crisis by establishing a triumvirate to replace Somoza as president. The deal gave Agüero one of the three places on this junta but left Somoza in command of the Guard. Later, following the December 1972 earthquake that devastated Managua, Shelton once again rushed to Somoza's aid. The ambassador urged Somoza to regroup the nearly disbanded National Guard. With the interim aid of CONDECA and U.S. forces, Somoza reestablished the control that had momentarily escaped him. When Dr. Agüero then protested Somoza's rule by decree, Somoza replaced him with a more pliable puppet—reportedly at Shelton's urging.

U.S. diplomatic support for Somoza began to erode in the mid-1970s. This change began when Richard Nixon resigned and continued with State Department efforts to reduce the embarrassing excesses of the Shelton years. The Panama Canal negotiations prompted a major reassessment of the geopolitical significance of Central America and of Nicaragua's alternate transisthmian water route. Intercontinental nuclear strategy, and the development of naval and commercial vessels too large for the existing canal, had vastly diminished Nicaragua's strategic importance to the United States, while the growing emphasis of Congress and the Carter administration on human rights began slowly to erode Somoza's U.S. support.

Informal U.S. backing had long helped the Somozas and became increasingly critical as formal U.S. backing weakened. Anastasio Somoza Debayle cultivated his U.S. military friends from his West Point days, as well as U.S. Congressmen John Murphy (New York), Charles Wilson (Texas), and Larry McDonald (Georgia). These soldiers and legislators visited Somoza in Nicaragua and defended the regime in congressional aid hearings and in the U.S. press. When even this help proved inadequate to keep the Carter administration's backing, Somoza expanded Nicaragua's long-standing public relations campaign in the United States by New York and Washington advertising firms.[13] Somoza also courted U.S. businessmen, most notably the eccentric Howard Hughes, who lived in Managua's luxurious Hotel Intercontinental from 1970 to 1972. Hughes made various Nicaraguan investments, including the purchase of one-fourth of LANICA, the Somoza family airline. As the following section details, these business ties helped balloon both the Somoza fortune and the dictator's incentive to stay in Nicaragua long after most ordinary tyrants would have fled to live off their spoils.

The Economy

Nicaragua's export-dependent economy rode an international price and investment roller coaster, the effects of which differed markedly before and after the 1972 earthquake. These economic cycles, plus certain progressive transformations, eventually built up great structural strains that precipitated a severe crisis in the late 1970s.[14]

Falling coffee and cotton prices after 1956 caused a sharp recession. This slump ended only in the early 1960s, when prices rose again at about the same time that new national and international investment policies stimulated growth. Fear of Cuba's revolution boosted U.S. economic aid and the formation of the Central American Common Market (CACM) under the umbrella of the Alliance for Progress. The Nicaraguan government began to push infrastructure programs such as highway building and electrification and created numerous entities to encourage economic development. These stimuli produced rapid industrialization and aggregate economic growth. Gross domestic product increased two and a half times from 1960 to 1975. In 1960 the manufacturing sector generated only 15.6 percent of the gross domestic product, a share which rose to more than 23 percent by the early 1970s, despite some 10,000 manufacturing jobs lost in the 1972 quake.[15] This CACM-spawned boom in light industry helped blunt the impact of a mid-1960s slump due to falling coffee and cotton prices. The early 1970s brought another upswing.

Nicaragua's industrialization had a peculiar cast, however. Nicaragua remained quite poor. Widespread poverty continued in part because the government repressed unions, kept wages low, and undertook no effective agrarian reform. Thus Nicaragua's internal market remained small, and most manufactures were exported. The new industries had to import much of the raw materials used, increasing external dependencies. Despite dramatic production increases, the highly capital-intensive nature of the new plants created few new jobs to absorb the rapidly growing labor force. Unemployment in Managua, seat of the nation's industry, reached 17 percent in 1974.[16] All told, then, industrialization under the CACM did not reduce but merely diversified Nicaragua's dependencies upon external markets and manufactures. Ironically, aggregate economic growth attained spectacular levels, but few benefits reached the lower classes. The wealth- and profit-generated share of national income (as opposed to wages and salaries) went up notably in the mid-1970s — an income shift to the wealthy (see Table 5.1).

For the 1973–1979 period Nicaragua's growth-recession cycles became much shorter and more intense. These accelerated cyclical changes, combined with the postquake development strategies and political problems, accentuated sharply the problems of certain social strata. In 1973–1974 heavy foreign borrowing and the massive reconstruction activity produced a small boom that benefited the upper classes by further concentrating wealth and ownership of production. The petty commercial and manufacturing sector of Managua suffered most from the quake. In

TABLE 5.1
Inflation, Wages, and Income Distribution Data, Nicaragua 1961–1980

| Year | Percentage Change Consumer Prices[a] | Real Wages Indices | | | Employee compensation as % of national wages[e] |
		Industry[b]	Construction[c]	Communication/transport[d]	
1961	0.2	100			
1962	-0.3	113			57.5
1963	0.8	118			55.1
1964	9.6	101			57.5
1965	3.9	106			65.0
1966	3.9	166			65.3
1967	1.6	174		100	65.3
1968	3.1[f]	181	100	96	65.3
1969	2.0[f]	177	104	94	65.6
1970	5.9	141	99	91	65.3
1971	5.6	134	99	89	65.5
1972	3.3[f]	135	89	86	65.6
1973	16.8[f]	123	66	81	69.7
1974	20.5[f]	117	78	72	58.9
1975	1.8	128	85	71	59.1
1976	2.8				
1977	11.4				
1978					
1979	36.0				
1980	-9.6[g]				

Sources: K. Ruddle and K. Barrows, eds. Statistical Abstract of Latin America (Los Angeles: UCLA Latin American Center Publications, 1972); J. Wilkie and P. Reich, eds. Statistical Abstract of Latin America, Vol. 19 (1978) and Vol. 20 (1980) (Los Angeles: UCLA Latin American Center Publications); Ministerio de Planificación, Programa de reactivación en beneficio del pueblo, 1980–1981 (Managua, 1980); Bureau of the Census, U.S. Department of Commerce, Statistical Abstract of the United States, 1978 (Washington, D.C.: Government Printing Office, 1978); Mario A. De Franco and Carlos F. Chamorro, "Nicaragua: Crecimiento industrial y desempleo," in D. Camacho et al., El fracaso social de la integración centroamericana: capital, tecnología, empleo (San José, Costa Rica: Editorial Universitaria Centroamericana, 1979).

[a] Based on Wilkie and Reich, Vol. 20, Table 2513, and De Franco and Chamorro, Table 7.

[b] Based on Wilkie and Reich, Vol. 20, Table 1400, and Ruddle and Barrows, Table 48.

[c] Based on Wilkie and Reich, Vol. 20, Table 1401.

[d] Based on Wilkie and Reich, Vol. 20, Table 1402.

[e] Based on Wilkie and Reich, Vol. 20, Table 1404, and Ruddle and Barrows, Table 53.

[f] Estimate from De Franco and Chamorro, Table 7.

[g] Estimate from Ministerio de Planificación, 1980.

1975–1976, in contrast, the economy declined because of lowered coffee prices and the labor unrest and political repression that frightened away investments. The government moved to counteract this trend by increasing its deficits, financed by even greater foreign borrowing. In 1976–1977 this public spending combined with revived coffee prices to spur yet another period of growth. Simultaneously, however, inflation spurted upward, reducing the real wages of the middle and lower classes precipitously, a problem further aggravated by the 1979 devaluation of the weakened córdoba. The increasing political violence of 1978 caused a 43 percent drop in investments, which in turn produced a 5 percent decline in the GNP. Trying to compensate for such problems while financing its military effort against the growing popular insurgency, the government pushed foreign debt up to $1.15 billion, worsening inflation still more. The late 1970s have been described as a "situation of apparent economic bonanza with a clear deterioration of the living conditions of the working classes [due to] unemployment, inflation, and the precariousness of social services."[17] Thus, Nicaragua entered the final economic crisis of the Somoza dynasty.

If not the lower and middle classes, then who did benefit from the post-1960 industrialization boom? First, Nicaragua's own bourgeoisie contributed heavily to the CACM-era growth, diversifying its holdings and profiting hugely. Two capitalist factions emerged in the early 1950s and grew rapidly. The Banco Nicaragüense (BANIC) group, with its origins among old-line Liberal landowners and the emerging cotton sector, and the Banco de América (BANAMERICA) group, tied originally to the Conservative oligarchy, both invested heavily in manufacturing, commercial enterprises, and real estate and construction activity.[18]

A third, or "loaded dice," group, the Somoza family and its closest collaborators, coalesced only in the early 1970s but grew both faster and bigger than its competitors. The late 1950s agricultural export slump had prompted the Somozas to modernize their huge agricultural holdings and to diversify into modern industrial investments. In order to take advantage of the CACM's reduction of trade barriers, the Somozas entered interregional commerce in construction materials, meat packing, tobacco products, shoes, rice growing and processing, and fishing and fish canning. They invested in domestic construction, real estate development, the mass media, auto products and automobile importing, and data processing. Ties between Anastasio Somoza Debayle and U.S. investors multiplied, both domestically and abroad. "Supported by funds extracted from the state and its autonomous entities—the National Bank, the National Light and Power Company, the National Lottery, the National Social Security Institute and others—the Somoza group entered full tilt into the competition for industrial development, incomparably better backed than BANIC or BANAMERICA."[19]

The Somoza group as it grew in the early 1970s surpassed the capacities of the BANIC and BANAMERICA groups and threatened their stability.[20] Its success stemmed from the advantages of unchallenged power over public institutions. The Somozas continued to use public funds and power—they abused the treasury, operated illegal businesses, created legal monopolies for themselves, and demanded bribes in cash or stock in businesses in exchange for licenses, concessions, and contracts. Anastasio Somoza Debayle skimmed off large proportions of international development loans and contracts.

The 1972 earthquake demolished Managua, but vastly enriched the Somoza group. Somoza, as director of the National Guard, ruled Nicaragua by decree and acted as

> president of the Emergency Committee and therefore administrator of international loans and aid, urban planner, demolisher of buildings, and manager of national resources. [He] restructured his traditional construction enterprises [especially cement and concrete products] and also organized a powerful new conglomerate capable of absorbing the whole reconstruction cycle and appropriating the hundreds of millions of foreign aid dollars that began to flow in for the rebuilding.[21]

Somoza invested in demolition, earth moving, heavy equipment, construction materials, premixed concrete, paving, metal buildings, pipes and tubing, real estate development, land, and housing. His greed and his willingness to take advantage of his compatriots' suffering seemed boundless. His wealth became heroic—one estimate placed Somoza's personal worth at $400 million in 1974.[22]

During the 1960s and early 1970s, the various factions of the Nicaraguan bourgeoisie seemed to converge toward unity.[23] The three capitalist factions developed myriad joint investments in several key areas of the economy. Representatives of the three united to found and direct both the Central American Business Administration Institute (INCAE) and the Jesuit-run Central American University (Universidad Centroamericana). Numerous pressure organizations formed among agricultural, industrial, commercial, and financial interests. These groups then united into the Superior Council of Private Initiative (Consejo Superior de la Iniciativa Privada—COSIP), which, like its components, pressed for influence and advantage with public institutions. By the mid-1970s, however, Anastasio Somoza Debayle's personal economic power and his ruthless methods had begun to alienate the other capitalist factions. Ultimately, many of the once-cooperative leaders of the BANIC and BANAMERICA groups, and even some former Somoza associates, joined in opposition to the regime.

The second major group of beneficiaries of Nicaragua's economy in the 1960s and 1970s consisted of foreign investors. The Alliance for Progress and the CACM dramatically increased foreign investment in Nicaragua, with twice as much of this investment going into manufacturing as elsewhere in the region. "Although foreign investment in

Nicaragua had never been truly large, its [recent] increase has been great."[24] Between 1959 and 1969 Nicaragua's share of total CACM foreign investment had doubled to 10.1 percent; this represented a 404 percent increase in the total foreign investment in Nicaragua.[25] Although 80 percent of Nicaragua's foreign investments came from the United States, this did not directly augment U.S. trade ties. Throughout the 1960s and early 1970s, the U.S. share of Nicaragua's exports and imports diminished, while trade with the CACM, Japan, and Europe grew. External indebtedness, both public and private, steadily rose, and the balance of payments consistently ran in the red, pushing up inflation.

Overall, then, Nicaragua's foreign and domestic investments stimulated industrial growth and diversified but did not decrease external dependencies. The cobeneficiaries of this process were foreign investors and the Nicaraguan bourgeoisie (especially the Somozas). The main loser in the industrialization boom was the poor majority — for whom too few new jobs developed, wages declined, and prices rose.

Social Structure

Theorists of social conflict have convincingly argued that rapid economic growth tends to destabilize less developed societies and that a widening gap between expectations and achievements can lead to violence and even revolution.[26] Ironically it is not always a decline in a group's fortunes that leads to social aggression, but sometimes changes relative to other groups, rapid short-run declines, or increased insecurity in the face of the improved expectations seeded by rapid economic growth. What follows reveals how social and economic factors moved the Nicaraguan pressure cooker ever closer to bursting during the 1960s and early 1970s.[27]

Nicaragua's population grew at a very high average rate of 3.5 percent per annum for 1955–1965, diminishing but slightly to a 3.3 percent yearly rate for 1970–1975. The total population rose from 1,410,289 in 1960 to 2,162,262 in 1975 and to an estimated 2,462,000 by 1979. During this period the urban population grew half again as fast as the overall population.

Of economically active Nicaraguans, the proportion in agriculture declined steadily from a 1964 peak of 58 percent to around 50 percent in 1975. Industrial employment increased from less than 10 percent in 1960 to a high of 11.6 percent in 1965, holding more or less steady for seven years. The 1972 Managua earthquake destroyed some ten thousand manufacturing jobs, mostly in cottage industries, reducing industrial employment in 1975 to the pre-1960 level of 9.7 percent. Tertiary sector (services, commerce, and government) activities rose steadily from around 26 percent in the mid-1960s to a 1973 peak of 32.4 percent, then dropped sharply following the quake to about 29 percent in 1974–1975. The quake-related job loss hit mainly petty commerce and services in the devastated heart of Managua. Although construction employment rose between 1973–1975 because of recovery efforts, this absorbed only about half the jobs lost elsewhere. Despite rapidly rising economic output, then, the population grew faster than the work force, so that unemployment increased constantly throughout the 1960s and 1970s, officially reaching 13 percent in 1977. The economic and political crisis of 1978–1979 then sharply pushed up unemployment to almost 30 percent in 1979.

Nicaragua's class structure underwent critical changes after 1960.[28] The traditional bourgeoisie, joined by new manufacturing investors, enriched itself and diversified its holdings on the rich diet of industrialization and high profits. The old bourgeois factions, ever more prone to collaborative ventures, grew less distinct. Vestigial political factionalism receded before the joint investments and the renewed co-optation of Conservatives into government by the 1971 Somoza-Agüero pact. Nevertheless, the capitalist class's convergence halted, then altered radically in the mid-1970s. Somoza's greed had become too great for the BANIC and BANAMERICA factions to tolerate, and they began to reject the Somoza regime. Political and labor struggles and unrest on the left ate away the confidence of both foreign and domestic capital. One early sign of this divergence was the 1974 appearance of the Democratic Liberation Union (Unión Democrática de Liberación — UDEL). UDEL included major businessmen of varied political backgrounds, among them certain former Somoza collaborators.

Two factors expanded the size of the middle class from about 11 percent of the population in 1960 to 15 percent in 1975. First, commerce and industry grew, boosting the number of managerial, clerical, and sales jobs. Second, the Nicaraguan government expanded its size and scope. The central government and several new autonomous institutions increased planning, development promotion, and social welfare programs of limited scope, raising the number of clerical, managerial, and technical employees in the public sector. Despite the loss of petty commercial employment due to the 1972 disaster, the overall trend was toward middle-sector growth. The quake and its aftereffects — inflation, sharpened recessionary cycles, and rising unemployment — worsened the lot of the petty bourgeoisie both in Managua and elsewhere. The salaried middle sector (and its university student aspirants) also suffered rising unemployment and declining incomes due to inflation in the mid-1970s (see Table 5.1 for consumer price trends). This sharpened labor conflicts and student opposition to the regime, which in turn brought increased repression.

Nicaragua's urban working classes experienced some improvement in conditions during the 1960s, but things became decidedly worse during the 1970s. The industrial proletariat grew at the same rate as the economically active population, and industrial productivity grew 280 percent from 1960 to 1975. However, real industrial wages increased only until the late 1960s, then began a rapid decline that accelerated during the inflationary spiral of the 1970s. The percentage of national income paid in wages and salaries (a rough measure of income distribution to all workers) first rose in the mid-1960s, then dropped sharply in 1975 (see Table 5.1). Labor organization and conflict, despite increased repression, grew notably after 1973. Worker militancy increased, then, when labor's share of the income pie and real wages dropped despite labor's mighty contribution to Nicaragua's rapid overall economic growth during the CACM boom. Unfortunately, data to pursue most of these trends past 1975 are not available, but both inflation and unemployment in the late 1970s were severe and both undoubtedly further reduced real working-class income.

While the agricultural sector increased its production 137 percent from 1960 to 1975, its share of the work force shrank from 58 to 50 percent between 1964 and 1975. As in industry, real wages and income declined for day laborers and small producers, so that increased productivity did not enhance the well-being of most campesinos. Falling agricultural employment and income stemmed in part from "agrarian reform" in which the government displaced campesinos from areas of FSLN guerrilla activity to remote forest reserve plots and from the continued technification of agriculture, which reduced the number of available jobs. Overall, agricultural unemployment climbed steadily after 1965, reaching 16 percent by 1977 and 32 percent in 1979. Evidence of rising anger among the rural poor includes land seizures, strikes, and the formation in 1977 of the Association of Rural Workers (Asociación de Trabajadores del Campo—ATC).

The surplus agricultural population drifted into the cities, especially Managua's miserably poor *barrios,* in hopes of finding work in industry. This urban migration outstripped job creation, thereby swelling the unemployed and underemployed lumpenproletariat. Managua grew to half a million residents and developed huge slums, a phenomenon exacerbated by the December 1972 earthquake that destroyed thousands of lower-class dwellings and the cottage industries and small commerce that sustained the poor. Suburban shantytowns bereft of services then sprawled around the capital and became a base for Nicaragua's urban guerrillas.

In conclusion, from 1960 until the earthquake, income distribution became less equal. The upper class and foreign investors absorbed a bigger share of the pie, the middle class and urban working classes held their own, but the poor's share shrank. The great aggregate growth of the economy fueled conspicuous consumption by the rich and their middle-class imitators. The apparent prosperity undoubtedly raised the aspirations of most urban Nicaraguans. In the countryside, well-being declined and dislocation and repression increased. Real wages for blue-collar workers began to decline in 1969–1970. The 1972 earthquake and its aftermath also worsened the lot of the middle sector and accelerated elite dissatisfaction with the regime. In sum, Nicaragua had the classical ingredients for unrest among important sectors of the populace, especially from the early 1970s on—rising expectations contrasted with increased insecurity or diminishing rewards. Aggravated by the political problems discussed below, the intensifying frustration engendered unrest and demands for change.

As a balance sheet on Nicaraguan society after the CACM boom, let us review some data from the 1970s. In the agricultural sector 58 percent of the farms covered only 3.4 percent of the farmland, while 0.6 percent of the farms covered 31 percent of the total agricultural area. The bottom half of Nicaraguan income earners together received 15 percent of the national income, while the top 5 percent of income earners received some 30 percent. Only about 49 percent of the population could read and write, and only 25 percent among the rural populace. Nearly half the country's housing (80 percent in rural areas) lacked indoor plumbing. The average Nicaraguan could expect to live only 53 years, the lowest life expectancy in Central America. Infant and child mortality rates were the second highest in Central America. The lack of potable water outside the cities caused epidemic intestinal diseases that led to almost one-fifth of all deaths. Nicaragua had the highest murder rate in Central America, a high accident rate, and Central America's highest alcoholism rate. The government spent less of its budget on health and education than any other nation in the region.[29] Overall, the data here and in Table 5.2 suggest that Nicaragua distributed services and wealth very unequally and that living standards for the majority were poor, even in comparison to most of the rest of Central America.

Political Institutions

The Nicaraguan government grew like Topsy during the Somoza Debayle era, but its core became more rotten with every passing year. The government created several agencies to ameliorate social strains, partly in fear that lower-class anger might threaten the dictatorship and

TABLE 5.2
Selected Social Indicators for Nicaragua and Other Countries

Index	Nicaragua	Costa Rica	El Salvador	Guatemala	Honduras	Mexico	United States
Physical quality of life, 1974[a]	53	87	67	53	50	75	96
Death rate among children 1-4 yrs.[b]	18.4	4.0	14.5	30.0	20.0	10.6	
Inhabitants per physician[b,f]	2014	1804	5101	4498	4085	1726	569
Daily caloric intake (DCI) as % of average daily requirement (ADR) (2,025 calories/day), 1974[c]	118	117	81	83	89	121	167
DCI/ADR, 1979[d]	117						
DCI/ADR, among poorest half of the populace, 1974[d]	79						
1979[d]	78						
Percent of 1977 central government budget spent[e] on							
a. Education	13	33	23	16	19		
b. Health	12	4	11	11	12		
c. Education plus health	25	37	34	27	31		
Life expectancy[f] at birth: males	51.2	61.9	56.6	48.3	52.1	62.8	68.7
females	54.6	64.8	60.4	49.7	55.0	66.6	76.5
Percentage of all deaths from intestinal diseases[g]	18.7	5.4	15.6	18.9	15.3	12.7	0.1
Percentage of gross domestic product for military expenditures[h]	1.5	0.5	1.7	0.8	1.7	0.7	6.1

TABLE 5.2 (continued)

Sources: K. Ruddle and K. Barrows, ed. Statistical Abstract of Latin America (Los Angeles: UCLA Latin American Publications, 1972); J. Wilkie and P. Reich, eds. Statistical Abstract of Latin America, Vol. 19 (1978) and Vol. 20 (1980) (Los Angeles: UCLA Latin American Center Publications); Ministerio de Planificación, Programa de reactivación en beneficio del pueblo, 1980-1981 (Managua, 1980); Bureau of the Census, U.S. Department of Commerce, Statistical Abstract of the United States, 1978 (Washington, D.C.: Government Printing Office, 1978); Mario A. De Franco and Carlos F. Chamorro, "Nicaragua: Crecimiento industrial y desempleo," in D. Camacho et al., El fracaso social de la integración centroamericana: capital, tecnología, empleo (San José, Costa Rica: Editorial Universitaria Centroamericana, 1979).

[a] An index including levels of infant mortality, literacy, and life expectancy, from Wilkie and Reich, Vol. 19, Table 101.

[b] Wilkie and Reich, Vol. 19, Table 106.

[c] Wilkie and Reich, Vol. 19, Table 110.

[d] Estimate based on Wilkie and Reich, Vol. 19, Table 110, and Ministerio de Planificación, p. 98.

[e] Wilkie and Reich, Vol. 20, Table 106.

[f] Wilkie and Reich, Vol. 20, Table 700; U.S. data from Statistical Abstract of the U.S., 1978.

[g] Wilkie and Reich, Voo. 20, Table 707.

[h] Wilkie and Reich, Vol. 20, Table 2513.

partly because of Alliance for Progress pressure. Anastasio Somoza Debayle himself grandiloquently declaimed: "We must have a direct dialogue with the people in order to know their needs and aspirations and, based on these, build a program of government that will effectively raise the standard of living of the governed."[30] Such programs included the Agrarian Institute, the National Agricultural Technology Institute, the Institute for Peasant Welfare, the Family Center for Rural Education, the Nicaraguan Housing Bank, and the National Housing Institute. These programs were mainly symbolic and siphoned off their resources to raise the standard of living not of the ruled but of the rulers.

In contrast, the government strongly promoted economic growth and industrialization, which directly benefited the bourgeoisie. Among development promotion entities were the National Development Institute (Instituto de Fomento Nacional — INFONAC), the National Foreign and Internal Commerce Institute, and several planning agencies and departments. A public works program emphasizing utilities and road building made infrastructural strides from the late 1950s on.[31] As shown above, the resultant rapid growth of the government expanded middle-class employment, while economic growth enriched mainly national and foreign capitalists without helping the Nicaraguan masses.

Why did Nicaragua's social tragedy worsen despite the expansion of the ostensibly developmental and ameliorative functions of the state? One important answer is that government growth subsidized mainly the personal fortunes of the members of the regime and its collaborators. Bigger government meant more resources to steal or with which to buy friends.[32] Corruption of all kinds abounded, diverting public resources to private ends. For example, more and more Somoza relatives held key public offices, and most observers agree that these relatives upheld their public trust with the same vigor and integrity that characterized the director of the National Guard. Thus the traditional forms of corruption, the main cement of the regime, continued — bribery, conflict of interest, embezzlement, theft, and fraud.

Some cases of corruption have a morbidly illustrative value. For example, the Somoza family owned the franchise for Mercedes Benz automobiles. This contributed to "law and order" in high style, as the Managua police drove nothing but Mercedes Benz prowl cars. Similarly, taking a page from the "remember your friends" textbook for public lending, INFONAC usually gave credit to those close to the regime. In one tobacco development scheme, INFONAC underwrote "officials of the regime who had never grown a leaf of the plant, but who had the pull to alter credit policy for their personal ends."[33]

Anastasio Somoza Debayle never removed his hand from the public treasury, whether the take was large or small. On the petty level, he unconstitutionally campaigned on the national radio system and used National Guard troops to pilot his commercial transport vessels on the Great Lake of Nicaragua. On the grand scale he had no equal as a real estate speculator. Following the 1972 quake, Somoza's Inversiones NICARAAO, S.A., bought some land just outside Managua for $30,000. Weeks later NICARAAO sold it to the National Housing Institute (Instituto Nacional de Vivienda−INVI) as a site for a housing relief project. The price was $3,000,000; a U.S. relief grant provided INVI the funds. INVI never built a house there.

Under the tutelage of the brothers Somoza, Nicaragua's political parties generally declined in cohesion and strength of purpose. The Liberal-Conservative interaction became a struggle "for power with one eye on the budget. The strictly followed rule has been: 'Onward, via public power, toward the public till and the businesses it can finance.'"[34]

The Liberal Nationalist party, the vehicle of the dictatorship, clearly suffered under the Somozas.[35] The PLN became enormously corrupt; many members sold heart and mind to the dynasty in exchange for lucrative government jobs and contracts. In return the PLN always delivered: The presidential nomination went to whomever the Somozas indicated−to Luis (1956); to René Schick (1962); and to Anastasio (1966, 1974). PLN dominance of public institutions assured fraudulent Somoza election victories and pliable courts and bureaucracies.

The decade of apparent liberalization under Luis Somoza raised certain hopes within the PLN that the dynasty might end. A cousin of the Somozas, Dr. Ramiro Sacasa, a wealthy businessman and former cabinet member, decided to seek the PLN presidential nomination for the term ending in 1971. But Anastasio's retention of control via the 1971 junta closed this avenue for Sacasa. He thus became a critic, left the fold, and helped Pedro Joaquín Chamorro found the bourgeois opposition group UDEL in the early 1970s.

The Conservative party, despite its traditional anti-Liberal hostility, often collaborated with the Somozas and the PLN. The willingness of Conservative leaders such as Emiliano Chamorro (1950) and Dr. Fernando Agüero (1971) to abandon principle for a share of power and its rewards rotted the heart of Conservatism and eventually destroyed the party. Such men would exhort the Conservative public to repudiate the dynasty at one moment, then later join league with the enemy. For example, around 1960 Fernando Agüero appeared on the Conservative scene and breathed new energy into the party with calls for social and political reform. In 1967 he and Pedro Joaquín Chamorro led a huge march to protest the upcoming presidential election of Somoza. When the National Guard fired on the crowd of more than forty thousand, three hundred people died, a hundred fell wounded, and the movement's leaders wound up in jail. Yet just a few years later Agüero accepted a deal offered by Somoza in order to quell unrest. The once-spirited reformer joined a PLN-dominated three-person junta, and the Conservatives gained a constitutional revision guaranteeing them 40 percent of public offices. Agüero's acceptance of the Gaustian bargain ruined his credibility and fragmented the Conservatives.

Such collaborationism, partly the result of the convergence of the upper classes, caused a wave of opposition within the party. An anti-collaborationist Young Conservative movement appeared in 1952, and some of its members took part in the insurrections of 1954 and 1959. One emergent strain of rebellious Conservative youth took on social Christian leanings. Many young Conservatives joined with leftists to form the Patriotic Youth (Juventud Patriótica) movement of 1959. Because Agüero had led in the Conservative efforts at revitalization, his later pact with the dictatorship aroused intense hostility and drove many children of the old Conservative establishment into the arms of the radical left.

The small Independent Liberal party, born in 1944 when certain Liberals rejected Somoza García's continuismo, remained committed to opposition. The PLI's mainly middle-class members espoused constitutionalism, Keynesian economics, and socialist economic egalitarianism. Led by such feisty individuals as Enrique Lacayo Farfán, the PLI supplied cannon fodder for several anti-Somoza conspiracies and uprisings. Its reformist refusal to play ball with the regime earned the PLI considerable repression, but it persevered, opposing the dictatorship to the end in 1979.

Communists founded the Nicaraguan Socialist party in the early 1940s. The PSN collaborated with Somoza García briefly during the fleeting period of his populist guise, then fled underground following the 1948 persecution and constitutional ban on a communist party. Struggling, the PSN maintained its base in the urban working class, especially the construction trades. The building upsurge in 1973 broadened the base of the PSN, but the party remained tiny and rather distrustful of the revolutionary potential of the masses and of the "premature" revolutionism of the FSLN.

Hardly worth mentioning as a true party, but nevertheless an interesting phenomenon, is the National Conservative party (Partido Conservador Nacional). This was an ad hoc creation of the Somozas, because of its parasitic character better known to Nicaraguans as the Partido Zancudo (Mosquito party). Whenever the Conservatives mustered the integrity to boycott an election (1957, 1963), the Somozas dusted off the Zancudo Conservatives to provide an illusory opposition. Always demolished by the inevitable Somoza landslide, this chimera would vanish just after the election to reappear only when needed.

In sum, the Somoza brothers combined co-optation and repression in order to manipulate Nicaragua's highly personalistic, conspiratorial, and opportunistic major party factions and personalities. By this manipulation, however, they unwittingly spawned more ideologically committed and disciplined reformist and revolutionary forces. From the early 1950s on, new ideas and new groups—Christian democracy, social democracy, Marxism—emerged from the rubble of the old parties (see Chapter 6).

The National Guard

The National Guard permitted Anastasio Somoza Debayle to control Nicaragua for his family for more than two decades. Yet the Guard became progressively more plagued by internal contradictions, the victim of its functions and its management. Ever better trained and armed for its repressive task, it became still more corrupt and less disciplined. Ever larger and more extended through Nicaraguan society, it became more and more isolated from it.

The Guard retained its multiple roles—armed force, customs control, police, tax collection, postal and telecommunications service. The institution grew from six to seven thousand troops (police, infantry, and air force) from 1970 to 1975. This growth, mainly a one-thousand-man increase in the infantry, was to help control the growing guerrilla threat. Nicaraguan military expenditures occupied an increasing share of the gross national product, rising from less than 1.5 percent before 1965 to 1.7 percent by 1973—almost always the highest in Central America. Military spending per capita rose from $5.60 in 1963 to $7.98 in 1973, a level consistently double that of any other Central American nation. The Guard's share of the 1975 Nicaraguan national budget (including military, police, customs, and diplomatic functions) came to 11 percent—more than $12.00 per capita.[36]

Anastasio Somoza Debayle, spending both Nicaraguan and U.S. cash, generally kept the Guard well trained and equipped. The military aid from the United States totaled $25.5 million from 1946 through 1975. Nearly five thousand Guardsmen trained in the Canal Zone. The Guard suffered some real budget cuts during the administration of René Schick, but after Luis Somoza died the budget recuperated steadily. About the only thing that ever impeded procurement was the director's fear that equipment might be used against him. Thus in the early 1970s the long-favored FAN suffered budget cutbacks that caused equipment to deteriorate somewhat. The popular insurrection of the late 1970s, however, caused a reversal of this trend.

The management of the Guard, as during the Somoza García era, had both positive and negative aspects (in organizational, not moral terms). Several techniques tended to improve the Guard's competence and its morale. Overall, its share of the national budget rose after 1967. This permitted higher pay; for instance, Somoza raised officer's salaries 50 percent and enlisted salaries 150 percent in 1972 (enlisted pay was still very poor, however). Training programs in the Military Academy and abroad improved military effectiveness. Somoza continued his father's paternalism, reinforcing loyalty with personal gifts and attentions throughout the ranks.

The negative side of management, however, eroded morale and discipline. Personal loyalty to the director in chief usually outweighed competence in promotions and assignments. Favoritism led to the protection of corruption to the point that internal discipline suffered. Manipulation of the command structure went on constantly to foil potential conspiracies: Somoza retired entire senior officer classes at once (usually at full pay and with government jobs) to eliminate potential competitors and to make room for junior officers. Especially popular or competent officers found themselves sent abroad as military attachés or retired. Corruption made major customs, police, or departmental commands extraordinarily lucrative. Nepotism continued, as Somoza's illegitimate half-brother José became a general and commanded the Third Battalion, the major infantry force. Anastasio Somoza Portocarrero, Somoza's son and heir apparent to the dynasty, commanded the Basic Infantry Training School (Escuela de Entrenamiento Básico de Infantería—EEBI). Spying within the Guard itself continued; trials, torture, imprisonment, and sometimes death awaited those who would conspire against the tyrant.

Such techniques hurt the organization's cohesion. Younger officers fretted about the lack of professionalism and the corruption in the upper ranks. Military Academy graduates, as always, resented the priority that Somoza family members and sycophants received in assignments. Illustrative of the deterioration of morale and discipline is a scandal that rocked the National Guard in 1968–1970. Somoza confidant Major Oscar Morales in 1968 beat to death a suspected dissident and former Guard lieutenant, David Tejada. When public outcry forced a trial, the tribunal convicted Morales for *besmirching the honor of the Guard* (overlooking the murder) and sentenced him to eight years in prison. Although supposedly confined, Morales continued to circulate freely in public. Some months later he publicly murdered a principal witness against him, Captain Fernando Cedeño. Opinion within the Guard divided sharply over the case, and tensions rose. In September 1969 the incident culminated in a gunfight between Morales's principal defender (Colonel Orlando Villalta, head of the FAN) and Major José Silva Reyes, Morales's prosecutor. This sordid spectacle weakened Somoza's hold on parts of the Guard, as did his increasing drinking problem at this time. Somoza felt sufficiently unsure of his control at this moment that he made the pact with the Conservatives in order to retain his hold on the system.

Nicaraguans knew too well the corruption of the Guard, but its behavior after the 23 December 1972 Managua quake stunned even the most cynical. The National Guard dissolved. Most soldiers abandoned their posts to attend to their families and belongings. Somoza could not rally even a company for two days, so that U.S. and other CONDECA forces came to keep order. Meanwhile, some officers and their troops looted, then sold the booty on the black market. After Somoza rallied the Guard, it entered into the wholesale theft and resale of international relief and reconstruction supplies. Guard elements and their families, of course, received priority in all medical and material relief efforts. Whatever minimal popular support for the Guard had survived the four decades of dictatorship thus yielded in 1973 to fear, contempt, and hostility.

Already alienated from the Nicaraguan people, the Guard grew still more so as a result of several deliberate policies. The dictator apparently feared lest his instrument of repression feel too much sympathy for its victims. Thus, he set the National Guard apart from society. Officials escaped paying most taxes. Members and their families received special medical care, housing, and food and clothing subsidies. Crimes by guardsmen normally went unpunished; if, as in the Morales case, the crime was serious enough, special military tribunals sometimes slapped the offending wrists. Finally, during the 1970s Somoza reportedly began to indoctrinate the Guard with virulent antiopposition, anticommunist ideology. This encouraged ruthlessness in the repression of all opposition.

Repression

The sons of Anastasio Somoza García refined, brutalized, and progressively increased the political repression their father had made a constant tool of power. Repression rose and fell according to the level of opposition activity — with major peaks during the late 1950s, the late 1960s, and from 1974 to the fall of the regime in 1979. The repression spawned ever greater opposition to the regime. This strengthened opposition in turn caused repression to spiral toward its horrifying zenith in 1978–1979.

International human rights conventions, represented here by the American Declaration of the Rights and Duties of Man signed by Nicaragua in 1948, recognize that citizens have certain inherent political and legal rights.[37] Some of these basic rights existed for some

Nicaraguans during portions of the Somoza Debayle years, but most rights were violated systematically and some never existed at all. Amnesty International investigated human rights violations in Nicaragua in 1976 after two years of martial law.

> The violation of human rights — political detentions, tortures, executions — is in large measure, directly or indirectly related to the suspension of constitutional protections of December 1974. The most relevant aspects of the decree are the extension of military court jurisdiction to civilians, and the right of the Executive Branch to censor the media. . . . The military tribunals . . . do not guarantee due process and impartial trials. . . . Many second level union and political activists have experienced repeated detentions for short [sic] periods of up to 180 days . . . for crimes of conscience. . . . Normally prisoners were held incommunicado from their arrest until freed, without opportunity to communicate with their families or attorneys. . . . Of over 200 campesinos said to have been detained between November 1975 and January 1977 in Zelaya Department alone, Amnesty International believes that none was legally processed; the whereabouts of the majority are unknown. It has been reported that military forces have fired in cold blood on many campesinos. . . . There is considerable proof to confirm denunciations of the torture of prisoners in the custody of the National Guard.[38]

Amnesty also listed several torture techniques commonly employed in the Model Prison at Tipitapa: beatings, rupturing of the eardrums, electric shocks, near drowning, hanging by the extremities, cigarette burns, threats of castration and other abuse of the genitals, hooding for periods up to months, and incarceration of nude prisoners in an extremely cold room for days.[39]

These repressive tactics had clear patterns. They rose in proportion to the strength, visibility, and success of opposition movements. They peaked during states of siege when constitutional guarantees were removed and the Guard had nearly total license to restrain individuals and commandeer property. The Office of National Security, the infantry, the police, Anastasio Somoza Portocarrero's EEBI, and certain paramilitary and parasecurity groups combined to carry out the repression.

In rural areas, especially the mountainous North, anti-FSLN counterinsurgency involved infantry mobilized by foot, helicopter, truck, and canoe. The Guard sought to disrupt the FSLN, to capture and kill as many guerrillas as possible, and to take reprisals against any campesinos who, willingly or not, supported the insurgents. The army often appropriated the resources of peasants without compensation. Whole regions underwent "agrarian reform" — population relocation to break up foci of guerrilla support. Suspected guerrilla collaborators suffered horrifying tortures. The Guard often murdered not only suspected FSLN collaborators, but their families as well. Estimates of the total number of peasants killed by the Guard begin at three thousand.

In urban Nicaragua the barbarity was sometimes less for cosmetic reasons, but no less repressive for that. OSN spies kept pressure on dissidents. Independent media suffered frequent violent attacks by "unidentified assailants." During the states of siege thousands were detained and tortured; hundreds were given kangaroo trials by military courts and/or exiled. Overt demonstrations of opposition often unleashed Guard attacks with tear gas and bullets. Few union or partisan opponents of the regime escaped detention or torture. When in the late 1970s the government began to suspect the FSLN of recruiting mainly teenage males, the Guard seized many—often barely more than children—from Managua's streets and executed them on the shore of the lake.

Conclusion

Of his role in this increasingly impoverished, divided, corrupt, repressed, and angry society, Anastasio Somoza Debayle said in his 1976 presidential campaign: "I am a man with a different mentality, who wishes different things for his country—by peaceful means."[40] Among the few who believed Somoza's claims was his friend U.S. Representative Charles Wilson of Texas, who had visited with Somoza in Nicaragua in 1977. Wilson testified to a U.S. House committee considering reducing aid: "There are no political prisoners that I know of. There have been no serious violations of human rights since early 1977."[41]

But the repression was terribly real. Many of those who actively opposed the regime felt Somoza's cruel hand; most of Nicaragua's current revolutionary leaders spent time in jail or suffered torture. But Somoza's repression backfired—it undoubtedly cowed and destroyed some opponents, but it increased the resolve and the numbers of others. Between this and the growing economic frustrations of the lower strata, even a committed and institutionally strong regime would have faced serious challenges. But forty years of Somocismo had swelled and corrupted the state, spoiled and divided the upper class, and perverted the instruments of security.

6
Social Class and Opposition to the Somoza Dynasty

The overthrow of Anastasio Somoza Debayle began on the night when General Tacho Somoza, his father . . . decided to execute Augusto Cesar Sandino.[1]

The opposition realized it lacked the power to overthrow my government; to try it was a sterile effort.[2]

— Anastasio Somoza Debayle, 1 June 1978

Anastasio Somoza García did indeed plant some of the seed that would help destroy his political edifice forty-five years later. The ruthlessness of his methods, the martyrdom of Sandino, and the alienation of Sandino's followers and admirers coalesced in that historic moment to produce both an anti-Somoza kernel in Nicaraguan political culture and a cluster of bitter and determined enemies. The dynasty's subsequent performance then slowly nurtured the hostility of these and other new opposition elements into an undeniable rage that swept Somocismo from Nicaragua.

Upper-Class Opposition

Nicaragua's upper class or bourgeoisie in the 1970s consisted of several elements: There were the major capitalists (such as the huge BANIC and BANAMERICA groups, a few smaller groups, the Somoza family and their closest economic associates, and foreign investors). Also in this sector were the owners of medium-sized local firms and moderate capital holdings. Foreign capitalists constituted a third important element,[3] and a fourth upper-class sector derived its wealth from its connections with the Somoza regime and from the corrupt exploitation of public capital or public power. Within the bourgeoisie, then, were not only the traditional upper-class owners of large and medium-sized landholdings, banks, and insurance companies, but also service and manufacturing entrepreneurs and corrupt public officials.

The Nicaraguan economic elite from the 1930s to the 1970s remained ambivalent toward the Somoza regime. This ambivalence derived from at least four partly contradictory factors. Pushing some portions of the elite away from the Somozas were two things. First, traditional political factionalism at times prompted leading Conservatives to try to capture political power from the Somozas (see next section). Second, the ever-growing economic power of the Somoza family threatened other bourgeois elements. The Somozas often used their political power to seize desired property, especially from political enemies. Moreover, the Somozas' access to capital and control of the national regulatory apparatus made them almost invincible economic competitors. On the other hand, two factors attracted the bourgeoisie to the Somozas: First was the very economic and political power that made the Somozas extraordinarily attractive business and political allies. Second, the Nicaraguan government under Somoza tutelage pursued economic policies that favored most of the wealthy—infrastructure development, laws promoting industrial development, close control of labor policy and labor unions, and regressive taxation.

Overall, the Somozas, like the proverbial bully on the block, represented to their weaker neighbors both a fearsome adversary and an attractive ally. Because of these sometimes conflicting factors, during the first four decades of Somoza rule there emerged a general pattern of bourgeois cooperation with the regime, broken by sporadic efforts to wrest power away from the family. The overarching power of the Somozas signaled to other upper-class elements that accepting political and economic alliance with the Somozas and staying flexible about partisan, regional, familial, or ideological principles constituted the best ways to protect or enhance one's wealth. This pattern held until the 1970s; by then the regime had become more a liability than an asset to most of the bourgeoisie.

The Conservatives

After the Conservative party adopted the tenets of economic liberalism during the late nineteenth century, popular allegiance to the party became not an ideological matter but a habit based mainly upon regionalism, socioeconomic power structures, and family ties.[4] To these reasons was added, especially since the 1940s, dislike for the Somoza regime and clan. The Conservatives sometimes tapped this anti-Somoza feeling among Nicaraguans at large, as evidenced in heavy popular electoral support for the party on several occasions. However, while the Conservative party did sometimes garner many popular votes, its leadership came predominantly from among the same few upper-class clans—the Chamorro, Cuadra, Zavala, Solórzano, and Pasos families.[5]

The Conservative party represented the interests of these families and their upper-class cohorts much more consistently than the interests of its occasional middle- and lower-class constituents.

Some wealthy Conservatives had supported Anastasio Somoza García in the 1930s because they believed that he might effectively control depression-spawned labor unrest. By 1944, however, many Conservatives were ready to rid Nicaragua of Somoza. Conservatives played an important role in the 1944–1948 opposition coalition against the regime, organizing, demonstrating, and electioneering for a common presidential candidate, Dr. Enoc Aguado. This energetic opposition prompted the nervous dictator temporarily to ally with the labor movement and the PSN. Having thus successfully wooed labor away from the opposition, Somoza escalated repression against all the opposition coalition parties. However, he then made key deals with Conservative party leaders Carlos Cuadra Pasos (1948) and General Emiliano Chamorro (1950), buying peace with the Conservatives with a constitutional amendment granting them one-third of the nation's congressional seats and judicial appointments.

Many younger Conservatives who in the mid-1940s had seen the party as a vehicle for change and had suffered imprisonment and exile for their anti-Somoza activities became disillusioned with the older leadership's willingness to accept co-optation. This younger generation contributed heavily to a social Christian movement to reform Conservatism from within (see below), as well as to at least three unsuccessful armed revolts against the regime (1954, 1957, 1959). The young reformists' Popular Christian Democratic Movement (Movimiento Popular Demócrata Cristiano—MPDC) took over the Conservative party leadership in 1960 and chose Dr. Fernando Agüero to run against Luis Somoza's Liberal party designate René Schick in 1962. Evidence of massive impending fraud caused the MPDC-dominated Conservative party to abandon its loyalist stance of the previous decade and to boycott the 1962 elections, thereby raising the party's credibility among the public at large.

Fernando Agüero led the Conservative presidential slate again in the 1967 presidential contest and was the sole nominee of the National Opposition (Unión Nacional Opositora—UNO) coalition. In this turbulent period following Luis Somoza's death, the Conservatives (then at the apogee of their popular support) and their social Christian and Independent Liberal allies mobilized widespread popular opposition to the first presidential candidacy of National Guard head Anastasio Somoza Debayle. The latter had himself elected by the usual fraudulent means, but his unpopular and repressive presidency kept unrest at a high level in the late 1960s. Therefore, following a time-tested model, Somoza Debayle sought to co-opt the Conservatives with a 40 percent share of the

Congress and other government posts. In the now established Conservative tradition, ex-reformer Fernando Agüero agreed in 1971 to serve on a three-person executive junta (1972–1974) pending a constitutional revision.

The decision of Agüero and his collaborators to cooperate once again with the regime in exchange for shared power and spoils alienated many Conservatives and splintered the party. There were heavy desertions to the Social Christian party (especially by the MPDC reformers) and to new groups: Pedro Joaquín Chamorro's Conservative National Action (Acción Nacional Conservadora—ANC), the Authentic Conservative party (Partido Conservador Auténtico) and the Democratic Conservative party (Partido Conservador Democrático). Moreover, some university-age youth from Conservative families renounced Conservatism entirely for much more radical alternatives. In sum, the opportunism of the Conservative leadership alienated successive generations of young Conservatives, eroded electoral support, splintered the party, and eventually left it dead and buried—by the hand of its own leaders.[6]

Dissident Liberals

The Liberal party,[7] finally returned to power in the 1930s after nearly two decades of U.S.-backed Conservative rule, apparently enjoyed a substantial majority of popular support and a significant following among the urban middle classes, especially professionals. At that time, however, the Liberal political apparatus was dominated by an upper-class elite. Among the more powerful Liberal clans were the Debayle, Sevilla, Sacasa, and Lacayo families. The Somoza family came from a second tier of poorer or downwardly mobile Liberal stalwarts. When Anastasio Somoza García became Guard commander and president (1934–1936) he began to take over the Liberal party. He did so by enhancing his family's rather insignificant economic base (a small coffee farm) and then by linking himself to other leading Liberals through a skillful mix of business, politics, patronage, persuasion, and coercion. By 1944 these methods had vouchsafed him control of the party, now rechristened as the Liberal Nationalist party. Although the PLN itself never constituted an opposition group, disgruntled Liberals rejected Somocista Liberalism on two important occasions.

The first big fissure within Liberalism opened in 1944, when Somoza García decided to seek "reelection." Many Liberals disliked the Somoza clique; led by General Carlos Pasos and Dr. Enoc Aguado, these dissidents tried to block Somoza's renomination bid. Frustrated, Pasos and Aguado founded the Independent Liberal party. Even when Somoza later decided not to seek another term, the PLI, in coalition with the Conservatives, ran Dr. Aguado against Somoza's designated PLN candidate, Dr. Leonardo Argüello. After his fraudulent election and in-auguration, Argüello tried to fire Somoza. The outraged general had the PLN-dominated Congress oust Argüello and quickly return himself to the presidency. Ironically, the schism that created the PLI and the subsequent Argüello debacle permitted Somoza García completely to dominate the PLN and thus establish it as one key organ of family control over the political system.

From the later 1940s until the death of Luis Somoza Debayle in 1967, the PLN became ever more identified with the Somozas' interests and objectives and progressively less ideological. The well-financed and well-organized party moderated and modernized somewhat under the leadership of Luis after 1956. However, after the 1967 ascendancy to power of Anastasio, the PLN began to decline. He reportedly surrounded himself with especially avaricious and corrupt cronies, demoralizing the party's more loyal cadres at the base. Though the PLN as a whole never rejected him, considerable disaffection did develop in the ranks in the 1970s. This led to the defection of Ramiro Sacasa Guerrero, a former Somocista cabinet member, who founded the Constitutionalist Liberal party (Partido Liberal Constitucionalista–PLC) and, in 1974, the Democratic Liberation Union, a coalition of opposition groups. Thus, by the 1970s, the negative impact of Anastasio Somoza Debayle had pushed the PLN near collapse.

Other Upper-Class Groups

Following the 1972 Managua earthquake, the rapid cyclical fluctuations of Nicaragua's economy, brought on in part by government responses to the quake, increasing labor unrest, escalating political violence, and Somoza Debayle's aggressiveness in capitalizing upon the earthquake recovery process, began to threaten numerous established interests. Economic and political crisis so alienated business support from Somoza that many national capitalists eventually worked to overthrow his regime.[8]

Nicaragua's principal industrial and commercial chambers–including the Chamber of Industries, the Chamber of Commerce, and groups of cotton, cattle, and coffee producers–united as the Superior Council of Private Initiative (Consejo Superior dé la Iniciativa Privada–COSIP). In the 1960s COSIP occasionally tangled verbally with the government over policy matters or while defending business interests from Nicaragua's corrupt regulatory agencies. COSIP also began to promote broader goals, however, seeking to ameliorate certain kinds of socioeconomic strains that more progressive business leaders feared might lead to revolution.

Under the aegis of the Alliance for Progress in the early 1960s, the

U.S. Agency for International Development (AID) helped COSIP start three reformist institutions: (1) the Nicaraguan Development Institute (Instituto Nicaragüense de Desarrollo—INDE) (1963) sought to attenuate growing socioeconomic inequities by promoting, via "democratic means and the free enterprise system," community development, cooperativism, education, improved public services, and community-government cooperation. (2) With funding from the Nicaraguan private sector and AID, the Nicaraguan Development Foundation (Fundación Nicaragüense de Desarrollo—FUNDE) was organized to foster cooperatives. FUNDE by 1979 reported forming fifty-eight production cooperatives with more than seventeen thousand members. (3) INDE also created the Educational Credit Program (Programa de Crédito Educativo—EDUCREDITO) to channel private-sector educational loans to students from poor families.

As the national crisis deepened after 1972 both COSIP and INDE, under the leadership of Felipe Mántica, Enrique Dreyfus, Alfonso Robelo Callejas, and William Baez, became much more critical of the government. In 1974 INDE and COSIP sponsored a convention of private-sector interests that demanded greater honesty in government and social reforms to assist the "great dispossessed majorities." Also at this juncture appeared the UDEL, supported by private capital and founded by Pedro Joaquín Chamorro and Ramiro Sacasa Guerrero. UDEL criticized the regime frequently, and this landed many of its leaders in jail from 1974 on.

The rift between the government and the private sector widened still further in 1977, when the regime removed certain business tax exemptions and imposed new business taxes, which INDE urged its members not to pay. In the same year COSIP and INDE promoted, in collaboration with the church, a "national dialogue" to seek a peaceful resolution of the political crisis. Most major business interests still preferred a "national unity" reform—ousting the Somozas but retaining the basic political structure, including the National Guard and the PLN.

One key group of Nicaraguan capitalists, however, helped broaden the revolutionary coalition and established business interest links with the FSLN. Among them were industrialist Emilio Baltodano Pallais, lawyer-businessman Dr. Joaquín Cuadra Chamorro, supermarket magnate Felipe Mántica, and international banker Arturo Cruz Porras. Their contacts with and mid-1977 endorsement of the FSLN allegedly led the guerrillas' leadership to propose them along with eight others for cabinet posts in a revolutionary government. This "Group of Twelve," exposed in 1977, fled Nicaragua for safety. From abroad, the Twelve began to lobby against international aid for Somoza and to organize the anti-Somoza coalitions within Nicaragua.

The assassination of Pedro J. Chamorro on 10 January 1978 convinced many reluctant capitalists and private-sector leaders that stronger steps should be taken. COSIP broadened its coalition of private-sector groups and changed its name to the Superior Council of Private Enterprise (Consejo Superior de la Empresa Privada—COSEP). Industrialist Alfonso Robelo Callejas organized a new opposition party of progressive business interests and professionals, the Nicaraguan Democratic Movement (Movimiento Democrático Nicaragüense—MDN) in March 1978. In May 1978 the Group of Twelve, the MDN, and the UDEL's organizations joined to form the Broad Opposition Front (Frente Amplio Opositor—FAO), which during the next ten months organized a series of general strikes (by both business and labor) that weakened the regime financially and politically and thus helped topple the dynasty.

The Press

The mass media, and in particular the daily newspaper *La Prensa,* played a complex role in the Somozas' Nicaragua.[9] Opposition papers and radio stations criticized or published news unfavorable to the regime. The Somozas generally countered such information via the controlled national radio and television stations, proregime private broadcast media, and their own daily newspaper, *Novedades.* But the independent and opposition media did not enjoy true press freedom, for they often experienced police searches, and their employees sometimes suffered arbitrary confinement and beatings. Many opposition papers did not survive for long, but *La Prensa*—owned by the powerful Conservative Chamorro clan—prevailed from its founding in 1936 and ultimately helped unseat the regime.

La Prensa cast a jaundiced eye upon the Somoza government; under the editorship of Pedro Joaquín Chamorro Cardenal from the late 1940s on, it repeatedly embarrassed the regime by exposing unsavory official behavior, by reporting opposition politicians' criticism, and by supporting opposition candidates. In the 1970s, Pedro Chamorro's leadership of UDEL and his highly critical daily political commentary provoked intensified repression against the paper. On various occasions unidentified assailants fired automatic weapons at *La Prensa's* plant. With the state of siege in 1974 came strict press censorship, banning criticism of the government and restricting reports of insurgent activity. Attacks against individual reporters escalated. In 1977 the paper published an exposé of a business owned by Somoza cohorts, including Anastasio Somoza Debayle's son Anastasio Somoza Portocarrero. The concern exported blood plasma badly needed in Nicaragua. In retaliation, the firm's owners reportedly hired assassins who murdered Chamorro. Subsequent investigations by the revolutionary government have claimed that President Somoza Debayle played no role in the assassination, but they have directly implicated his son.[10]

La Prensa and the slain editor's widow, Violeta Barrios de Chamorro, helped mobilize the massive protest demonstrations that followed the assassination. This campaign and the reporting of other independent media led to two more machine gun attacks on *La Prensa's* plant and to the closure of two radio stations (including that of the Catholic archdiocese) within the next eight months. External criticism of such acts prompted Guillermo Sevilla Sacasa, Nicaraguan ambassador to the United States, to affirm in late June 1978: "In Nicaragua . . . there is absolute freedom of the press."[11] But in August and September the National Guard suspended publication of *La Prensa* for twenty-five days. On 11 June 1979 the air force bombed the paper's printing plant in northern Managua, thus silencing the paper for good until after the revolution's triumph the next month.

Given the degree of criticism directed toward the regime by opposition media, one must ask why the dictatorship tolerated it at all and for so long. Two factors account for this partial press freedom: First, the Somozas' hold on power was occasionally rather tenuous; they periodically needed to ally themselves with leading Conservatives. Permitting the survival of *La Prensa* helped keep the influential and rebellious Chamorros and their Conservative allies at bay at least some of the time. Second, the Somozas usually paid lip service to constitutional formalities such as press freedom because backing from the United States thus came more readily. Retaining such an important (albeit vexatious) symbol of press freedom was therefore expedient. In the mid-1970s, however, under siege from all sides, Anastasio Somoza Debayle eventually went to war with the opposition press, thus inadvertently creating a powerful symbol on which mass hostility could be focused.

Middle-Class Groups

The Nicaraguan middle strata consist mainly of salaried private-sector employees, government employees, professionals, small business people, teachers, and university and secondary school students. Many members of the Nicaraguan middle class and organizations representing middle-class concerns came to oppose the Somoza regime—more with each passing decade: students from the 1930s on, the Independent Liberals from the 1940s on, the social Christians in the 1950s and 1960s, and middle-sector unions in the troubled 1970s.

Independent Liberal Party

The PLI, largely supported by professionals, salaried workers, and small business interests, spun off from the Liberal Nationalist party in

1944 (see above).[12] The new party raised as its standard the democratic traditions of Liberalism and advocated "Keynesian economics, socialist economic reformism, and Jeffersonian democratic politics."[13] The PLI and the Conservative party jointly nominated Aguado for the presidency in 1946. From that moment forward the PLI's opposition to the regime remained unrelenting, at times costing its militants dearly at the hands of the National Guard. By exposing its activists to repression, the PLI radicalized several individuals who later came to play a major historical role against the Somoza dynasty.

The PLI opposed the Somozas in several ways. In the electoral arena, the party waged strong campaigns against the PLN in 1946, 1956, and 1967. In 1946 and 1967 the PLI allied with Conservatives and other smaller parties behind a single presidential candidate. The Somozas' use of electoral fraud, however, frustrated each of these efforts. One of the PLI's most important strengths was organization. During the 1946 campaign the party's student arm, the Democratic Youth Front (Frente Juvenil Democrático – FJD) played an especially active role in the northern areas of traditional Liberal support. The FJD mobilized high school and university students to electioneer and to demonstrate against the regime. In the FJD's paper, *Vanguardia Juvenil,* one young PLI militant wrote in 1946 of "reactionaries, idolators, and cowards whose ideal is to keep in power the Nicaraguan Fuhrer and his Gestapo. . . . The Democratic Youth Front calls upon all brave Nicaraguans to refuse to join the organization that serves Anastasio Somoza García."[14] Tomás Borge Martínez penned these fiery lines; fifteen years later he helped found the Sandinista National Liberation Front.

Over the three decades of PLI opposition, numerous party figures paid for their activism with imprisonment, internal exile, torture, or death. For example, a 1954 rebellion cost several PLI participants their lives. Following the assassination of Somoza García in 1956, the enraged Anastasio Somoza Debayle jailed and interrogated every known PLI leader; some were tortured. The list of victims included the elderly Dr. Enoc Aguado, PLI leader Enrique Lacayo Farfán, and Tomás Borge Martínez. By then a law student in Managua, Borge was tortured and tried and convicted on false testimony of conspiring in the assassination. Once again in 1967, PLI leaders went to jail following an opposition rally turned rebellion, and numerous PLI supporters fell among the estimated three hundred dead.

Although the PLI as an organization normally pursued its goals by legal channels, not all its adherents always acted peacefully or legally. The most notable of the PLI supporters to turn to violence was Rigoberto López Pérez, who assassinated Anastasio Somoza García in 1956. Others included the PLI sympathizers, some of them National Guard officers, who mounted an unsuccessful invasion and coup in 1954. Later, in the effervescence after the fall of Cuba's Batista and Venezuela's Pérez Jiménez in 1959, PLI supporters tried several times, independently of each other, to overthrow the dynasty. Carlos ("Chale") Haslam Herrera, a Matagalpa farmer, died in an unsuccessful guerrilla campaign against the regime. Manuel Díaz y Sotelo, a reporter for several opposition newspapers and a regime torture victim, also mounted an unsuccessful revolt and was killed. Enrique Lacayo Farfán and others took part with Conservatives in the well-financed but abortive 1959 invasion at Olama and Mollejones.

Despite such repeated setbacks, Independent Liberals continued to oppose the dictatorship. The PLI joined the UDEL in 1974 and the FAO coalition in 1977. When the FAO's largely upper-class leadership began to vacillate during the coalition's negotiations with the regime late in 1978, the PLI withdrew from the FAO in protest and joined with the more radical, FSLN-linked National Patriotic Front (Frente Patriótico Nacional—FPN). In this way the PLI upheld its tradition of consistent opposition to the Somoza dynasty, unpunctuated by periods of collaboration like those of the Conservative party.

Although never able to win a mass base in the working classes and thus by itself unable to oust the Somoza family from power, the PLI continually worried and irritated the regime. Through association with the PLI, numerous important opponents had sharpened their techniques, clarified their ideas, and tested their mettle. Not all of them remained Independent Liberals, however: some, like Tomás Borge, sought more effective organization and more radical ideology; others simply took up arms with a quixotic disregard for organization. In sum, by its early and persistent opposition to the Somoza dynasty, the relatively small PLI catalyzed major opposition coalitions that demonstrated the futility of peaceful struggle against Somocismo and socialized many rebels and revolutionaries.

The Social Christian Movement

The Nicaraguan Social Christian party (Partido Social Cristiano Nicaragüense—PSCN) originated in the dissatisfaction of elements of both the traditional Conservative and Liberal factions with their own parties. Christian democracy first blossomed as the tiny, reform-oriented National Union of Popular Action (Unión Nacional de Acción Popular—UNAP). Established in 1948 by Antonio Téfel Vélez, *La Prensa* editor Pedro Joaquín Chamorro Cardenal, and others, UNAP foundered during the postassassination repression of 1956–1957. In 1957, however, the smaller of two groups of former UNAP members formed the Nicaraguan Social Christian party. The PSCN was not confessional (i.e., a political arm of the church); indeed, the Catholic hierarchy of Nicaragua supported the Somozas and frowned upon the PSCN. The party was a secular, reformist, prodemocratic organization pledged to peaceful social change. It advocated "communitarian corporatism" (cooperatives, community development, Christian labor unions), reformist state intervention in the economy, and political reform as the keys to greater social justice. Throughout its history, the PSCN has drawn members mainly from among working-class affiliates. From 1957 to 1962 the party grew rather slowly, but steadily improved its organization.

A second and larger group of UNAP social Christians drifted into the Conservative party after 1957 and formed within its ranks the Popular Christian Democratic Movement. Shortly afterward, several MPDC leaders, including Pedro J. Chamorro and Antonio Téfel, broke dramatically with the Christian democratic nonviolent creed by attempting to overthrow the Somoza brothers by force in the abortive 1959 invasion at Olama and Mollejones. The MPDC faction, nevertheless, continued its efforts within the party, and in 1962 it won control of the Conservative party convention and major party leadership positions. From this position the MPDC pledged the Conservative party to the ideals of Christian democratic reformism, overriding objections by the party's older leaders. The MPDC leadership launched the Christian Democratic Youth (Juventud Democrático Cristiano — JDC), which by 1963 was rapidly gaining ground in university student politics against the waning influence of the student left. The MPDC also organized a Christian labor union, the Nicaraguan Autonomous Union Movement (Movimiento Sindical Autónomo de Nicaragua — MOSAN). In 1963, however, Fernando Agüero, who had risen to head the Conservative party via the MPDC, changed sides to back the old-line Conservatives whom the MPDC had just edged out of power. Although a handful of social Christians (including Pedro Joaquín Chamorro) decided to remain in the Conservative party, the Christian democratic experiment within Conservatism had ended. To protest Agüero's move, most of the MPDC faction joined the PSCN.

The MPDC influx into the Social Christian party in 1963 accelerated the party's growth, although its platform and traditional commitment to politics by legal means remained unchanged. With the aid of leadership training and consultation from international Christian democratic organizations, the PSCN after 1963 increased its organizational capabilities. It promoted a new youth organization in the universities, the Christian Democratic Front (Frente Democrático Cristiano — FDC), which soon led many energetic recruits into the PSCN itself and won control of university student governments in León and Managua in 1966. In the

1967 elections the PSCN joined the PLI and the Conservatives in the UNO opposition coalition. Although UNO lost the presidency to the Liberals' Anastasio Somoza Debayle, the PSCN did win one seat each in the House and Senate. From this platform the PSCN goaded the political establishment and aired national problems to a previously unknown degree through vigorous debate and the introduction of reform legislation.

As the Social Christian party entered the 1970s, observers believed that it offered promise as an agent of political reform in Nicaragua. When the progressive Miguel Obando y Bravo became archbishop of Nicaragua in 1968, the church began to give the party moral support. But just as the PSCN's chances for political influence began to brighten under the status quo ante, history began to outrun the PSCN. The rapid deterioration of the civic order after 1973 began radicalizing other elements that might have backed a reformist PSCN in more peaceful times. More radical unions stole MOSAN's thunder. Students progressively abandoned the FDC for more revolutionary groups. In 1974 the PSCN affiliated with the UDEL to press for more sweeping, yet still peaceful, reform. The internal tension over methods and ideology grew, and in the mid-1970s a leftist faction broke from the PSCN to form the People's Social Christian party (Partido Popular Social Cristiano—PPSC). As violence had grown and more and more groups opposed the regime, the PSCN had become just one of many groups advocating change, rather than the leading opposition force. In 1978 the PSCN joined the FAO coalition as part of the UDEL. The PPSC, however, joined the pro-Sandinista National Patriotic Front coalition in early 1979. Thus, despite having entered the 1970s as the leading reformist party, the PSCN was eclipsed and divided because it remained reformist during revolutionary times.[15]

Students

University students, and sometimes secondary school students, provided a nearly constant thorn in the side of the Somoza dynasty. As early as 1939, for example, several anti-Somoza students in León were jailed for burning a campus portrait of Anastasio Somoza García. A 1943 clash occurred when the dictator attempted to impose a campus festival queen. From such inconsequential beginnings, students went on periodically to force themselves into national politics. Whole student leadership generations—in 1944-1948, 1959-1961, and 1970-1979—had their lives shaped by clashes with the regime during the periods of national unrest.[16] Students have served as organizers, mobilizers, rioters, plotters, and guerrillas.

A first student generation took shape in the 1944-1948 struggle to oust Somoza García and to implement greater political democracy. The movement involved students from different party backgrounds; some gave up their freedom and a few even their lives in the efforts. One Conservative university activist was Pedro Joaquín Chamorro, who got himself briefly exiled to the Corn Islands for antiregime activity in 1944. The Independent Liberals' student wing, the Young Democratic Front, mobilized many disgruntled young Liberals into politics against Somoza from both the high schools and the universities. For example, in the anti-Somoza northern region, where Sandino's memory still aroused powerful positive feelings, Matagalpa high school students, such as Tomás Borge Martínez and José Ramón Gutiérrez Castro worked with the FJD. Later, in the National Autonomous University of León in 1947–1948, Borge participated actively in a student movement, becoming more and more critical of the regime. In 1948 this activity in León came to a head in several large antiregime demonstrations that were violently put down by the National Guard. Numerous student leaders went to jail or into exile.

The student movement of the 1940s began to subside after 1948, partly because of repression and partly because of the 1948 and 1950 agreements between Anastasio Somoza García and Conservative leaders. As the Conservatives accepted sharing the spoils of government with Somoza's PLN, some Conservative student leaders opted to return to the now richer fold, thus eroding one important wing of the University movement.

At the Matagalpa high school (Instítuto Nacional del Norte), students' anti-Somoza efforts did not subside, however. Tomás Borge's activist friend José Ramón Gutiérrez Castro went to revolutionary Guatemala[17] for three years and returned in 1953 to introduce Carlos Fonseca Amador to Marxism. Fonseca and his companion Silvio Mayorga were tremendously influenced by socialist ideas and adopted them as a guide for their activism. Fonseca in 1954 founded *Segovia,* a student newspaper.[18] He also joined the Socialist party (then underground) and started a Marxist study group in Matagalpa. The study group's members would help disseminate their revolutionary ideas throughout the university student movement in 1959–1961.

Following the assassination of Somoza García in 1956, many student leaders and former students (including Borge and Chamorro) suffered imprisonment, torture, and exile at the behest of Somoza's sons and as a consequence became increasingly disgruntled with peaceful means of opposition. In the late 1950s and early 1960s, leaders of the 1944–1948 generation together with the early 1950s Matagalpa contingent helped forge a second generation of student opponents to the Somoza dynasty.

When Fidel Castro overthrew Cuba's Batista in January 1959, student leaders saw in the Cuban experience hope for change in Nicaragua. Students of diverse political backgrounds soon organized the Nicaraguan Patriotic Youth (Juventud Patriótica Nicaragüense – JPN). The JPN expanded its goals to include the destruction of the Somoza dynasty. Student demonstrations in 1959 provoked violent repressive measures by the National Guard, which in turn apparently convinced numerous student activists to emulate the Castro model of guerrilla insurrection. A number of Nicaraguan activists, as ideologically diverse as Pedro J. Chamorro and Carlos Fonseca, visited Cuba in 1959–1960 to seek aid and training. The nature and amount of Cuban assistance still remain obscure, but several of those who visited Cuba (including both Fonseca and Chamorro) returned soon afterward to attempt guerrilla insurgencies. Students from the JPN joined in several of these initiatives. The only guerrilla movement that prospered, however, was the Sandinista National Liberation Front, founded in 1961 by Carlos Fonseca Amador, Tomás Borge Martínez, and Silvio Mayorga.

The student revolutionist movement of 1959–1961 became quiescent after 1962. Unrest abated as the U.S.-sponsored Alliance for Progress promoted socioeconomic reforms to forestall "more Cubas." Under the leadership of Luis Somoza and his protégés, Nicaragua joined the Central American Common Market, implemented (largely symbolic) rural welfare and land reform programs, and permitted some hints of political liberalization. Such domestic and international policies combined with a period of economic prosperity to produce optimism about the legal road to change and, consequently, reformism within Conservatism and Christian democracy. Much popular discontent calmed—even in the universities—and violence diminished before this illusory dream of peaceful change. Most leftist student leaders who had committed themselves to the guerrilla struggle were wiped out by the National Guard's counterinsurgency campaign by 1962. The FSLN itself suffered major military setbacks in 1963 and later in 1967, yet it escaped obliteration by learning from its mistakes (see Chapter 7).

But after several years of relative calm, a new student revolutionary generation emerged in the 1970s from the growing political malaise precipitated by Anastasio Somoza Debayle's assumption of complete ruling power in 1967. He was more ruthless and less politically adroit than either his late brother or father; his faction of the PLN soon proved both more corrupt and less competent than Luis's. He quickly dashed opposition hopes for peaceful change by arranging to keep himself in office through 1981 and by escalating repression of his critics. Meanwhile, the Managua quake of December 1972 shattered the capital and laid bare the enormous corruption of Somoza, his cohorts, and the National Guard.

As these events unfolded, leftist and revolutionary ideologies replaced the reformism of the 1960s in university student organizations. Despite counterpressure by the regime, the Student Revolutionary Front (Frente Estudiantil Revolucionario—FER) supplanted the Christian Democrats' reformist FDC in the leadership of student governments in the early 1970s. Many frustrated Social Christians defected to the revolutionary left as the church and the PSCN's community activism gave them contacts with the FSLN. The FER — radical, heavily influenced by Marxism, and closely linked to the FSLN[19] — gave the guerrilla organization critical support. After the Agüero-Somoza pact of 1971, revolutionary student groups began to attract more youths from upper-class backgrounds, both Liberal and Conservative.[20]

In 1974 an FSLN hostage taking (see Chapter 7) resulted in a three-year state of siege (until 1977) under which all civil rights were suspended and the police were given special powers. The National Guard went on a rampage to wipe out the subversives, with students as an important target. When a state of siege was again declared in 1978, the Guard's violence against the young became epidemic. The Inter-American Commission on Human Rights described the situation as "a general repression by the National Guard against male youth between 14 and 21."[21] Hundreds of young men detained in random roundups from buses, homes, and private vehicles later were found dead, their bodies often mutilated. Despite heavy emigration by young people to escape such terror, the student movement grew. The National Federation of Youth Movements formed to coordinate student opposition. Other groups developed direct links to the guerrillas. High schools also began to experience antiregime unrest. In July 1978, for example, students occupied most of Nicaragua's secondary schools. They demanded the release of political prisoners, the removal of regime spies from the schools, and general political reform.

As three FSLN factions emerged in the 1970s, each developed its own student organizations, but all continued to coordinate their actions. After 1974 students stepped up the number of demonstrations, conducted still more propaganda activities, and organized neighborhood groups against the regime. Groups with FSLN links also committed acts of antiregime sabotage and terror, raised money, and recruited for the guerrillas. By 1978 nine of twenty-two affiliates of the pro-FSLN United People's Movement (Movimiento Pueblo Unido — MPU) were student groups; two of these represented high school students.

In summary, student reformers and revolutionaries from Conservatives to Marxists plagued the Somozas for forty years and ultimately played a critical role in the overthrow of the dynasty. Several features of student opposition to the Somozas bear emphasis here. First, each of the revolutionary student generations drew activists from diverse partisan origins, including Liberalism; Second, although the bulk of student revolutionaries have come from the middle class, there have also been major leaders from the working class and from the upper class. Third, in each revolutionary generation, initial nonviolent criticism of the regime elicited heavy-handed repression that radicalized the student movement, thus producing violence. Many who survived jail or torture by Somoza became implacable opponents of the regime, including Pedro Joaquín Chamorro, Carlos Fonseca, and Tomás Borge.

Fourth, the student movement, to some degree, matured with each successive generation. In 1944–1948 the national political parties heavily manipulated the student opposition for partisan ends. Student revolutionaries in 1959–1961, however, led by a few veterans of 1944–1948, overcame such manipulation via the independent, revolutionary JPN. The 1970s generation of student opposition to the regime, now led by veterans of both earlier generations, combined partisan independence, revolutionary ideology, and the sophisticated FER-FSLN-MPU organization with an armed insurrection. One final distinctive feature is the role in the Nicaraguan revolution of a handful of 1944–1948 leaders from Matagalpa—Fonseca, Borge, and Mayorga. This Promethean group helped lead the 1959–1961 generation, founded the FSLN, and then nurtured the guerrilla movement through a decade of clandestine existence and several military disasters. The group resurfaced in the 1970s, fortified by its 1959–1961 recruits, to guide the third student revolutionary generation and the Sandinista military insurrection.

The universities and some of the professors also contributed to the opposition movement during the 1970s.[22] The public universities in León, Granada, and Managua and some of their provincial satellite campuses served as sanctuaries for student organizations. University autonomy from state intervention usually kept the National Guard out of university campuses. The Guard occasionally violated autonomy to search facilities or to disrupt meetings and demonstrations, but it resorted mainly to spies for information about university radicals. This caution undoubtedly reflected the high risk of massive student violence if major breaches of university autonomy occurred. Such violations became much more frequent in the late 1970s and left the National Autonomous University of Nicaragua (UNAN) in León heavily damaged.

Tolerance of revolutionary activism on campus by university officials such as Carlos Tunnerman Bernheim, rector of UNAN from 1964 to 1974, greatly facilitated student organization against the regime. Tunnerman has called university autonomy "one of the great contributions to the revolution" and said it put the universities "in cooperation with the people."[23] Although the private, Jesuit-run Central American University (Universidad Centroamericana—UCA) experienced somewhat less antiregime activity, there too student organizations worked against the regime.

University faculty did not merely sit and watch their students make a revolution. Many activist university professors of the 1970s were veterans of earlier student radical generations, especially the 1959–1961 group. Some university faculty actively collaborated with student revolutionaries and with the FSLN. The most important example of this is the four university professors in the Group of Twelve—Fernando Cardenal, Sergio Ramírez Mercado, Carlos Tunnerman Bernheim, and Ernesto Castillo.

Middle-Sector Unions

The Nicaraguan labor movement experienced long periods of manipulation and repression under the Somozas. Nevertheless, unions representing middle-class groups—teachers, private-sector and government employees, health workers—began to act with increasing independence during the 1970s, eventually contributing to the destabilization of the regime.[24]

The middle-class unions and groups, located mainly in the cities of the populous Pacific zone, included such organizations as the National Association of Educators of Nicaragua (Asociación Nacional de Educadores de Nicaragua—ANDEN), the Federation of Nicaraguan Teachers (Federación de Maestros de Nicaragua—FMN), the National Employees Union (Unión Nacional de Empleados—UNE), and the Association of Women Confronting National Problems (Asociación de Mujeres ante la Problemática Nacional—AMPRONAC). Prior to 1973, while the economic and public-sector growth of the 1960s still benefited the middle classes (see Chapter 5), such organizations had done little to press their demands with the state. However, after the December 1972 catastrophe in Managua, the boom-and-bust economic cycles, rapid inflation, and ballooning middle-sector unemployment combined to anger certain middle-class groups. Moreover, national postquake emergency legislation boosted the workweek from forty-eight to sixty hours and forced all public employees to contribute a month's salary per year as a special reconstruction levy.

Such events and policies increased the number and the activity of middle-class groups—especially unions—which in turn demanded higher wages and protested the emergency austerity measures. Government intransigence before these demands led to a wave of strikes by middle-sector unions in 1973 and 1974, including teachers, hospital workers, and health workers. When Somoza declared martial law in 1974, union leaders began to disappear or to suffer torture or imprisonment. Such repression, added to the unresolved economic problems of the middle sector, began to radicalize the middle-class unions. They began to alter their demands from specific economic benefits for their members to calls for broad political reform or revolution. By 1977 most of the middle-class unions and AMPRONAC were demanding sweeping political reforms and the release of the several thousand political prisoners accumulated in the nation's jails since 1974. Most of the middle-class groups (UNE, ANDEN, and AMPRONAC) first joined the moderate FAO opposition coalition, then left it for the revolutionary MPU coalition in early 1979. Mobilized through these coalitions, middle-class unions supported, and their members took part in, the general strikes of 1978 and 1979. Even substantial numbers of nonmilitary public employees boycotted their jobs, in spite of regime threats of retribution. These and other middle-class organizations also took part in protest demonstrations. Overall, such activity contributed significantly to the general destabilization and economic resistance that weakened the Somoza regime during 1978 and 1979.

The Petty Bourgeoisie

Analyzing the role in the revolution of Nicaragua's small business interests (petty commerce, services, and manufacturing) provides a difficult task.[25] Commonly victimized by police and bureaucratic corruption, many members of this sector today express great joy at the passing of the Somozas. For instance, taxi drivers and hotel keepers, once subject to constant police shakedowns to keep licenses or to avoid fees or fines for often imaginary infractions, were typically bitter opponents of the dictatorship and its corrupt agents. However, the very visibility and smallness that made such enterprises so vulnerable to corrupt officials also kept them atomized and disorganized. Moreover, such individuals were often quite economically conservative and susceptible to regime appeals that portrayed political unrest and the FSLN as threats to their property. For these reasons, petty bourgeois responses to the regime remained individualistic, relatively poorly organized, and formally uncommitted. Although some petty entrepreneurs fought the Somozas in one way or another and others supported them actively, most probably remained neutral as much as possible.

Lower-Class Opposition

Never unified nor coherent, lower-class opposition to the Somoza regime from the 1930s on varied tremendously in its forms, intensity, and locus. Indeed, some lower-class elements, such as the organized proletariat and the Nicaraguan Socialist party, actively collaborated with the regime of Anastasio Somoza García during the 1940s. In contrast, many northern peasant smallholders in the regions once frequented by Sandino remained steadfastly unsympathetic toward the regime. Despite the variety of working-class responses to the dynasty, the nationwide deterioration of economic conditions and the growing governmental repression in the 1970s turned many of the lower class against the regime by converting their narrowly focused economic grievances into more clearly defined antiregime positions and action.

The Socialists

Founded in 1944 while Nicaragua was still at war with the Axis powers and allied with the Soviet Union, the Socialist (Communist) party enjoyed the tolerance of the government. Anastasio Somoza García, besieged by determined Liberal, Conservative, and student opponents in their 1944–1948 thrust for democracy, adopted a populist stance toward organized labor and toward the Socialists in order to keep the party and unions on his side. The PSN operated openly and promoted unions; meetings of members and public workers' meetings occurred, and the party's paper circulated with some freedom.

But when in 1948 Somoza arranged his truce with the Conservatives, in effect buying off his toughest opposition, he no longer needed the Socialists' backing. Somoza also had detected the increasingly anticommunist drift in U.S. foreign policy. As Somoza was momentarily out of U.S. favor, he decided to try to secure U.S. approval by breaking with the left, a move now made safe by his alliance with the Conservatives. He thus shifted rapidly to the ideological right in the late 1940s and early 1950s, dramatically altering the fate of the Socialist party and the labor movement. He had the PSN and Communist party affiliation outlawed in the 1950 constitution and imprisoned or drove into exile most Socialist leaders.

PSN leaders surreptitiously maintained ties with the construction trades in Nicaragua, where their support had previously been strong. The party was slowly rebuilt during the 1950s and the more liberal 1960s, although it remained underground and illicit. The PSN attracted some supporters from the middle class and some among peasant day laborers but drew its main strength from the urban proletariat. Constrained by the conservatism of its Soviet-bloc communist allies, the PSN regarded the Nicaraguan masses as retrograde and lacking revolutionary potential. This posture caused Carlos Fonseca to leave the party in 1959 because of his own rapidly evolving hopes for promoting a Cuban-style revolution. The PSN denounced as utopian the guerrilla movements of the late 1950s, in particular the FSLN. The party remained committed in theory and practice to await the maturation of social conditions for revolution and to continue organizing the proletariat.

In the early and middle 1970s the PSN suffered internal strains that split it three ways. One small splinter became the Communist party of Nicaragua (Partido Comunista de Nicaragua – PC). The remainder divided behind clashing personalities into two groups, both retaining the original name; one incorporated most of the old political apparatus, the other centered in the labor wing. In 1974 the more conservative (political) PSN faction joined the UDEL and then in 1978 the Broad Opposition Front. After the FSLN's military success and the breadth of the popular insurrection of 1978 clearly demonstrated how badly the now-split Communists had misjudged both, the PC and the labor PSN faction in 1979 joined the revolutionary MPU and FPN coalitions.[26] They did so, however, as mere followers rather than as leaders of revolution.

The Original Sandinistas

One sporadic source of lower-class resistance to the Somozas came from the original followers of Augusto César Sandino.[27] Sandinista resistance in the North continued for a few years after Sandino's death in 1934 but eventually died out. Subsequently, however, survivors of the Sandinista insurrection took part in several armed uprisings against the Somozas. For example, Juan Gregorio Colindres was killed by the National Guard in a 1948 anti-Somoza rebellion with Conservative backing. Other Sandinistas also took part in a 1954 uprising. In 1958 Ramón Raudales (then 68) and Heriberto Reyes joined a group of Nicaraguan exiles in an effort to liberate Nicaragua via revolutionary guerrilla war. Their small force infiltrated Nicaragua in September 1958 but was soon discovered and cut up badly by the Guard; it eventually succumbed completely in 1961.

Perhaps the most important of the original Sandinistas was Santos López, once a member of Sandino's "angels' chorus." After Carlos Fonseca's initial failure to establish a guerrilla movement in 1960, he recruited the aging López to teach the fledgling guerrillas of the FSLN the craft of surviving in the mountainous jungles of the North. This instruction in the tactics and strategy of guerrillla warfare helped the largely urban novice guerrillas to survive long periods of isolation and persecution by the National Guard.[28] By training the Front so that it survived when no other guerrilla group of the late 1950s could do so, Santos López forged a continuity of tactics and methods between the Sandino of the 1930s and the revolutionaries of the 1960s and 1970s.

Peasants

Economic pressures have long left Nicaraguan peasants poor, disorganized, and manipulated. Economic changes since 1950 weakened even more the position of many cultivators, exposing them more directly to market pressures and forcing many to migrate in search of work or arable land. Moreover, the traditional regional identification with the Liberal and Conservative parties had become ingrained in many peasants under decades of pressure from their landlords, patrons, or regional

Figure 6.1: Agricultural regions and zone of FSLN development 1961-77.

strong men. Such allegiances long permitted the political manipulation
of the peasantry by the traditional parties. To peasants with the temerity
to protest such economic or political realities, the Somoza regime and
large landholders consistently responded with repression. Thus, prior to
the 1970s Nicaraguan peasants generally remained politically disorganized and passive. Nevertheless, peasants from at least three regions contributed in important ways to the anti-Somoza struggle during the 1970s.
A comprehensive analysis of this story is not possible here, but the
following passages outline some of what occurred in parts of the
Nicaraguan countryside.

Zone I (see Figure 6.1) included the southern and central Pacific
lowlands (the departments of Rivas, Managua, Granada, León, and
Jinotepe).[29] After 1950, the rapid spread of cotton cultivation in much of
this region forced thousands of former smallholders to sell their plots
and become agricultural day laborers. As both cotton production and a

simultaneous modernization of the sugar industry concentrated land ownership and replaced manual labor with machines, the number of rural jobs for Zone I peasants diminished rapidly after 1950 (by more than half in certain areas), causing a huge labor surplus. More traditional cultivation in other parts of Zone I (e.g., coffee and livestock) could absorb neither this labor oversupply nor its own surplus working-age population. Some who could not find jobs migrated to the cities, others to new agrarian colonies in other regions. The Zone I labor surplus and the economic power of the large landowners kept rural wages low and living conditions abysmal.

In response to these conditions and to the growing commitment of the Nicaraguan clergy to social activism on behalf of the poor (see Chapter 7), in 1969 the Jesuits formed the Evangelistic Committee for Agrarian Promotion (Comité Evangélica de Promoción Agraria — CEPA) to train peasant leaders to organize self-help projects and to promote demands upon public institutions. CEPA's early work, centered in Zone I, evolved into political organization with an anti-Somocista focus. The CEPA and other organizations, including the PSN and the FSLN, thus planted the seeds of peasant organization in Zone I during the early 1970s.

Because rural day laborers suffered somewhat more from inflating food prices than did subsistence cultivators, the rapid inflation that began in 1973 hit peasants in Zone I, which had a higher percentage of day laborers than other regions, particularly hard. Encouraged by rural organizers, some peasants responded to their shrinking real incomes with labor organization, strikes for higher wages, and land seizures. Such efforts met stiff resistance from both the regime and landowners, a fact that helped to radicalize many peasants as well as CEPA's rural organizers and to increase their ties to the FSLN. One important case of peasant unionization occurred on the massive San Antonio sugar plantation and mills. During the lengthy struggle to organize its workers, the enterprise dismissed strikers and organizers, and the Guard employed force against strikers. Despite such repression, however, the struggle culminated in a 1977 walkout by some five thousand workers — mostly cane cutters — who won wage gains and improved working conditions.

Out of the San Antonio strike grew the Association of Rural Workers (Associación de Trabajadores del Campo — ATC). Promoted by the FSLN and staffed in part by former CEPA organizers, the ATC began to organize peasants elsewhere in the Pacific region in the late 1970s, concentrating on day laborers in sugar, cotton, and coffee. The ATC promoted peasant organizations, and through them demands for better working conditions and wages, land seizures, and political demonstrations. Via the ATC, several CEPA activists entered the FSLN as combatants. Although the high population density and relatively open terrain of Zone I did not permit a permanent guerrilla presence there, through the ATC and other groups the FSLN developed an important organizational resource.[30]

Conditions differed greatly in Zone II, the north central portion of the country (Estelí, Matagalpa, and Nueva Segovia departments). This largely mountainous area had important concentrations of peasant smallholders cultivating at least partly for subsistence. The north central zone experienced less dramatic post-1950 shifts in cultivation than Zone I, yet it did undergo increased coffee cultivation, which raised land prices and thus increased pressure on small farmers to sell their farms. That pressure, together with a population growing faster than the regional economy could absorb it, created a migratory outflow and depressed wages for day laborers and sharecroppers.

The CEPA was also active in Zone II, helping to train peasant leaders to make political demands. As in Zone I, the CEPA radicalized itself and established links with the FSLN. In fact, the active presence of guerrilla bands was a critical factor in the zone from 1958 on. Because this had been Sandino's territory, the regime distrusted and mistreated its campesinos. Repression of peasants by public officials, and especially by the Guard, became quite commonplace in the 1960s and 1970s. Such abuse further alienated the populace from the government. When guerrilla activity in the north picked up notably in the 1970s, regime coercion against Zone II peasants also escalated. "Agrarian reform" programs relocated peasants away from "infested" zones. Thousands of peasants were also tortured and killed by the National Guard in order to discourage support for the FSLN. Many examples of the extent of such activity came to light during testimony in postrevolutionary trials of National Guard troops for crimes committed under the Somoza regime. One enlisted man related tortures of peasant prisoners conducted by a Korean mercenary officer and his Nicaraguan troops: "He cut chunks of their own flesh from the campesinos with a knife. . . . He fried the flesh and gave it to them to eat, yelling 'Swallow it! Swallow it! Swallow it!'"[31] Executions of entire families became commonplace during the mid-1970s. National Guard Lieutenant José Antonio Robleto Siles described a typical "cleanup operation": "About thirty-five peasants were executed, including some women. . . . In general, when a campesino confesses that he cooperates with the guerrillas, he knows one or two more, and that's how the chain is formed. Some are executed without having confessed. The Guard follows the technique of seeding doubt among the peasantry."[32] Overall, then, a traditional admiration for regional hero Sandino, a pronounced anti-Somoza feeling, organizational efforts by the CEPA, and the brutal excesses of official repression in Zone II appear to have been the main factors that led or drove Zone II peasants into the arms of the FSLN. Among the campesinos from this region who joined the FSLN was Germán Pomares Ordóñez, an early recruit who rose to a key guerrilla command before his death in June 1979.

Zone III (including the eastern portions of Boaco, Juigalpa, Matagalpa, and Nueva Segovia departments, plus the northwestern portion of Zelaya's little-populated public lands) was a major attraction point for peasant migration from Zones I and II. The landless went there to government land reform projects or, more commonly, to squat on the abundant virgin public land. But rather than enjoying some independence, many Zone III peasants suffered exploitation by such local officials as the *juez de mesta*. Usually a peasant himself and appointed for his loyalty to the Somozas, the juez de mesta spied for the government and exercised certain police powers. It became common for many jueces to abuse their influence in order to steal newly improved agricultural plots from squatters, whose shaky land titles made them highly vulnerable to anyone close to the government.

Lt. Robleto Siles, on patrol in Zone III with the Guard, reported the following incident involving a group of peasants taken prisoner by another patrol:

> They were cadaverous, ill from their tortures. Several had cigarette burns on their bodies, or their wrists raw from the pressure of handcuffs. Three had large head wounds. One man of about sixty was spitting up blood, it was all around him.
>
> "Why are you prisoners?" I asked, but nobody replied. "Somebody tell me. Don't be afraid."
>
> "They accuse us of giving food to the guerrillas," said one.
>
> "Everyone?"
>
> "Others for other things," replied another. . . . "I was denounced by a juez de mesta so that he could take my land."[33]

Such reports from the northern countryside became commonplace, as did reports of systematic killings of campesinos. Amnesty International, the Inter-American Commission on Human Rights and others estimated peasant deaths numbering in the thousands during the 1970s.

There were two factors in Zone III that attracted this fierce National Guard repression. First, the Capuchin Fathers had organized a lay wing known as the Delegates of the Word to serve the spiritual and socioeconomic needs of the peasants of Zelaya. These nine hundred community organizers quickly became targets of National Guard repression. When delegates and peasants with whom they worked began to disappear, many of their peers turned toward the FSLN and gave it active support. Similary, some Catholic parish priests and Protestant ministers also became active in promoting peasant organizations, and they too promoted ties between their parishioners and the FSLN. Second was the presence of the FSLN itself in Zone III. The torture, extortion, and killings enraged many peasants and convinced them they had nothing to lose by joining the FSLN, especially if they were already suspected of collaboration. The FSLN thus recruited successfully in this region, and the guerrillas' collaboration with the local peasants ultimately became excellent. One campesino related how he came to join the FSLN: "I began to know the *muchachos* when I lived in Pancasán. At first I thought they were bandits, but then I realized that they took an interest in the peasants. They began to teach us to read, to live more cleanly, to plant better. They are good people. . . . We realized that they came to fight for us, for the poor people. I was one of several who joined them."[34] Zone III was a major focus of guerrilla activity from the 1960s on, and peasant collaboration and participation grew steadily during the 1970s.

Labor Unions

From 1935 to 1944 strikes and union demonstrations by diverse worker groups occurred several times, and an incipient nationwide union confederation formed. Somoza García's response took a consistently repressive path during this era. From 1941 to 1944, however, he tolerated local communists because of the wartime alliance with the Soviet Union. These leftists had union ties and helped form a labor confederation at about the same time they founded the Nicaraguan Socialist party. When Somoza saw that the unions and the PSN might ally with him against the incipient prodemocracy movement of 1944, he stopped directly repressing them and began to manipulate and co-opt them. Somoza curried favor with union confederation leaders, corrupting many in order to gain their backing. In 1945 he implemented an advanced labor code to cement this support among labor's rank and file. These tactics secured labor backing for Somoza during his 1944–1948 struggle to keep power. But in 1948 when the dictator consolidated his position vis-à-vis the Conservatives, the PLI, and students, he betrayed the labor movement. With a wave of repression he dismantled the main national confederation and drove a fledgling independent federation underground. Many independent-minded labor leaders had to flee Nicaragua, and union activity was greatly curtailed. Once he had dismantled the old labor movement, Somoza permitted in 1949 the establishment of a new confederation – the General Confederation of Workers (Confederación General de Trabajadores – CGT). Pro-Somoza leaders and regime agents heavily infiltrated the CGT, giving the government extensive control over the labor movement. The CGT did form a fair number of new unions, but its corrupt leadership responded primarily to the interests of the regime rather than of the workers. Clandestine labor groups survived the repression of the 1950s only with great difficulty.[35]

After this low ebb in the 1950s, organized labor began a long, slow comeback. The 1960s and Nicaragua's membership in the Central American Common Market brought rapid industrialization and economic growth, accompanied by some political liberalization. Unionization of workers spread and began to bypass the officialist CGT; several important strikes occurred. In 1962 the Social Christians, the MPDC, and international Christian labor organizations helped found MOSAN, which later (1972) affiliated with a wider, reformist confederation known as the Nicaraguan Workers' Confederation (Confederación de Trabajadores de Nicaragua—CTN). In 1963, dissident unions split from the official CGT to create the Independent General Workers' Confederation (Confederación General de Trabajadores—Independiente—CGTI), which had close ties to the Socialist party. In 1968, under the auspices of the Interamerican Regional Workers' Organization (Organización Regional Interamericana de Trabajadores—ORIT), sponsored by the U.S. government and the AFL-CIO, yet another federation formed—the Council for Union Unity (Consejo de Unidad Sindical—CUS). The CUS adopted a moderate, mainly job-related, and apolitical set of goals.

The Nicaraguan labor movement thus entered the 1970s fragmented into four main confederations of divergent ideology. After the split in the early 1970s in the Socialist party created the Communist party, the PC founded its own labor federation, the Center for Union Action and Unity (Centro de Acción y Unidad Sindical—CAUS). Altogether the various confederations represented only some thirty thousand workers, about 5.5 percent of the work force. But although divided and small, organized labor had become increasingly dynamic. After the Managua earthquake of late 1972, the union movement began to play an increasingly prominent national role. The postquake reconstruction program raised the work week from forty-eight to sixty hours and froze or cut wages. Simultaneously, inflation began to escalate rapidly, causing real wages to decline.[36]

Such economic blows catalyzed the unions to demand better wages, a process that began with a major construction workers' strike in 1973. Unionization and strikes spread in 1974 as basically unchanged government labor policies continued to erode the standard of living of the proletariat. The independent confederations soon broadened their major goals from merely job-related issues to political reform, a shift made evident by the affiliation of the CGTI and the CTN with the anti-Somoza reform coalition UDEL in 1974. Declaration of martial law late the same year made strikes illegal and permitted the police an unrestrained hand against union organizers and activists. This repression reduced strikes in 1975 and put many union activists in jail. An Inter-American Commission on Human Rights inspection team declared bluntly that "trade unions are severely restricted by means of the persecution and jailing of a great number of union organizers."[37] Nevertheless, strikes, now accompanied by antiregime demonstrations, became more frequent in 1976 and 1977 in spite of martial law. Union demands now routinely called for the release of political prisoners, among whom were several important labor leaders.

In 1978 labor activity continued to escalate and to become more openly revolutionary. After the assassination of Chamorro the UDEL called a general strike for 24 January. Affiliated unions supported this nationwide suspension of economic activity, which on its first day idled an estimated half of Nicaragua's six hundred thousand workers. Workers also participated in related political demonstrations despite government threats to deny social security benefits to strikers and despite the Guard's widespread use of force against demonstrators. In July several small revolutionary unions joined several left-wing groups and the FSLN to form the United People's Movement. The CGTI joined the openly revolutionary MPU soon afterward.

Following the successful FSLN capture of the National Palace in late August 1978, organized labor supported another general strike called by the FAO. This time both moderate unions (CUS, CTN) and the more radical CGTI supported the four-week strike, which idled well over half the work force and precipitously reduced Nicaragua's foreign export earnings and tax collections. However, when the FAO began to vacillate in its commitment to dismantling the National Guard during the regime-opposition negotiations in late 1978, parts of the labor movement assumed a more radical posture in favor of change. The Social Christian-affiliated CTN joined the MPU in early 1979. The ORIT-affiliated CUS, however, remained with the increasingly discredited FAO and even denounced the use of violence against the regime in late 1978. When the third nationwide general strike was called in May 1979, the vast bulk of Nicaragua's organized workers participated in these massive acts of economic subversion that cut away the regime's financial base. Labor unions also continued to conduct antiregime demonstrations.

In sum, important changes occurred in unions' goals after 1976. Moderate labor confederations first adopted a reformist stance, then followed the leftist unions to a revolutionary posture by 1978–1979. The major divisions in the Nicaraguan labor movement persisted throughout this process, but diverse union confederations did begin to work in parallel against the regime through the antiregime coalitions. Organized labor, by participating in the general strikes, demonstrations, and such organizations as the UDEL, FAO, MPU, and FPN, contributed significantly to the decline of public order and undermined the economic

Figure 6.2. Housing conditions typical of much of poor urban Nicaragua in the 1970s; this scene is from suburban Managua. (Photo by the author)

base of the government, thereby weakening the dictatorship's capacity to resist the military offensive of the Sandinistas.

The Urban Poor

During the late 1960s, the Nicaraguan Catholic church became heavily influenced by "liberation theology" (see Chapter 7), and many Catholic organizations and parish priests formed organizations for community self-help and political demand-making in the poor urban barrios. These organizations of poor people became steadily more politicized, especially because of their experience following the 1972 Managua earthquake when Somoza, the Guard, and the Liberal party exploited relief efforts and supplies for economic and political advantage.[38] The quake displaced huge numbers of poor people from Managua's center into sprawling shantytowns ringing the city. In following this clientele, Catholic relief and community improvement efforts spread rapidly and brought more and more urban poor people into contact with such groups.

The earthquake also marked an important turning point for the work among the poor of Nicaragua's previously apolitical Protestant churches. The Protestants, of various denominations, formed a nationwide relief organization that soon became a permanent agency to promote self-help organization among the poor. The Christian Committee for the Promotion of Development (Comité Evangélico Pro-Ayuda al Desarrollo — CEPAD) grew rapidly and began organizing local committees and projects in more than two hundred poor neighborhoods nationwide.

Christian social action programs in the 1970s, then, created hundreds of groups among the urban poor. Such organizations became progressively more involved in making political demands, seeking government assistance and service improvement. Deteriorating economic conditions after 1973 spread such organizations ever more widely among the urban poor, who were becoming increasingly caught between the pincers of spiraling inflation and shrinking real wages (see Chapter 5). The regime's lack of sympathy for or resistance to such demands often led to confrontations and to the repression of activists among the urban poor. Experiencing such repression eventually radicalized many of the organized urban poor. Moreover, the contacts of the FSLN with both Catholic (from the early 1970s) and Protestant (in the late 1970s) community organizers began to create in the urban slums an important organizational base for the guerrilla movement. As a consqeuence the FSLN often operated in friendly territory in Managua's slums. By the late 1970s many neighborhood organizations had become covert FSLN support groups, stockpiling food and medicine. During guerrilla operations in many such areas in 1978 and 1979, residents frequently built barricades, fed and ministered to the Sandinistas, and often fought alongside them with whatever weapons were at hand.

One dramatic uprising by an urban poor community involved the Indians of the barrio of Monimbó of the city of Masaya, where smouldering hostility toward the National Guard spontaneously exploded in an attack on its nearby headquarters on 23 February 1978. Over the next year popular revolts against the National Guard also occurred in Rivas, Chinandega, Matagalpa, Estelí, León, Managua, and elsewhere.

Summary

Each major Nicaraguan social class made significant contributions to the breakdown of the Somoza dynasty regime. The regime—Somoza, his cohort, the PLN, and the National Guard—had become so isolated that eventually only brute military force held the government in power. Anastasio Somoza Debayle had driven away many of his erstwhile allies among the upper class with his disastrous economic policies, his political maladroitness, and his greed, all of which threatened the economic well-being of the propertied and entrepreneurial class. A panoply of economic and political difficulties had progressively alienated the middle and lower classes. When they expresssed their concerns by organization and demands for change, the government answered with bullets and torture. The regime's excessive use of coercion caused the most significant organized elements of both classes to shift from more individualized efforts at self-improvement or from narrow demands for reform to overt, broad-gauge revolutionary opposition.

The Somoza dynasty's hold upon political power in Nicaragua had always been somewhat tenuous, never totally secure. As a consequence, the Somozas had relied upon three techniques to sustain their regimes. First was coercion by means of controlling the instrument of force and power. This coercive capability raised the stakes of opposition for all opponents and could easily crush an isolated opponent. Second was a careful juggling of internal political forces. Somoza García and his son Luis Somoza skillfully manipulated political groups, aligning at different times as the need arose with organized labor, the Socialists, the Conservatives, and the bourgeoisie. Such allies—won by co-optation—helped counterbalance the opponents of the movement, preventing the development of a broad coalition of dissident forces capable of effectively challenging the coercive power of the Guard. Third was the manipulation of external support. Externally derived power (moral support and economic and military assistance) from the United States figured importantly in the Somoza equation for retaining power. So too, to a lesser degree, did the cooperation and friendliness of neighboring regimes in Central America. When Anastasio Somoza Debayle took power in 1967, however, the balancing game among these three factors went out of kilter.

7
Foreign and Domestic Opposition

Our nation was truly delivered into the hands of the Marxist enemy by President Jimmy Carter. . . . His most active accomplices were Venezuela, Panama, and Cuba.

In the Jesuit schools, the seeds of discontent and, basically, the seeds of Communism, were sown. Their doctrine was spread to the children from affluent families and with many, the doctrine was accepted.
                                               —Anastasio Somoza Debayle[1]

This chapter rounds out the overview of opposition by examining additional elements alluded to by Somoza above—other nations, religious institutions, and the FSLN, as well as the coalitions that eventually drew much of the disparate opposition together in 1979.

Foreign Governments

Other nations played a significant role in the Nicaraguan insurrection—some with enthusiasm, others with reluctance. In no case was external intervention decisive, but the policies of foreign governments generally weakened the Somoza regime and strengthened the insurgents. The regime, however, was certainly not without international support. Some military aid came from Guatemala, El Salvador, and Honduras, but it was restricted mainly to logistical assistance and to the denial (not always successful) of sanctuary to the FSLN. A few countries (e.g., Portugal, Israel, and Spain) sold weapons to the Nicaraguan government, some up until the final weeks.[2] International lending institutions such as the International Monetary Fund and foreign private banks continued until 1979 to extend the regime development credit, much of which was used to acquire arms, and to provide liquidity to Nicaragua's banks so that Somoza and his cohorts could drain foreign monies until July 1979. Nevertheless, on balance foreign elements played a role much more negative than positive for the stumbling government of Anastasio Somoza Debayle, especially after September 1978, when the regime's brutality became widely apparent.

TABLE 7.1
Mean Annual Aid from the United States to Latin America and Nicaragua (dollar amounts in millions of U.S. dollars)

	Period			
Latin America (overall)	1953–61	1962–66	1970–75	
Economic assistance	181.02	1024.18	702.00	
% change over previous period[a]		427	-52	
Military aid	58.24	131.42	149.00	
% change over previous period[a]		102	-20	
Nicaragua	1953–61	1962–66	1974–76	1977–78[b]
Economic assistance	3.74	13.64	25.53	9.29
% change over previous period[a]		230	39	-75
Military aid	0.21	1.48	3.33	2.76
% change over previous period[a]		543	67	-43

Sources: G. Pope Atkins, Latin America in the International Political System (New York: Free Press, 1977), pp. 166-167, 183; and Congressional Research Service, "Human Rights and United States Foreign Assistance: Experiences and Issues in Policy Implementation (1977-1978)," Report to the Committee on Foreign Relations, U.S. Senate (Washington, D.C.: Government Printing Office, 1979), Table I, p. 194.

[a]Correction for inflation between 1953 and 1962 is 1% per annum; between 1963 and 1974 3% per annum; and between 1975 and 1978 is 10% per annum.

[b]Includes the transition trimester for changeover to the new fiscal calendar between 1976 and 1977.

The United States

The Nixon and Ford administrations supported the Nicaraguan government as the FSLN and other opposition groups grew in numbers and strength. Although overall economic and military aid to Latin America from the United States declined in the 1970–1975 period, military and economic aid to Nicaragua increased dramatically. Even when corrected for the high rate of inflation in the 1970s, the average annual U.S. military assistance to Nicaragua in the 1974–1976 period was 67 percent higher than for the 1962–1966 period (see Table 7.1). However, with the growing consciousness of human rights in the U.S. Congress and the Carter administration beginning in 1977, U.S. aid to Nicaragua began to decline. For 1977–1978, the annual average economic assistance dropped some 75 percent in real terms, and military aid fell about 43 percent. Growing administration and congressional awareness of the behavior of the Nicaraguan National Guard, together with growing domestic and external lobbying against further aid to the Somoza government, ultimately brought about the complete termination of all new U.S. aid in the 1979 budget. (Previously appropriated U.S. economic aid, however, continued to be delivered up through Somoza's ouster.) Although the Carter administration strongly opposed the Sandinistas and other radical elements among the insurgents, it nevertheless gradually but substantially reduced assistance to the Somoza regime.[3]

The effects of these changes in U.S. policy were twofold. First, the resolve of many backers of the regime began to flag. Bitter denunciations of the United States and its "interventionist" human rights policy by the regime became commonplace after 1977. For example, Francisco Urcuyo Maliaño, a high official and Liberal Nationalist leader, affirmed that Jimmy Carter's "foreign policy, supposedly in favor of human rights, was a cynical instrument of pressure applied selectively to Nicaragua, which has no oil. . . . President Carter . . . merely lamented the presence of Castro in Africa, but he employed direct action against Somoza in Nicaragua."[4] Somoza Debayle himself stated that most Nicaraguans believed that "it is in Washington where the decision is being made about the survival or disappearance of Somocismo or of Somoza himself."[5] Former economic (and even political) allies of the Somozas drifted toward the opposition as growing instability threatened their interests. The rebels, meanwhile, feared less that they might have to confront the United States in combat and became bolder as the dictatorship's political edifice crumbled. The second major effect of the U.S. human rights policy was to reduce National Guard resources and to diminish the regime's military capability. Moreover, Somoza had to turn to increasingly desperate international borrowing and internal fiscal measures to raise money to buy arms and to pay the Guard.

One should not conclude, however, that the Carter administration favored the revolutionaries, as Somoza charged. The United States opposed the Sandinistas and preferred moderate reforms to revolution. Nevertheless, the administration never understood well either the FSLN or the situation in Nicaragua. U.S. policymakers significantly misjudged the organizational strength of the opposition in general — in particular on the left — and misperceived the opposition's basic goals and biases. The United States consistently sought a moderate political resolution of the conflict via negotiated settlement between the regime and its centrist, upper- and middle-class opposition forces. Although the United States finally resigned itself in 1978 to the removal of Somoza, two of the "moderating" institutions the United States consistently pressed to retain were the PLN and the detested National Guard, Somoza's principal instruments of power. Confronted with such anathema, the rebels vitriolically denounced this enormously insensitive policy as *somocismo sin Somoza* (Somocism without Somoza).

The U.S. administration often conducted even its putatively more humane policies with remarkable maladroitness. For instance, when Somoza lifted the state of siege in October 1977 and then invited a visit by the Inter-American Commission on Human Rights in mid-1978, President Carter commended the dictator for improving Nicaragua's human rights situation. This act flabbergasted the persecuted Nicaraguan opposition, thousands of whom continued to feel the regime's lash. There were howls of both outrage and cynical derision as to the sincerity of the policy. In sum, although "the United States did not defeat Somoza,"[6] U.S. policy gradually eroded the regime's coercive strength and its support. Yet it did so in such a manner as to alienate both incumbents and insurgents, leaving the revolutionary government that came to power in July 1979 profoundly suspicious of the United States.

Costa Rica

Nicaragua and its southern neighbor have clashed many times since the 1824 annexation by Costa Rica of Nicaragua's Nicoya province. Later came a long-running dispute over waterway rights to the Río San Juan, Costa Rican tolerance of Augusto César Sandino's forces operating from Guanacaste, and Anastasio Somoza García's grant of asylum to the losers of the 1948 Costa Rican civil war, as well as his support for vain efforts in 1948 and 1955 to overthrow Costa Rican president José Figueres and Figueres's return of the favor in 1959. Although international mediation had prevented open war between the two nations on several of these occasions, the chronic conflict and interference in each other's affairs had left a legacy of mutual hostility. Costa Ricans, smug about their democratic political tradition and pacific image (Costa Rica having abolished its armed forces), regarded the Somoza dynasty with considerable contempt.

As the FSLN insurgency developed in the 1960s, tensions between Nicaragua and Costa Rica grew because the FSLN used Costa Rica's isolated North for sanctuary and bases. This led to clashes along the border between the Nicaraguan National Guard and the Sandinistas, to border violations by the Guard, and to Nicaraguan harassment of Costa Rican travelers. In the mid-1970s, Anastasio Somoza Debayle accused Costa Rica of violating a treaty concerning the Río San Juan, and Costa Rica seized three Nicaraguan tuna boats for fishing in Costa Rican waters. Such incidents kept Costa Rican public opinion seething with anti-Somoza chauvinism, a fact not lost on Costa Rican politicians.[7] The governments of José Figueres (1970–1974) and Daniel Oduber

(1974–1978) had permitted the FSLN fairly free rein, with an occasional symbolic roundup or prosecution of guerrillas for consumption by the international press.[8]

When Rodrigo Carazo Odio assumed the Costa Rican presidency in May 1978, he surprised many by reversing his position with respect to the Nicaraguan insurgents. Carazo had denounced his predecessors' soft policies toward the FSLN. However, apparently motivated by opinion polls revealing great public sympathy for the Nicaraguan revolution, Carazo once in office systematically favored the rebels. Costa Rica permitted the FSLN to operate training bases and to stage strikes into Nicaragua from Costa Rican soil. Arms shipments to the FSLN entered Costa Rica from Panama by truck and by air and were convoyed by Ministry of Public Security personnel.[9] Most of "los Doce" (the Group of Twelve) resided in San José, from where they conducted their anti-Somoza propaganda and international lobbying efforts. Numerous other Nicaraguan opposition figures regularly received political asylum in Costa Rica, including Sandinista guerrillas escaping across the border with the Nicaraguan Guard in hot pursuit. Because of repeated violations of Costa Rican territory by the Nicaraguan armed forces, the Carazo government borrowed weapons from Panama and Venezuela to strengthen its northern defenses. This act, however, also effectively protected the FSLN camps in the north.

As the conflict within Nicaragua grew in late 1978 and 1979, Costa Rica became even more openly supportive of the rebels. FSLN recruiters worked openly on the streets of San José, which were papered with Sandinista propaganda. One widespread poster proclaimed: "Costa Rica too is Sandinista." Costa Ricans enlisted in the FSLN, raised money for the rebels, and aided the thousands of Nicaraguan refugees streaming into the country. Nicaragua's denunciations of Costa Rican support for the rebels in the Council of the Organization of American States fell largely on deaf ears and brought Costa Rican counter-charges of Nicaraguan violations of its own territory and demands for sanctions. President Carazo officially wept crocodile tears for the Somoza regime and invoked a policy of neutrality, which was observed mainly in the breach: "We have made the greatest effort to maintain the neutrality of the Government in the conflict suffered by our sister republic Nicaragua."[10] Such declarations notwithstanding, on 23 October 1978 Costa Rica severed diplomatic ties with Nicaragua. In May 1979 Costa Rica permitted the FSLN and its coalition organizations to establish a revolutionary government in exile. Soon afterward Costa Rica extended this junta diplomatic recognition as a belligerent force equal to the Somoza government. Costa Rica ultimately recognized the junta as the legitimate government of Nicaragua. When Somoza finally fell, jubilant Costa

Ricans danced in the streets, and Rodrigo Carazo visited Nicaragua to a hero's welcome.

Without the sanctuary, the training camps, and the moral, diplomatic, and logistical support of Costa Rica, the Nicaraguan rebels would undoubtedly have required much longer to oust Somoza, had they been able to do so at all.

Other Latin American Nations

Several other nations aided in the demise of the Somoza regime. Honduras, apparently despite its government's intentions and efforts to control the rugged area along the Nicaraguan border, served as a sanctuary for the FSLN's northern front. The military government of Honduras opposed the FSLN and the revolution but nevertheless tolerated a certain amount of pro-Sandinista organizing in university and intellectual circles. Honduras refused to come overtly to the Somoza regime's aid in June 1979, probably fearful of diplomatic reprisals by the United States.[11]

Panama directly assisted the rebels by serving as the entry point for arms purchased from Cuba and elsewhere by the FSLN. The weapons were then transported to Nicaragua via Costa Rica. Panama granted asylum to the FSLN assault team that captured the Nicaraguan National Palace in August 1978, then permitted the guerrillas to return to the struggle. The government of Omar Torrijos also lent weapons and pledged military assistance to Costa Rica should Nicaragua attack. As noted, this Panamanian defense of Costa Rica assisted the FSLN indirectly by protecting its camps in northern Costa Rica. The infuriated Anastasio Somoza Debayle repeatedly denounced Panama as a communist tool engaged in the plot to overthrow him.

Several other nations took diplomatic action against the Nicaraguan government, especially in the Council of the Organization of American States (OAS). Probably the most consistent critic of the Somoza regime and its human rights record was Venezuela. Beginning in early 1978, Venezuela repeatedly called for OAS sanctions against Nicaragua, criticized Nicaragua's incursions into Costa Rica, and called for investigations of the deteriorating human rights situation. Nicaragua's ambassador to the OAS, Guillermo Sevilla Sacasa, and Anastasio Somoza Debayle frequently criticized Venezuela for interfering in Nicaraguan affairs. In May 1979 Venezuela called for all Andean Pact members to sever diplomatic ties with Nicaragua. Venezuela's leadership ultimately succeeded, persuading Colombia, Ecuador, Peru, and Bolivia to withdraw their recognition from the Somoza government and to recognize the provisional revolutionary junta in San José.

Mexico, too, actively opposed the Nicaraguan regime in international circles. Mexico's past support for Sandino and its own revolutionary history favorably disposed the Mexican government toward the Nicaraguan revolutionaries. With a large Nicaraguan exile community, Mexico became a center for rebel fund-raising and coordination activities. By late 1978, Mexico had begun to criticize Nicaragua in the OAS and to press international financial institutions such as the IMF to suspend credit to Nicaragua. Mexico broke diplomatic relations with Nicaragua in May 1979 and then stepped up its calls in the OAS for the ouster of Somoza and for international recognition of the rebel junta.

The international opponents of Somoza used the Organization of American States in a variety of ways. The OAS Council provided a forum for criticism and served up repeated warnings against Nicaraguan threats of military action against Costa Rica. The OAS sent an inspection team to Nicaragua in October 1978 from its subsidiary, the Inter-American Commission on Human Rights (IACHR). Its report galvanized several OAS members into more active opposition to Somoza. The OAS also sent an inspection team to Costa Rica to seek evidence of support there for the FSLN, but Costa Rican security officials carefully engineered the visit to hide their role. At U.S. urging, the OAS sought to mediate the conflict in Nicaragua following the August–September uprising of 1978. An OAS negotiating team worked feverishly through December 1978 but failed to reconcile the intractable Anastasio Somoza and the FAO. Finally, the OAS apparently helped restrain Nicaragua's more conservative neighbors from intervening on behalf of Somoza, who repeatedly asked them for help in 1978 and 1979.[12]

Cuba, the nation most widely accused of helping to overthrow Somoza, in fact appears to have contributed less to the insurrectionary effort than is widely believed. Cuban support for guerrilla efforts to oust the Somozas had predated the formation of the FSLN. Not only Carlos Fonseca, but others, including Pedro Joaquín Chamorro, visited Cuba in 1959 seeking aid and arms from Fidel Castro's fledgling revolutionary government. In the 1960s Cuba did provide some aid to the FSLN; even after Cuba cut back such help in the 1970s FSLN elements continued to train in Cuba.[13] However, in the final three years of struggle, overt contacts between Castro's regime and the FSLN remained limited. Somoza and his supporters in the U.S. Congress frequently denounced Cuban arms shipments to the FSLN. This existence of such aid was subsequently confirmed by Costa Rican police who helped ferry arms from Havana to the FSLN in northern Costa Rica. The U.S. State Department and Central Intelligence Agency, however, argued that such Cuban assistance was relatively minor in the overall arms flow to the insurgents.

The Sandinistas themselves have denied that they received massive Cuban arms aid or direction. FSLN commander Henry Ruiz, for exam-

ple, has stated: "We didn't receive international aid . . . except at the end
from international solidarity committees. . . . We did enjoy the solidarity of the international revolutionary movement [for] instruction, experience, and military training, etc.; we also took part in some guerrilla
schools."[14] But as for Cuba, apparently Fidel Castro believed that any
major Cuban aid to the FSLN could have brought U.S. intervention to
frustrate the revolution. FSLN commander Edén Pastora quoted Castro
as saying: "The best help I can give you is not to help you at all."[15] Cuba,
therefore, refrained from intervening in a major way. On balance, then,
Panama and Costa Rica contributed more to overthrowing Somoza than
did Cuba.

Religious Groups

The Catholic Church

The Nicaraguan Catholic church identified quite strongly with the
Conservatives during the nineteenth and early twentieth centuries, but it
eventually shifted its support to the Somozas. Under Archbishop Alejandro González y Robleto during the 1960s, the church hierarchy strongly
supported the regime and opposed reformist and opposition movements,
including the Social Christian party. However, when Miguel Obando y
Bravo replaced González as archbishop in 1968, the Nicaraguan ec-
clesiastical hierarchy's policy toward the regime altered sharply. Monsignor Obando sold for the benefit of the poor Somoza's gift of a
Mercedes Benz in 1968. In 1971 he refused to register to vote in upcoming municipal elections and thereby to "dignify" the inevitable fraud. In
1972 Obando and the bishops boycotted the inauguration of the special
bipartisan triumvirate that Anastasio Somoza Debayle had created to
succeed him. Such symbolic acts to distance the church from the regime,
however, were merely signs at the level of the hierarchy of profound
changes already well under way in Nicaraguan Catholicism. These
changes soon made the church and its faithful a moving force in the overthrow of the Somoza dynasty.[16]

The political transformation of the Nicaraguan Catholic church
originated in the early 1960s following the 1962 Second Vatican Council.
Vatican II affirmed the Roman Catholic church's greatly strengthened
commitment to promote the interests of the world's poor and thus
stimulated the development of a new "theology of liberation." Attracted
by the immediate relevance of liberation theology and even blending it
with Marxian revolutionary precepts, clerics throughout Latin America
began to promote social justice for the poor, reversing a lengthy tradition
of encouraging submission to and acceptance of poverty and the extant

political order. Similarly moved, at first a handful but eventually many reformist Nicaraguan clergy initiated projects to help the poor promote for themselves and to demand from the government improvements in social and economic conditions. By the time of the 1968 Latin American Bishops' Conference in Medellín, Colombia, much of the Nicaraguan clergy had felt the influence of liberation theology's call for social action. The Medellín conference strongly endorsed such social and political activism, a further encouragement to the movement in Nicaragua that was also reinforced by the appointment of the progressive Monsignor Obando y Bravo. Thus, unlike in many other Latin American nations, where the liberation movement among lower clergy met stiff resistance from a conservative hierarchy, in Nicaragua such social activism was encouraged. When students occupied churches to protest government policies and repression in 1970–1972, Monsignor Obando several times endorsed the protesters' position. In their "Pastoral Letter from the Bishops of Nicaragua Concerning the Principles of Political Activity of the Church," the archbishop and bishops criticized the government for human rights violations; there were other critical pastorals, as well.

In the late 1960s and early 1970s, Catholic religious orders, including the Jesuits, Maryknolls, Capuchins, and Trappists, organized hundreds of study groups, youth clubs, and "Christian base communities" (comunidades evangélicas de base—CEBs) to promote spiritual growth through social action, community improvement, and pressure upon government for better services. The CEPA began training peasant leaders to solve problems and make political demands, first in the coffee-producing areas around Masaya and Carazo, later in the region from León to Estelí. During the 1970s the CEPA became increasingly committed to radical sociopolitical change. The Capuchin order in the eastern department of Zelaya began to train lay workers known as delegates of the Word to perform certain sacramental functions and to help organize peasant communities. Like the CEBs and the CEPA, the delegates also came to regard political change as a key to improving the lot of the rural poor.

Political repression was instrumental in politicizing and radicalizing these Catholic organizations and their community groups. The National Guard interpreted as subversive and discouraged violently organization among the poor. Beginning in the late 1960s, Christian organizers and community activists began to disappear—murdered by the Guard. Such violence increased steadily during the 1970s, eventually leading both the church hierarchy and various orders to denounce internationally the numerous human rights violations against clerics and followers. This confrontation with the regime's determination violently and ruthlessly to resist pressure for greater social justice radicalized more and more Christian activists, who concluded that only by replacing the Somoza regime could needed change come about.

Clerics working in poor barrios, in the countryside, or with university and high school student protesters became contact points between the FSLN and the Christian neighborhood organizations throughout Nicaragua. In the early 1970s, and especially following the Managua earthquake, CEBs and other groups became foci of antiregime mobilization. Father Uriel Molina's Christian Revolutionary Movement, founded in 1971 in the poor parish of Fátima, led numerous youths directly into the FSLN. By the mid-1970s, regime repression and violence had risen to such a level that many clergy and laypersons previously reluctant to associate with the insurgents came to do so. Christian groups became a key organizational and logistical resource for the guerrillas—raising money, stockpiling food and medical supplies, and mobilizing residents for demonstrations and even for combat. Church buildings served as sanctuaries for activists and for the FSLN, and a few became revolutionary armories. The CEPA's peasant organizers helped the FSLN found the ATC peasant union in 1977, with several CEPA activists eventually moving over to the new organization (see Chapter 6).

Indeed, some priests even joined the FSLN as combatants. The most celebrated was Sacred Heart Father Gaspar García Laviana of the parish of Tola, Rivas. The Spanish priest's early, peaceful efforts in the poverty-ridden community caused him only frustration:

> I tried to improve the situation in a Christian manner, in the pacifist ways of human social promotion. . . . But I realized that all that was a lie, all falsehood; people continued living the same way. For that reason I joined this violent movement. [I did it] because this is a just war. . . . To my Christian conscience it stood for a struggle against a state of things that is hateful in the eyes of our God, The Father.[17]

García Laviana rose to a position of command in the FSLN southern front and died in combat with the National Guard in December 1978. Other priests worked with the opposition in political organization. Among these were Ernesto Cardenal, a pioneer of the liberation theology movement in Nicaragua and organizer in the opposition, and Maryknoll father Miguel d'Escoto Brockman, international spokesman for the opposition coalition and the provisional revolutionary government. Both men came to hold ministerial portfolios in the revolutionary government.

Although significant portions of the church at its base had thus become deeply committed to the Sandinista insurrection, the church hierarchy itself remained somewhat ambivalent. On the one hand, Archbishop Obando firmly opposed the regime and the violent tactics of the National Guard and denounced them repeatedly. This position so outraged the Somocistas that they began referring to the archbishop as "Comandante Miguel," after the fashion by which FSLN guerrillas referred to their commanders. Obando, however, had substantial reservations about the FSLN, its violent methods, and the Marxist ideology of some of its leaders. As head of a Coordinating Commission for National Dialogue, Archbishop Obando continually promoted a "national dialogue" among parties to the conflict. Two early efforts, in November 1977 and January 1978, failed because Somoza Debayle refused to negotiate in good faith. Such discussions, now also urged by the United States and the Organization of American States, finally began in October 1978. The church hierarchy hoped a settlement would remove Somoza from power well before an FSLN military victory, thus leaving moderates in control of the new government. These negotiations, too, collapsed in early 1979.

Protestant Churches

Evangelical Protestants in Nicaragua were far fewer than Catholics, yet they too played a role in the insurrection. Prior to the Managua earthquake the Protestant churches, mostly concentrated in poorer urban and rural areas, were generally conservative and apolitical. The quake and Protestant relief efforts, however, led to rapid growth in Protestant affiliation and a growing consciousness of the need for social action. Protestant groups organized the Evangelistic Committee for the Promotion of Assistance to Development, which promoted numerous community organizations not unlike the Catholic CEBs. Eventually these groups, too, radicalized and developed FSLN contacts and revolutionary commitments. One report estimated that at least ten Protestant ministers joined the FSLN. Ultimately, Protestants played a role in the rebellion similar, although on a smaller scale, to that of the Catholics.[18]

The Sandinista National Liberation Front

The history of the Sandinista National Liberation Front is in many ways more remarkable than that of Fidel Castro's guerrilla army in Cuba. Castro fought a crumbling and irresolute Cuban army for a mere three years. The FSLN survived eighteen years of struggle with the National Guard, which was numerically superior, better equipped, and trained in counterinsurgency. The Cuban guerrillas captured power with relatively little fighting and relatively little popular participation in combat. The FSLN's struggle ended with a year of intense, direct combat that involved thousands of Nicaraguans. Nevertheless, important parallels exist between the two revolutions. The Cuban model inspired and informed the FSLN's strategy and tactics. In Nicaragua as in Cuba much of the success of the insurgents stemmed from the development of the support and loyalty of the peasantry in key zones. Both movements conducted a massive organizational and political struggle after the military victory to win and hold political power and popular support. (The FSLN, however, had an advantage over Castro's rebels in this process, because the Sandinistas had mobilized mass support during the insurrection.)

Origins

The FSLN originated in the anti-Somoza student movements of 1944–1948 and 1959–1961 (see Chapter 6). Its prime mover was Carlos Fonseca Amador, a student activist socialized into Marxist-Leninist beliefs in the Nicaraguan Socialist party (PSN). Fonseca, born in 1935 as the illegitimate son of a Matagalpa domestic servant and a laborer for one of the Somoza family enterprises, was reared by his mother in straitened circumstances, although probably not penury. In 1950, Fonseca enrolled in Matagalpa's high school and soon won renown for his intelligence and leadership. He was introduced to Marxism and joined the PSN during this period, and he soon met many of Nicaragua's communist leaders.

In 1956 Carlos Fonseca went to Managua to study at the National Autonomous University. There he fell in with other leftist intellectuals, including another former Matagalpa high school activist, law student Tomás Borge. Fonseca became a leader in the Centro Universitario (student government) and edited *El Universitario,* a student paper. After the 1956 assassination of Somoza García, the regime arrested Fonseca, Borge, and other student leftists. Although he was tortured by the police during his month in prison in 1956, Fonseca escaped rather lightly. By contrast, Tomás Borge spent many months longer in prison and was tried and convicted for his contacts with members of the alleged conspiracy. The PSN sent Fonseca to the Soviet Union in 1957, after which he wrote a pamphlet extolling socialism. Back in Nicaragua Fonseca renewed his activism, now on behalf of Tomás Borge's release from prison; Fonseca was arrested several times and then in 1958 was deported to Guatemala, whence he traveled first to Mexico and then on to Cuba in 1959. Entranced with Castro's revolution, Carlos Fonseca Amador began traveling surreptitiously among Cuba, Costa Rica, Mexico, and Nicaragua, organizing revolutionary opposition to the regime. Fonseca believed that Cuba's insurrectionary experience held promise for ousting the Somozas, but the conservative, Moscow-line PSN leadership rejected such an effort. In June 1959 Carlos Fonseca took part in the abortive invasion of Nicaragua at El Chaparral from which, wounded, he escaped to Honduras.

The failure at El Chaparral strengthened Fonseca's belief in guerrilla revolution. In frustration, he quit the balky PSN and redoubled his organizing. At this time the nationwide student movement under the leadership of the JPN was gathering momentum. Fonseca, now operating completely underground, met in San José, Costa Rica, in 1960 with old friends Silvio Mayorga and Tomás Borge (recently released from prison), and formed the Nicaraguan Revolutionary Youth (Juventud Revolucionaria Nicaragüense – JRN). From the JRN, Borge, Mayorga, and another radical Matagalpa friend, Marcos Altamirano, infiltrated the JPN. Although the JPN became quickly radicalized under this influence, it failed to achieve its revolutionary goals. The numerous guerrilla insurrections of 1960–1961, too, succumbed one by one.

Carlos Fonseca Amador, however, pressed on; he organized a clandestine revolutionary network and cultivated Cuban support. In 1961 Fonseca, Borge, and Mayorga founded the Sandinista National Liberation Front. The fledgling guerrilla group robbed a few banks to finance itself, then repaired to the relative safety of Honduras to commence its struggle. In 1961 the neophyte guerrillas slipped into Nicaragua near the Bocay River in the North, but they immediately tangled with the National Guard. Under the guidance of Santos López, a veteran of Sandino's army recruited by Fonseca, the survivors escaped to Honduras, reorganized, and then surreptitiously reentered Nicaragua. Although pledged to armed struggle against the Somozas and to social revolution, the tiny guerrilla column now wisely avoided the National Guard until its skills, backing, and organization could sustain even small-scale operations. Survivors of these early years report many blunders and tactical errors, including major military setbacks in 1963 and 1967. Nevertheless, the founders' resolve and their commitment to acquire guerrilla skills and to organize and build slowly permitted the movement to survive where dozens of other armed movements had failed before them.[19]

Evolution, 1962–1974

From these beginnings, with fewer than twenty novice guerrillas in 1961, the FSLN painfully learned its way in the enterprise of revolution.[20] Its founders regarded the organization as a revolutionary vanguard, totally divorced from the traditional Liberal-Conservative conflict. They believed that the FSLN "assured both the leadership of the struggle that had been crushed with the assassination of Sandino in 1934, and the *strategy of popular revolutionary war* that the vanguard put in practice, thus following the path blazed by the General of Free Men."[21] Sandino's guerrilla strategy—recently validated in Cuba—provided a method for overthrowing the dynasty.

From 1961 to 1963, the FSLN remained quite small and had a minimal urban support organization. The guerrillas kept mainly to remote northern areas or to southern Honduras and thus did not develop much support among the rural population. This strategy cost the Front sorely when in 1963 it attempted an offensive campaign in the Bocay region. Lacking peasant logistical support, intelligence, and knowledge of the local terrain, the guerrillas proved vulnerable. The Guard's effective response dealt the FSLN heavy casualties. This military defeat caused the FSLN to retrench militarily for nearly three years in order to develop better urban and rural support systems. Careful work in the north central mountains began to improve peasant links. The urban support network also grew, including a university student organization, the Student Revolutionary Front, to recruit and train new members and to raise funds. Initiatives toward broadening its public base led the FSLN to form some labor unions, to recruit peasants, and in 1965 briefly to ally with the opposition parties in the short-lived Republican Mobilization (Movilización Republicana) movement.

In 1966-1967 the FSLN returned to the offensive—once again too soon. An urban campaign beginning in 1966 consisted mainly of numerous successful bank holdups, and the assassination (*ajusticiamiento,* in the words of the FSLN, meaning "bringing to justice") of Gonzalo Lacayo, a National Guard torturer. However, when the FSLN attempted a major military campaign in the northern zone around Pancasán (east of Matagalpa) in 1967, the Guard reacted very effectively. By deploying patrols quickly by helicopter the Guard soon decimated much of the FSLN's rural organization, killing many Sandinistas, including Silvio Mayorga, as well as their peasant collaborators. Once again the FSLN retrenched its attacks against the National Guard, but it stayed in the public eye through periodic terrorism and bank holdups (referred to as "recuperations" of wealth believed to be ill-gotten from the people). Despite the 1967 military reversals, the FSLN continued to grow and to become more pragmatic. In 1968-1969 the national leadership met outside Nicaragua to elaborate new principles, statutes, and strategies. In one setback, Costa Rican police in 1969 captured several Sandinistas, including Carlos Fonseca, who remained in jail in Costa Rica until 1970.

By 1970 the FSLN's rural organization had rebuilt sufficiently to mount another important military initiative. The Zinica campaign involved several successful raids on National Guard outposts in the north central region. With the Zinica operations the FSLN passed a tactical and organizational watershed: "For the first time the guerrilla column was not destroyed, and was able to elude the surround-and-destroy campaigns launched by the enemy."[22] The campaign succeeded because it had both the backing and the participation of peasants. "We had found the way to recruit the campesino; we had taken away his distrust of the city man. . . . What happened there was almost completely a peasant movement."[23] After Zinica, a reassured and more confident FSLN lowered its military profile to concentrate once again on building its base.

By 1970, then, the character of the Sandinista Front had changed from a small, isolated, and bumbling guerrilla band to a larger, much better-supported, and better-integrated insurgent force. From 1970 on the National Guard began to respond differently to the FSLN. Recognizing the Front's improved ties to the peasantry, the Guard initiated systematic repression in zones of guerrilla presence. However, this strategy of intimidating FSLN supporters by random torture and murder began to backfire. The systematically excessive brutality soon made peasants actively hostile toward the regime and much more prone to cooperate with the rebels.

In the early 1970s, the FSLN drew still closer to peasants in the north central region. "To win over the peasantry it was necessary to live as a part of it. That is what we did—lived with the campesino, lived his problems, became one more member of his family. . . . All their reluctance ended when we made ourselves their brothers. By 1972 we had won their confidence totally, and we built an organizational network, which we called *a chain*."[24] Using the familial and godparenthood ties regarded as virtually sacred by Nicaraguan peasants, Sandinistas living with the peasants would win the confidence of one person, who in turn linked them to others. The obligations of familial ties assured the confidentiality and good will of the members of the chain, so that geographically dispersed extended families became FSLN recruits and collaborators. Improved relations with peasants and the increasing brutality of the National Guard began to bring the FSLN more rural recruits.

In the cities, the burgeoning 1970s student opposition movement swelled the Sandinista support organizations. In 1971–1973 the FSLN campaigned for the release from jail of Sandinista prisoners. In 1971 students demanding political reforms occupied several churches. In 1973 public demonstrations called for political reform, and relatives of Sandinista prisoners conducted a hunger strike. In response to both the 1971 and 1973 demonstrations Somoza released several Sandinistas from prison as a gesture of magnanimity.

The December 1972 Managua earthquake upset the whole national political applecart, so that 1973 and 1974 were years of rising labor unrest, high inflation, disquiet among the economic elite, and growing political dissatisfaction because of Somoza's efforts to engineer his return to the presidency. In 1974 the FSLN resumed the military offensive, now backed by a stronger organizational network in the city and countryside and with a seasoned military arm. The return to the offen-

sive began with an extremely risky operation that promised—if successful—an enormous propaganda coup. The spectácle, planned to coin-
cide with Somoza's reelection as president, was an assault on a party on
27 December 1974 at the house of José María ("Chema") Castillo Quant,
a wealthy cotton exporter and former minister of agriculture. The event
was to honor U.S. Ambassador Turner B. Shelton, and many luminaries
of the regime and diplomatic circles attended. Ambassador Shelton
himself had just departed when at 10:50 P.M. a well-drilled assault team
of thirteen Sandinistas attacked and took the entire party hostage.
Castillo ran to his bedroom where he found the party's musicians in
refuge. He tried to organize them to counterattack with arms from his
private arsenal. When the musicians wisely demurred, Castillo grabbed a
machine gun from his closet to fight the attackers alone, an act that cost
him his life. By the time the National Guard reached the scene at 11:10
P.M., the guerrillas controlled the situation and repelled the Guard with
automatic fire from one of Castillo's own weapons.

The hostages included Guillermo Sevilla Sacasa, Nicaragua's ambassador to Washington and Somoza's brother-in-law; Alejandro Mon-
tiel Argüello, the foreign minister; Guillermo Lang, Nicaraguan consul
in New York; Danilo Lacayo Rapacciolli, head of ESSO Nicaragua;
Noel Pallais Debayle, first cousin of the president and president of the
National Economic Development Institute; and Alfonso Deneken Die,
ambassador from Chile. The FSLN demanded the release from prison of
various Sandinistas (including Daniel Ortega Saavedra), a $5 million ran-
som, and the publication of a message from the FSLN to the Nicaraguan
people. Anastasio Somoza Debayle, in Miami en route to Spain, rushed
back to Managua for several days of tense negotiations mediated by
Archbishop Obando. Somoza finally acceded to most of the demands,
released eighteen Sandinistas, and provided an airliner to fly the guerrillas, released prisoners, and hostages to Cuba. Nicaraguan radio stations and newspapers published two lengthy communiqués from the
FSLN. The archbishop, the apostolic nuncio, and the ambassadors of
Mexico and Spain served as replacement hostages to guarantee the safety
of the guerrillas.

Evolution, 1975–1978

The hostage-taking of 1974 gave the FSLN a huge symbolic victory,
won the freedom of several key Sandinista leaders, and raised a large
sum of money.[25] The FSLN stepped up both urban and rural actions in
1975–1976. Yet despite the increase in guerrilla activity, the Front remained rather small and poorly armed. For example, Henry Ruiz re-
counted coming down from the mountains to lend his automatic weapon
to the team for the 1974 assault. Among other weapons used in the raid

were such primitive hunting arms as shotguns and a .22-caliber rifle. The FSLN probably numbered around a hundred or a hundred and fifty armed guerrillas at this juncture.[26]

December 1974 also hardened the regime's position toward all opposition. Repression increased so greatly that it soon forced a turning point in the struggle. Somoza continued martial law indefinitely and gave the National Guard great license to intimidate or to eliminate the opposition however it chose, thus rapidly escalating regime violence in 1975–1976. This increased governmental pressure caused the guerrillas some setbacks, but the FSLN continued to grow in both members and supporters as regime violence made opponents of more and more Nicaraguans.

These pressures by the regime and the movement's own growth split the FSLN into three factions in 1975–1976. As government pressure forced ever greater security precautions upon the rebels, parts of the Front became isolated from each other. Ideological colorations also crept in with the recruits from the generation of the 1970s, and tactical differences developed. Considerable conflict arose among the factions, or "tendencies." The tendencies were:

1. The *Proletarios* (proletarian) wing. The first clearly to differentiate itself, this group emerged from the urban guerrilla front in 1975. Influenced by the intellectual Jaime Wheelock Román and rejecting excessive "voluntarism," the Proletarios formed a new student arm, the JRN, and sought to broaden the movement's mass base by organizing unions in factories, in poor neighborhoods, and among new classes emerging from industrialization. The other factions criticized the Proletarios for excessive "propagandism," for adherence to a "traditional Marxist line," and divisiveness.

2. The *Guerra Popular Prolongada* (Prolonged People's War— GPP) faction. The GPP was heir to the original FSLN rural organization and such leaders as Tomás Borge and Henry Ruíz. The GPP, with mainly rural operations, abandoned the "foco" strategy, which was followed by Fidel Castro's forces in the Cuban Sierra Maestra, and preferred the cautious strategy of accumulating forces advocated by guerrilla-war theorists Mao Tse Tung of China and Vo Nguyen Giap of Vietnam. The other factions criticized the GPP as being too cautious militarily and prone to isolate itself from the daily life of the people. The FER remained the student wing of the GPP.

3. The *Terceristas* (third force) faction. This group, which appeared in 1976–1977, was also called the Insurreccionales (insurgents)

and the Christian wing because of its apparent ideological pluralism. The Terceristas' leaders, some expelled from the GPP, included Daniel and Humberto Ortega Saavedra and Victor Tirado López. The Terceristas relaxed the original FSLN's requirement for Marxist-Leninist orthodoxy and rapidly increased their ranks with social democratic, social Christian, and bourgeois recruits, although the leaders remained Marxist-Leninists. The Terceristas' student wing was the Sandinista Revolutionary Youth (Juventud Revolucionaria Sandinista). Tactically and militarily much bolder than the other factions in 1977–1978, the Terceristas pressed the urban and rural insurrection with vigor. The other tendencies criticized them for excessive boldness if not adventurism, and for a lack of ideological purity.

The growth of each wing continued despite the internal rift, and some contact among them continued. However, despite later statements designed to downplay the extent of these internal strains, the divisions were intense if one takes seriously the principals' own words during the schism.[27]

What saved the FSLN from splitting apart entirely was the rapid escalation of popular opposition to the Somoza dynasty. The internecine vituperation of 1977 melted away before the rising heat of mass hostility to the regime. In early 1978 mass protests against the killing of Pedro Joaquín Chamorro and the spontaneous rebellion in Monimbó revealed a popular revolutionary animus far greater than most FSLN leaders had expected. Again in August, more spontaneous popular uprisings occurred in Matagalpa, Jinotepe, and other cities. This startled the three factions into reunification talks. The failure of the OAS-sponsored mediation effort between the FAO and Somoza in January 1979, and the subsequent fragmentation of the FAO itself, strengthened the FSLN's hand within the opposition. Thus, the lead of the Nicaraguan people together with the smell of possible success drew the FSLN back together—provisionally in December 1978, then to full formal unity on 3 March 1979. The reunited Front thus vastly enhanced its ability to wage a coordinated national military and political campaign.

In 1978–1979 each of the FSLN's three wings grew rapidly, while the military strategy altered substantially. In early 1978 the Terceristas abandoned their rural front in the North and reassigned those veterans to urban areas in order to enrich the combat experience of the fast-growing urban movement. In the most spectacular incident of the insurrection, on 22 August 1978 a command of twenty-five Terceristas led by Edén Pastora (Comandante Cero)[28] daringly seized the National Palace, seat of the Congress and several government ministries, taking more than two thousand hostages. Among the captives were numerous high government officials, many relatives of President Somoza himself, and twenty reporters who found themselves with the scoop of their lives. As in December 1974, the action was an enormous military, political, and propaganda success. The commandos achieved nearly all their objectives and escaped to Panama with sixty Sandinistas freed from prison and a half million dollars in ransom (see Chapter 8). One reason for the action was to create a military crisis for the National Guard that would forestall a coup d'etat that was rumored to be in the works. The coup would have removed Somoza in order to permit a government of reconciliation between proregime and opposition elements that would exclude the FSLN and its more radical collaborators. The expected military takeover never materialized, although whether it was blocked by the National Palace incident remains a matter of speculation.

The FSLN's combat forces had been relatively few in number before the National Palace incident. Humberto Ortega reported that the Terceristas committed one hundred and fifty soldiers to the September 1978 uprising. When the GPP initiated armed actions in Estelí that same month, only thirty-five guerrillas participated, and in Chinandega there were only eleven. Thus all three FSLN tendencies combined probably numbered between five hundred and a thousand armed regulars in mid-1978. After the August-September uprising of 1978, however, the guerrillas' ranks swelled rapidly: "Though 150 of us took part in that insurrection, from that moment on we quickly multiplied into greatly superior numbers—three or four times that number and with the potential to recruit thousands more. Thus, we grew in men and we grew in armament, because we seized [weapons] from the enemy."[29]

From then on, not only did the number of Sandinista regulars snowball, but irregular volunteer popular participation in combat also burgeoned. By late 1978 the Terceristas alone had roughly two thousand men under arms. Especially in the North where popular support for the guerrillas was so great, the FSLN also helped to train, organize, and lead the people, who were "throwing themselves into the struggle."[30] For example, the GPP's Henry Ruíz (Modesto) reported that "the campesinos came down to join the struggle in the cities. In Chinandega, for example, our safe houses were [constantly] full giving three hour militia classes. The people were going into the streets. It was the people who went at the vanguard of the struggle."[31] In addition to capitalizing on the rage of the Nicaraguan people against Somocismo, the reunited FSLN in 1978 and 1979 coordinated its activities with other opposition elements to an unprecedented degree. The formation of the two great pro-Sandinista coalitions, the MPU in 1978 and the FPN in 1979, gave the FSLN a major leadership role in the final political struggle to overthrow Somoza.

Sandinista Ideology

The FSLN draws much of its ideology from the ideas and example of Sandino. Augusto César Sandino lacked a well-developed ideology, but he consistently called for armed resistance to U.S. occupation and interference and for populistic social policies, including workers and peasant cooperatives and land reforms.[32] Sandino also excoriated Nicaragua's sham electoral republicanism, calling it a farce. The ideology of the FSLN has consistently contained similar elements. The Front, however, has articulated a much clearer, broader, and more coherent program than did Sandino, mainly because its founders believed in the basic premises of Marxian socialism as modified by Lenin regarding the possibility of national (as opposed to worldwide) revolution.[33] The Marxist-Leninist vein predominated in the FSLN until the mid-1970s, when the rapid alienation of ever broader sectors of the Nicaraguan people brought many non-Marxists to the FSLN's door. The decision to admit such elements caused the ideological pluralization of the Tercerista wing and swelled its ranks and financial support. In the process of reunifying the three tendencies and forming the MPU and the FPN in 1978–1979, the FSLN's rhetoric changed to accommodate these new internal and external allies, thus losing some of its Leninist flavor. Nevertheless, although references to "Marxism-Leninism" were absent from the June 1978 proposed agreement among the three tendencies, the FSLN remained committed to "opening a popular democratic process permitting . . . the enjoyment of full democratic liberties as the most appropriate framework . . . for the march toward full national liberation and socialism."[34] Especially because of the Terceristas, the FSLN came to contain different strains of socialists, as well as nonsocialists.

The ideology and program of the FSLN evolved from 1961 to 1979 as the movement changed from a tiny armed conspiracy pledged to a lengthy struggle for power into a major contender for rule in need of broad backing from other opposition groups. In the beginning the leaders' Marxist-Leninist faith in the revolutionary vanguard helped sustain the energy of cadres in the face of overwhelming odds. In later years, however, Sandinista leaders developed an increasingly sophisticated understanding of the geopolitical and economic context of the revolution. This understanding led them to adopt an extremely pragmatic program stressing a mixed economy and political pluralism. Moreover, the rapidly broadening ideological pool of non-Marxist recruits and the prospects of widespread mass opposition to the regime led to an FSLN program designed to attract many different groups victimized by Somoza. The program appealed to peasants and factory workers denied fair wages and unions, to victims of political repression, to the many denied access to decent public services, to the urban poor, to residents of the isolated and critically poor Atlantic coastal zone, and to many others. Moreover, because of the strategy of uniting with a broad coalition of other forces, overt references to socialism and to nationalization of property other than that of Somoza had vanished from the published FSLN program. For example, rather than call for nationalization of banks—a policy feared by many entrepreneurs and investors—the FSLN promised only that "the resources of banks . . . will be at the service of the interests of the development of Nicaragua and the welfare of the people."[35]

Given the programs enacted by the FSLN from 1979 to 1984, one must conclude that the ideological evolution of the FSLN was profound. Nicaragua's Sandinistas had developed a new Marxist revolutionary program that retained such Leninist features as a mobilizing vanguard party and profound socioeconomic transformation to benefit the working classes but was also innovative in that it institutionalized political opposition, preserved a large private sector, and established traditional civil liberties (see Table 7.2).

Organization

Beginning with fewer than twenty militants in 1961, the FSLN probably never numbered more than a hundred armed guerrillas before 1967.[36] The Front operated mainly as a clandestine rural organization, usually from Honduras. The guerrilla column imitated Sandino's military field tactics, but it established only limited contact with the Nicaraguan peasantry. In 1962 small training operations began in both Managua and the countryside, and the FSLN published its first propaganda organs, *Rojo y Negro* and *Trinchera*. After 1963 the FSLN did much of its recruiting through the urban, university-based FER. The FSLN and the FER operated in the classical clandestine cell mode. Members used code names and knew little about each other in order to minimize the risk to other cells in the event of a security breach.

Following both the 1963 Bocay and 1967 Pancasán setbacks, the FSLN curtailed military action to reorganize and rebuild. In 1964–1965 it tried a brief and unprofitable alliance with other opposition groups.

TABLE 7.2
The Program of the FSLN

--Nationalization of the Somozas' and their cohorts' goods and property

--Agrarian revolution, including reforms of land redistribution, sale, tenancy, and rental

--Improved rural working conditions and pay

--Improved working conditions (pay, hours, vacations, and social security for miners, factory workers, teachers, and government and private-sector workers)

--Free unionization for all workers, both urban and rural

--Control of living costs, especially basic necessities (food, clothing, and medicine)

--Improved and generalized availability of public services (public transportation, electricity, water, health care, sanitation, social security, and recreation)

--Rent control and improvement of housing conditions

--Improvement of education (mandatory, free through high school); schools available to the whole national population; national literacy campaign

--Nationalization and protection of natural resources, including mines

--Development of the Atlantic Coast region and its integration into the nation

--Elimination of organized crime, delinquency, and police corruption

--Abolition of torture and political assassination

--Full panoply of democratic liberties (freedom of expression, political organization and association, and religion; return of political exiles)

--Equality for women

--Free, nonaligned foreign policy and relations; end of foreign interference in Nicaraguan affairs

--Formation of a new, democratic, and popular army under the leadership of the FSLN

Source: FSLN declaration of goals and program, quoted in José Fajardo et al., Los Sandinistas (Bogotá: Editorial La Oveja Negra, 1979), pp. 245-257.

The FSLN also formed unions in Matagalpa, Jinotega and Estelí, as well as neighborhood organizations and Popular Civic Committees (Comités Cívicos Populares) among sympathetic popular elements in both rural and urban areas. Regrouped guerrilla columns developed closer ties with peasants, seeking them out both as militants and as supporters. In 1968-1969 the FSLN de-emphasized rural armed actions and gave the urban guerrilla arm new emphasis, conducting a series of bank robberies and acts of sabotage to undermine confidence in the regime.

Although in 1970 a few FSLN elements trained in guerrilla tactics with the Palestine Liberation Organization and others occasionally trained in Cuba and elsewhere, external assistance remained rather meager during most of the 1970s. Guerrilla commander Henry Ruíz described how the FSLN supported itself with little foreign backing: "The city acted as a sort of lung for the rural operations, but directly from abroad we received nothing. . . . Our requirement of the urban wing was arms . . . which were bought with money collected by committees . . . of *compañeros,* two, three, four, five, who clandestinely obtained money to buy munitions, arms and medicine."[37] The FER raised funds using teams of three to board city buses. One would keep watch, the second would make a brief pitch for aid for the compañeros fighting Somoza, and the third would collect donations. The three would then jump from the bus between stops to elude police. The combination of hundreds of such forays monthly with other money-raising activities among students, business people, and unions kept cash flowing into FSLN coffers. This was supplemented with bank robberies and ransoms from a few hijackings. According to the FSLN, it was only in 1978–1979 that international solidarity committees supplied significant amounts of external funds.

The FSLN high command consisted of a National Directorate that met periodically to establish general strategy. The National Directorate, including major political strategists and guerrilla commanders as well as field commanders, steadily expanded to include distinguished younger militants in addition to veterans. For this reason, the arrests of Tomás Borge, Carlos Fonseca, and Daniel Ortega and the deaths of Silvio Mayorga, Camilo Ortega, and even Fonseca himself posed only momentary difficulties for the Front. The FSLN divided itself among operational zones referred to as "fronts" named after fallen comrades or heroes (see Figure 7.1), with a general command staff below which the command structure was rather informal. Unit size depended upon the mission—twelve to fifteen for a military mission, five for a supply mission, and five for an armed propaganda mission.

In the jungle, armed propaganda consisted in temporarily occupying a house or a hamlet, where we talked about the objectives of our struggle. We used small squads to facilitate our withdrawal. . . . We never carried out a local action without keeping moving, which disconcerted the enemy. We were a small enemy, but very feared and above all very mysterious.[38]

During 1978–1979 the FSLN's growth rate skyrocketed. The spontaneous popular uprisings of 1978 revealed that the Front lagged

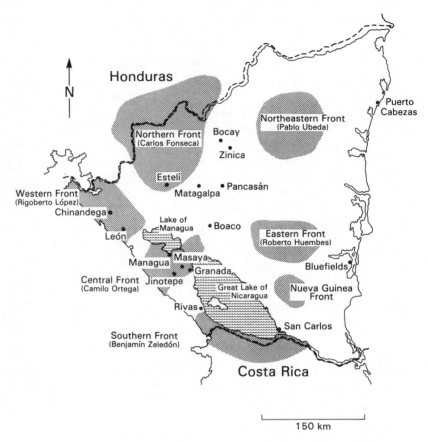

Figure 7.1: The Fronts of the FSLN 1977-1979

behind the people of Nicaragua in readiness for a major offensive; this hastened the expansion of the ranks. Training camps in Costa Rica, Honduras, and Nicaragua swelled into substantial operations. The overall number of FSLN troops thus ballooned from between five hundred and a thousand in early 1978 to nearly three thousand by late 1978 to around five thousand by July 1979. To incorporate the many irregular volunteers, the FSLN also ran short combat-training sessions for citizens when Sandinista columns occupied a neighborhood. These trained volunteers were the core of the popular militia. In 1978 Radio Sandino began to broadcast, at first from Costa Rica but later from within Nicaragua. Radio Sandino helped coordinate military actions and popular support and gave pro-Sandinista news on the war.

Seeing the victory looming closer, the National Directorate in May 1979 organized in San José, Costa Rica, its provisional government junta, which laid plans for governing Nicaragua after the expected victory, conducted foreign relations for the rebels, and operated a sophisticated propaganda machine. FSLN coordination with other opposition groups also escalated rapidly (see below).

Membership

By the late 1970s the membership of the FSLN had changed markedly from its early days. The founding Sandinistas came mainly from lower- and middle-class urban backgrounds. Most had been leftist student activists from the 1944–1948 and 1959–1961 generations who for their militancy had suffered detention, torture, or exile by the government. A few peasants joined the early Sandinistas, recruited through rural operations. During the late 1960s and early 1970s, recruitment of northern campesinos increased as the Front better integrated itself into rural society. During the 1970s urban recruits came from two main sources: (1) The burgeoning student movement supplied especially left-wing students at first, but later recruits were increasingly ideologically diverse. Student militants were predominantly middle class, but in the late 1970s increasingly came from upper-middle-class and upper-class backgrounds. (2) Urban lower-class youth—some as young as twelve to sixteen years—were mobilized into the Front by the barrio self-help organizations and civic defense committees or were self-recruited because of the regime's systematic repression of young people.[39]

Women played a major role in the FSLN in the 1970s. Women entered the organization in the same ways as men. They took an active part in combat, eventually making up a quarter of the troops, and rose to positions to power. Dora María Téllez, Mónica Baltodano, and Leticia Herrera, for example, "played a very important role, not just in support of the revolutionary struggle, but as conductors of the struggle in its military, and political aspects."[40] Téllez commanded the entire Rigoberto López Pérez western front, one of the most important of the war.

Arms

The Sandinistas have described themselves as poorly armed and quite dependent for the acquisition of weapons upon the fund-raising success of the urban support system from the 1960s until 1978.[41] Many of the rural columns of the 1960s patrolled and entered combat equipped with .22 rifles and shotguns, and with as few as five or six rounds apiece. Ancient military carbines and a few M-1 rifles

Figure 7.2. Compañera Betty (left) and other Sandinista regulars. Participation in the FSLN by women and youth was widespread. (Photo by John E. Newhagen)

were commonplace. Automatic weapons were treasured; more so-phisticated, heavier weaponry was almost unknown. In most of the assaults upon National Guard patrols and posts, capturing arms and munitions ranked equally with other military and political objectives.

In the battle for the cities, the Sandinistas and their thousands of volunteers utilized contact bombs, bullets, and Molotov cocktails manufactured in rude clandestine factories. As neighborhoods and towns rose in support of the FSLN guerrilla columns, citizens retrieved weapons from hiding. These and captured National Guard weapons were used to arm both the guerrillas and their volunteer militia ranks.

As the war escalated in the late 1970s, the Front's arms supply increased. The operation of base camps in Costa Rica and Honduras facilitated arms acquisitions. This was especially true of Costa Rica after 1978, when the government of President Rodrigo Carazo not only permitted but encouraged arms shipment to the FSLN. Sandinista weapons purchases went first to Panama, then on to the FSLN by air or ground via Costa Rica. The Costa Rican Civil Guard sometimes even convoyed FSLN arms shipments. Private arms dealers in Costa Rica also supplied the FSLN, often flying the weapons to FSLN bases inside Nicaragua.[42] As the combat assumed the nature of a conventional ground war in 1979, the FSLN both purchased and captured more sophisticated weapons, including mortars, bazookas, heavy-caliber automatic weapons, rockets, and even a few antiaircraft guns. A major arms-smuggling scandal in Costa Rica has subsequently revealed that in May–July 1979 twenty-one flights by Costa Rican civilian transport planes brought a total of 320 tons of arms from a Havana military base to the FSLN via the airfield at Costa Rica's northern town of Liberia. The cost to the FSLN of this assistance was Costa Rica's retention of half the arms.[43] Virtually every known model of light combat arm manufactured in the United States and Western Europe found its way into the FSLN armory. Light civilian aircraft flown from Costa Rica even dropped a few bombs on National Guard positions late in the war.

The Opposition Coalitions

Four major opposition coalitions developed in Nicaragua in the years following the 1972 earthquake. The first two—UDEL and FAO—reflected the dissatisfaction of certain well-established economic and political interests with the Somoza regime and their efforts to reform it. The latter two coalitions—the MPU and the FPN—mobilized and consolidated a new configuration of more radical opponents, allied with the Sandinistas and seeking revolution rather than reform.

Democratic Liberation Union

This coalition, forged in 1974 by major leaders of several Conservative and Liberal splinter factions, as well as by other minor parties and some labor unions,[44] sought reform of the system rather than revolution (see Chapter 6). Although the UDEL's members came from both working and middle class in addition to the disaffected bourgeois groups, the upper-class interests tended to predominate. The UDEL's calls for political reform and for the end of the Somoza dynasty earned its leaders increasing persecution by the regime, especially during 1978–1979.

Broad Opposition Front

In 1978 this coalition merged the UDEL with several other opposition organizations, mainly of middle- and upper-class origins.[45] The FAO represented a considerable expansion of the anti-Somoza front. Among the new groups was Alfonso Robelo's Nicaraguan Democratic Movement, an organization of smaller business and professional interests. Also in the FAO were the Group of Twelve, the Social Christian party, and three Conservative factions.

The FAO broadened the middle- and upper-class reformist opposition to Somoza yet fell short of proposing a revolutionary reorganization of society. It called for political democracy, an end to political corruption, freedom to organize, a vaguely defined agrarian reform, and broadened social welfare guarantees. Its access to anti-Somoza press support from the Catholic church helped to mobilize huge public demonstrations against the regime in 1978.

The FAO actively sought a negotiated settlement with Somoza from September through January 1979, encouraged by the United States and the OAS. Internal concessions to Somoza, the PLN, and the National Guard split the FAO in late 1978 and early 1979. The growing military power of the FSLN and the FAO's failure to settle with Somoza further hurt the FAO. By early 1979 it had lost its momentum and several key organizations, thus permitting the MPU/FPN coalitions to supplant it as the main rebel political front.

United People's Movement

As the FSLN pulled itself back together in late 1978 and early 1979, it struggled to broaden its public base. At first during the FAO-Somoza negotiations, the FSLN withheld its objections as long as a settlement might get rid of Somoza, the National Guard, and the PLN. However, when this chance began to fail the FSLN rejected the settlement talks and helped form the United People's Movement under the leadership of Moisés Hassán. Founded in 1978 and broadened in early 1979, the MPU eventually included twenty-two unions and civic and political organizations representing students and youth, urban workers, and organized peasants, teachers, and intellectuals mobilized against Somoza.[46] Among the MPU's student groups were the FSLN's university support wings. The MPU's agenda of revolutionary goals was virtually identical to the program of the FSLN itself. Many of the MPU organizations, especially on the more radical left, represented lower- and middle-class Nicaraguans. The MPU helped organize barrios and rural communities to rally popular support and to facilitate the FSLN's war effort.

National Patriotic Front

The National Patriotic Front, formed 1 February 1979, gave final shape to the FSLN's policy of alliance with other groups as the battle with the dynasty escalated toward its climax. The decline of the FAO left a critical organizational vacuum among opposition political forces, giving the FSLN leadership of the opposition by default—yet the FSLN had no well-established broad front organization. To fill this void the FSLN organized the FPN, which united the MPU revolutionary coalition with several other opposition groups, including the Independent Liberals, the Popular Social Christian faction, the Group of Twelve, and several unions.[47]

Given its broader political base, the FPN's formal program contained somewhat less far-reaching reform proposals than that of the MPU. Lest critics denounce the FSLN and the MPU for selling out their revolutionary principles to other forces, however, the FSLN justified the watered-down FPN program as necessary to unite disparate forces seeking a common anti-Somoza objective.

Summary

This chapter has delineated the critical role played in the formation of opposition to the Somoza regime by non-class or cross-class forces in the Nicaraguan revolution. Foreign governments, some unintentionally and others deliberately, weakened the regime and strengthened its opponents. U.S. ambivalence about Somoza, ironically, first weakened his regime and encouraged his enemies, then ultimately helped prolong his bloody hold over Nicaragua during the months of the U.S. search for a solution to the conflict that would leave out the FSLN. The dilatory U.S. behavior in late 1978 and early 1979 provided additional months for political maneuvering during which the FAO fell apart and the Sandinistas reunited themselves and forged their own political coalitions. When repressed by the regime for their tentative efforts at social action, clergy, laypeople, and to some extent even the churches themselves were politicized and became important sources of opposition personnel, organization, talent, and support. The FSLN survived seventeen years of weakness, repeated setbacks, and eventually internal divisions to assume the political leadership of a popular rebellion of remarkable spontaneity. Of the opposition forces, the Sandinistas alone had the military capacity to challenge the National Guard and the flexibility to respond with sufficient speed to the rapidly changing circumstances of the unfolding insurrection.

8
The Insurrection of 1977–1979

Somoza is finished.
—Edén Pastora, 1 June 1979[1]

I will not resign.
—Anastasio Somoza Debayle, 11 June 1979[2]

The Somoza dictatorship's opposition evolved rapidly during 1977–1979, a process in which the more radical, FSLN-led lower- and middle-class forces among the rebels eclipsed the bourgeois reformists. The Nicaraguan people fought successfully to free themselves from the dynasty, but they paid a terrible price. For although the dictatorship had decayed so that it could no longer rule, it wielded an awful capacity for destruction until the very last.

The First Wave of the Insurrection (1977)

The three-year state of siege, first imposed by Anastasio Somoza Debayle during the December 1974 Castillo house raid, set the stage for the 1977–1979 insurrection. The state of siege suspended most civil liberties, permitted military trials for civilians, imposed curfews, and generally freed the hands of the National Guard. The Guard employed this license to terrorize real and suspected opponents of the regime—especially peasants, rural religious organizers, and youths. More visible, urban-based opposition parties, unions, and interest groups also experienced harassment, illegal detentions, and—although less commonly than did peasants—torture and murder. Antiregime hostility steadily intensified among ever wider sectors of the society.[3]

Although overall real economic growth rates were officially tabulated at a mean of 5 percent annually between the 1972 earthquake and 1978, the economy cycled through quick booms and busts while inflation escalated rapidly. Political corruption diverted the quake-recovery efforts into private pockets and left the seismic damage scarring the capital. Economic strains intensified labor unrest among middle- and lower-class groups and alienated the national bourgeoisie despite the great repressive energy expended by the regime. Nicaragua had become an overheated boiler with no safety valve. Some pressure might have been reduced had the National Guard tried judiciously to contain unrest while the government made economic and political adjustments to lower the heat. But judicious behavior was as foreign to the Somoza regime as integrity with the public purse. The National Guard's excessive coercion itself became a source of hostility toward the regime, and Somoza's government produced no meaningful reforms.

The violent denouement of these massive social strains began in 1977. From 1975 through early 1977 the FSLN was divided and lost much personnel because of a major National Guard counterinsurgency campaign. The FSLN did manage, however, to continue to raid Guard posts, to rob banks, and to conduct propaganda missions. Despite their losses from 1975 to 1977, the Sandinistas returned to the attack in early 1977. This prompted Somoza to form in May 1977 special anti-FSLN units, the Special Antiterrorist Activity Brigades (Brigadas Especiales Contra Actividades Terroristas – BECATs). They would be trained by the EEBI, established earlier under the command of the heir apparent to the regime, Anastasio Somoza Portocarrero, nicknamed "el Chigüín" (the Kid). In January 1977 Somoza suffered a diplomatic setback when Jimmy Carter became U.S. president. Carter reversed his predecessors' policy of diplomatic, economic, and military assistance to the dynasty, and the Department of State began to press Somoza for human rights reforms, in particular to lift the state of siege.

On 28 July 1977, the hard-drinking, overweight Anastasio Somoza Debayle suffered a serious coronary attack. He was flown to Miami for treatment. Many Somoza cohorts believed that the gravely ill dictator would never return to Nicaragua. This prompted a spree of embezzlement of public funds so serious that it suggested to many the imminent collapse of the regime. Somoza's surprise return to Managua on 10 September pulled the government and the PLN back together, although the scandal brought about the ouster of Dr. Cornelio Hüeck, then president of the Congress. While still hospitalized in the United States, Somoza had learned of Amnesty International's damning report on human rights in Nicaragua. To counter the unfavorable publicity and to mollify the United States, Somoza ended the state of siege on 9 September 1977.

Anastasio Somoza settled into a rehabilitation regimen at the family's Montelimar estate and hoped for relief from internal and international pressures. However, lifting of the state of siege aggravated tensions in Nicaragua by releasing a tremendous amount of pent-up citizen hostility. The FSLN Terceristas in October launched attacks on National Guard posts at San Carlos, Ocotal, Rivas, Granada, and elsewhere. The GPP, too, staged attacks in Managua, Masaya, and in the rural North. The Guard responded by crossing both the Costa Rican and Honduran borders in pursuit of the guerrillas. These border incidents elicited diplomatic protests from both nations, followed by U.S. and Venezuelan snubs at a hemispheric military meeting held in Managua in late 1977. Civic opposition to the regime also rose. *La Prensa* trumpeted the scandals in the government and among Somoza cohorts. Conservative and social Christian factions increased their demands for political reform. In October 1977 captured FSLN documents allegedly named the Front's proposed revolutionary cabinet. Its dozen members, the Group of Twelve (los Doce), fled to exile, and endorsed the revolutionaries. The political and military situation became so grave that Archbishop Miguel Obando y Bravo in November called for a national dialogue between the regime and moderate opposition forces. Somoza tentatively accepted, but reaffirmed his intention to finish his full term (to end in 1981), despite demands for his resignation.

The guerrilla actions of October–November 1977 soon subsided, and Somoza's confidence in his ability to defeat the FSLN recovered. The Guard was strong: The regime had imported some $10 million worth of arms in 1977 — more than 1 percent of total national imports — and with some seven thousand troops the expanding and reorganized Guard outnumbered the insurgent military forces roughly tenfold. However, Somoza recognized clearly his growing isolation. He increasingly railed against his enemies, calling them "communists" — whom he saw in the Catholic church, other political parties, the international media, the Carter administration, and the U.S. Department of State. Events would soon demonstrate to the cocksure dictator that the 1977 turmoil was but a warning ripple before a tidal wave.

The Second Wave (1978): The People in the Vanguard

The Chamorro Assassination

One critical catalyst of rebellion for many Nicaraguans was the assassination of *La Prensa* editor Pedro Joaquín Chamorro Cardenal on 10 January 1978.[4] *La Prensa's* exposé of the exportation of scarce Nicaraguan blood plasma by Plasmaferesis apparently led this firm's owners, among them Cornelio Hüeck and Anastasio Somoza Portocarrero, to have Chamorro disposed of. The ambush assassination by Silvio Peña Rivas and several accomplices electrified Managua: Within hours some fifty thousand mourners and demonstrators had gathered outside the slain editor's home. Thousands more turned out for the funeral procession, while angry mobs totaling thirty thousand burned Plasmaferesis, numerous vehicles, and several Somoza family businesses. Spontaneous mass unrest spread nationwide and continued for days, leading to the reimposition of martial law in some areas.

Chamorro's assassination convinced many upper-class interests, previously reluctant to declare publicly against Somoza, to join the opposition at last. Their protest took shape as a business-initiated general strike, called by the UDEL for 24 January 1978. By 25 January the general strike had idled about 80 percent of the country's economy. Accompanied by widespread acts of protest and violence, the general strike lasted until the second week of February. In other protests, the official wing of the Conservative party boycotted the February municipal election (turnout was only 20.3 percent), called for Somoza's resignation, and renounced its long-standing pact with the regime (although the party did not pull out of the government).

International response to the Chamorro assassination took several forms. In the Organization of American States, Venezuela called for the Inter-American Commission on Human Rights to investigate Nicaragua. The United States canceled a scheduled visit by State Department special envoy Terrance Todman because of the postassassination unrest. On 30 January the United States announced that because of human rights violations Nicaragua's 1979 military assistance loan had been canceled — the only nation so penalized that year. A few days later, the Department of State announced U.S. support for "democratic government" in Nicaragua — a criticism of the dynastic dictatorship — and denied intentions of military intervention on behalf of the Somoza regime.

The Monimbó Uprising

Residents of Monimbó, an Indian community within the colonial city of Masaya, 28 kilometers southeast of Managua, decided in early February 1978 to rename a small plaza in honor of Pedro Joaquín Chamorro. The National Guard disrupted the commemorative mass, attended by some two thousand residents of Monimbó; the crowd responded by fiercely attacking the soldiers with fireworks and stones and routing the Guard. Euphoric, the crowd spontaneously barricaded the approaches to Monimbó and declared it free territory. Poorly organized, poorly armed, and untrained, the people of the barrio held off the Guard's tentative nighttime forays for two weeks — without the aid of the FSLN. Finally, on 26 February the Guard attacked; it opened up with heavy weapons fire and aerial bombing for several hours, then followed through with a massed ground attack. After hours of intense house-to-house combat, the Guard retook Monimbó. The lone Sandinista who had finally arrived to help organize the neighborhood struggle, Camilo

Ortega Saavedra, died in the Guard assault, along with more than two hundred residents of the barrio.

The ferocity of the National Guard's actions against Monimbó spawned other uprisings. A second spontaneous revolt occurred in Diriamba on 26 February. On 3 March the Subtiava Indian community in the city of León also rebelled. In both Diriamba and Subtiava, the regime copied its strategy at Monimbó, holding back until well reinforced and prepared for attack, then throwing heavy ordnance and air strikes at the community prior to a massive ground action to regain the territory and to mop up lingering resistance. As in Monimbó, civilian casualties were very high.[5]

Growing Political Opposition

The Chamorro assassination had stirred a rebellious outburst against the government by many different elements of Nicaraguan society, including formerly timid or even pro-Somoza bourgeois elements. Monimbó, Subtiava, and Diriamba reinforced the disaffection by showing concretely how the regime would respond to public rebellion. Several frantic months (March–July 1978) of intense political activity followed as various political and economic groups began to work for Somoza's ouster and sought a unifying organizational framework.[6]

After a relatively calm last half of March, overt opposition suddenly rose as protesting students occupied forty-eight churches. Then mothers of imprisoned Sandinistas went on hunger strike to demand an end to solitary confinement for the prisoners. Soon after, high school students led by the Secondary Students' Association (AES) struck their institutions, affecting some thirty thousand pupils in about fifty schools nationwide. Later in April thousands of members of industrial, transport, construction, and hospital workers' unions staged a forty-eight-hour protest strike against the regime.

The government's response was mixed. On the moderate side, Somoza released from solitary the FSLN prisoners, undermining the protest. He also defused the school strike by making certain concessions. He began to speak of a forthcoming general program of political reform. On the other hand, the National Guard acted heavy-handedly: It fired on a group of peasant hunger strikers on 17 April, wounding fifteen. A 1 May 1978 demonstration by the UDEL brought the arrest of several labor union leaders and of Rafael Córdoba Rivas, the UDEL's president. In numerous other clashes in Managua, Masaya, and Jinotepe, protesters died from National Guard bullets. On two occasions automatic-weapons fire from moving vehicles raked the plant of *La Prensa;* on another an independent radio station was the target.

Opposition to the regime, however, grew rapidly despite Somoza's talk of reform. Alfonso Robelo Callejas formed his business- and professional-based, proreform MDN. In May, the MDN joined the UDEL and the Group of Twelve to form the Broad Opposition Front. The Agüero faction of the Conservatives and the Social Christian party joined the FAO in early July.

In early June 1978 President Somoza bowed to U.S. pressure and announced that the Twelve could freely return to Nicaragua; he also invited the Inter-American Commission on Human Rights to visit the country (see below). The Twelve soon announced their intention of ending their exile, causing several demonstrations to support them that culminated in a gigantic airport welcome rally in July. About the same time Radio Sandino began to broadcast, attracting an eager audience and providing yet another source of criticism of Somoza. To protest the killing of three students in Jinotepe by the National Guard, the FAO and UDEL called for 19 July 1978 a one-day general strike that idled some 70 percent of the nation's businesses and factories.

Somoza's decision to permit the Group of Twelve to return to Nicaragua and to invite the IACHR inspection had resulted from international pressure. Venezuela, for example, had repeatedly blocked Nicaraguan efforts to seek OAS sanctions against Costa Rica for harboring the FSLN. Venezuela frequently denounced the Nicaraguan human rights situation in the OAS, where the Venezuelan ambassador once said: "Somoza believes that God has given him Nicaragua for an hacienda, and its citizens as its peasants."[7] Somoza Debayle became so distressed by the pressure that he secretly visited Venezuelan president Carlos Andres Pérez to plead unsuccessfully for cooperation rather than criticism.

U.S. pressure had also helped persuade Somoza to make the minor human rights concessions of June 1978. In a secret June 30 letter to Somoza, Jimmy Carter offered congratulations for inviting the IACHR, for proposing amnesty for political prisoners, and for permitting the return of the Group of Twelve. Somoza interpreted this congratulatory missive as an endorsement of his regime and was stunned when the Department of State declared within days: "The fact is, we're against Somoza."[8] Somoza's memoirs recall this as the moment of his decision for a massive arms buildup in order to fight the rebels, regardless of international cooperation or sanctions.

Ironically, the Carter letter had alienated the moderate opposition that had been building in the March–July period almost as much as it did Somoza. Although little of substance had changed in the National Guard's treatment of the opposition, President Carter had written to Somoza: "I look forward to hearing of the implementation of your decisions, and appreciate very much your announcement of these constructive actions."[9] When someone leaked the letter in July, its congratulatory tone convinced many Nicaraguan moderates that they had no ally in the United States, despite U.S. statements supposedly supporting the reformers. Then, to reinforce the moderates' skepticism came the U.S. release of $12 million in economic development aid budgeted for 1978. Many moderate anti-Somocistas thus decided that U.S. policy supported the old regime, a perception that began to undermine the FAO even as it was aborning.

The Assault on the National Palace

Patterns of opposition activity changed little during early August. The Nicaraguan Council of Bishops called for Somoza's resignation and for a national dialogue to end the violence. On 21 August the FAO announced its political program, which called for a broad array of reforms. The regime likewise struggled to strengthen itself. On 23 August the Chamber of Deputies of the Congress met in the National Palace, one of the few buildings still standing in the heart of the desolate Managua quake zone. Set for debate was the budget, instrumental to Somoza's decision to beef up military spending.

Sandinista columns had conducted a handful of operations in early August, but the Front remained locked in internecine conflict. The FSLN's GPP and Proletario wings remained pledged to their respective strategies of accumulating forces and of building up mass support organizations. Led by the surviving Ortega Saavedra brothers, Daniel and Humberto, and by Edén Pastora, the Terceristas, however, chanced a heroic gamble to accelerate popular revolutionary momentum and to regain the military initiative from the regime—an attack on the National Palace.[10] Humberto Ortega recalled the Terceristas' reasoning:

> We knew that the mass movement was developing, and preferred that it come rather than not come [an oblique reference to the GPP's accumulation of forces strategy]. The important thing was to block an imperialist [U.S.] maneuver planned for August, a coup d'etat to install a civil-military junta that would undercut the revolutionary struggle. . . . We knew that because we lacked a great partisan organization and because we didn't have the working classes organized in a block, the only way to establish a political presence was with arms. . . . Thus it was a military action, but it obeyed the necessities of the political, rather than military, situation.[11]

The enormous risks could be repaid many times over should what they dubbed "Operation Pigsty" (Operación Chanchera) succeed.

On 23 August 1978, twenty-five Sandinistas armed and disguised as an EEBI patrol boarded a truck painted military green and at 12:30 P.M. drove boldly up to the National Palace. Feigning President Somoza's arrival with shouts of "Make way, the Chief is coming!" Edén Pastora (Comandante Cero) led his troops to the entrances, calmly relieved the police guards one by one, then entered the building. An identical ploy worked several times at interior guard posts, but finally one Guard captain awoke to the deception. Shots fired by the captain brought a burst of return fire from the Sandinistas that left him dead and signaled the guerrillas at the street doors to secure the entrances. Pastora's squad then entered the Blue Room of the Chamber of Deputies to find sixty-two deputies staring at him in astonishment. Fearing recognition, he shouted, "This is the Guard. Everybody on the ground!" All complied instantly except the president of the Congress and Luis Pallais Debayle, Somoza's first cousin, who was speaking to the president himself by phone. At this instant two other squads led by Hugo Torres Jiménez (Uno) and Dora María Téllez (Dos) entered the Blue Room by other doors. Both at first saw only an empty room and feared the operation had somehow failed, but then they realized that the missing deputies were merely meekly prostrate in the belief that the operation was a National Guard coup. An assault from outside by an alerted passing Guard patrol was repulsed with a few shots and a grenade. The building and occupants had been completely secured with minimal resistance and loss of life—within the planned three minutes.

The more than two thousand terrified hostages included most members of the Chamber of Deputies, twenty journalists, several high ministerial and judicial officials, hundreds of public employees, and hundreds of citizens there on business. Some employees and civilian hostages escaped, but a majority remained throughout the two-and-a-half-day ordeal. Dora María Téllez conducted all the negotiations with Somoza by phone. She secured the Roman Catholic bishops as mediators and gained various critical concessions, including the withdrawal of troops from nearby. Over the next two days, Téllez won a cessation of Guard helicopter and sniper attacks on the palace, publication of a manifesto calling for popular insurrection, the release of key Sandinistas from prison, $500,000 in ransom, and safe passage out of the country of the assault team, a handful of key hostages, the sixty freed prisoners (including Tomás Borge), and the guerrillas. The presence of the hostage reporters, who were permitted telephone contact with their media, gave Nicaragua and the world a window on the drama. The 25 August convoy of the assault team and hostages to the airport became a triumphal procession as thousands cheered the successful raiders.

The September Insurrection

Electrified by the National Palace incident, Nicaragua exploded in a paroxysm of anti-Somoza activity.[12] The Terceristas had gambled and won; they had realized their major objectives. First, they forestalled a Guard coup against Somoza, who arrested eighty-five members of the Guard for plotting against him in late August. Second, they caused overt popular resistance to the regime to balloon to a degree that stunned even the FSLN. Both spontaneous and organized acts of popular rebellion snowballed, building into the September mass insurrection. To illustrate, on 28 August a spontaneous anti-Guard uprising occurred in Matagalpa. This revolt involved mainly poor people, youths, and women, who held off the Guard for three days. On 1 September, however, the National Guard overran the city with a thousand troops; casualties topped two hundred and fifty, including some fifty dead. Similar violence also flared in Jinotepe, and smaller incidents occurred elsewhere. Employees of the Somoza family airline, LANICA, as well as construction workers, walked off their jobs in late August, joining health workers, who had already been on strike for four weeks.

To take advantage of the public's anger, the Terceristas and the FAO coordinated two major actions: First, the FAO called a general strike for 28 August. Thirty-four of thirty-six national business and industrial chambers endorsed the strike, which the Ministry of Labor promptly declared illegal. The pro-Sandinista MPU coalition first appeared in early September and endorsed the strike. Because the general strike closed down some 75 percent of business in Managua and other cities, national government revenues eroded quickly. To counter the lost revenue — needed to buy arms — the Congress passed a new business tax. The Nicaraguan Development Institute (INDE) and the National Chamber of Commerce then urged their members not to pay the new levy. The government reacted to this rapidly increasing opposition by arresting hundreds of spokesmen of participating groups, including leaders of the FAO, PLI, INDE, UDEL, and several unions.

The second action was national armed insurrection, quickly coordinated among all three FSLN tendencies. The spontaneous Matagalpa and Jinotepe rebellions of late August showed the Front that it could count on considerable mass support. The regime's handling of the Matagalpa uprising also revealed the need for simultaneous multiple attacks in order to prevent the Guard from concentrating its firepower at any single location. On 9 September 1978, columns of Sandinistas attacked and overran National Guard stations in León, Managua, Masaya, Estelí, Chinandega, and Chichigalpa. In each case, small numbers of guerrillas led previously organized local supporters and volunteers, who together captured and held a certain amount of territory in each city. For example, in León, the FSLN overran most of the city with the aid of mostly youthful volunteers armed with weapons supplied by residents.

Somoza immediately declared martial law in several cities, then extended it nationwide and imposed military censorship of the press. This prompted the church to threaten to excommunicate the entire National Guard if it acted as it had during the 1974–1977 state of siege. The war and the general strike caused shortages of vital commodities, especially food. The strike itself continued until late September. Fighting in several cities damaged or destroyed many businesses and factories. Cotton plantings were abandoned. Those who could spirited their wealth and business capital out of Nicaragua, causing the córdoba to drop from the official rate of seven to the dollar to a black-market rate of ten to the dollar. Urban refugees began streaming from their smashed neighborhoods to urban and rural camps and into Costa Rica and Honduras.

The National Guard, protected from public scrutiny by the press blackout, followed the strategy of retaking one city at a time. In each instance, the Guard would concentrate a large portion of its forces at the target town or barrio. It would then surround the target zone and cut off utilities and all traffic in order to curtail the insurgents' ability to withstand a siege. Next came anywhere from hours to days of artillery shelling and aerial strafing and bombing, with both explosives and incendiaries. This shelling and bombing usually came with no warning to the civilians within the target zone and thus injured or killed many more bystanders than guerrillas. Then the Guard would launch its ground assault to retake the rebel area. In each case the FSLN and much of its militia eventually abandoned the resistance and withdrew, escaping via their support networks. The Sandinistas claimed to have lost very few troops in the September uprisings. Civilian casualties, however, were very high: More than a hundred died in the retaking of León on 15 September; more than three hundred died in Masaya; the recapture of Estelí during the final week of September left four to five hundred dead. Overall, the suppression of the September insurrection cost from fifteen hundred to two thousand lives.

During the insurrection the Guard had (despite its misleading casualty figures) suffered heavy losses that gravely undermined its morale and discipline. During the October "mopping up" operation, atrocities by National Guard troops—random murders, rapes, destruction of property, looting, and brutality toward any opposition suspect—reached epidemic proportions. No type of person or institution escaped as the Guard ran amok—it searched and vandalized schools, hospitals, health centers, and churches; it attacked people of all ages and both sexes. The Guard executed many scores of preteenagers and repeatedly attacked Red Cross ambulances and their crews.

Despite the domestic press censorship, the international news media, eyewitnesses, refugees, and religious institutions soon spread the horrible tale of September and October. The violence of Somoza's response to the insurrection prompted a steadily growing international reaction. Early September brought new Venezuelan calls for an Inter-American Commission on Human Rights visit to Nicaragua. The OAS accepted this proposal and asked Nicaragua for permission for the inspection. Hot pursuit of FSLN columns into Costa Rica and border fighting repeatedly involved the National Guard in violations of Costa Rican territory. Costa Rica consistently denied that the FSLN used its territory, denounced Nicaraguan aggression, and sought protection from the OAS and individual nations. On 15 September Venezuela signed a defense pact with Costa Rica; then both Venezuela and Panama lent the Costa Rican Civil Guard some sophisticated weaponry to help deter the Nicaraguans from further border transgressions.

Venezuela called for OAS mediation of the Nicaraguan conflict, a motion supported by the United States. Later in September, after heavy but fruitless U.S. pressure upon Somoza to accept mediation, President Carter sent U.S. naval cruisers to patrol near Nicaragua, and the Senate struck $8 million in economic assistance for Nicaragua from the 1979 budget. (Previously appropriated U.S. assistance continued, however.) The mounting pressure upon Somoza to introduce reforms and to accept international mediation of the bloody conflict finally paid off in late September, after the Guard had contained the rebellion. Somoza accepted the IACHR inspection and released 350 political prisoners. He also agreed to OAS mediation by the United States, Guatemala, and the Dominican Republic—after rejecting participation by Colombia and Mexico.

International Mediation

Both parties to the conflict and the mediators had vastly divergent objectives. Some of the opposition sought anti-Somoza reform, others desired a full-blown social revolution. Somoza himself sought only to buy time to regroup his forces and thus to remain in power. The mediators themselves were hardly neutral; they sought Somoza's ouster and mild reforms but opposed revolutionary changes in Nicaragua. These differences doomed the negotiations from the start because Anastasio Somoza's goals could not be reconciled with those of either the mediators or the opposition.[13]

The OAS mediation team commenced its efforts in early October 1978. The FAO and FSLN had agreed in early October on two absolutely nonnegotiable conditions for any settlement: (1) no direct negotiations with the regime or Somoza and (2) Somoza's resignation and exile from Nicaragua. They also demanded the end of martial law and press censorship. To pave the way for the negotiations, Somoza reduced certain censorship restrictions, permitting *La Prensa* to resume publication, eased curfews and the use of military courts, and agreed to talk only through the mediators. These concessions from the regime prompted the FAO to agree to begin the talks.

The initial negotiating positions of each party were the following: The FAO's nonnegotiable demand was for Anastasio Somoza Debayle's resignation and the departure of the dictator and his entire family from Nicaragua. Other FAO demands included a three-year interim government under a three-person FAO junta, new elections in 1981, an advisory council of state (to include Somoza's Liberal party), and a new constitution to be drafted by popularly elected representatives. Somoza, speaking through the PLN, demanded that he be allowed to finish his term of office (until 1981), that direct FAO-PLN negotiations be held without prior conditions, that the extant constitution be retained, and that regular 1981 national elections be held under OAS observation. The OAS mediators proposed that Somoza resign and cede power to a junta that would include both the PLN and the National Guard; Congress would elect Somoza's successor. The critical differences among these proposals involved the resignation and departure of Somoza and the role of the PLN and of the National Guard in the new government.

By mid-October 1978 the negotiations began to break down. The FSLN objected to the foreign mediators, especially the United States. On 26 October, the FSLN-linked Group of Twelve quit the FAO to protest U.S. advocacy of interim junta slots for the Liberal Nationalists and the National Guard. Then in early November the FSLN signaled its complete repudiation of the mediation by resuming the armed struggle. The CTN, a major labor confederation, also quit the FAO to protest concessions to the regime. While the opposition coalition fragmented, the regime's stance hardened. In early November the PLN categorically rejected Somoza's resignation or exile as a violation of both Nicaragua's constitution and the Somoza family's human rights. The regime's newfound concern for human rights must have elicited great sympathy for the Somozas from many of their victims.

Anastasio Somoza's refusal to resign stalled the mediation completely in mid-November. Seeking to break the logjam, the mediators proposed a foreign-supervised plebiscite on whether Somoza should finish his presidential term, but the regime rejected any such election. Having found no formula by which Somoza might relinquish power, the FAO broke off negotiations on 21 November 1978. About this time the FSLN, its strength now near twenty-five hundred and on the road to reunification, renewed its military offensive. The resumption of combat spurred the mediators to press for concessions that might salvage the talks. Somoza capitulated on certain human rights issues; he proposed a general amnesty for Sandinistas who would lay down their arms and the release of all political prisoners. In exchange, however, he demanded face-to-face talks with the FAO, a provision counter to that group's internal agreements. On 10 December, the FAO's leaders bowed before international pressure and accepted direct talks. This, however, drove yet another wedge into the FAO. One critic later declared that this decision rendered the Broad Opposition Front "neither a front, nor broad, nor opposed to imperialism."[14] The FAO then suffered more defections, which further discredited its role as the leading opposition representative. The FAO-regime negotiations collapsed in late December and could not be revived, despite efforts in January 1979 by the United States.

In late 1978, both regime and insurgents prepared to resume combat. The FSLN's new awareness of its potential for victory had promoted progress toward reunification. The FSLN also began to build coalitions that might supplant the degenerating FAO and rally lower- and middle-class support. The Front had also embarked on a major buildup to prepare for another, bigger offensive.

The regime, too, was building its strength. Anastasio Somoza Debayle regarded the end of the September insurrection as a great triumph for the regime: "We had won a military victory and an economic victory, because the second business strike failed."[15] Fighting for survival, Somoza recruited heavily to build the National Guard up to a strength of fourteen thousand. The EEBI rushed thousands of new recruits through basic infantry training and a brutalizing ideological indoctrination; it treated the often reluctant troops more as prisoners than as soldiers. Somoza made huge arms purchases in late 1978, especially from Israel and Argentina, financed by foreign loans for development projects.

Despite such support the international environment in general became less friendly toward the dynasty in late 1978.[16] The November publication of the IACHR's report on the situation of human rights in Nicaragua stunned world opinion. Seeking to mollify other Latin American leaders, Somoza sent secret envoys throughout the region to plead his cause. The ploy proved largely unsuccessful. Soon afterward, the United States vetoed a $20 million International Monetary Fund loan to Nicaragua, announced that it favored Somoza Debayle's resignation, and strongly criticized the regime's human rights records. Following yet another border incident, Costa Rica on 21 November 1978 became the first nation to sever diplomatic ties with Nicaragua. In late December Somoza threatened to invade Costa Rica to wipe out the Sandinistas, prompting a 31 December OAS warning to Nicaragua not to threaten other member states. In one week in mid-December, both a UN special commission and the General Assembly itself censured Nicaragua for its human rights violations by nearly unanimous votes.

While the fate of Nicaragua's government became an international political football, the country's economy crumbled.[17] Capital flight, tumbling export revenues due to the strikes' impact on cotton and coffee production, and the havoc caused by combat did massive economic damage. Economic growth for 1978 was nil, down from a two-decade average of 5.5 percent per annum. The overall economic loss for 1978 was estimated at more than $60 million. Inflation reached 18 percent. Shortages of many items became critical, contributing to panic buying, hoarding speculation, and looting. Medicine became scarce because of the shortage of hard currency. In sum, many Nicaraguans went without sufficient food, and health conditions were deplorable. Although some two thousand died in the September insurrection, seven times as many Nicaraguans (mainly children) died in the following gastroenteritis epidemic. The bombing of Masaya, Matagalpa, Estelí, Jinotepe, León, and Diriamba left thousands homeless. To the still unrepaired earthquake damage of 1972, then, the fighting of 1978 added the devastation of war.

The Gathering Storm (January–May 1979)

Major reformist, upper-class economic interests had largely dominated the opposition political struggle of 1977–1978 through the UDEL and the FAO. The consolidation of these bourgeois forces with groups representing other social classes badly sapped the regime's backing, material resources, and morale. This early preeminence of upper-class interests had occurred partly because of support by international actors who preferred reform to revolution in Nicaragua and partly because the radical forces remained divided during much of this period. But in August–September 1978, popular repudiation of the dynasty boiled over into spontaneous rebellion. This convinced revolutionary opponents to collaborate in order to rally working- and middle-class opposition behind the FSLN. However, despite immense strides toward realigning the opposition, the radical forces' consolidation remained incomplete as the new year began. The first five months of 1979 brought continued realignments that favored the rapidly strengthening revolutionaries at the expense of the reformists, while the regime itself steadily decayed.

The Decline of the Regime

The dynasty's political deterioration accelerated from January on.[18] Supporters of the regime began to emigrate to safety, especially to the United States, Guatemala, Honduras, and Costa Rica. January's steady outflow of dependents and exportable wealth became a torrent of panicked Somocistas by May. Top officials developed a siege mentality, their morale plummeted, and corruption spiraled. Many officials sent their families off to Costa Rica in Nicaraguan government Mercedes Benzes, mobile baubles that alone made a comfortable grubstake.

The Liberal Nationalist majority in Congress supplied the government with the legislation it needed to conduct the war, especially in fiscal matters. Meanwhile, the increasingly critical congressional Conservatives underwent a protracted leadership crisis while temporizing over precisely what role to play in the government. On 5 April 1979, Congress named a triumvirate of Liberals to replace Somoza Debayle in case of his resignation, a sure sign of growing pessimism. Congress also passed a resolution imploring God "to find a quick, peaceful, civil, and constructive solution" to the national crisis so that "all Nicaraguans might live in a climate of true peace and brotherhood,"[19] perhaps at last recognizing that the Somozas, the PLN, and the National Guard were unlikely to provide such a solution. When FSLN military activity reached unprecedented intensity in May 1979, most remaining members of the Congress and other key regime officials moved into the luxurious Hotel Intercontinental on the flank of Managua's Tiscapa volcano. Located adjacent to the EEBI and Somoza's fortified headquarters (known as "the Bunker"), the Intercontinental became the seat of government because most other locations had become unsafe for the regime.

The president's emotional state reflected progressively greater tension and insecurity during the early months of 1979. Anastasio Somoza Debayle's public statements ranged from bravado and bluster about winning "by blood and fire" to threats and imprecations against his internal and external enemies, both real and imagined. Somoza repeatedly claimed that a majority of Nicaraguans supported him loyally and that communists and Jesuits were seeking to drive him from office. Although he appeared increasingly strained and tired, the cornered dictator kept to his postcoronary diet and exercise program and remained in good health.

Economic chaos accompanied the progressive political malaise of the regime. Tax revenue had nearly collapsed because of the decline in economic activity arising from the general strikes and the war and because of the entrepreneurial tax-evasion movement. Public expenditures had become completely subservient to the growing cost of the war. The regime increasingly diverted loans from both private banks and international public agencies to purchase arms and munitions. Congress raided the budgets of other public agencies and programs in order to finance the rapid 1979 buildup of the National Guard.

In March 1979 the Central Bank defaulted on interest payments of $65 million to international private banks, adding to the $23 million interest payment already missed in December 1978. The regime's pleas for help to the International Monetary Fund brought an IMF investigation team to

Managua to assess the fiscal viability of the regime. In late April the IMF announced that the Nicaraguan government would have to reduce drastically its military expenditures in order to receive from the IMF the nearly $270 million necessary to reorganize the outstanding debt. No such policy change could be made by this desperate government, which could survive, if at all, only by force of arms.

On 8 March 1979 the Central Bank devalued the córdoba by 43 percent from seven to ten per U.S. dollar, and simultaneously suspended free conversion to dollars in order to stem the outrush of foreign reserves needed for the purchase of arms. A storm of opposition protest ensued because devaluation immediately boosted the price of most basic consumer goods. Price increases permitted for many basic commodities were well above the 25 percent boost later decreed in the minimum wage. Commodity hoarding and speculation increased, making periodic shortages of foodstuffs and fuel the daily fare of most Nicaraguans.

The regime's diplomatic isolation grew steadily in early 1979. The year began with the OAS mediation team's unsuccessful last-ditch effort to restart the talks; the effort ended in mid-January. Despite strenuous efforts by the "Somoza lobby" in the United States, both the U.S. Congress and the administration had now clearly decided to abandon the struggling dictator. In February, the United States withdrew its military attachés, Peace Corps volunteers, and some diplomats and suspended the delivery of appropriated but undelivered 1978 aid. In April, Great Britain recalled its ambassador to Nicaragua, an event credited to successful lobbying in London by the Group of Twelve. The OAS Council repeatedly admonished Nicaragua and its Central American neighbors to preserve regional peace. This OAS pressure frustrated Somoza's efforts to win major military intervention by Guatemala, Honduras, or El Salvador, whose military presidents he visited several times each in early 1979.

Escalating fighting between the National Guard and the FSLN in May brought numerous new incidents of indiscriminate regime terror and military brutality. With a broadside denunciation of such conduct, Mexico severed diplomatic relations with Nicaragua on 20 May 1979. During the following week the OAS Council in Washington called for Anastasio Somoza's resignation, and Brazil, Ecuador, Grenada, and Panama all suspended relations with Nicaragua. In late May the United States withdrew its remaining nonessential diplomatic personnel, and the Department of State opined that only Somoza's resignation and departure could end the Nicaraguan conflict. Also in late May, presidents of the Andean Group nations met to analyze the Nicaraguan crisis and described it as threatening the peace of the Americas.

The military performance of the Somoza regime in early 1979 revealed a decline in National Guard morale and capability, despite the massive effort made to strengthen the army. Growing Guard casualties in combat with the ever more numerous and better-armed FSLN, plus periodic Sandinista assassination of Guard officials involved in torturing rebel prisoners, sapped Guard morale. The desertion rate grew steadily from January to May; some former Guard officers even joined the FSLN and others conducted antiregime propaganda via Radio Sandino. Unable to keep its ranks full with Nicaraguans, the Guard turned increasingly to mercenaries. Now fully at war with the Nicaraguan people, the National Guard used its destructive capacity with a willful disregard for civilian life. Barbarity against ordinary citizens became so commonplace as to suggest a substantial breakdown of discipline. The FAN regularly bombed (even with incendiaries) civilian neighborhoods and rural villages suspected of sympathy for the FSLN or of harboring guerrillas. The Guard repeatedly violated the borders and airspace of Honduras and Costa Rica while pursuing fleeing guerrillas, striking at FSLN bases, and interdicting enemy supply routes.

The Growing Rebellion

The first months of 1979 saw the growth of the pro-FSLN MPU coalition, the formation of the pro-FSLN FPN broad front, and the definitive reunification of the FSLN itself. The revolutionaries coordinated escalating Sandinista harassment of the Guard with increased civil disobedience by the member organizations of the MPU, FPN, and FAO.[20]

In mid-April, the reunited FSLN launched an offensive in the North and West. A Sandinista force of two hundred and fifty captured Estelí on 9 April 1979, and with strong popular backing, held the small city for five days. The Guard moved several major units to Estelí while bombing and shelling rebel positions—and much of the city—to ashes. As the Guard mounted its ground assault, the FSLN force in Estelí decided to retreat rather than risk annihilation by the vastly stronger Guard force. Despite the army's cordon around the city, most of the guerrillas escaped. The Estelí uprising took about a thousand lives, more than 80 percent of them civilians, a grisly pattern that was to repeat itself many times in the coming months.

On 1 May 1979, an opposition demonstration turned out some twenty-five thousand protesters. As he had a year earlier, Somoza arrested the May Day organizers, including Alfonso Robelo of the MDN, Rafael Córdoba Rivas of the UDEL, and some forty labor leaders. The National Guard fired upon an FPN rally, killing three demonstrators. May also brought a series of rebel uprisings in León, Matagalpa, Nueva Guinea, and suburban Managua. The combat in May, although severe, was less intense than that of September 1978 and involved less loss of life. Although the National Guard was at its greatest numerical strength ever (fourteen thousand), it now consisted largely of new, hastily trained draftees. The Guard had strained itself sorely to recapture the rebel-held towns one at a time during April and May. Badly in need of rest, reinforcements, and munitions, Guard officers and troops must have heard with dismay the FSLN's announcement on 30 May 1979 of a "final military offensive" and Radio Sandino's call for mass civilian support.

This announcement was dramatic evidence of the new political strength of the FSLN-led opposition. The FAO, MPU, and FPN jointly called another general strike. In San José, Costa Rica, the FSLN and other opposition forces now worked on a postwar reconstruction program, sparking rumors that the revolutionaries would soon name their government.

In sum, from their 1978 standing as only one among many opposition sectors—and divided at that—by May 1979 the Sandinistas had pulled themselves together, seized the political initiative from the reformists, forged a strong lower- and middle-class organizational network, hammered together a broad front movement that backed the FSLN, and greatly increased their military power.

The Final Offensive (June–July 1979)

The announcement of the final FSLN offensive and the call to mass insurrection signaled the beginning of a coordinated nationwide escalation of combat against the regime.[21] From three fronts—the north central (Carlos Fonseca), western (Rigoberto López), and northeastern (Pablo Ubeda)—the Front struggled to capture and secure the North for the rebels. In little more than a week the FSLN easily controlled the northern third of the country, including the cities of Estelí, Jinotega, Matagalpa, and Chinandega (see Figure 8.1). Popular participation in combat alongside the FSLN troops was notable, as it was to be in much of the coming struggle. Fighting also escalated in Managua's suburbs and in the Atlantic Zone. In the south, the FSLN's Benjamín Zeledón front, commanded by Edén Pastora, launched a major attack northward from Costa Rica. In what was the toughest fight of the final offensive, the FSLN forces on the southern front battled the National Guard in a largely conventional war. The armies struggled back and forth over the territory between Rivas and the Costa Rican border for more than a month.

Anastasio Somoza Debayle, his son, Anastasio Somoza Portocarrero, and General José Somoza fought desperately for survival. The National

The Insurrection of 1977–1979

Figure 8.1: FSLN controlled zones and lines of attack, June 1979.

Guard's troops proved insufficient, so that in early June the president called for former Guard members to reenlist. Heavy casualties and desertions forced Somoza Debayle to call up reserves and to ask for a thousand volunteers in late June. Neither effort sufficed, for on 7 July the president ordered all reservists to report for active duty because troop strength had dropped to only ten thousand. Few answered these calls.

The regime's military strategy was simple. Early in June the Guard conceded control of the hostile North to the FSLN and consolidated its forces elsewhere. Thereafter, the Guard fought on three main fronts — to hold back the southward push by the FSLN's northern forces, to block Pastora's army in the south, and to recapture several Managua suburbs. The Guard had three main tactical advantages: numbers of regular troops, superior mobility (ground and air), and air support. The Guard suffered, however, from deteriorating morale and discipline, high casualties and desertions, the hatred of the populace, some reduction of munitions due to diplomatic pressure, and harassment behind its lines by the FSLN's underground.

In contrast, the FSLN enjoyed the advantages of high morale, excellent discipline, great popular support and cooperation, secure bases in Costa Rica and in the Nicaraguan North, little opposition behind its own lines, and a growing flow of arms and volunteers. The Front's disadvantages—insufficient equipment and arms, numerical inferiority, lack of air support, and low tactical mobility—tended to diminish in importance almost daily as the FSLN deployed antiaircraft weapons in the southern front, captured Guard weapons and transport vehicles, and inflicted heavy casualties on the Guard. Although the National Guard always remained numerically superior to the Sandinista regulars, it dropped from a rough 2.5:1 advantage in early June to an edge of 1.8:1 or less by early July. The FSLN's numerical disadvantage was greatly offset by its massive popular support in organization, logistics, and combat. In almost every battle in a populated center, the Front found its numbers multiplied severalfold by volunteers.

The battle in the South was brutal and long because the Guard made its major stand there. Despite reinforcement by the Colombian Socialist Workers party's Simón Bolívar Brigade and a contingent of Panamanian volunteers, the Front suffered a major reverse. The Sandinistas hoped quickly to capture the key town of Rivas, where they would install their rival government. The FSLN combined guerrilla infiltration behind the Guard lines with an attack from the southeast to overrun half of Rivas on 20 June. Meanwhile, Pastora's push from the border area broke through Guard lines at Ostallío and El Naranjo. But the Guard rallied enough reinforcements to retake Rivas and then to push the FSLN back toward the border three days later. From then on, the FSLN fought bitterly for every yard of territory won in the southern zone. To take and hold Rivas required two more full weeks of bitter combat. Once retaken in early July, however, Rivas and its southern hinterland gave the FSLN a transport center, clear supply lines southward, and relatively easy terrain for the northward push.

On the northern front a Sandinista column struck southeast from Chinandega; it reached León and dug in in part of the city on 19 June. But Guard resistance was so determined that the Front spent two more weeks pushing the enemy out of León. Meanwhile, another FSLN column fought its way south toward Managua from the Matagalpa area.

The central (Camilo Ortega) front involved two major struggles—for Managua's suburbs and for Masaya. The FSLN overran Masaya on 25 June. Despite repeated National Guard counterattacks after heavy incendiary bombing of Masaya, the Front held firm. In early July, the rebels installed a provisional revolutionary municipal government in Masaya, in a ceremony attended by Moisés Hassán, representing the rebel Governing Junta of National Reconstruction. As a rebel stronghold, Masaya served as the staging base for the battle of Managua. The FSLN had dug in in large numbers in several Managua neighborhoods in early June, not to be budged by Guard ground attacks. This prompted a systematic FAN air war against these positions—often in the poor residential neighborhoods throughout the city's eastern industrial strip along the Inter-American Highway. This bombing caused massive casualties—some nine thousand dead in Managua alone by mid-June—and demolished much lower-class housing and dozens of factories. By 29 June the Front could no longer hold its Managua positions and thus retreated southeastward to Masaya.

In early July, then, the National Guard (now less than ten thousand strong) had routed the FSLN from Managua and controlled the capital, but the FSLN held firm in Masaya and its hinterland. The North, now including León, was under Sandinista control, as was Rivas. Thus, by 5 July the military advantage had shifted to the Sandinistas. The Front held some 80 percent of the national territory, including twenty-three major towns and cities. As the FSLN commenced its final campaign to capture Managua, the cornered Guard began coming apart one unit at a time through desertion; principal officers fled the country to escape the expected rebel retribution. (Indeed, during early 1979, and especially in June, FSLN units had captured and executed various regime and Guard figures, including Cornelio Hüeck, and called for the execution of numerous others.) By 13 July the Front securely controlled all the major roads to Managua, cutting off the National Guard from outside help except by air. At this juncture the Front suspended the offensive, expecting Somoza's imminent surrender. All that remained between the rebels and victory were the frantic negotiations under way between Anastasio Somoza Debayle, the rebel junta, and the United States.

Politics and Diplomacy

The opposition political strategy for the final offensive had three facets—armed insurrection, a general strike, and coordinated civil disturbances and demonstrations.[22] Somoza responded to this campaign by fighting back savagely and by refusing to quit (well into mid-June). The dictator's resolve still showed in his attempts to call up Guard reserves, the FAN's destruction of *La Prensa*'s printing plant, and the fierce military resistance to the rebels.

On 20 June a National Guard unit had wantonly murdered ABC television correspondent Bill Stewart before his own camera crew. This event stunned the world and stripped away most of the remaining international

Figure 8.2. FSLN squad at the end of the insurrection shows FSLN regulars (well armed and uniformed, in center) and volunteers. Note the extreme youth of all. (Photo by John E. Newhagen)

support for the Somoza regime. Panic among Somocistas followed, as hundreds of remaining regime officials and collaborators crowded Las Mercedes airport in a rush to leave. This final demoralization of the bankrupt regime appears to have persuaded Somoza to give up. On 30 June 1979 he announced his conditions for resignation: preservation of the Liberal Nationalist party and the National Guard. On 6 July Somoza declared that his resignation awaited only the order of the United States. Somoza placed his resignation in the United States's hands to give the Carter administration a trump card with which to wrest concessions from the rebels.

Meanwhile, from the Costa Rican capital the revolutionaries announced on 10 June 1979 the existence of the Governing Junta of National Reconstruction, its membership still secret. The junta began planning to assume power, to organize a government, to establish new public policy. On 9 July a rebel spokesman announced that the junta was negotiating with the United States concerning Somoza's resignation. Two days later, the junta publicly announced its membership, program, and

Figure 8.3. Barrio Monimbó in Masaya after National Guard FAN bombing in 1978 and 1979. (Photo by John E. Newhagen)

tentative cabinet. Members of the new governing Junta were Sergio Ramírez Mercado, U.S.-educated novelist and intellectual and member of the Group of Twelve; Moisés Hassán, leader of the MPU and a U.S.-trained scientist; Violeta Barrios, widow of Pedro Joaquín Chamorro; entrepreneur Alfonso Robelo Callejas, head of the MDN and a key private-sector leader; and Daniel Ortega Saavedra, veteran Sandinista (Tercerista) commander. The junta also announced outlines of its proposed policies and reforms.

Conducting the junta's frenetic foreign policy and international relations was Miguel d'Escoto Brockman, a Maryknoll priest. The rebels and the junta sought further to isolate the Somoza government. In early June they successfully lobbied the OAS to block Somoza's attempted invocation of the provisions of the Inter-American Reciprocal Assistance Treaty concerning military aid. By 18 June, at least fifteen nations had recognized the junta or suspended relations with the Somoza government. During the third week in June, the United States proposed that the OAS send a multilateral peacekeeping force to Nicaragua to end the crisis, an initiative blocked definitively on 22 June—once again by successful FSLN lobbying in the OAS. The junta's sense of its growing international support and military potential rapidly bolstered rebel confidence. To U.S. proposals in late June for a cease-fire and a government

Figure 8.4. Sandinista in action. Slogan reads: "Workers and peasants forward in the war for the victorious insurrection (FSLN Proletarios)." (Photo by John E. Newhagen)

of reconciliation of "all democratic sectors" – i.e., including the National Guard and PLN but excluding the FSLN – the junta responded with an unconditional rejection. The rebels' refusal to compromise with the United States regarding the structure of the junta became the hallmark of their policy during the last three weeks of the war. The junta viewed victory as both inevitable and imminent and therefore refused to include two major pillars of Somocismo in the new regime merely to shorten the war by a few days.

The confrontation between the rebel government's steadfast realism and the U.S. government's hopeless diplomatic pressures to shape the new regime prolonged the war for some two weeks.[23] Ironically, the United States had, by cutting its support for the Somoza regime and by reducing its economic and military aid from abroad, weakened the government so that its demise was inevitable. Yet now the Carter administration sought to force rebel concessions by forestalling the regime's final collapse. This threat was hollow, as the government and its armed forces were by then clearly crumbling. U.S. emissary William Bowdler conducted the negotiations with the junta in San José. He first proposed an interim government by a "committee of notables" that would include Somocistas and exclude the FSLN. The rebel junta rejected this proposal, too, labeling it "Somocismo without Somoza."

On 7 July, however, the United States gave in on the major point of FSLN representation in the government. The United States still insisted, however, on including the PLN and the Guard in the new regime. The junta again refused to accept Somocistas in the government. From 7 July until 13 July, Bowdler talked frantically with Ambassador Lawrence Pezzullo in Managua, with the Department of State, and with the junta, seeking some crack in the rebels' refusal to negotiate on the final sticking point. But the military success of the FSLN grew daily, further shrinking the already minuscule disposition of the junta toward compromise. On 15 July the Carter administration at last recognized the worthlessness of its trump card. Somoza's resignation was not a matter of necessity to the revolutionaries; it was merely a matter of convenience. The United States then capitulated and informed Anastasio Somoza Debayle that the end had come without Guard and PLN representation in the government.

Somoza convened the remnants of the Nicaraguan Congress at the Hotel Intercontinental on 16 July and submitted his resignation. The Congress named Dr. Francisco Urcuyo Maliaño as interim president for the transition to the new regime. Somoza later blamed his resignation not on military defeat by the rebels but on the 23 June 1979 OAS resolution calling for his resignation. His recollection of the end has touches of both the bravado and the pervasive unreality that marked his whole regime:

> I wanted all of my people to know that I was not leaving because of fear, I was leaving because I had seventeen nations against me in the OAS and they were demanding my resignation.
>
> In my administration, I had always adhered to the Constitution. In that trying and desperate moment, I refused to bypass the Constitution and ignore the proper protocol. If I were going to resign the presidency, I wanted to do so properly and with class. Those tenets had been my trademark, and in that time of personal frustration, I would not abandon those principles.[24]

Early in the morning of 17 July, the last Somozas—Tachito, El Chigüín, and José—the remnants of the Guard general staff, and the PLN leadership and congressmen hurried to Las Mercedes airport and flew to exile in Miami. The dynasty had ended.

In an astonishing footnote to the collapse of Somocismo, interim president Dr. Urcuyo Maliaño attempted to remain in power.[25] He named a new head of the National Guard, General Federico Mejía González, called on the armed forces to defend the government, and announced that he would complete the remaining two years of Somoza's term of office. Astounded by this unexpected turn of events, the United States demanded Urcuyo's resignation. To signal their displeasure, other states, including Mexico and the Andean Group, recognized the rebel junta and the cabinet (which was preparing to embark from San José). The FSLN immediately resumed its military campaign to capture Managua.

The Urcuyo regime proved ephemeral indeed. The National Guard, its command and ranks decimated, promptly collapsed as the new general staff recommended immediate surrender to President Urcuyo. Thousands of soldiers and junior officers fled across the border to Honduras; thousands more sought refuge in Red Cross camps and at the Managua airport. At Jimmy Carter's insistence, ex-President Somoza telephoned Urcuyo from Miami at 7:00 A.M. on 18 July to tell him to cede power to the rebel junta. Later that day, the United States threatened to sever relations with the Urcuyo government. Thus besieged, Urcuyo at last recognized the hopelessness of his position and gave up. Guatemalan president General Romeo Lucas García granted Urcuyo's plea for transportation out of Nicaragua. Thus the remnants of Nicaragua's last prerevolutionary government and a handful of remaining Guard officers abandoned Managua at 8:00 P.M. on 19 July 1979 aboard three Guatemalan Air Force planes. Francisco Urcuyo Maliaño had been president of Nicaragua for forty-three hours, one hour for every year that a Somoza had ruled Nicaragua.

Later that night, Mexico's presidential jetliner flew the cabinet of the new government to Nicaragua. In Nicaragua's rubble-strewn streets people danced for joy, cheered the victorious Sandinistas, and smashed symbols of the hated dynasty. FSLN columns moved through the capital, took control of the city, confined remaining Guard troops in camps, and sought to establish a semblance of order. On 20 July 1979, members of the junta arrived in Managua from already liberated León to commence rebuilding a Nicaragua laid waste by war.

Epilogue

The new rulers of Nicaragua encountered destruction almost beyond belief[26] — the war had rent the last shreds of the social and economic fabric of the nation. Martial law in June and July had made civilians mere expendable props—if not an outright enemy—in the military crisis confronting the National Guard. The seven-week general strike, reinforced by FSLN intimidation, had paralyzed most of the urban economy. In early June, the war had prompted most airlines to suspend all flights to Nicaragua, and they were slow to resume after the Sandinista triumph. In mid-June, famine had appeared in the cities and towns as the last bits of hoarded food ran out. The starving populace had then sacked every food store and warehouse in Managua for supplies that ran out within days. Fuel supplies too were virtually exhausted. The Nicaraguan Red Cross and international agencies had begun to distribute food in early July. In Managua alone, a hundred thousand a day had lined up for rations; a family of eight received daily one kilogram (2.2 pounds) of rice and a half kilogram each of sugar and milk. Nevertheless, relief workers estimated that six hundred thousand hungry people received no relief at all. Various epidemics had spread as the public water supply became contaminated, health services broke down, and medical supplies ran out. By 19 July, bodies of the thousands of recent dead were decomposing in Managua's streets and in the rubble of houses, spreading contamination and disease to the living.

What was the cost of ridding Nicaragua of Somoza? By 19 July, Nicaraguan refugees in Honduras and Costa Rica numbered some one hundred twenty thousand. Internally, Managua alone had one hundred fifty thousand refugees, living in Red Cross camps, impromptu squatter settlements, and the rubble of earthquake-damaged buildings. At least that many more refugees—the displaced of Estelí, Rivas, León, Chinandega, and other towns and villages by the dozen—could be found outside the capital. FAN bombing of FSLN positions had destroyed huge amounts of residential, commercial,, and industrial property in virtually every important population center. Per capita production had been set back to 1962 levels by the destruction of property worth $470 million. The foreign debt inherited from Somoza was $1.6 billion and the treasury was empty. Officials estimated that some six hundred thousand people had been left homeless or with badly damaged housing at the war's end. Civilian casualties in the insurrection included some three hundred thousand wounded. The fighting of June and July took three to four hundred lives per day—perhaps fifteen thousand overall. The war and related epidemics between 1977 and 1979, it is estimated, killed between forty and fifty thousand Nicaraguans.

The rebellious Nicaraguan people and the red-and-black-scarved Sandinistas had triumphed. Relief from the horror of war and the terror of the dictatorship was so great that, despite their personal losses, most Nicaraguans celebrated, dancing in the ruins of their homes and their cities.

The Beginning: Government in Revolutionary Nicaragua

For the bloodshed which occurs daily and for the bloodshed which surely will follow . . . many tears were shed in Nicaragua, and some of those tears were mine. Now, tears are shed daily for those 8,000 loyal young men of the National Guard who languish in prison.
—Anastasio Somoza Debayle, 1980[1]

When they tried to lynch the [Somocista] prisoners who were in the Red Cross building, I personally went to see the relatives of our martyrs . . . and convinced them not to do it by saying, "So why did we make this revolution, if we are going to do the same things they used to do?"
—Tomás Borge Martínez, 1979[2]

Nicaragua's new government confronted monumental problems from its first moment. The new rulers had clear goals, a fairly elaborate program, and personnel to confront their problems. But they had also attracted worldwide attention and thus struggled not only with Nicaragua's vast needs but with the many conflicting meanings attributed to the revolution by others and with efforts to manipulate and to undermine it. After five years in power, the revolutionary government had made major steps toward institutionalizing itself.

The Goals of the Revolution

By consensus, the revolutionary coalition led by the Sandinistas sought, in the short run, first to assure the destruction of the Somoza regime and its economic power base and to replace the old regime's exploitation of and brutality toward the people with a more humane relationship. Second, the Sandinistas and their allies wished to reconstruct the national economy, which had been left reeling by the war. Third, the government wanted to replace the corruption of the old regime with an ethos of public honesty, frugality, and service to the public.

There was sharp divergence, however, over longer term goals. The leaders of the FSLN sought an eventual transition to socialism in order to reduce class inequality and to improve the standard of living and economic influence of the lower classes. They also sought to establish a direct, participatory form of democracy—increased popular participation in decision making and implementation, protected by expanded human rights. By democracy, however, the Sandinistas did not mean liberal, representative constitutionalism, but a broader and corporatistic participation, under the leadership of the Sandinista vanguard, in political and economic arenas (including the workplace). Electoral democracy would have to await the establishment of national institutions capable of defending the revolution.[3] The FSLN's ultimate goal has been summarized as follows: "to construct an egalitarian collectivist community of selfless men and women," a historical fulfillment of the "true freedom and the material and spiritual conditions which socialism will create."[4]

Other rebel coalition members—moderates, conservatives, social democrats, the Catholic hierarchy, and many people in the private sector—hoped for less drastic reforms and for more political power than the Sandinistas. These groups believed that their influence and ends would be best served if a representative, liberal-constitutional regime were quickly established. The Sandinistas prevailed from the outset, however, prompting an increasingly bitter dispute over goals, institutions, and policy that eventually split the rebel coalition into warring camps.

The Revolutionary Government

The government of revolutionary Nicaragua must be studied both from the perspective of formal structures and from that of the political role of the new system's most powerful political group, the FSLN. The formal government, established by accord within the broader rebel movement prior to Somoza's ouster, and many key personnel in it, represented most of the anti-Somoza economic and political groups. The FSLN, however, not only set overarching policy through its National Directorate but also controlled key ministerial and bureaucratic posts, including the entire security system.

The Governing Junta of National Reconstruction

The Governing Junta of National Reconstruction (JGRN) was the chief executive council of Nicaragua, a collegial presidency that included major leaders from the broader rebel movement. The junta, which legislated by decree until the Council of State was established in 1980, constituted itself and other formal government institutions by its own decree, the Fundamental Statute of the Republic of Nicaragua, on 22 August 1979. This revolutionary charter abolished the previous constitution and constitutional laws and dissolved the former Congress, Supreme Court of Justice, courts of appeals, labor courts, and "remaining structures of Somocista power."[5] The Fundamental Statute provided that the junta be designated "from among the distinct political and socioeconomic sectors of Nicaragua."[6]

The first junta included Sergio Ramírez Mercado of the Group of Twelve; Violeta Barrios de Chamorro, widow of Pedro Joaquín Chamorro and a major stockholder of *La Prensa;* Moisés Hassán Morales of the MPU; Alfonso Robelo Callejas, industrialist, private-sector leader, and head of the MDN; and Comandante Daniel Ortega Saavedra, a member of the FSLN National Directorate. Served by a large staff of technical experts, trained public administrators, and social scientists, the junta elaborated public policy along the lines determined by or with the FSLN Joint National Directorate (Dirección Nacional Conjunto—DN) and executed that policy through the various government ministries. During the first year following the fall of Somoza the junta legislated by unappealable decree under emergency powers.

Despite the diverse political orientations of the junta's members, the body usually made decisions by consensus and without formal votes. Although give and take occurred between the FSLN Directorate and the junta, the DN set the general guidelines for the revolution, and the junta worked out the details for their execution. The link between the DN and the junta was Daniel Ortega, junta chairman since 1981, who met with both and conveyed the FSLN's wishes to the junta. Both Alfonso Robelo and Daniel Ortega portrayed the DN as the highest political authority. In late 1979 Robelo said that "the FSLN Directorate is the head of the revolution. The vanguard." Ortega agreed: The National Directorate of the FSLN "is the highest conducting [leadership] organ of the Revolution. The Government of National Reconstruction reflects the line established by the National Directorate."[7] Violeta Barrios concurred that coordination and cooperation between the two bodies was permanent and at a high level.

Membership in the junta evolved between 1979 and 1981. In early 1980 Violeta Barrios resigned from the body, avowedly for personal reasons, although later comments indicated dissatisfaction with the emerging FSLN policy. Alfonso Robelo also resigned shortly afterward to protest an expansion of the membership of the new Council of

State (Consejo de Estado) to include groups that tipped the balance of power in that body to the Sandinistas. Robelo and Barrios de Chamorro were replaced by Rafael Córdoba Rivas, a rancher and a leader of the Democratic Conservative party (PCD) and UDEL, and by Arturo Cruz Porras, international banker and member of the Group of Twelve. In 1981 the junta was reduced to three members when Arturo Cruz went to Washington as ambassador to the United States and the OAS and Moisés Hassán took a cabinet post. By 1983 Daniel Ortega clearly played the leading role in the junta.

The Cabinet and Bureaucracy

The Nicaraguan government executed policy through ministries (e.g., foreign relations, housing and human settlements, defense) and autonomous agencies (e.g., the Institute of Agrarian Reform, Central Bank).[8] Cabinets included a broad array of anti-Somoza political points of view; many top bureaucrats did not have previous FSLN ties. Cabinet reorganizations through 1984 maintained this pluralism while increasing FSLN influence. Non-Sandinistas occupied the more technical, less political portfolios, but FSLN leaders headed such critical ministries as defense, interior, agrarian reform–agricultural development, and planning. The makeup of the cabinet was remarkably stable after 1981, as the only change was when Fernando Cardenal replaced Carlos Tunnerman Bernheim as minister of education upon the latter's appointment as ambassador to the United States in mid-1984 (see Table 9.1).

Planning played a key role in the reconstruction efforts of the Nicaraguan government. The Ministry of Planning, headed since early 1980 by Henry Ruíz of the FSLN National Directorate, coordinated public-sector plan preparation between its own *técnicos* (experts) and those from the other ministries. Broad discussions of national versus individual ministerial goals occurred in these working sessions and in the meetings of a dozen policy area coordinating committees. Although planning participation by technical experts was extensive, popular influence was at first more limited than the Planning Ministry had hoped, and citizen input has on occasion been at odds with revolutionary policy. Planning caused several ministerial reorganizations to improve agency performance, such as the fusion of the Ministry of Agricultural Development and the National Agrarian Reform Institute (Instituto Nacional de Reforma Agraria—INRA) and the division of the Ministry of Commerce into more specialized Foreign Commerce and Internal Commerce ministries.

The great expansion of the public sector (nationalization of Som-ocistas' properties, foreign commerce, insurance, and banking) re-

Table 9.1
Organization and Officials of the Nicaraguan State, 1984

FSLN Joint National Directorate (DN)

Tomás Borge M.	Humberto Ortega S.	Luís Carrión C.
Daniel Ortega S.	Jaime Wheelock R.	Henry Ruíz
Bayardo Arce C.	Carlos Núñez T.	Victor Tirado L.

Governing Junta of National Reconstruction (JGRN)

Daniel Ortega S.	Sergio Ramírez M.	Rafael Córdova R.

Ministerial Positions

Interior: Tomás Borge M.
Defense: Humberto Ortega S.
Finance: Joaquín Cuadra Ch.
Transport: Carlos Zarruck
Industry: Emilio Baltodano
Labor: Virgilio Godoy
Planning: Henry Ruíz
Construction: Moisés Hassán M.
Internal Commerce: D. Marenco
Foreign Affairs: Miguel D'Escoto B.

JGRN Secretariat: Rodrigo Reyes
Education: Fernando Cardenal
Health: Lea Guido
Agriculture: Jaime Wheelock R.
Culture: Ernesto Cardenal
Housing: Miguel Ernesto Vigil
Justice: Carlos Argüello G.
Foreign Commerce: Alejandro Martínez
Coordinator of Regional Assemblies:
   Mónica Baltodano

Council of State (CE)

President: Carlos Núñez T.   Vice Presidents: Dora M. Téllez,
Secretary: Rafael Solís C.   Domingo Sánchez, Plutarco Anduray

Supreme Electoral Council (CSE)

Leonel Argüello R.	Amanda Pineda	Mariano Fiallos O.
Carlos García C.		José María Icabalceta

Sources: Stephen M. Gorman, "Nicaragua," in Jack Hopkins, ed., Latin American and Caribbean Contemporary Record, Vol. 1 (New York: Holmes and Meier, 1983), Table 1; Barricada Internacional, 9 April 1984, p. 1-4; 14 May 1984, p. 1.

quired considerable public institution building. The junta's own staff—including public administration experts and social scientists in the Department of Government Information and Promotion (Dirección de Información y Gestión Estatal—DIGE), Ministry of Planning officials, and planners from the affected agencies—played key roles in the government's reorganization. Press reports and documents published by Nicaraguan government agencies indicated ongoing evaluation, "self-criticism," and reform in many agencies and policy areas.[9]

The planning process generated as its final product an annual plan setting forth goals, projecting revenues and expenditures, and outlining policies. Economic planning for the private sector, which in 1980 produced 59 percent of gross national product (GNP), was largely "indicative"—it guided the private economy with state–private industry production agreements; regulatory, fiscal, and monetary measures; credit policy; and trade and price controls. Later policies increased control over the private sector.

During its first years in power the JGRN extensively reworked the basic structures, personnel, laws, and procedures of the Nicaraguan state. Of over 600 laws promulgated by the junta in 1979–1980, some 179 created or modified public agencies, established norms for civil servants, created taxes, or regulated the handling of public funds.[10] Many old autonomous agencies became parts of central cabinet ministries, and several new decentralized agencies were created for various purposes (e.g., to operate water and sewer services, produce electricity). Moreover, between 1979 and 1982 many agencies underwent repeated modifications of their laws and administrative procedures. An overall decline in administration-related legislation in 1983–1984, however, revealed that the frenetic reorganization of the national bureaucracy was slowing during the revolution's fourth year.[11]

Such changes affected not just the central government but municipalities as well, as their governing statutes were altered three times in 1979–1980. Moreover, in 1982 a program of administrative decentralization went into effect, partly in an attempt to improve the state's capacity to operate in the event of an invasion. These reforms profoundly altered Nicaraguan government personnel and performance on the local level.[12]

The execution of public policy in Nicaragua remained in many of the same bureaucratic hands as before the revolution. For the first few days after the victory public administration was chaotic. The rebel forces and their new government literally had to locate government offices and find their keys; they discovered that many files and records had been destroyed to hide corruption. The Sandinistas who took over dozens of agencies and Somoza businesses at first had the assistance of only teenage guerrillas-cum-bureaucrats; one reported "making a million mistakes."[13] But the junta called back former lower- and middle-level public employees, and some 90 percent returned to their posts, greatly reducing the administrative disruption of the change in power. Even certain second- and third-echelon Somocistas retained their posts, especially in such ministries as health, construction, and telegraph and post. Those former government employees who were not welcomed back had held politically responsible posts or had been Somoza henchmen. The revolutionaries, however, took over all the key policymaking and supervisory jobs and placed rebel loyalists throughout the government.

The revolutionaries appeared to have partially succeeded in creating a new administrative culture among public employees that stressed productivity, sacrifice, honesty, and a strong public-service orientation. They promoted such values by example, exhortation, office and agency newsletters, staff meetings, and the organization of voluntary study groups, employee associations, and even militia units.

Tensions inevitably developed between old and new public employees, despite determined efforts to foster cooperation and harmony. Furthermore, as the extent of the revolutionary transformation of the Nicaraguan bureaucracy became clear, further tensions arose within many agencies between activist public employees who were politically aligned (*alineados*) with the revolutionary process and others who were less interested in politics and who complained of a politicization of technical processes and a bias that meant that the alineados received preference for promotions over people who were merely technically competent.[14] Administrative corruption still occurred sometimes, but in the words of one informant, corruption was "reduced dramatically and instantaneously" after 19 July 1979.[15] One possible example of such corruption was indicated in a report by the U.S. government in mid-1984 that alleged that certain Sandinista security officials participated in smuggling cocaine to the United States.[16]

The Council of State

The revolutionary government of Nicaragua inaugurated its consultative representative assembly, the Council of State, on 4 May 1980.[17] Its membership had originally been negotiated among the broad revolutionary coalition prior to Somoza's fall, but it was modified in April 1980. The council was originally slated to have thirty-three representatives, with twelve for the FSLN and its closest political allies, but the FSLN Directorate and the junta later added fourteen new delegates, twelve from pro-FSLN groups. Critics, especially the Nicaraguan Democratic Movement, charged that this change was a violation of the fundamental agreement among the insurgents made at Puntarenas and a power grab that gave the FSLN control of twenty-four of the forty-seven council votes. The Sandinistas responded that the newly represented organizations (such as the ATC peasant union and the July 19th Sandinista Youth) had either appeared or grown greatly since the triumph and that to exclude them would be unfair. Alfonso Robelo Callejas, head of the MDN, resigned from the junta to protest this change, but the MDN retained its seat on the Council of State and kept supporters at their posts within the national bureaucracy. Other groups were added to the Council of State by an amendment to the Fundamental Statute in 1981: the Ecumenical Axis (MEC-CELADEC), the Social Christian party, and the National Union of Farmers and Cattlemen (Unión Nacional de Agricultores y Ganaderos—UNAG). The Center for Union Action and Unity (CAUS) received one additional seat (see Table 9.2).

The Council of State's (CE) role was "colegislative"—it shared a consultative and legislative function with the junta. The council provided the major formal channel for the participation in public-policy making by organizations that supported the insurrection. Geographical representation occurred only via the nine regional delegates of the Sandinista Defense Committees. The Council of State served as a "national forum for political and ideological debate . . . an expression of the democratic pluralism of the Sandinist revolutionary process based on a policy of national unity, and a concrete manifestation of popular power, exercised in original form, and guaranteed by the active participation of the mass organizations."[18]

Under the Fundamental Statute, the Council of State had the following powers: to approve or propose reforms to laws submitted to it by the JGRN, to initiate its own legislation, to reform administrative subdivisions (at the initiative of the JGRN), to authorize the functioning of civic and religious entities (i.e., concede full legal status), to write an electoral law and a draft constitution (at the initiative of the JGRN), to ratify treaties and conventions concerning boundaries and maritime limits, to regulate all questions of citizenship and patriotic symbols, and to require information from cabinet ministers and agency heads.[19] Junta-passed decrees submitted to the CE for approval took effect within ten days if not acted upon. If the council made nonbinding recommendations for revisions to a junta draft decree within ten days, the draft returned to the JGRN, which could accept or reject the council's proposals. The junta often accepted CE amendments. Although the junta dominated legislative initiatives in 1980–1981 by introducing the bulk of the legislation considered by the council, by 1983–1984 the CE's own initiatives more than doubled the junta's initiatives in the previous legislature.[20]

The Council of State was not a strong legislature as authority over many administrative matters, budgets, and the extensive emergency powers begun in 1981 resided exclusively with the junta, which also had an absolute veto over CE-initiated legislation. The council, however, was more than a rubber stamp—it frequently influenced junta-initiated legislation, and well over a hundred CE bills had become law by 1984. Three indexes of the CE's policymaking im-

Table 9.2
Membership and Voting Strength in the Council of State, 1981-1984

	Number of seats
Political parties	
* Sandinista National Liberation Front (FSLN)	6
Independent Liberal party (PLI)	1
* Nicaraguan Socialist party (PSN)	1
* People's Social Christian party (PPSC)	1
Nicaraguan Democratic Movement (MDN)	1
Democratic Conservative party (PCD)	1
Nicaraguan Social Christian party (PSCN)	1
Liberal Constitutionalist Movement (MLC)	1 a
Popular organizations	
* Sandinista Defense Committees (CDSs)	9
* July 19th Sandinista Youth (JS-19)	1
* Nicaraguan Women's Association (AMNLAE)	1
Labor organizations	
* Sandinista Workers' Central (CST)	3
* Rural Workers Association (ATC)	2
Independent General Workers' Confederation (CGTI)	2
Nicaraguan Workers Confederation (CTN)	1
Council for Union Unity (CUS)	1
Center for Union Action and Unity (CAUS)	2 a
* Federation of Health Workers (FETSALUD)	1
Guilds and other social organizations	
* Armed Forces	1
National Association of Clergy (ACLEN)	1
* National Council of Higher Education (CNES)	1
* Association of Educators of Nicaragua (ANDEN)	1
* National Journalists Union (UPN)	1
Unity of the Miskitu, Sumu, Rama, and Sandinistas (MISURASATA)	1
* National Confederation of Professional Associations	1
* National Union of Farmers and Cattlemen (UNAG)	2 b
Ecumenical Axis MEC-CELADEC	1 a
Private sector organizations	
Nicaraguan Development Institute (INDE)	1
Nicaraguan Chamber of Industries (CADIN)	1
Confederation of Chambers of Commerce (CCCN)	1
Nicaraguan Chamber of Construction (CNC)	1
Union of Nicaraguan Agricultural Producers (UPANIC)	1
Total representation	51

Sources: Consejo de Estado, Instauración Tercera Legislatura (Managua,
4 May 1982), pp. 8-15; and John A. Booth, The End and the Beginning: The
Nicaraguan Revolution (Boulder, Colo.: Westview Press, 1982), Table 9.1,
p. 188.
*   Normally voted with FSLN.
a   One seat added in 1981.
b   New as of 1981; one of these seats formerly belonged to the ATC.

portance were the length of its sessions (from May through December
of each year, plus extended sessions as in early 1984), the extent and
intensity of delegates' debate of policy matters, and the degree of
opposition influence upon legislation.

    The council's leadership resided in a president and an executive
committee[21] elected by simple majority from among the membership.

The president after 1981, Carlos Núñez Téllez, exercised several important duties, including presiding over plenary sessions, naming the members of working commissions, and directing the CE's staff. Representation on the CE was corporate, not geographical, and open to Nicaraguan citizens eighteen years or older to be designated by the organizations represented (see Table 9.2). The CE was organized into nine standing commissions for initial consideration of proposed laws: Defense and Interior; Justice; External Affairs; Labor and Social Security; Health and Welfare; Education and Culture; Community Services, Urban Reform, and Human Settlements; Production and Agrarian Reform; Finance and Popular Consumption.

Overall the volume of legislation considered by the Council of State declined in each of its second and third sessions. Meanwhile, the proportion of bills introduced at the initiative of the junta declined from about 60 percent in the first legislature to about 25 percent in the third. The subject matter of legislation also evolved in the early years as the second legislature's heavy emphasis on administration shifted more toward political matters in the third and fourth legislatures. Taken together, the declining volume of legislation and the shift away from administrative subject matter suggests that the principal base of the Sandinista revolutionary program had been established by 1984. Moreover, the rising proportion of Council of State legislative initiatives indicates an increasing independence and maturity of this body vis-à-vis the executive.

During its first session in 1980, the council had no formal opposition bench (1) because it included no sector opposed to the ouster of Somoza or to major reforms and (2) because the government's revolutionary goals required national integration and consensus building. In fact, however, an opposition to the FSLN began to take shape in late 1980 and 1981, led by the MDN and including business groups and other small parties. Some of the opposition representatives, including the MDN, boycotted their council seats for certain periods to protest FSLN policies.

By the 1981 session of the council, however, a clear opposition bloc had formed. Styled the Democratic Coordinating Committee (Coordinadora Democrática—CD), it included the Nicaraguan Social Christians (PSCN), Nicaraguan Democratic Movement (MDN), Constitutionalist Liberals (PLC), Social Democrats (Partido Social Demócrata—PSD), five private-sector groups, and two unions—the social Christian CTN and the ORIT-affiliated CUS. Pro-Sandinista forces also organized into a National Patriotic Front (Frente Patriótico Nacional—FPN), which included the FSLN, the People's Social Christians (PPSC), the Independent Liberals (PLI), and the Nicaraguan

Socialists (PSN). As divisions within the council arose, several CD member groups opted not to designate a representative to the Council of State for certain periods, so that some of the potential CD votes (always a minority) could not be cast.

Council debate over many issues—especially the Political Parties Law, Electoral Law, and Draft Law—was often sharp and protracted. Since the CD opposition coalition was consistently a minority, it rarely prevailed on all its points when it directly confronted the FPN or the FSLN and its affiliates. The proregime coalition, however, did not entirely disregard the minority opposition's concerns. When council debate revealed intense CD opposition to a bill's particulars, the FSLN and the FPN often conceded important points to the CD. For instance, 30 percent of the Parties Law approved in 1983 reportedly had been altered by the council because of opposition to the FSLN's draft proposal.[22]

Neither the Council of State's opposition nor the proregime coalition was monolithic. The discussion of the Electoral Law in early 1984, for example, opened fissures in the ranks of both the FPN and the CD over specifics of the bill. The effect of the November 1984 election upon the Council of State's two coalitions may well have been still more corrosive. In addition to acrimony within both coalitions over the date of the elections (late 1984 versus 1985), there was disagreement within the CD about whether to participate in the elections at all. The PLI, moreover, withdrew from the National Patriotic Front to pursue its 1984 campaign independent of the FSLN.[23]

The Courts

The revolutionary government, although zealous to promote its programs without interference, also wished to enhance the capability of the courts and the quality of justice. Revolutionary systems have historically made courts tools of revolutionary public policy, yet in Nicaragua the court system both improved its jurisprudence and became more independent. Because of the widespread corruption in the judiciary, the rebels rebuilt the court system almost from scratch, with jurists chosen for their expected competence and honesty, not necessarily for automatic agreement with the FSLN. These often independent-minded judges have since ruled against the government in various instances. On various occasions, for example, the Ministry of Interior has obeyed habeas corpus rulings to release supposed Somocistas in spite of popular and media clamor against their release. The junta in April 1980 promulgated a national law of *amparo* empowering the courts to order redress of administrative excess or error. With this law, then, the new regime explicitly expanded the judicial review power of the courts. The persistence of economic recovery difficulty into late 1981, however, led to a one-year suspension of amparo in economic emergency matters.[24] The state of emergency declared in 1982 extended the suspension of amparo, and continuation of the war with counterrevolutionary forces into 1984 brought repeated extensions of the suspension until 1984, when amparo was reinstated as part of the preparations for the November presidential and legislative elections.

In another area, however, certain courts exercised far less autonomy from the revolutionary leadership. Special tribunals created to try Somoza henchmen and National Guardsmen for war crimes began to function in December 1979.[25] Highly political in nature, these courts served (1) to educate the Nicaraguan public about the virtues of the revolution, in contrast to the vices of the old regime, and (2) to punish the dynasty's criminals in an orderly manner. The procedures, rules of evidence, and protection of the accused's interests in the special tribunals would probably have offended a U.S. civil liberties advocate. For example, in exploratory interrogations by the three-judge panels, prosecutors questioned the accused for the record without counsel, which was available only for the actual trial. Questions were often highly leading or laden with intense moral and political value judgments to which a defendant's attorney would surely have objected. One of the three judges of each court was an attorney or law school graduate, but the other two were ordinary citizens. Many court officials were victims of the Somoza regime's repression and were hardly likely to be impartial in judging war crimes.

Several factors, however, counteract the impression that the special tribunals were kangaroo trials. First, the press (including international media) had free access to all proceedings, which clearly acted as a restraint on the proceedings. Second, the prisoners manifested no signs of mistreatment and appeared in good health. Prisoners' accusations of mistreatment referred almost exclusively to the relatively brief postvictory interlude before the FSLN had reestablished public order and full discipline over its troops. Third, a public defender represented indigent prisoners. Fourth, the junta decreed that Nicaragua's traditional constitutional bar to the death penalty—previously observed in the breach by the National Guard—would apply even to war criminals and the special tribunals. The maximum combined sentence possible for all crimes (genocide plus delinquent association) was thirty-four years. The law applied was not written ex post facto but was the previously extant penal code. Finally, of some 4,550 defendants, 267 were acquitted, and charges against 30 were dropped for lack of evidence. Some 38 percent of those convicted were sentenced

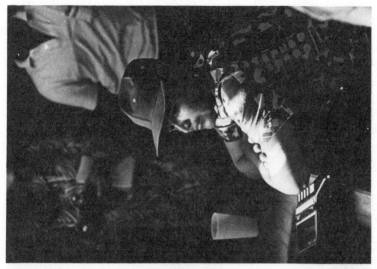

Figure 9.1. Two faces of the revolution: (left) junta members (left to right) Daniel Ortega Saavedra, Moisés Hassán Morales, and Sergio Ramírez Mercado under a portrait of Sandino; (right) a Somoza agent on trial for war crimes in the special tribunals. (Photos by the author)

to five or fewer years, 29 percent from twenty to thirty years, the maximum permitted under Nicaraguan law.[26]

By 1982 the major problems cited concerning the courts involved technical problems and severely overcrowded criminal dockets. In 1983 the nation's jury courts were reformed, with their jurisdiction reduced to only the most severe felony crimes in order to free crowded jury-trial dockets. Also in 1983 most other crimes were assigned to the jurisdiction of the regular courts of justice. In 1983 exclusive criminal jurisdiction (except in crimes requiring accusations by the victim) was given to the attorney general and new, more modern criteria of proof were adopted in criminal proceedings. Several revisions of legal codes concerned with criminal matters were decreed between 1979 and 1984, with the general goal of modernizing and improving judicial practice.[27]

The FSLN's Role in Government

The FSLN National Directorate set the principal policy guidelines for the revolution.[28] Its mandate to rule was partly moral, deriving from the FSLN's eighteen years of anti-Somoza struggle and military victory over the dynasty's National Guard, and partly practical, as FSLN Directorate members dominated the revolutionary security forces upon coming to power. Only brief references in the revolutionary constitution, the Fundamental Statute of the Republic of Nicaragua, embodied the DN's formal authority. The junta was to be "designated by the Revolutionary Movement,"[29] which after the fall of the old regime in effect meant the DN. The Fundamental Statute also "substitute[d] for the National Guard of Nicaragua a new National Army . . . to be formed by the combatants of the Sandinista National Liberation Front [and other appropriate citizens and] provisionally commanded by the military chiefs and leaders of the armed movement that put an end to the dictatorship,"[30] an obvious reference to the FSLN.

As strategy for the insurrection had been one important difference among the three tendencies in the FSLN, the victory over Somoza eliminated much of the internal strain. Certain ideological differences persisted in the early policy statements of individual DN members, but most were later retracted. For example, agrarian reform head Jaime Wheelock Román first announced a radical farm nationalization program—a Proletario preference. Wheelock soon modified this posture under the pragmatizing influence of the whole directorate, which opted for a more modest nationalization. Despite persistent ideological shadings among members of the FSLN's three tendencies, the DN's collegial decision making and firmly held policy against personality cults continued to moderate internal differences and to give revolutionary policy a markedly pragmatic cast (see Table 9.1 for a list of DN members). Decisions on issues that evoked sharp internal debate within the DN were reportedly taken by only a six-vote majority. Continual speculation about a major split within the DN or a radicalization of the revolution under the lead of one faction or another failed to prove valid.

The FSLN held key government positions in order to shape revolutionary policy and to control national defense and public security. Most DN members occupied important administrative or political positions: Daniel Ortega Saavedra chaired the junta; Humberto Ortega Saavedra was minister of defense; Luis Carrión Cruz, vice-minister of defense; DN chairman Tomás Borge Martínez was minister of interior (police and security); Bayardo Arce Castaño, president of the Council of State (1980); Henry Ruíz, minister of planning; and Jaime Wheelock Román was minister of agrarian reform and agricultural development. Other top Sandinista leaders also held or have held key positions: For example, Omar Cabezas Lacayo, Dora María Téllez, Federico López, Carlos Zamora, and Rafael Tijerino were all members of the Council of State; Hugo Torres Jiménez was secretary of that body; and Moisés Hassán Morales first served on the junta and then became minister of construction. The DN's Carlos Núñez Téllez headed the Council of State from 1981 through 1984.

The FSLN National Directorate constantly worked to shape the revolution and avoid obstacles in its path, as some examples illustrate. First, the Sandinistas were initially committed to broad participation in the government and to organizational freedom among anti-Somoza elements. Thus the cabinet and national bureaucracy included people of many parties and points of view. Rather few administrative purges had occurred through mid-1984, and diverse views still found representation in the junta and the government. Although various parties remained in the government in 1984, growing internal and external opposition to the FSLN—including violent subversion, sabotage, and outright acts of war—had reduced the Sandinistas' tolerance of opposition. Tensions between the domestic opposition and the regime had become extreme by mid-1984, as Nicaragua prepared for that year's November election.

Between 1980 and 1984 there were several important protest resignations from the government. The least surprising involved relatively conservative interests. In addition to Robelo, the more significant resignations were by Arturo Cruz Porras as ambassador to the United States (early 1982) and by the immensely popular Edén Pastora Gómez (Comandante Cero) as vice-minister of interior (in 1981). Social democrat Pastora had been marginalized from decision making within the FSLN. He left Nicaragua rather quietly, reportedly in disagreement with the DN. After ten months of silence, Pastora surfaced in San José, Costa Rica, in April 1982 and attributed his break with the Nicaraguan regime to dissatisfaction with "excessive foreign influence" on the revolution. He excoriated the DN for imitating the Cuban revolution rather than pursuing a purely self-developed model, for needlessly provoking confrontation with the United States by acquiring Russian tanks (primarily offensive weapons), and for adopting extravagant life styles like the Somocistas. Soon after, Alfonso Robelo joined Pastora's movement; Arturo Cruz eventually associated himself with the external opposition as well and returned to Nicaragua in mid-1984, supposedly to be the CD's presidential nominee. Cruz's demands for an immediate dialogue with the external opposition's military leaders were rejected by the regime. Cruz never filed for president and ended his brief candidacy in protest of alleged regime intransigence. Regime supporters, however, argued that Cruz merely acted as a foil for U.S. efforts to discredit the November 1984 elections.

The FSLN's early commitment to maintaining a broad front was also shown by its response to the frequent attacks upon such sometimes critical groups as COSEP, INDE, the MDN, or the newspaper *La Prensa* by pro-FSLN media such as *Barricada, El Nuevo Diario,* or national television in the 1979–1981 period. The DN typically cooled down the zealots' demands to rid the country of such "troublemakers" with moderate statements. The DN's tendency to restrain such criticism, however, diminished notably after 1981, when incidents of harassment of opposition groups and media by pro-FSLN crowds or vandals increased.

In general, however, when labor trouble threatened important industries (e.g., the Texaco refinery and *La Prensa*), the DN itself mediated in order to get the businesses back into production. Indeed, the government had become so concerned about economic recovery by late 1981 that a new economic emergency law banned strikes for one year (a ban that was continued until 1984). When the Nicaraguan entrepreneurial sector expressed fear about the status of private property and further nationalizations in early 1980, the DN negotiated with COSEP and INDE to guarantee property and profits and to keep businesses operating, despite strident criticism from the radical left both internally and abroad.

Evidence of the limits of the FSLN's tolerance of opposition can be found in other incidents. When the radical faction Workers' Front

(Frente Obrero), the Popular Anti-Somocista Militia (Milicias Populares Anti-Somocistas—MILPAS), and *El Pueblo,* the newspaper of the Workers' Front, continued in late 1979 to agitate for strikes and for seizures of factories and farms by workers, the FSLN took this as a threat both to economic recovery and to the revolutionary program. The FSLN moved against the radicals in January 1980; the police seized MILPAS arms, closed *El Pueblo,* and jailed several Workers' Front leaders for counterrevolutionary agitation. The limits of tolerance became clearer in 1981 and 1982 when proregime crowds or mobs (*turbas*) began to harass certain opposition groups and regime critics. Perhaps the most controversial example of the regime's treatment of its opponents involved Father Bismarck Carballo, an archdiocesan official and fervent anti-Sandinista. In 1983 Carballo was arrested by security police during a tryst with a woman acquaintance, and he was paraded nude in front of television cameras. The police claimed that they had rescued the fleeing priest from an irate husband; regime critics said the incident had been fabricated in order to embarrass Carballo and the church's supporters. Regardless of the merits of either version of the incident, the presence of television for the event strongly suggests either an extraordinary coincidence (a happenstance presence of a news crew in a quiet residential neighborhood) or an awareness on the part of the security police of an opportunity for such an incident so that they alerted the news media.

The FSLN was by 1979 the preeminent political party in Nicaragua. During the insurrection the Front organized Nicaraguans for the armed struggle and coordinated the struggle against the regime with other political opponents through the broad front organizations. After the victory the FSLN worked to expand and to integrate its own mass base of allegiants in order to successfully compete with other political groups. The DN's early 1980 decision to postpone elections from 1982 until 1985 was widely seen as buying the Front additional time to further consolidate its organization, popular base, and role in the government.

The FSLN established an elaborate organization stretching from the Managua headquarters to every corner of the nation. The national headquarters generated copious literature, propaganda, plans, and programs. The FSLN organized neighborhood Sandinista Defense Committees (Comités de Defensa Sandinista—CDSs), modeled loosely on the Cuban Committees for the Defense of the Revolution, to mobilize citizen support for revolutionary policies. CDSs had both administrative functions (assisting in the implementation of various health and educational programs) and political functions (recruiting support for the FSLN). In late 1979 the FSLN briefly gave CDSs some police functions (helping maintain public order in their neighborhoods and providing security references for applicants for visas to leave the country), but this so rankled many Nicaraguans that most such functions were soon removed. By mid-1980 somewhat fewer than half the original CDSs still functioned, mostly in the lower- and middle-class barrios where the Front had had its strongest support during the insurrection. When counterrevolutionary attacks from Honduras and guerrilla activity within Nicaragua escalated rapidly in 1982 and 1983, the CDSs again assumed an important role in the administration of public policy. They handled the distribution of certain basic commodities and ration permits during the periodic commodity shortages, served as the basis for organizing a neighborhood-by-neighborhood "revolutionary vigilance" (*vigilancia revolucionaria*) program of nighttime street patrols, and constructed civil defense works.

There were other mass FSLN organizations: The Luisa Amanda Espinosa Nicaraguan Women's Association (Asociación de Mujeres Nicaragüenses Luisa Amanda Espinosa—AMNLAE) was formerly AMPRONAC. The July 19th Sandinista Youth (JS-19) united the various student arms of the FSLN with the secondary student group AES, assuring the Sandinistas an enormous influence in the universities and high schools. The Front also promoted the ATC peasant organization, which grew rapidly in 1979 and 1980, and a Sandinista Workers' Central (Central Sandinista de Trabajadores—CST). A workplace-based militia was organized in 1980, reaching a membership of more than a hundred thousand. In 1981 the ATC split into two groups: The ATC itself retained agricultural workers, and the National Union of Farmers and Cattlemen (UNAG) gathered together small farmers, whose ownership of farms had put them increasingly at odds with the ATC's wage laborers.

Other Parties and Interest Groups

Other political parties also functioned openly in Nicaragua, including the Independent Liberals, People's Social Christians, Nicaraguan Democratic Movement, Democratic Conservatives, Social Christians, Social Democrats, and two communist parties—the Nicaraguan Socialist party and the newer Nicaraguan Communist party. Most of these parties had changed little since before the revolution. The revolutionary government's Fundamental Statute recognized and legitimized such party diversity by including "distinct political sectors" on the junta and by granting Council of State representation to seven parties other than the FSLN.[31] These parties (see Table 9.2) held

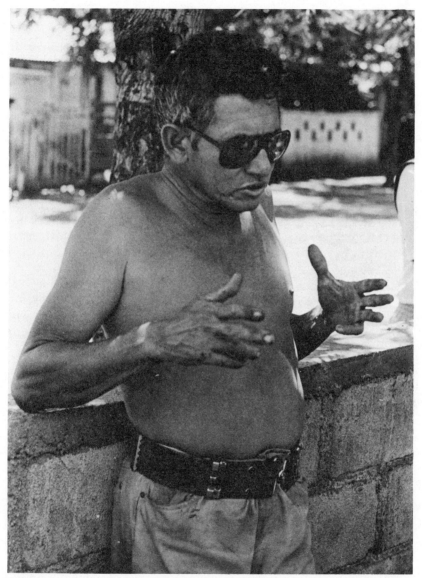

Figure 9.2. CDS leader in Ciudad Sandino, a poor neighborhood on the outskirts of Managua, discusses his neighborhood (1984). (Photo by the author)

posts in the junta, cabinet, bureaucracy, and the Council of State. Even after several parties and other organizations coalesced into a formal opposition group, they continued to participate in national political life.

In 1979–1982, the most significant political party other than the FSLN was the MDN,[32] which Alfonso Robelo Callejas had established in 1978 as a middle class–bourgeois anti-Somoza opposition movement. In early 1980, however, the MDN transformed itself into a political party and adopted a social democratic platform. By 1981 it had evolved into an opposition party. It criticized the postponement of elections, the altered makeup of the Council of State, the more openly Marxist-Leninist policy line of the FSLN's National Directorate, and the confusion between the FSLN and the state (e.g., the Sandinista Police, Popular Sandinista Army). The MDN, however, retained its seat on the Council of State despite Robelo's protest resignation from the junta. The MDN's criticism of the FSLN and the MDN's bourgeois support brought on the party in turn harsh criticism by the FSLN and its media. Previous MDN criticism notwithstanding, the party backed the government's declaration of a national emergency and suspension of constitutional rights in 1982 as a response to a U.S.-backed counterrevolutionary campaign against Nicaragua. However, shortly after that, Robelo went into exile with other key MDN leaders and joined forces with Edén Pastora to form the Revolutionary Democratic Alliance (Alianza Revolucionaria Democrático—ARDE) in Costa Rica. This action devastated the MDN as a legal political force within Nicaragua, and its influence and presence suffered irreparable damage.

Nevertheless, except for the radical Workers' Front and the Somozas' Liberal Nationalist party, the political parties mentioned above operated openly and each had a seat on the Council of State. The Democratic Conservative party was also represented on the junta by Rafael Córdoba Rivas. Although the opposition never dominated public policymaking after 1979, it did influence administration and policymaking. Even under censorship (1982–1984) opposition parties' critiques of proposed policy were regularly presented and discussed in the Nicaraguan press. Prior to the 1984 election the junta eased censorship and meeting restrictions to facilitate party contact with the public.

The Nicaraguan revolution at first won the national labor movement new freedom.[33] Organized labor increased its ranks a minimum of tenfold over the early 1979 level of twenty-five thousand. Perhaps a hundred thousand rural laborers were mobilized through the ATC. The several prerevolutionary union confederations still existed, but the FSLN promoted greater proletarian unity with the new Sandinista Workers' Central. About 79 percent of the roughly five hundred industrial unions recognized by the Ministry of Labor in the first year following the victory (three hundred of them new) affiliated with the CST, 9 percent with the Christian democratic CTN, 5 percent with the CGTI, and 4 percent with the conservative, ORIT-affiliated CUS.[34]

The CST and the other labor groups differed in their goals. The Sandinista unions hewed closely to government guidelines on moderate wage demands and emphasized increased production, gains in social benefits, and better working conditions. In contrast, the CGTI and CTN were more militant on salaries and criticized the CST for heavy-handedness and for ignoring legitimate worker demands. On occasion, CST locals ousted their Sandinista leaders and split with the CST in disputes over wage demands, a sign of organizational freedom. Regardless of the affiliation of their plants' unions, management of public-sector (nationalized) industry permitted unions some participation in decision making for the firms, a novelty in Nicaraguan labor relations. Despite the formation of the National Interunion Council (Consejo Nacional Intersindical) in January 1980 (including the CGTI, CAUS, and CST), the plural character of the labor movement continued into mid-1984. Labor unity grew slowly, accompanied by a vitriolic dispute between the CST and the other confederations.

Persistent economic difficulties, first in promoting economic recovery from the war (1979–1981) and subsequently because of external economic pressures and the counterrevolutionary offensive (1982–1984), brought the suspension of the right to strike in 1981 (continued until August 1984). Deterioration of real wages owing to an austerity-induced end of certain food subsidies (1982–1983) cooled the independent unions' interest in affiliation with the CST. Pressures upon independent unions and upon the non-Sandinista confederations (CGTI, CTN, CAUS, CUS) took on more intimidating forms in 1983 and 1984, including harassment of leaders by security officials. On 2 June 1984 two CTN officials were arrested and charged with counterrevolutionary activity in violation of the Law for the Maintenance of Order and Public Security.[35]

Many of Nicaragua's largest businesses were nationalized in the confiscation of the Somoza group's property in 1979, so that the remaining bourgeoisie owned modest-sized enterprises. Confiscation of firms owned wholly by the Somozas received widespread support among the reformist bourgeoisie, but nationalization also caused conflict and apprehension when some businesses in which the Somoza group had only a partial interest were also taken. Labor unrest fueled nervousness among industrial investors, and peasant mobilization by the ATC, spontaneous land invasions, and early ambiguities about agrarian reform also aroused the fears of larger landholders. As the capitalists' hopes for major political influence waned with progressive Sandinista consolidation of power, businessmen's anxieties grew and their willingness to risk investment and make long-term commitments diminished.

Private investors and their oganizations (INDE, COSEP, and the various chambers of commerce, industry, and agriculture) grew quite restive in late 1979 and early 1980 and called for the government to clarify its policies vis-à-vis the private sector.[36] The United States backed the business groups by proposing a $75-million AID recovery loan to Nicaragua, $30 billion of which was to be earmarked for private-sector loans. In March and April 1980 the business groups called on the regime to spell out and to stabilize its policies on further nationalization, strikes, and agrarian reform. The FSLN Directorate responded with several concessions: It legitimized private ownership of the means of production, conceded greater press freedoms, ended seizures of property, and set forth the law of amparo, which gave citizens and businesses redress in the courts for wrongful administrative actions. This defined the new economy as a mixed system and sought to give private investors some of the stability they wanted in order to rebuild and to operate, as well as legal tools with which to defend themselves. In the words of one Sandinista official, "We have to permit the bourgeoisie to reactivate the economy in order to protect the revolution. We must feed the people or they will throw us out like they did Somoza."[37]

Despite the early 1980 business-government understanding, by late 1980 some capitalists were again expressing dissatisfaction with the regime.[38] In October and November a heated dispute arose between the business faction and the pro-FSLN faction in the Council of State. In early November COSEP and several of the more conservative parties and their unions withdrew their delegates from the council as a protest against the postponement of elections and in an effort to rally the private sector for stronger opposition. In May and June 1980 the Democratic Action Front (Frente de Acción Democrática—FAD), backed by several entrepreneurs and ranchers, began armed harassment of the regime. On 5 June 1980 the police broke up the FAD and arrested some of its leaders. Soon after, however, Jorge Salazar, head of the Union of Nicaraguan Agricultural Producers (Unión de Productores Agrícolas Nicaragüenses—UPANIC) and vice-president of COSEP, died in a shoot-out with police. Subsequent investigations linked Salazar to a counterrevolutionary conspiracy tied to former National Guard elements based in Honduras. This armed resistance, however, discredited the more radical bourgeois opponents of the FSLN and the revolution and brought private-sector affirmations of support for the revolution and the FSLN.

As of mid-1982 one greatly changed factor for the Nicaraguan private sector involved the new U.S. administration. President Carter and the U.S. Congress had lent Nicaragua $30 million in 1980 to stimulate private enterprise. President Reagan, however, soon suspended most U.S. aid programs, including those 1980 private-sector loan funds that had not yet been disbursed. This policy cost the Nicaraguan entrepreneurial sector both an important external ally and some important economic backing. Moreover, the Reagan administration's encouragement and support of anti-Sandinista intervention in 1981 and 1982 apparently involved some of the same business elements that had backed the FAD. This increased distrust and tension between the FSLN and the Nicaraguan entrepreneurial sector.

On 19 July 1981 the junta announced the nationalization of thirteen additional businesses for "decapitalizing and boycotting the national economy."[39] But the junta simultaneously suspended strikes for one year and announced new government supports for "nationalistic entrepreneurs" and small businesses in an attempt to lift the nation out of its persistent economic slump. The relationship between Nicaragua's capitalists and the Sandinista regime remained tentative and uncertain, but the Sandinistas after three years in power appeared still committed to rebuilding the economy with the assistance of a substantial private sector.

The regime's vows to maintain a mixed economy and its policies of providing credit for key economic sectors, controlling labor unrest and wages, and making production agreements with businesses failed to allay nervousness about the socialist leanings of the FSLN leadership and the regime's control over banking and external commerce. As private-sector representatives became more clearly aligned with political opposition to the regime, then, pressure on particular firms and key private-sector leaders grew. Proregime mobs vandalized MDN leader Alfonso Robelo's home; his decision to leave Nicaragua and go to Costa Rica brought about the nationalization of his holdings. External encouragement of opposition to the Sandinistas, especially by the United States, aroused suspicions, probably well founded in some cases, that the private sector was collaborating with people who were endeavoring to subvert the revolution. Neither regime policy or assurances, the troubled sociopolitical environment, nor the perceptions of the anti-Somocista bourgeoisie inspired investor confidence.

Private investment ran considerably less than either the government or the business sector had initially hoped for, which slowed economic growth and recovery.

Political Opposition

External Opposition—the Contras

During 1981 the Reagan administration began to assist anti-Sandinista forces in Honduras. The so-called *contras* (counterrevolutionaries)—given arms and funds by the United States, training and intelligence support by the CIA, and sanctuary and tolerance by Honduras—grew steadily in number and capacity during 1982. During 1983–1984 this buildup and the military activity of the contras redoubled in an apparent effort to topple the Sandinista regime. Although the regime did not fall (and some Nicaraguans actually rallied more strongly behind it out of nationalism), the heavy external pressure sorely taxed the regime's economic capacity, human rights performance, and popular support.

The two major contra groups were the Honduras-based Nicaraguan Democratic Forces (Fuerzas Democráticas Nicaragüenses—FDN), composed mainly of former members and officers of Somoza's National Guard, and the Guard's allies. Alfonso Callejas, a vice-president under Somoza, and Adolfo Calero, ex-president of Coca-Cola of Nicaragua, headed the FDN's political wing. Also allied with the FDN was the Nicaraguan Revolutionary Armed Forces (Fuerzas Armadas Revolucionarias Nicaragüenses—FARN), which was headed by Fernando Chamorro and included elements of various Conservative factions and a wing of the Miskitu group MISURA (Miskitu, Sumu, Rama) headed by Steadman Fagoth. Ex–National Guard elements, Nicaraguan campesinos and refugees in Honduras, Miskitu Indians, and FSLN militia deserters made up most of the troops, but by 1984 U.S. mercenaries were also fighting with the FDN. Well financed by the CIA (aid apparently exceeded $100 million between 1981 and 1984), the FDN forces grew from perhaps five thousand in 1982 to a level variously estimated at between ten thousand and fifteen thousand by mid-1984. The FDN at first mainly conducted raids into Nicaragua, but in early 1983 it moved thousands of its troops into Zelaya department. It then launched major ground actions in northern and eastern Nicaragua with intelligence, command, and logistical assistance from the CIA and the Honduran armed forces.

Operating out of Costa Rica, the Revolutionary Democratic Alliance was made up of ex-junta member Alfonso Robelo's Nicaraguan

Democratic Movement (MDN), a political party; ex-Sandinista leader Edén Pastora Gómez's Sandinista Revolutionary Front (Frente Revolucionario Sandinista—FRS); and Brooklin Rivera's faction of the Miskitu MISURA organization. After several false starts, because of funding problems and a lack of support, ARDE's military wing, the FRS, grew rapidly to perhaps three thousand troops when financing by the CIA and the participation of former National Guard elements were provided in early 1984. The FRS-ARDE forces, which included former Sandinistas and large numbers of Costa Rican campesinos, captured the southeastern coastal town of San Juan del Norte in April 1984, but they were soon dislodged by the Nicaraguan army.[40]

In May 1984 there were reports of an imminent alliance between ARDE and the FDN, arranged by the CIA. Edén Pastora strongly opposed formal union with the Somocista and ex–National Guard elements of the FDN and threatened to withdraw his FRS forces from ARDE. On 30 May 1984 a bomb that was supposed to assassinate Pastora exploded during a press conference at his field headquarters in southern Nicaragua, but he escaped with minor injuries. He received medical attention in San José before the Costa Rican government deported him to Venezuela. Attributions of responsibility for the bombing, which killed five persons including two journalists, ranged from Costa Rican president Luis Alberto Monge's mention of Sandinista infiltrators to Pastora's blaming the CIA—allegedly to block his plan to withdraw from ARDE. Subsequent to the assassination attempt Alfonso Robelo announced the expected FDN-ARDE union, and Pastora pulled the FRS out of ARDE. ARDE returned the favor by ejecting Pastora.

On 24 July 1984 FDN and ARDE leaders signed a pact of union in Panama. But ARDE was in disarray by then, and the Nicaraguan armed forces made significant gains against ARDE forces in July and August 1984.[41] By late October 1984 Brooklin Rivera and some MISURA leaders were back in Nicaragua, traveling through northern Zelaya and exploring the possibility of a truce and settlement with the government. The FDN suffered serious setbacks in the United States when the White House capitulated in July 1984 to the U.S. House of Representatives' refusal to authorize further funding for contra operations in 1984, and again when a CIA-prepared guerrilla manual surfaced instructing contra troops in sabotage, terrorism, and assassinations ("neutralization") of Sandinista officials. The FDN responded to its shrinking resources by seeking sources of private funding, by threatening to escalate its military offensive before supplies ran out, and by shifting a reported twenty-five hundred troops to northwestern Costa Rica to replace FRS and MISURA forces.[42] By late 1984 the contras were concentrating mainly on economic sabotage, terrorism, and harassment of election officials; the FDN had begun to receive private aid amounting to a reported $500,000 per month from U.S. conservative groups.[43]

Domestic Opposition

Governments at war tend to be highly suspicious of their domestic critics, and modern revolutionary movements have rarely tolerated any open opposition—much less institutionalized it. This fact made the continued existence of the opposition to the FSLN, not to mention its participation in national political life, an extraordinarily distinctive aspect of the Nicaraguan revolution. Tensions growing out of the contra war against the Sandinistas and the sharpening criticism of the regime by its domestic critics, however, appeared to many observers to call the ultimate survival of the opposition into question. In 1982 and 1983 FSLN sympathizers on occasion intimidated and harassed certain opponents, especially with action (disruption of meetings, vandalism, and physical intimidation) by pro-Sandinista turbas. Turba activity then declined markedly in 1984, albeit without disappearing. The state of emergency also restricted domestic opponents, especially the press and political parties, but the opening of the 1984 election campaign saw curtailed intimidation of other parties, greatly eased press censorship, and the restoration of habeas corpus, the right to strike, and most other rights that had been suspended during the state of emergency. These changes permitted, contrary to the impression promoted by the administration in the United States, a free-swinging election campaign in which the opposition strongly criticized the government and its policies. Overall, the freedom of the domestic opponents of the FSLN appears to have varied in inverse proportion to the level of external pressure experienced by the Sandinistas. The election campaign, however, sharply reversed this pattern when the government took what regime spokesmen described as a gamble to legitimize the government domestically and internationally in order to forestall an expected U.S. invasion.[44]

Because a coalition of parties and groups overthrew Somoza, the revolutionary government's Fundamental Statute legitimized party diversity in revolutionary Nicaragua by providing for the participation of various parties both on the junta and in the Council of State.[45] Representatives of several parties other than the FSLN also served in cabinet posts and in the bureaucracy. As noted earlier, by 1980 two political coalitions had developed. The National Patriotic Front (FPN), which supported the Sandinistas, included the FSLN, PPSC, PLI, and the PSN. The opposition Democratic Coordinating Committee (CD) included the PSCN, MDN, PLC, PSD, five private-sector groups, and two unions, the CTN and the CUS. Although always a minority in the government, the CD did influence public policy in several important instances, and even under press censorship opposition criticism of FPN policy proposals were discussed in the press.[46]

As the 1984 national election approached, fissures appeared in both coalitions. The CD became divided internally over whether to take part in the elections and eventually chose not to file for candidacy. The PLI, PSN, and PPSC each withdrew from the FPN to contest the presidency and National Assembly races with the FSLN. The PLI's candidate was the former labor minister (1979–1984) Virgilio Godoy Reyes. He emerged as the main opposition candidate when the CD decided not to contest the presidency, but he eventually withdrew his candidacy one week before the election.[47] The 1982–1984 state of emergency had undoubtedly weakened the opposition parties, but they received some relief during the 1984 election when the junta eliminated censorship on all but security issues, permitted the parties to hold public meetings and campaign rallies, and gave the parties considerable access to television and radio.

Another major opponent of the Sandinista government was the hierarchy of the Catholic church, led by Archbishop Miguel Obando y Bravo and represented formally by the Council of Bishops. The Nicaraguan church hierarchy had supported the reformist movement against Somoza, and many clergy and laypeople, both Catholic and Protestant, had taken part in the insurrection for religious reasons.[48] After the overthrow of Somoza, it seemed that the Catholic hierarchy generally favored the new government and its policies. Archbishop Obando and the Council of Bishops appeared publicly with Sandinista leaders and in late 1979 issued the following statements.

> As in the past we denounced the violation and repression of human, personal and social rights as contrary to evangelical precepts, now we wish to reaffirm that we recognize the profound motivation for the struggle for justice and life. . . . At the head of the diverse social forces of the revolution is the Sandinist National Liberation Front, which has won its place in history. To keep this place its main task is, in our judgment, to continue involving the entire people in forging its own history through decided and multiple participation in national life.[49]

The bishops explicitly expressed no fear of a socialism in Nicaragua that meant the preeminence of the interests of the majority of Nicaraguans and a nationally planned economy . . . , power exercised on behalf of the great majority and increasingly shared by the organized people so that it evolves toward a true transfer of power to the people . . . , and the awakening of the dignity of our masses and their courage to take responsibility for themselves and to demand their rights.[50]

The pastoral letter also recommended that the FSLN respect political pluralism and work toward electoral democracy. In July 1981 Archbishop Obando reiterated these stands.[51] (Some five hundred Protestant ministers also strongly endorsed the revolution in an October 1979 conference.)

Numerous Roman Catholic clergymen held government positions, including Minister of Foreign Relations Miguel d'Escoto Brockman, a Maryknoll priest, and Minister of Culture Ernesto Cardenal, a Trappist father. Moreover, many of the insurrection's activist clergy later became employees of INRA or social welfare agencies. Some powerful secular government figures, including Tomás Borge, openly professed strong religious sympathies. Hundreds of Christian activists, both Protestant and Catholic, took part in the literacy crusade. Catholic schools and churches provided facilities to crusade workers. Many observers affirmed that religious profession in Nicaragua increased because of the religious participation in the crusade.

Tensions existed, however, between the government and the Catholic church. A great debate ensued within the government over religious participation in the literacy crusade; some officials feared that proselytizing might interfere with literacy training and political socialization. The DN, however, permitted Christian literacy teachers to take part and to proselytize as a supplementary activity. The government also encouraged popular participation in religious holidays and made much of the fact that key Sandinistas and junta members took part.

Within the Catholic church many worried about links to the government and the potential tensions between the Marxism of many Sandinista leaders and religious institutions. Some voiced concern lest the Catholic church lose its identity by supporting the new regime too closely; others saw such fears as groundless and even counterrevolutionary. One widespread concern was that the strains introduced by such disagreements might fragment the church itself. Archbishop Obando criticized specific policies as not in keeping with the spirit urged in the 1979 episcopal pastoral letter on the revolution. Such criticisms and the hierarchy's dissatisfaction with the revolutionary government increased rapidly after 1982. Although many Protestant clergy and many Catholic religious and laypeople remained supportive of the revolution, the Catholic church hierarchy made common cause with the government's conservative opponents and greatly escalated its once muted criticism.

The visit of Pope John Paul II to Nicaragua in April 1983 deepened the regime-hierarchy split. Negotiations between the government and hierarchy over details of the papal visit had been very tense. The intensification of the anti-Sandinista war in early 1983 had prompted increased censorship (including some of Archbishop Obando's homilies) and restrictions on all manner of outdoor public meetings. Although the government provided for massive public access to the pontiff's activities, during his visit John Paul II himself adopted a posture that was intended to convey disapproval of the regime. He publicly chastised Culture Minister Ernesto Cardenal for participating in the government, and at the Managua mass the pope refused to offer a public prayer requested by the mothers of several fallen militiamen for their sons' souls. When antiregime demonstrators at the mass began chanting "We love the Pope!" (*Queremos el papa*), proregime elements in the huge crowd—many associated with the popular church movement that was supportive of the revolution—began to counterchant, "We want peace!" (*Queremos la paz*). The hierarchy's partisans were shouted down, and the mass was so disrupted that the pope called several times for silence. The image televised to the external world was one of a deliberate, organized disruption of the mass by the Sandinistas. The FSLN's propaganda catastrophe gave the church hierarchy a great public relations coup.

Following the demonstration at the pope's mass, the Catholic hierarchy pressed its propaganda advantage by stepping up its criticism of the regime. Other regime opponents rallied behind Obando, and church functions became more overtly political in 1984. According to Enrique Bolaños Geyer, president of COSEP, "The church is by far the most important source of encouragement for those of us who don't like what is happening. Mons. Obando is by far the most important leader we have."[52]

The church was particularly concerned about the Patriotic Military Service Law which was first publicized in August 1983. The junta had proposed a universal military draft for males aged eighteen to twenty-five, modeled on legislation in various Western nations, but the fusion between the partisan FSLN and the armed forces became a bone of contention. The Council of Bishops denounced the proposal in a letter published in all newspapers: "No one should be obliged to take up arms to defend a given ideology with which he is not in agreement, nor to perform obligatory military service for the benefit of a political party."[53] Other opposition groups rallied behind the church's position on the draft and also criticized the FSLN–armed forces fusion, Sandinista ideology and indoctrination, and the sexual integration of the army.

Pro-Sandinista elements responded to such criticism by increasing pressure on antiregime forces in the church, and the conflict escalated. In October 1983 groups hostile to the hierarchy's position interrupted masses in several churches that had conservative priests, and an auxiliary bishop was injured. Soon afterward, the regime ejected two Spanish priests from Nicaragua for antiregime political activity, and the Council of Bishops responded with a declaration of a national day of fasting and mourning. Apparently alarmed by the degree to which opposition had coalesced around the Catholic church, regime representatives met in November with the Council of Bishops in an effort to ease tensions. Despite a brief respite in those tensions, in April 1984 the Council of Bishops called upon the regime to engage in dialogue with the contras, and soon afterward the president of the bishops, Monsignor Pablo Antonio Vega, made declarations that appeared to endorse foreign military intervention in Nicaragua to overthrow the Sandinistas.[54]

On 21 May 1984 Archbishop Obando offered a mass that resembled an antiregime rally. Accusing the Sandinistas of being "capable of any barbarity," Obando stated: "To those who say that the only course for Central American countries is Marxism-Leninism, we Christians must show another way. That is to follow Christ, whose path is that of truth and liberty."[55] When asked about U.S.-backed attacks on Nicaragua in an interview by the FSLN daily *Barricada,* Obando stated, "I believe that Nicaragua suffers an ideological aggression by Russian and Cuban imperialism, as well as other imperialisms."[56] Obando did not, however, criticize the United States for its pressures on Nicaragua, nor did he soften his posture vis-à-vis the regime.

Ten foreign priests (four Spaniards, two Costa Ricans, two Italians, one Canadian, and one Panamanian) took part in an Obando-led protest march against the regime in early July, but when these priests shortly afterward began to organize the Christian Renovation Movement (Movimiento de Renovación Cristiana) to support the hierarchy in its confrontation with the government, they were quickly deported for antiregime activity by foreigners. In early December 1984 the provincial superior for Central America of the Society of Jesus (the Jesuit order) dismissed Fernando Chamorro from the order.[57] In comments illustrative of the bitterness of some church sectors, Vega fulminated against the elections in a personal pastoral letter on 24 October 1984; he later publicly stated that he believed a recent contra terrorist attack that had killed several children "was better than [the Sandinistas'] murdering children's souls."[58] Church-regime relations were at their nadir as this book went to press in 1985.

The newspaper *La Prensa* at first supported the revolutionary government, but by 1981 the paper had become a bitter opponent of the regime and a forum for its critics. Under the state-of-emergency censorship initiated in 1982, *La Prensa* continued to operate, but under restrictions that were more stringent than those imposed on other papers—the Interior Ministry even suspended the paper's publication for a day or two on several occasions. For example, publication was halted for one day in August 1983 to punish the paper for publishing without permission an account of vandals attacking the house of Violeta Barrios, former junta member and widow of Pedro Joaquín Chamorro, *La Prensa*'s former publisher. The paper's own editors elected not to publish on several other occasions because of the extent of cut copy. Censorship eased notably beginning in November 1983 and still more in early 1984 as election preparations began. *La Prensa*'s editorial line became markedly more critical of the regime as censorship eased. In early 1985 Pedro Joaquín Chamorro Barrios, son of the slain editor and himself editor of *La Prensa,* went into voluntary exile in Costa Rica to protest continued censorship. Chamorro soon made appearances with FDN leaders to criticize the Sandinista regime.[59] The paper continued to publish despite his departure.

The Electoral System and the 1984 Elections

Under discussion almost immediately after the fall of Somoza, the system for electing national and local officials finally took shape in mid-1984. Debate over the Political Parties Law in 1982 and 1983 had ended when the CE approved the law with several key amendments demanded by the opposition.[60] Full access to the mass media for campaign purposes and open recruitment, restricted in the FSLN draft law, were provided for in the final version. Also included was a definition of parties that included "vying for political power" rather than "participating in public administration" as in the first draft.[61]

Debate on the Electoral Law had also been intense. Major disagreements within and between the CD and FPN coalitions included the date of elections, the voting age, and the timing of elections for president and for the National Assembly. The opposition parties generally preferred a 1985 election date to give them more time to organize for the election. The FSLN prevailed, however, setting the election for 4 November 1984 and inauguration for 10 January 1985 in order to predate slightly corresponding events in the United States. The FSLN also won a sixteen-year-old voting age, which the opposition denounced as an effort to take advantage of the party's popularity among youth. The opposition had advocated an interim presidency for 1985–1987, during which time an elected constituent assembly would write a new constitution, to be followed by the presidential election. The JGRN in March 1984, however, announced that the assembly and presidential elections would be simultaneous owing to external aggression and to the high cost of holding separate elections.[62]

Although popular organizations and communities had elected members of municipal reconstruction juntas since 1979, no formal national elections were held until 4 November 1984. The Fundamental Statute had provided that the JGRN should call elections for a National Assembly "whenever the conditions of national reconstruction might permit."[63] The Electoral Law of 1984 provided for the simultaneous election of a president, vice-president, and a ninety-member National Assembly, all for six-year terms. The presidency would go to the party with a relative majority (the most votes). The Assembly was to have legislative power and would also draft a new constitution to replace the Fundamental Statute. The Assembly's constituency was to consist of ten multimember geographical districts with a proportional representation of parties according to their share of the total vote. Voting was to be for parties, each of which would determine its own candidates' positions on the ballot. Elections would be overseen by a fourth branch of government, the Supreme Electoral Council, which would establish the voter registry and conduct the actual balloting. The vote would be popular, direct, and secret for all Nicaraguans sixteen years of age or older. Parties that failed to register to contest the 1984 election would lose their legal certification to operate (*personería jurídica*).[64] Municipal elections were to take place at a later date.

Voter registration ended on 31 July 1984. The Supreme Electoral Council (CSE) reported that 1,560,580 people had registered. Presidential and vice-presidential candidates for the FSLN were Daniel Ortega Saavedra and Sergio Ramírez Mercado, respectively. The PLI ticket included Virgilio Godoy Reyes, former labor minister, and Constantino Pereira Bernheim; the Democratic Conservative party ran Clemente Guido and Merceditas Rodríguez de Chamorro. The Democratic Coordinating Committee announced that it would nominate Arturo Cruz and Adán Fletes, but when the government refused to include contra leaders of the FDN in a "national dialogue," the CD chose not to file by the 5 August deadline.

Soon, however, the CD appeared to reverse field; it sought to establish a national dialogue again, this time without requiring presence by the FDN, but this initiative also failed. The CD and the regime continued to negotiate possible postponement of the elections as late as mid-October. The FSLN's Bayardo Arce and Arturo Cruz in Rio de Janeiro actually signed an accord for a postponement negotiated through the good offices of Socialist International leaders Willy Brandt and Carlos Andrés Pérez. This deal, which gave the CD virtually everything it had asked for, reportedly collapsed when Cruz's private-sector backers in Managua demanded additional delays and conditions. This turn of events deeply disappointed the CD's Social Christian party, which wanted to run.[65] It also led to speculation by some observers, including a high-ranking U.S. diplomat in Nicaragua, that the CD had never intended to run at all but merely wanted to disrupt the election. Virgilio Godoy and the PLI national committee also voted to withdraw, very late in the campaign, but this action prompted a revolt, and vice-presidential candidate Pereira and most of the PLI National Assembly delegates still ran for office. During the campaign, U.S. diplomats repeatedly visited with leaders of the more conservative opposition parties (PLI, PPSC, PCD), urging them to withdraw from the election.[66]

With only twelve weeks to campaign, the opposition parties bitterly complained about the terms of the elections, the restrictions upon the press, and the state of emergency, which hampered their ability to reach their constituents. Conservative opponents, including the church hierarchy, COSEP, and several parties, also demanded that the regime should enter into a dialogue with the counterrevolutionary opposition and permit its leaders and combatants to take part in the election.[67] As the campaign got under way, there were numerous problems. *La Prensa* accused the FSLN of using public vehicles in conducting its campaign while opposition parties had to rely on personal vehicles and were hampered by gasoline rationing and a parts shortage. Archbishop Obando criticized the continuation of the state of emergency until 20 October (although restrictions on meetings, movement, and propaganda were lifted on 6 August) and hinted that the church might encourage an election boycott.

The early problems of campaigning had diminished sharply by the sixth week according to opposition party and CSE spokesmen, a fact confirmed by the author's scrutiny of the CSE's complaint files.[68] Each party received about $1.5 million from the CSE to finance its campaign, and most parties received private and foreign support as well. Each party had twenty-two hours of free television time, forty-four hours on state radio (and could buy additional time on private

Figure 9.3. Scenes from the 1984 election campaign: (above left) FSLN demonstration; (above right) giant dolls symbolizing Nicaragua's resistance to U.S. intervention through the election; (below left and right) propaganda, both formal and informal. (Photos by the author)

radio), and an equal share of thirty tons of paper and ink provided by the CSE. Nicaragua was blanketed with party propaganda, and most parties admitted that no significant irregularities—including turba activity or systematic intimidation—had seriously hampered their campaigns.[69] Somewhat improbably, stern-visaged Daniel Ortega began to campaign like a U.S. politician, visiting poor barrios and kissing babies. Campaigns varied in style—the FSLN, PLI, PCD, and PSN emphasized large public rallies while the PPSC relied mainly on television. Of the tiny leftist parties, the Communist party of Nicaragua (PC) emphasized radio in its campaign, and the Marxist-Leninist Popular Action Movement (MAP-ML) concentrated on person-to-person campaigning in poor barrios.[70]

The election itself, scrutinized by over a thousand foreign and press observers, appeared scrupulously conducted under procedures (designed by Swedish electoral advisers) that maximized secrecy of the ballot, prohibited pressure on or retaliation against voters and nonvoters alike, and effectively barred fraud. Turnout, despite confusion about the PLI's participation and church and CD statements encouraging abstention, was slightly over 75 percent. As expected, the FSLN won about 67 percent of the vote and the presidency. The PCD ran a distant second, Clemento Guido receiving 14 percent of the vote, and Virgilio Godoy of the PLI won 10 percent of the votes, despite withdrawing from the race at the last moment (see Table 9.3).

In voting for the National Assembly, the PCD won fourteen seats, the PLI nine, and the PPSC six of the seats not taken by the FSLN. The radical parties (PSN, PC, MAP-ML) combined won only six Assembly seats, and one for each party was a bonus seat for its presidential candidate. The FSLN's voting strength came in the North, the poorer urban neighborhoods, and the countryside. The opposition vote and abstention were greatest in southern Nicaragua and urban middle- and upper-class areas.[71]

International observers and the press[72] generally reported that the election was orderly, open, and fairly conducted. Given the generally high quality of the elections, the Sandinistas appeared to have gone a long way toward legitimizing their rule of Nicaragua and toward institutionalizing the revolution.

The newly elected government was inaugurated on 10 January 1985, the seventh anniversary of the assassination of Pedro Joaquín Chamorro. On the platform with President Daniel Ortega Saavedra and Vice President Sergio Ramírez Mercado were: the presidents of Yugoslavia, Sinan Hassani, and Cuba (Fidel Castro); the vice presidents of Argentina and the Soviet Union; the foreign ministers of the Contadora countries; and the secretary general of the Organization

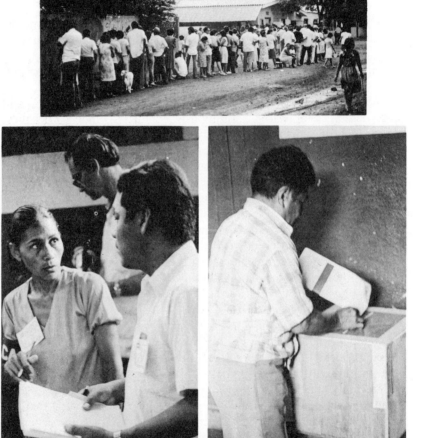

Figure 9.4. Election day 4 November 1984: (above) voters in line as poll opened at 7:00 A.M.; (below left) poll watchers; (below right) man deposits ballot in a sealed wooden ballot box. (Photos by the author)

Table 9.3
Results of 1984 Nicaraguan National Election

A. Turnout

Registered	Voted	Turnout	Null ballots
1,560,580	1,170,142	75%	71,209 (6%)

B. Presidential election

Frente Sandinista Ortega/Ramírez	Democratic Conservatives Guido/Rodríguez	Independent Liberals Godoy/Pereira
% 67	14	10
N 735,967	154,327	105,560

C. National Assembly [a]

Party	Number of seats	Percent of seats
FSLN	61	64
PCD	14	15
PLI	9	9
PPSC	6	6
PC	2	2
PSN	2	2
MAP-ML	2	2
Totals	96	100

Sources: Consejo Supremo Electoral, Managua; New York Times, 15 November 1984, p. 8; "Report of the Latin American Studies Association Delegation to Observe the Nicaraguan General Election of November 4, 1984," Latin American Studies Association Forum, November 1984, Table 3, pp. 14, 17.

[a]Ninety Assembly seats were by district; one additional seat went to the presidential candidate of each of the losing parties.

of American States (João Baena Soares). President Ortega's inaugural address sharply criticized U.S. policy toward Nicaragua, called for normalization of U.S.-Nicaraguan relations through the bilateral talks at Manzanillo, Mexico (broken off by the United States soon afterward), and renewed Nicaragua's offer of amnesty to those contras who would lay down their arms.

Table 9.4
Organization of the Nicaraguan State, 1985

FSLN National Directorate

Tomás Borge M.	Humberto Ortega S.	Luis Carrión C.
Daniel Ortega S.	Jaime Wheelock R.	Henry Ruíz H.
Bayardo Arce C.	Carlos Núñez T.	Victor Tirado L.

President

Daniel Ortega Saavedra

Vice-President

Sergio Ramírez Mercado

Cabinet

Foreign Relations: Miguel d'Escoto
Interior: Tomás Borge; First Deputy
  Minister, Luis Carrión C.
Foreign Cooperation: Henry Ruíz
Presidency: Rene Núñez T.
Foreign Trade: Alejandro Martínez
Domestic Commerce: Ramón Cabrales
Construction: Mauricio Valenzuela
Justice: Ernesto Castillo
Labor: Benedicto Meneses F.

Defense: Humberto Ortega
Housing: Miguel E. Vigil
Agriculture: Jaime Wheelock
Industry: Emilio Baltodano
Transportation: William Ramírez
Finance: William Hupper
Health: Lea Guido
Education: Fernando Cardenal
Culture: Ernesto Cardenal

Ministerial rank agency and office heads

Presidential Secretary of Planning and Budget: Luis E. Figueroa
Presidential Administrative Secretary: Rodrigo Reyes
Adviser to the President of the Republic: Dionisio Marenco
Presidential Director of Information and Press: Manuel Espinoza E.
President of Central Bank: Joaquín Cuadra Ch.
President of Social Security Institute: Leonel Argüello R.
Director of Nicaraguan Energy Institute: Emilio Rappaccioli
Director of Nicaraguan Waterworks Institute: Otoniel Argüello
Director, Telecommunications and Postal Institute: José M. Alvarado
Director of Nicaraguan Fishing Institute: Alfredo Alaníz
Director of Nicaraguan Mining Institute: Ramiro Bermúdez M.
Director of Nicaraguan Social Security and Welfare Institute: Reynaldo A. Téfel
Director of the Nicaraguan Tourism Institute: Herty Lewites R.
President, National Council of Higher Education: Joaquín Solís P.
Comptroller General of the Republic: Emilio Baltodano P.
Mayor of the City of Managua: Samuel Santos López

Regional Government Delegates

Region I: Carlos Ml. Morales	Region II: Alonso Porras
Region III: (not available)	Region IV: Javier Moncada
Region V: Edwin Zablah	Region VI: Diogenes Martínez

Special Zone I: Mirna Cunningham
Special Zone II: Thomas Gordon
Special Zone III: Alejandro Guevara

National Assembly Executive Committee*
(with party affiliation)

President: Carlos Núñez (FSLN)

Vice-Presidents
First: Leticia Herrera (FSLN)
Second: Clemente Guido (PCD)
Third: Mauricio Díaz (PPSC)

Secretaries
First: Rafael Solís (FSLN)
Second: Domingo Sánchez (PSN)
Third: Constantino Pereira (PLI)

Source: Barricada Internacional, 17 January 1985, pp. 4-5.

* Officers were provisional until Assembly drafted its rules and procedures.

The new cabinet sworn in on 10 January 1985 returned most former ministers to their previous posts (see Table 9.4). FSLN DN members kept their cabinet portfolios except for Henry Ruíz, who took the new position of minister of foreign cooperation. His old Planning Ministry was abolished; its functions were assumed by the new Secretariat of Planning and Budget reporting to the president. René Núñez Téllez became minister of the presidency; his ministry, created to provide direct staff support to the presidency, incorporated several offices of the former JGRN and the Office for Regional Affairs. The new National Planning Council was established to formulate and monitor key development programs; it included the president, vice president, the Central Bank president, the planning secretary, and the ministers of agriculture, industry, and foreign cooperation.

The National Assembly elected a team of provisional leaders (Table 9.4) headed by Carlos Núñez Téllez and Rafael Solís, FSLN delegates who had headed the former Council of State. Also elected to the Assembly's provisional executive council were leaders of four other parties. Only thirteen women held Assembly seats, twelve of them from the FSLN and one from the PCD. In the first sessions of the Assembly, opposition parties clashed among and within themselves over procedural and ideological issues.[73] As this book went to press in early 1985 it was too early to determine whether an opposition coalition would form in the Assembly.

The makeup of the presidency, cabinet, and National Assembly leadership promised a high degree of continuity of procedures and policy in the new government. Comments by key members of the administration, cabinet, and National Assembly[74] suggested that the FSLN had not significantly altered its basic strategy and programs and that Nicaragua's new leaders viewed the constitution drafting to be carried out in 1985 as a process of consolidation of the revolution.

Policies and Performance of the Revolutionary Government

The government of Nicaragua has imposed a new dictatorship . . . it has refused to hold the elections it promised and has attacked the opposition . . . it has seized control of all media except a lone newspaper . . . it has stifled the private sector and independent trade unions.
—Jeane J. Kirkpatrick, U.S. UN envoy, 1983[1]

[U.S. ambassador to Nicaragua Anthony Quainton] said that Nicaragua is not a totalitarian society at present and that in his opinion, if there were free elections in Nicaragua now the Sandinistas would easily win.
24 November 1982[2]

Like the governmental structures, public policy evolved during the revolution's first five years. The original goals of the revolutionary coalition shifted to reflect the predominance of the FSLN over other groups, and increasing conflict between the regime and its emergent opposition shaped policy along lines favoring the Sandinistas' constituencies. As the mystique and romance of the armed struggle were replaced by political and practical necessity, public policy was shaped by the reality of rule. Revolutionary ideological purity and planners' ideas about efficiency repeatedly succumbed to political pragmatism and expediency.

Public Order

The restoration of public order and the establishment of a police service constituted a thorny problem for the revolutionary government.[3] The entire police system had gone over the border with Somoza, his cohorts, and the National Guard. The collapse of Somoza's police was a boon, given its corruption and repressiveness, but the Sandinistas still confronted four major problems: violence by counterterrevolutionary bands, a highly armed and violent populace, high levels of crime, and the FSLN's own lack of police experience. Several steps were taken in response to these problems: FSLN patrols had captured, killed, or forced into exile most of the renegade Somocistas by late 1979. The ministries of Interior and Defense countered the problems of private armament and violence by conducting a "depistolization" campaign to reduce the number of arms in private hands and by carefully controlling arms bearing by off-duty soldiers and police. By early 1980 the violence was so reduced that private security guards and others were again licensed to carry weapons to protect property from criminals.

Crime itself proved more difficult because the FSLN lacked police experience. Nicaragua's criminal underworld, tolerated—and in some cases actually managed—by the National Guard police under Somoza, found itself virtually unrestrained in late July 1979. The new Sandinista Police (Policia Sandinista—PS) lacked police training, experience, and knowledge of the nature and personalities of Nicaraguan crime and were rather prone to react with excessive force. Knowledge of Nicaragua's criminal element developed with time, and crime overall (especially narcotics and vice) appeared to have diminished by 1980. The Ministry of Interior heavily stressed police training by bringing in foreign experts (from Costa Rica, Panama, and elsewhere) to teach police methods to hundreds of new peace officers. The ministry also cleaned its own house: By January 1980 more than six hundred and fifty police had been dismissed for use of excessive force, and soon afterward an internal investigation department began to investigate and to prosecute police lawbreakers.

During 1980 police began to conduct raids against "known delinquents" responsible for high levels of street crime, drug traffic, and robberies. The success of this practice became evident as crime rates fell steadily. The PS received assistance in many areas from the militias, including neighborhood policing in areas of militia strength and protection of the literacy crusade brigades from counterrevolutionary attacks. Still further crime reduction came about in 1983 and 1984 when neighborhood CDSs organized revolutionary vigilance programs. The revolutionary vigilance groups conducted evening and nighttime patrols in communities throughout Nicaragua to guard against saboteurs and terrorists. Their nearly ubiquitous presence discouraged ordinary criminals and vastly facilitated the work of the police. The author witnessed this fact in November 1983 when patrolling neighbors prevented two armed and drunken private security guards from shooting each other because of a long-standing quarrel. Police success with such minor crimes as violations of liquor sales laws and prostitution was limited and infractions were often overlooked, but traffic control efforts slowed and civilized Managua's once rambunctious traffic.[4]

Human Rights

Personal Security

Seeking to end the Nicaraguan tradition of human rights abuses by public authorities, Interior Minister Tomás Borge Martínez, a Somocista torture victim, kept human rights violations very low, especially during the period from 1979 to 1981. Following this early "consolidation" phase of the revolution,[5] however, the regime's human rights performance deteriorated under the pressure of counterrevolutionary attacks. In the earlier period, just after the fall of the old regime, both Sandinista troops and the general public killed some captured Somocistas, and the FSLN summarily executed a few counterrevolutionary terrorists until the terror subsided in late 1979. The total number of all such killings, however, was very low—probably fewer than a hundred nationwide—because Sandinista leaders ordered troops not to mistreat captured Somocistas. Despite rumors to the contrary, international human rights and media representatives found little violent repression. The Ministry of the Interior forbade cruelty to prisoners and dismissed and prosecuted violators. Due process of law was developing slowly, owing in part to the disorganization of the police and prison system after the insurrection.

Overall the revolutionary government determinedly sought to reestablish public order and to promote revolutionary goals without reviving the abuses of Somocismo. The revolution generally respected human rights, both rhetorically and in fact. The revolution's unleashing of aggressive social behavior certainly led to some errors, yet this very social context made the demonstrated restraint all the more remarkable. Nicaragua remained open and sensitive to international scrutiny. For example, in 1980 the government closed the independent Permanent Commission on Human Rights because it was considered superfluous (the government itself had a similar body) and because it had become politicized by its Social Christian director. However, after protests by Amnesty International, the IACHR, and others, the organization was permitted to renew operations. An IACHR team visited Nicaragua in 1980; its findings were favorable.

During the second "defensive" phase of the revolution, human rights performance deteriorated. Especially in 1982 and 1983 was there a marked change in the previously highly regarded human rights practices. Reports of violations of rights, disappearances, arbitrary detentions, and intimidation of political opponents and independent labor leaders increased sharply in those years.[6] Although many of the disappearance reports registered by the independent Permanent Commission on Human Rights (Comisión Permanente de Derechos Humanos) during this period proved unfounded (alleged victims simply having moved or left the country), there can be no doubt that human rights violations escalated. One particular problem arose in the government's dealings with the Miskitu Indians. The regime's treatment of and relations with this population of roughly seventy thousand became a source of great controversy both within Nicaragua and internationally. The Miskitu (and other inhabitants of the Atlantic coastal department of Zelaya) had historically been isolated from the society and governments of the densely populated Pacific coast. One major concentration of Miskitu was on both sides of the Río Coco, which demarcates a lengthy stretch of the Nicaraguan-Honduran border. The Sandinistas' early dealings with the Miskitu were marked by insensitivity and created several sources of tension, leading to Miskitu participation in protests against the regime as early as 1980.

When counterrevolutionary activity began to escalate near ex–National Guard camps in Honduras along the Río Coco, some Miskitu joined the contras, and many others became victims of the war and of pressure to emigrate to Honduras. Because the population was endangered by the increasing violence and military operations in the area, the government hastily evacuated about eight thousand Miskitu from the border area in 1982—burning houses and fields and killing livestock to ensure compliance with the ordered move. The Indians were marched on foot and resettled in inland camps at Tasba Pri, where it took over a year for agricultural land, schools, health care, and other services to become sufficiently developed for life to stabilize. The psychological impact of the relocation—the removal from the river environment, destruction of homes and valuable animals, use of Moravian and Catholic church buildings for military headquarters, and confinement of some Miskitu to camps—was intense.[7]

Sandinista troops apparently committed numerous human rights violations in their dealings with the Miskitu, especially in 1982 and 1983. The Inter-American Commission on Human Rights of the OAS investigated the regime's dealings with the Miskitu and concluded in a report released in early June 1984 that "hundreds of Miskito Indians have been arbitrarily detained without formalities, under vague accusations of counterrevolutionary activities" and that many "were placed in isolation for long periods, and in some cases, the commission verified they were tortured and illegally punished." The commission also reported that "the Nicaraguan government illegally killed a considerable number of Miskitos as a reprisal" for the deaths of soldiers fighting the rebels.[8]

After late 1983, however, reports generally indicated that the regime and its forces in the zone were greatly controlling such abuses and that relations with the Miskitu had improved markedly. Among the regime's efforts to improve relations with the Miskitu were the replacement of certain officials who had been involved with the human rights violations, extensive contacts with Catholic and Moravian clergy to assist in mediating differences, continued efforts to upgrade services in the Miskitu camps, and a 1 December 1983 amnesty to any Miskitu person who had "committed crimes against Public Order and Security" after 1 December 1981, whether in prison or at large.[9] Hundreds of Miskitu benefited from the amnesty, and tensions and abuses declined, but the government failed to account for the Indian disappearances and deaths of 1982. As this book went to press in 1985, it remained difficult to evaluate the full extent of the clearly serious abuses of the Miskitu's rights by the Sandinista regime. This difficulty in part stemmed from the regime's reluctance to discuss the problem and from the problems of contra kidnapping and terror of the Miskitu and of immensely distorted propaganda by the United States, the FDN, and other interested parties seeking to discredit the FSLN.

Despite the sharp deterioration in 1982 and 1983, human rights performance improved substantially in 1984, and even at its worst, the Nicaraguan revolution still involved much less postinsurrection violence and human rights abuse than did recent revolutions and coups d'etat in Cuba, Mexico, Bolivia, Iran, Chile, Liberia, Ethiopia, and Uganda, for example. Indeed, at its worst, the regime's performance was clearly better than that of the neighboring regimes of Guatemala, El Salvador, and Honduras.[10]

Press Freedom

With regard to freedom of the press,[11] the junta decreed a 1979 press law that attracted considerable criticism from the Inter-American Press Association (IAPA) and elsewhere for restricting the practice of journalism and excessively penalizing unfounded criticism of the revolution or government. Nicaragua's television channels were government-FSLN controlled, but there were several independent radio stations and one clearly independent daily newspaper, *La Prensa,* as well as the FSLN's *Barricada* and the highly proregime *El Nuevo Diario.*

La Prensa in 1980 began to criticize particular government actions within a general editorial policy of support for the revolution. The paper also supported the private sector and political party pluralism. On several occasions the revolutionary government suspended publication of *La Prensa* for a few days for knowingly or irresponsibly publishing false information damaging to the government. Each such suspension stirred denunciations by the IAPA, foreign papers, the Nicaraguan capitalists for whom *La Prensa* provided a voice, and critics of the Sandinistas. Despite these suspensions, the FSLN's DN also supported *La Prensa*. In early 1980 the daily's own employees shut it down in a dispute over editors and editorial policy. The DN settled this conflict and returned *La Prensa* to publication by arranging for the insurgent staff and editor to form *El Nuevo Diario*. In general, during 1979–1981 Nicaraguans enjoyed considerable access to information from a variety of perspectives via the mass media after the revolutionary victory. By comparison to other revolutions, and even to many nonrevolutionary conservative or socialist regimes, Nicaragua permitted a relatively open press.

As the revolution entered its defensive stage with the declaration of a state of emergency in 1982, the government instituted prior censorship of the mass media for security reasons. Most of the media experienced censorship in one form or another, including even minor Sandinista publications and each of the three major newspapers— *La Prensa* (with daily circulation of about fifty-five thousand), *El Nuevo Diario* (circulation about thirty thousand), and *Barricada* (circulation twenty-five thousand). The Ministry of the Interior suspended publication of *La Prensa* for one or two days several times in 1982 for unauthorized reporting of unverified incidents of sabotage or of shortages. Beginning in 1982 the major dailies began to publish editions that were restricted in size because of the cost of importing newsprint. All papers regularly had material cut by Ministry of Interior censors, but censorship of *La Prensa* was heavier than for the proregime papers. *La Prensa* was again suspended for one day in August 1983 for publishing unauthorized material, but its editors decided several additional times in 1983 and 1984 not to publish an edition because of extensive cuts by the censors. In November 1983 the regime eased censorship, according to some observers to reduce any pretext for increased U.S. military pressure against the regime. Following an announcement that *La Prensa* was about to shut down for lack of newsprint, the government authorized the release of scarce foreign currency to import the needed paper. *La Prensa* reporter Luis Mora Sánchez was arrested in 1984 on charges of working for ARDE. Mora, in a television broadcast, admitted to receiving $1,400 from

ARDE to recruit collaborators, paint slogans, publish leaflets, and conduct sabotage. He awaited trial as this book went to press.[12]

Broadcast media operated under extensive regime control, especially in 1982 and 1983. The government ran the only two television channels, which had a mainly urban audience. Although programs that originated in the United States constituted about a fourth of the material broadcast, political opposition had virtually no access to television until the 1984 election campaign. Radio, with forty-nine stations and an audience estimated at nearly two-thirds of the national populace, was less controlled. The regime operated a network of stations that broadcast under the name Radio Sandino. Several of the approximately twenty-eight privately owned stations broadcast their own, independent news programs or programs produced by one of four private news services. The amount of regime control of radio news varied. In 1982 and 1983, private news programs were reportedly subject to censorship, and some news programs were suspended; in late 1983 and 1984, in contrast, Nichols reported that "none [of the private news programs or news services] was subject to prior censorship."[13]

In 1983 and 1984 freedom of access to the media became a subject of intense debate between the regime and the political opposition. One focus of the debate was a proposed revision of the media law, which would have required membership in a journalists' union for reporters. In June 1984 regime supporters withdrew the draft law from the Council of State after intense opposition criticism of provisions limiting reporters' confidentiality and placing media under Ministry of Interior regulation. The 1984 Electoral Law provided for substantially increased press freedom during the four-month campaign that preceded the November 1984 election. Although barring the advocacy of electoral abstention, the law provided for the uncontrolled printing of all campaign materials, freedom to conduct public events and purchase time on radio and television, and equal party access to television and radio. Opposition spokesmen found the television access inadequate and expressed great reservations about the potential for true liberalization during the campaign.[14]

In summary, press freedom in Nicaragua after 1979 varied from being extensive in the first two years, to being rather limited by prior censorship in 1982 and 1983, to an intermediate position in 1983 and 1984. Divisions of opinion within the FSLN's DN were reportedly sharp concerning the institution of censorship, but Sandinista leaders have publicly manifested a commitment to the perpetuation of "pluralism" in the mass media. Students of the media and human rights groups have assessed the Nicaraguan case in ambivalent terms,

criticizing restrictions upon freedom of the press but finding considerable evidence that diverse points of view that were independent
of the regime were amply disseminated. Nichols, for example, in
comparing Nicaragua to other Third World, poor, and revolutionary
nations, and especially to other nations at war and other countries
with Marxist-Leninist regimes, argues that "the range of public
discussion tolerated in Nicaragua during the first five years of the
revolution was remarkable. . . . The diversity of ownership [of media]
and opinion was unusual. . . . Also books, periodicals, and other
publications were printed by political parties, university groups, and
other non-government organizations. Billboards with messages from
opposition political parties were commonplace around the country."[15]

National Culture

The revolutionaries hoped to forge a new national ethos conducive
to the psychological, economic, social, and political well-being and
development of all Nicaraguans.[16] Selfless and socially responsible
collaboration should replace individualistic striving. Nicaragua should
become an integrated whole, incorporating fully and equally such
marginal zones as the Atlantic region and such long-victimized social
groups and strata as women, Indians, peasants, and the urban poor.
The revolution should be both truly revolutionary (not reformist)
and Sandinist, with the FSLN as the vanguard, arbiter, and main
agent of social change within an environment of political liberty and
ideological pluralism.

To promote these cultural goals for Nicaragua, the FSLN engineered
a massive propaganda effort. The Front itself conducted numerous
propaganda activities through its periodicals (*Barricada, Poder Sandinista*), its broadcast media, the publications and productions of the
Secretariat of Propaganda and Political Education and its popular
organizations. The Ministry of Culture, dominated by the FSLN,
operated the nationalized television channels and radio stations,
subsidized the arts, organized historical and cultural programs, and
operated museums.

The Culture Ministry's single biggest early socialization effort was
the National Literacy Crusade of 1980, conducted with the Ministry
of Education to teach basic reading skills to the 50.2 percent of
Nicaraguans aged ten or older who had been found to be illiterate
in a late 1979 census.[17] The crusade was carried out mainly by student
volunteers; the teaching materials used pro-FSLN messages to teach
illiterate Nicaraguans the rudiments of the Sandinista vision of "the
new Nicaragua."

The literacy crusade has been widely praised for its immediate success in teaching literacy on a rudimentary level. It has been followed by policies designed to assure that the newly literate continue to develop and benefit from their new skills—adult education classes on the community level, follow-up programs on national radio to continue skill development, and a major expansion of primary school construction in rural areas. The crusade itself helped forge for many of its participants a new sense of national social solidarity. Both volunteer teachers, mainly middle-class urban youth, and class participants, largely rural poor people, reported that sharing living and learning experiences with other Nicaraguans (whom they would probably have otherwise never met) resulted in a life- and value-transforming adventure. Many observers and participants believed that the literacy crusade's impact on Nicaraguan culture could serve as the nucleus of the new national ethos sought by the Sandinistas, but the regime's critics attacked it as a propaganda effort and an assault on traditional social and political mores.[18]

Other government ministries also used propaganda both to educate the public about their programs and to proclaim the value of these programs in the new scheme of things. As the revolutionaries sought to replace an entrenched system of values, the propaganda was both straightforwardly hortatory and voluminous. Nicaragua was plastered with billboards and posters bearing such messages as:

Every year is the Year of the Child in the New Nicaragua.
Everyone to the Literacy Crusade! Literacy is Liberation!
Sandino yesterday, Sandino tomorrow!

As contra military pressure against the government increased in 1982 and 1983, some slogans took on a more militaristic flavor:

They [the contras] shall not pass!
All arms to the people!

In 1984, the fifth anniversary of Somoza's overthrow, slogans continued to emphasize defense and material sacrifice:

Everything for the war front, everything for
 our combatants!
Death to Yankee imperialism!

Other, more didactic themes were also common:

Irresponsible driving can lead to homicide.
Your vote decides.

The Ministry of Culture and the FSLN encouraged numerous traditional and new types of expression as tools to promote the transformation of social and political values. Nicaraguans have shared a national passion for poetry since the days of the poet Rubén Darío, but the revolution resulted in an astonishing outpouring of poetry and publishing (and workshops and contests) that was unprecedented anywhere on earth. Artists, artisans, and writers formed a Sandinista Cultural Workers' Association (Asociación Sandinista de Trabajadores de la Cultura—ASTC) to promote revolutionary goals through their work and to discover and preserve indigenous forms of artistic expression. Musicians and composers developed and the mass media popularized songs extolling new values and affirming the revolution. Under the Ministry of Culture's patronage and independently, painters developed a flourishing political art—expressed in murals, billboards, and posters—that exhorted support for the revolution, extolled revolutionary values, and dramatized the insurrection and struggle against the counterrevolutionaries. Literacy *brigadistas* and other groups collected folk plays, stories, and songs to conserve them and incorporated elements of these once little-known traditions into new dramas. Each of the major newspapers published a cultural supplement each week that reflected the deepening divisions along class lines between regime supporters and opponents.[19] Nicaraguan cultural life and expression under the revolution clearly began, not a renaissance, but a first major flourishing, heavily infused with the values and goals of and the tensions between those people who were committed to the Sandinista vision of the revolution and its critics.

Integration of the Atlantic Zone

One cultural goal difficult to achieve was the integration of the Atlantic zone into Nicaragua. The Atlantic region had long been isolated from the populous Pacific region. The various Indian groups (Miskitu, Sumu, Rama, and others) and English-speaking black Protestants of the zone had historically regarded the Spanish-speaking population (including Sandino, who raided foreign enterprises and thus destroyed jobs) as alien exploiters. Under the Somoza regime enclave foreign mining, fishing, and lumber companies provided many jobs, and Anastasio Somoza Debayle had cultivated the zone's Moravian missionaries, who promoted anti-FSLN sentiments among the populace.

The revolution brought an influx of "Spaniards" from the Pacific region to the Atlantic region and disrupted established patterns. In particular, the nationalization of the mines, lumber operations, and fisheries made the government the patron of newly organized unions demanding numerous improvements in wages and working conditions. Other tensions arose over the MISURASATA (Unity of the Miskitu, Sumu, Rama, and Sandinistas) Indian organization's demands for recognition of land titles dating back to the British protectorate era and over the resentment by the local black commercial elite of the domination by "Spaniards" of the plethora of new government agencies. Resistance developed in 1980–1981, including riots in Bluefields and Puerto Cabezas and a thwarted conspiracy to kill FSLN leaders. This hostility toward the revolution, which was popular elsewhere, stunned government and FSLN personnel, very few of whom had come from, or even visited, the Atlantic zone before the victory.[20]

Problems grew in 1981 and 1982 as anti-Sandinista forces based in Honduras exploited the antiregime sentiments and activists in the Atlantic region in order to increase their sabotage and raids within Nicaraguan territory. The government responded with the relocation program. The Reagan administration in early 1982 produced photographs purporting to prove that the Sandinista Popular Army (Ejército Popular Sandinista—EPS) was systematically killing and torturing the Indians and characterized the program as one of extermination rather than of relocation. The photos, however, were proved bogus within a few days (they dated, in fact, from the Somoza era). Numerous Nicaraguan and international observers (even some critical of the relocation program) also denied the validity of the U.S. claims of torture and extermination of the Indians.

By late 1984 tensions between the government and EPS and the Miskitu people had diminished greatly, and social, agricultural, and economic programs in the relocation zones had begun to function much better. Government spokesmen and some others expressed optimism about the potential for economic development in the Atlantic zone and for the integration of the region's people into the national culture and society. The legacy of bitterness from the excesses and errors of 1979–1982, however, undoubtedly presented a formidable obstacle for the cultural and ideological incorporation of the Miskitu and other Atlantic cultures into the "new Nicaragua."

Integration of Women

Things went somewhat better with efforts to integrate women into society.[21] Women's strong role in the insurrection and in the FSLN ranks, the FSLN's programmatic commitment to women's emancipation, and the Statute of Rights and Guarantees of Nicaraguans decreed by the junta in 1979 all portended significant new roles and possibilities for women, but traditional religious and social values as well as practical constraints upon the new regime provided significant barriers to such change. Machismo, an ethos of male dominance, pervaded Nicaraguan sexual and social values; many women suffered from abandonment by the father of their children, 60 percent illiteracy, legal discrimination, and concentration in unstable and low-paying jobs—a daunting array of problems for the new regime.

The principal vehicle for promoting women's rights within the revolutionary process was AMNLAE, which had five major goals and areas of activity. Molyneux has employed these goals of AMNLAE as a useful framework for summarizing the evolving role of women in Nicaraguan society and in the revolution.[22] Regarding defense of the revolution, women had made up as much as 40 percent of the FSLN ranks and 6 percent of its officers; six women had attained the rank of guerrilla commander (*comandante guerrillero*) in the reorganized EPS in 1980. Women, however, were gradually shifted to noncombat roles or into the Sandinista Police, prompting protests that led first to the establishment of several all-female combat units and later to integrated battalions. Women made up about 45 percent of the militia in 1984, and one estimate placed the number of women guards in the revolutionary vigilance program at fifty thousand, some 80 percent of the total. Women's defense roles, then, tended to shift toward indirect, support, and civil defense efforts and away from combat, but female mobilization increased substantially from 1979 to 1984.

In the area of promoting political awareness and participation, the FSLN claimed 22 percent female membership, with over a third of its leaders being female. However, no women sat on the National Directorate, and only a few held top government posts. In the mass organizations, AMNLAE itself had eighty-five thousand members by 1984 and had organized hundreds of committees to encourage participation and ideological awareness in the workplaces, schools, and neighborhoods. The peasant organization ATC had few women until 1983 and 1984, when an AMNLAE campaign increased female membership to about 40 percent. CDSs and the JS-19 organization had some 50 percent female membership. Women participated extensively in the literacy crusade as teachers, support workers, and students, though proportionately fewer women than men learned to read. Women constituted 80 percent of the activists in the 1980–1981 Popular Health Days (Jornadas Populares de Salud), which inculcated basic hygiene, conducted neighborhood cleanup campaigns, and vaccinated over a million people against polio and other diseases.

In the area of combating institutional inequalities and discrimination against women, the junta banned sexist exploitation of women in advertising and mandated equal pay for men and women performing equal work, full-pay maternity leaves for pregnant women, and industrial job safety improvements. Rural women and children over fourteen were required to be paid directly by employers, abolishing a practice of paying family wages only to the male head of family. A 1981 law equalized women's rights and privileges in custody cases with those of men and recognized the legal rights of illegitimate children. However, a 1982 draft provision law introduced by AMNLAE in the Council of State to legally obligate deserting fathers to support their children and to increase a male spouse's duties within the home stirred up a blizzard of objections and protests from men. Although passed by the Council of State in late 1982, the law had not been ratified by the junta by late 1984.

Improving women's economic and social positions proved rather difficult to achieve in the short run, given the harsh economic situation of the reconstruction and war against the contras. Women had increased from making up only 17 percent of the economically active population (EAP) in 1971 to composing 40 percent of the EAP by 1982, a greater share than the average in Latin America, but women workers remained in low-income jobs—agriculture, petty marketing, and personal service. AMNLAE strove with some success to assist the most deprived women through the establishment of production collectives producing such items as clothing and pottery, the promotion of family and communal gardening, and the distribution of agricultural land to rural women. Other efforts involved promoting educational improvements for women; female university enrollment, for example, doubled to roughly 40 percent between 1979 and 1984. Although successes in these efforts were notable, women still fell far behind men in economic status, and the slow recovery of the economy delayed further improvements.

Both economic and cultural conditions provided obstacles to promoting an appreciation of domestic labor and developing child care facilities for working women. The hotly debated and unimplemented provision law called for males to share in domestic labor; its moribund status two years after its passage testified to the difficulty of altering entrenched cultural biases against such sharing. AMNLAE and the FSLN promoted family frugality and resource conservation during the difficult years of 1982 and afterward, a reflection of the revolutionary movement's ambivalence toward the traditional family and domestic roles of women. Efforts to promote birth control and to legalize abortion remained very limited because of the intense opposition to such programs from the Catholic church. Finally, over forty child care and development centers were established in urban and rural areas, serving some four thousand children by 1984, and children's lunchrooms began to provide a daily main meal to several thousand poor children. However, such programs were only a small beginning in a society in which tens (if not hundreds) of thousands of families and children needed such services, yet the war against the contras and the burden of defense spending blocked their expansion.

In summary, women in the Nicaraguan revolution made important symbolic and legal advances in status and modest relative progress in material conditions and reduced discrimination. Institutional decisions, similar to those concerning other social programs, subordinated immediate and dramatic advances in women's status to the defense of the revolution as a whole. As Molyneux observed,

> The fate of women in Nicaragua in the first five years [was conditioned greatly] by external forces. These limited the capacity of the government and organizations like AMNLAE to implement a far-reaching reform program. Yet the paradox of the war was that while it certainly divided many women, not only along class lines, it also created the conditions in which women were increasingly mobilized in support of the revolution's gains. The spontaneous mobilizations of women in the prerevolutionary period were . . . transformed in the first five years into an organized and institutionalized defense of the regime they had helped bring to power.[23]

Economic Policy

The economic problems facing Nicaragua's revolutionaries in 1979 were formidable. The new government inherited several grave problems from the Somoza regime, including dependency on the export sector for about a fourth of all production, a tradition of financing large government deficits through foreign borrowing, and a chronic trade deficit. Nicaragua's 1975–1978 external balance averaged a deficit of $355 million per year, and government deficits increased from 37 percent of the $300-million 1975 budget to 51 percent of the $439-million 1978 budget. Of the $1.44-billion total public expenditure from 1975 to 1978, Nicaragua had financed 31 percent ($459 million) through foreign borrowing.[24] The new government came to power with the foreign accounts of the treasury drawn down to zero and with an international public debt of $1.6 billion.

The revolutionary government pursued, with varying success, three major goals for the economic system: (1) to rebuild the devastated economy; (2) to redistribute income and economic influence toward the lower classes and to reduce inequalities in wealth; and (3) to dismantle the economic base of the old regime. Some of these goals, however, worked against each other in the short run. For example, some policies favoring income redistribution (land reform, increased labor organization and militancy, nationalizations) caused short- to medium-run disruptions that reduced overall production and slowed the recovery.[25] Recovery still lagged badly in 1984. Moreover, U.S. economic pressure after 1981 severely damaged both economic recovery and new development efforts.

Transformation of the State and Its Economic Role

The Sandinistas divided their economic program[26] into several problem areas, the first of which was the transformation of the state and its economic role.[27] Nationalizations by the revolutionaries increased the public sector's share of the GNP from the 1978 level of 15 percent to 41 percent in 1980, with further small increments to reach about 45 percent by 1984. Most affected were natural resources (mining, lumber, and fishing), construction, manufacturing, services (banking, insurance, and transportation), and (although rather less than the others) agriculture. The approximately one hundred and twenty firms and two thousand farms (800,000 hectares) in the People's Property Area (Area Propiedad del Pueblo—APP) experienced both unexpected technical difficulties and critical shortages of managerial and technical talent. As many nationalized firms had been Somoza-owned, many of their managers had fled Nicaragua in mid-1979. After the victory, the austerity of life in Nicaragua caused other, prorevolutionary managers and technicians to emigrate to greener and less turbulent pastures elsewhere. The higher education system was being reorganized to provide needed technicians, but this solution would require several years to take effect.

Much was changed to improve the integrity and capacity of public administration. The Ministry of Planning directed government reorganization and guided public-policy planning with the collaboration of the other ministries and interagency program-coordinating commissions. Fiscal policy and public financial management were overhauled to improve revenue generation. To the delight of the new government, in 1979 and 1980 Nicaraguans greatly increased their voluntary tax payments of all sorts. This public vote of confidence and the reduced graft kept public revenues running well ahead of expected levels in 1980. Tax increases after that date were applied mainly to consumer luxuries such as beer, soft drinks, and tobacco. The national bureaucracy grew rapidly in 1980, so the junta cut the number of public employees by 5 percent in 1981. By 1984 there were several signs that the expansion of the state had ended and that failing some major crisis that might force further realignment, the public sector of the revolutionary regime was entering a phase of consolidation.

Any assessment of the economic performance of the Sandinista regime must consider not only the revolutionary program but also the external pressures emanating from the United States. After 1981 the United States sought to disrupt the Nicaraguan economy with the following policies: suspension of the final $15 million of a $75-million economic aid package approved during the Carter administration, suspension of wheat shipments, blocking Inter-American Development Bank loans to Nicaragua, and persuading the World Bank to suspend all its International Development Association loans to Nicaragua. The United States cut Nicaragua's sugar quota by 90 percent in May 1983, which resulted in a revenue loss of $23 million. The United States impeded trade with Nicaragua by restricting exports of chemical feedstocks, by applying "inconsistently scrupulous and exaggerated agricultural inspections," closing Nicaragua's U.S. consulates, pressuring U.S. firms to stop trading with Nicaragua, and directly pressuring U.S. banks to block loans to Nicaragua.[28] Despite the successful renegotiation of Nicaragua's long- and middle-term debts to U.S. financial institutions, Reagan administration pressure on banks caused a precipitous decline in credit to Nicaragua. The overall amount Nicaragua owed U.S. banks declined from $449.8 million in December 1980 to $322.2 million in December 1983. More important, short-term credit, essential to finance exports and key imports, had shrunk from about 55 percent of the total owed to about 20 percent for 1982–1983.

The U.S.-backed guerrillas and CIA campaign of economic sabotage increasingly damaged Nicaragua's economy through activities that included air and sea attacks upon pipelines and oil storage facilities, the mining of Nicaragua's harbors, and attacks upon farms and crops. Nicaragua estimated the material damage to property from such attacks at $220,000 in 1981, $23.5 million in 1982, $166 million in 1983, and $15 million in the first quarter of 1984. Other estimates of the costs of the war ranged as high as $1 billion overall, including lost production.

The war forced the government "to create secure channels of food distribution in order to guarantee basic products to the entire population; to put an end to speculation. . . . We have established greater centralized control over our resources and have strengthened our means for managing the economy in . . . foreign exchange and food distribution. We have allotted our foreign exchange more efficiently to priority areas: defense, the supply of basic goods, health care and production."[29] Inflation, repeated shortages of basic consumption items due to speculation, and a doubling of the black-market exchange rate for the córdoba (from fifty to the dollar in 1983 to over one hundred in 1984) were the by-products of the war for Nicaragua's businesses and consumers.

Agrarian Reform and Increased Agricultural Production

The new government faced prodigious problems in agriculture. The extensive Somoza family cotton holdings had been abandoned by their managers, and the workers had commenced a lengthy "vacation" in the absence of any coercion to work. Production of key crops had plunged because of abandonment and the war—beans by 29 percent, corn by 20 percent, sugar by 14 percent, milk by 50 percent (estimate), and cotton by a devastating 82 percent. The largest farms (over 500 manzanas—750 acres) represented only 0.6 percent of the total but occupied over 41 percent of the cultivable land, while poor peasants (with fewer than 10 manzanas) made up 58 percent of the landowning farmers but held only 2 percent of the land.[30] Landless seasonal workers and permanent wage workers (each about a fifth of the economically active rural population) lived in penury because of low wages, lack of land, and high unemployment. Much good land was committed to the capital-intensive production of the speculative export crop cotton, while domestic food production failed to meet national needs. Small and medium farmers produced most basic food grains, but many of them lacked sufficient credit, fertilizer, machinery, and technical assistance to produce efficiently.

Goals for the agricultural sector included rebuilding production to prewar levels; reforms in agricultural development, credit, and marketing to minimize the negative effects of the agro-export system; and the promotion of the interests of small producers and agricultural workers through a major transformation of the system of land tenure.[31] The agrarian reform was designed to break the economic power of the old regime and to respond "to the needs and involve the participation of the small peasant farmer and landless rural worker."[32] The idea was to establish a mixed agricultural economy that sought, rather "than control of the means of production, [control of] the economic surplus in order to distribute justly the nation's wealth."[33] To execute agricultural policy, the Ministry of Agricultural Development and the new National Agrarian Reform Institute combined in 1980 into the Ministry of Agricultural Development and Agrarian Reform (MIDINRA) under the leadership of intellectual and Sandinista DN member Jaime Wheelock Román. Although Wheelock was at first viewed as one of the DN's radicals, many observers eventually came to agree that under his leadership MIDINRA's agrarian reforms were quite flexible and pragmatic.[34]

Agrarian reform during 1979–1981, under terms of two JGRN decrees (numbers 2 and 38), swiftly reduced the number of private latifundia and established many state-owned farms. The new public agricultural enterprises, a key part of the new state economic sector known as the People's Property Area (APP), numbered fifteen hundred and encompassed 800,000 hectares (about 2 million acres), almost a quarter of Nicaragua's cultivable land. The regime placed a high priority on successfully managing the state farms—large, modern properties seized mainly from the Somoza family and its cohorts—because they produced one-fifth of the key revenue-generating exports such as coffee, cotton, and beef. The regime assured the remaining private farmers and ranchers—who were fearful about their security—that they could continue to own and cultivate their properties, regardless of size, as long as they obeyed labor laws and did not leave their land idle.

Rural wages were increased, and day laborers on both state and private farms and peasant smallholders were organized by the ATC, which had fifty-nine thousand members by late 1979 and about one hundred twenty thousand by mid-1980. The ATC became both an effective lobbyist and a union for peasants and also helped the FSLN and MIDINRA train peasants in new techniques and political values. To stimulate production, the government passed decrees in early 1980 that lowered land rents by 85 percent and barred eviction of tenants. MIDINRA also doubled the acreage receiving basic agricultural credits for 1980-1981 and quadrupled credit in such basic grains as corn, beans, and rice. Special efforts were made to extend credit to the poorer peasants: Smallholders in cooperatives and independent smallholders received preferential interest rates (as did state farms), but private agriculture also received ample credit. These policies stimulated both cooperative formation (over twenty-five hundred had appeared by mid-1980) and grain production. However, the late arrival of credit, poor marketing facilities, bad weather, and limited technical assistance destroyed the crops of many smallholders and left them saddled with heavy debts. Export crop production, disastrous in the war-year harvest of 1979-1980, had recovered substantially by 1980-1981 but remained inadequate for national needs.

By 1981 several strains had appeared in the agricultural sector. Despite government credit, a seat on the Council of State, and regime assurances, people involved in large- and medium-scale private agriculture, represented by the Union of Nicaraguan Agricultural Producers (UPANIC), remained restive and reluctant to invest in new production. UPANIC began to organize smallholders against the ATC and became an overt opposition political force. Angered by the rental law, large-holders reduced land rentals to small producers and evicted some tenants. These actions prompted landless and land-poor peasants to increase their demands for land and to invade both public and private holdings. Internally, increasingly irreconcilable tensions developed in two areas of the ATC: between its functions as a union for wage laborers and as a representative of small owners, two very different constituencies, and between MIDINRA's preference for state farms and increasing peasant pressure for land distribution.

These growing problems led the JGRN to decree the 1981 Agrarian Reform Law[35] and to adopt a series of policies that ushered in the second major phase of the agrarian reform. In order to satisfy private agriculture's security concerns, the decree limited expropriation to only idle or underutilized lands in excess of 500 manzanas (750 acres) in the Pacific area and 1,000 manzanas elsewhere. Agrarian courts, which included peasant members, were established to adjudicate and compensate expropriations. In 1982 many of MIDINRA's operations were decentralized into sixteen regional offices, giving local peasants better access to policy planning. MIDINRA, at first committed to a strategy of favoring state farms, shifted gears and began to parcel out land to peasants, with different approaches predominating in different zones. MIDINRA, however, strongly favored cooperative production arrangements, so co-ops received almost four-fifths of the 421,000 manzanas distributed among twenty-six thousand families from 1981 to late 1983. Land confiscations (over 60 percent of them for inefficient use) and redistribution were accelerated in 1983 because of attacks by the counterrevolutionaries on the theory that land-reform beneficiaries would defend both the regime and their new property. The agrarian reform program continued to result in a redistribution of land at an aggressive pace in 1984.

Other aspects of the second phase of agrarian reform included the enactment of the National Food Plan (Plan Alimentario Nacional) in 1981 to promote national self-sufficiency in food staples, improve agricultural marketing, and improve prices to small and medium producers for their crops. Most of Nicaragua's food grains had been produced by these smaller farmers on poor land and with inadequate credit and technical assistance. Under the National Food Plan,

MIDINRA increased land redistribution and services to smallholders, and the Ministry of Commerce sharply raised producer prices of basic grains in order to make them more attractive to and profitable for small farmers. MIDINRA invested in several extensive, modern, irrigated corn and bean cultivation projects to supplement smallholder production. MIDINRA also undertook major agricultural investment programs for milk (production had plummeted after 1979 when ranchers butchered their dairy herds), export tobacco, and several tropical products. The government forgave smallholder debts acquired in 1980–1981 and reformed the granting of credit to smallholders.

In response to the small producers' dissatisfaction with the ATC, a new agricultural association was formed. Small and medium owners and cooperative members formed the National Union of Farmers and Cattlemen (UNAG) in April 1982. UNAG promoted the small-holders' interests—pressing especially for secure land titles—and worked to counteract UPANIC's recruitment of peasant owners into opposition to the regime. Organized around local committees and represented on most government councils and agricultural policy boards, UNAG grew very rapidly (to a reported forty-six thousand members by 1983) and became quite influential in regard to agrarian reform policy. MIDINRA's decisions to deemphasize state farms in favor of distributing more land to cooperatives and individuals and to accelerate land redistribution and titling in 1983 and 1984 both reflected UNAG's policy influence.

The effects of these policies can be measured in the extensive land redistribution to the benefit of poorer peasants: Private holdings over 500 manzanas had dropped from 41 percent of the cultivable land in Nicaragua in 1978 to only 12 percent by 1983. Small holdings (zero to 50 manzanas) had increased from 15 to 18 percent of cultivable land and cooperative farms from zero to 7 percent in the same period. State farms, of which there were none in 1978, occupied 23 percent of the cultivated land by 1983. Other effects included producer price increases for corn, beans, rice, and sorghum ranging from 50 to 125 percent between 1980 and 1983, which increased peasant income and stimulated production increases in rice (55 percent) and beans (64 percent) between the 1980-1981 and the 1982-1983 harvests. The production of coffee, tobacco, pigs, chickens, and eggs had also increased notably by 1982-1983. Cotton, cattle, and milk production, however, remained sharply below 1978-1979 levels.

Considering that extensive agrarian reform typically lowers production during its early stages, Nicaragua's production figures after only four years of revolution were remarkably good. The reforms had not made Nicaraguan peasants rich, but they appeared to have laid the groundwork for eventual real improvements in living conditions for the rural poor. The reforms avoided the extensive bureaucratization of agriculture while strengthening peasant organization, policymaking participation, and support for the FSLN. Thome and Kaimowitz argue that the government and MIDINRA revealed

> a capacity to subsume ideological goals and values in favor of political pragmatism, economic reality, and result-oriented policies. While this process created some tensions within the FSLN, particularly between those who favored centralized planning as against those who supported a more decentralized and participatory process, . . . Nicaragua's agrarian reform process nevertheless progressed toward . . . maintaining agricultural productivity in the context of profound transformations in income and resource distributions.[36]

Unfortunately for Nicaragua, the international prices of its major export crops—coffee and cotton—declined steadily throughout the first five years of the revolution, sharply reducing vital foreign earnings despite production advances and structural reforms.

Rebuilding Industrial Production

The Ministry of Industry sought to rebuild industrial productivity[37] in both the nationalized sector (the People's Industrial Corporation—COIP) and in the private sector. With 1979 GNP at only about two-thirds of 1978 levels because of the war's damage to industrial plants, the government's major industrial objective was to reactivate manufacturing facilities and thus to rebuild industrial employment. Priority was given to traditionally strong export items and to products badly needed for internal consumption (medicines, shoes, clothing, and construction materials). The government sought private-sector cooperation through production accords (*convenios de producción*). Under these agreements between the Ministry of Industry and private firms, entrepreneurs contracted to produce needed goods at negotiated prices, quantities, and schedules in exchange for public credit and raw materials imports. In 1979–1980 the regime invested more than $230 million to rebuild industrial production, 90 percent of which went to essential industries. Overall capital expenditure (projected) for 1980 alone—including private-sector investment—was $235 million, a powerful stimulus to the manufacturing economy. However, both public-sector and private-sector investment in manufacturing declined beginning in 1981; net private investment was strongly negative. After 1981 the state allocated progressively less foreign exchange to industry for importing inputs (something that was happening throughout

Central America), thus increasing the number of idle factories. By 1983 manufacturing output had fallen to 1980 levels (some 20 percent below the peak year of 1978) and appeared to be declining further for 1984 and beyond.[38]

As in the agrarian sector, the revolutionary regime had reserved a significant role for private capital—75 percent of manufacturing, 30 percent of construction, and 45 percent of services. The junta wholly nationalized banking, insurance, and water and electrical utilities. But from April 1980 until September 1981 no new nationalizations occurred (except for thirteen firms that had been decapitalized by their owners). Several multinational companies operated in Nicaragua after the revolution, but others did not reopen and little new foreign private capital was invested. The slowness of economic recovery in mid-1981 brought a temporary suspension of recourse to amparo, a disadvantage for private capital, but the junta compensated for that move with stepped-up credit and other assistance to businesses, plus a one-year moratorium on strikes. Government incentives to investment by the private sector in the form of special exchange rates for exports were widely refused by capitalists, and the black-market dollar price surged rapidly in 1982, indicating that private investors were rushing to export, not their products, but their capital. Although the regime confiscated a few firms for decapitalization, it chose not to carry out a massive reorganization of the industrial sector, apparently for political reasons connected with its international image and domestic opposition.

The roots of this failure in industrial policy have been identified by Weeks.[39] Two important factors preceded the revolution and the war. First, in the late 1970s a virtual collapse of the CACM sharply reduced the external demand for Nicaraguan manufactured goods. Second, the sharp increase in the price of foreign inputs to manufacturing that accompanied the córdoba devaluations and inflation of 1979 and 1980, plus a marked increase in the need for imported inputs for manufacturing, severely limited both state and private manufacturers' ability to rebuild production. In summary, Nicaragua's industrial sector would have shrunk in the early 1980s with or without the revolution.

However, additional barriers to industrial recovery appeared after the Sandinista victory. Domestic capitalists engaged in practices that hurt recovery, such as the export and slaughter of dairy and beef herds, which lowered domestic inputs to the milk product and leather goods industries. Moreover, the private sector largely refused to take advantage of government incentives to invest, decapitalized existing firms, and pressured other investors not to invest and to reduce production. Finally, the persistence of a market economy and the random nature and minority position of the state's investments in manufacturing made it impossible for COIP to manage, control, or rationally plan an industrial policy. In effect, between domestic and international political constraints on industrial reorganization and the relatively weak position of government-owned enterprises in the economy, the state owned about a third of the industrial sector but could not control even its own portion effectively. As of 1984 prospects for improvement appeared very slim.

Foreign Commerce

The regime's objective for foreign commerce[40] was to continue to generate traditionally profitable foreign exports, but for a share of their profits to accrue to the state rather than the bourgeoisie. The government thus nationalized foreign commerce, diversified commercial relations to include new markets among the nonaligned and socialist countries, established careful import and foreign currency controls to reduce the trade deficit, and renegotiated the enormous foreign debt inherited from the Somozas. Some of these goals would prove very elusive, but Nicaragua made modest progress in the diversification of its foreign trade. Table 10.1 reveals clear patterns of declining U.S. trade: Exports to the United States fell from 23 percent in 1977 to 18 percent in 1983 while imports from the United States declined from 29 percent to 19 percent. Some of the declining trade with the United States occurred because of Reagan administration policies to block commerce with Nicaragua, including a 90 percent reduction of Nicaragua's sugar quota, closure of Nicaraguan consulates, and altered meat inspection standards. Nevertheless, in 1983 Nicaragua still exported most of its bananas, meat, and fish to the United States.

Trade with the Central American Common Market fell by half during the same period because of several factors already mentioned and because of the disruption of production and consumption brought about by regional conflicts. Exports to the CACM dropped from 21 percent to only 8 percent between 1977 and 1983; imports from the CACM declined somewhat less, from 22 percent to 15 percent. Exports to Mexico and Venezuela declined slightly from 3 percent to 2 percent between 1977 and 1983, but Mexican and Venezuelan imports, mainly oil provided on concessionary terms, had risen from 15 percent in 1977 to 24 percent by 1983. Venezuela stopped its oil sales to Nicaragua after 1982, leaving Mexico to take up some of the slack and the Soviet Union the rest. Nicaraguan exports to Japan rose about a third under the new regime, but imports plummeted from 10 percent

Table 10.1
Selected Trade Data for Nicaragua, 1977-1983

	Trading partners (percent of total trade)									
	1977		1980		1981		1982		1983	
Region	Ex	Im	Ex	Im	Ex	Im	Ex	Im	Ex	Im
Central American Common Market	21	22	17	34	14	21	13	15	8	15
United States	23	29	36	28	26	26	22	19	18	19
Mexico and Venezuela	3	15	.1	20	2	26	4	27	2	24
Japan	11	10	3	3	11	3	11	2	15	2
Socialist bloc (COMECON)	1	.3	3	.2	7	3	7	12	13	17

	Indicators of Terms of Trade (1970=100)				
	1977	1979	1980	1981	1982
Terms of trade for goods	112	92	90	83	73
Buying power of exports of goods	117	141	85	90	70

Source: Sylvia Maxfield and Richard Stahler Sholk, "External Constraints," in
Thomas W. Walker, ed., Nicaragua: The First Five Years (forthcoming),
Chapter 11, Tables 1 and 2.

in 1977 to only 2 percent in 1983. Not reflected in these data was
increased trade with other Third World countries as diverse as Taiwan,
Algeria, and Iran.

Nicaragua began increasingly to trade with socialist countries after
the Sandinistas' victory. Exports to the socialist bloc rose from only
1 percent in 1977 to 3 percent in 1980 and then to 13 percent in
1983; imports from the socialist economies rose from nearly nothing
in 1977 to 17 percent of Nicaragua's total in 1983. By no means,
however, did Nicaragua become an integral part of the socialist
economic system; the country remained "overwhelmingly dependent
on trade with the capitalist world and the U.S. continued to be the
country's single largest trading partner."[41] Of particular importance

to Nicaragua, a very large share of its most critical imports of chemicals, spare parts, and raw materials continued to come from U.S. suppliers.

The small, modestly industrialized Nicaraguan economy depended heavily upon imports for many key parts of its economic life and depended upon exports to pay for them. The new government hoped eventually to reduce its twin dependencies on imports and agricultural exports and to inject new life into the stagnant subsistence sectors of the economy. In order to do so,

> Nicaragua needed to diversify its exports and promote those exports which, through linkages with production of other goods and services, would help the entire domestic economy. However, the economy could not be transformed overnight . . . and the need to earn foreign exchange to pay debts and to buy vital imports was more urgent than the need to diversify.[42]

The regime thus decided to turn to the traditional foreign exchange earner, agriculture, to finance vital imports and pay the nation's foreign debts. Responding to the programs outlined above, agricultural production and the volume of exports rose. Additionally, the government imposed stringent import restrictions upon nonessential and luxury goods, which drastically curtailed the outflow of foreign reserves. However, despite these largely successful domestic policy measures, Nicaragua's terms of trade (the prices received for its exports) declined sharply from those of 1977 (see Table 10.1). Thus, even though the agro-export volume rose, the total value of exports declined.

To counter these import-export problems, the government took several steps. It selected several nontraditional agricultural products (including sesame seeds, melons, mangoes, ginger, garlic, and onions) and aggressively promoted their production and export—they increased in export value from $14 million in 1979 to $39 million in 1983. It also promoted import substitution programs such as the cultivation of African palm for cooking oil and of cacao. A thermal energy project to tap the heat of the volcano Momotombo began to operate in 1983, apparently reducing national oil import needs by something over 10 percent. The regime with certain, much trumpeted success encouraged workers and firms to develop domestic substitutes for parts and equipment. A multiple exchange rate (ten córdobas to the dollar at the official rate, twenty-eight to the dollar at the parallel rate) was established to subsidize certain exports and to tax heavily nonessential imports. The nature of imports shifted away from luxury consumption items (automobiles, home furnishings, small appliances) toward items for lower-class consumption (basic food imports tripled after 1980) or of productive utility (trucks, buses, inputs for the construction industry).

The trade deficit fell from about $450 million in 1980 to $350 million in 1983, but this drop was due mainly to import reductions. The projected trade balance for 1984, however, was that $461 million in exports would cover slightly less than half of the $940 million spent for imports.[43] This depressing reality required that the regime continue to borrow heavily from abroad (and continue to pile up foreign debt) in order to finance imports and other key aspects of its programs and national defense.

Investments

The government heavily concentrated its 1979–1980 investments[44] in infrastructure development for the economy and in social services. Investments went mainly into construction, which created thousands of jobs and reduced the unemployment rate from 28 percent in 1979 to 17 percent in 1980. In 1980 alone the junta spent $150 million to build roads, streets, housing, parks, utilities, hospitals, and health centers. Another $120 million went to import equipment, especially for construction and public transport. Thus, public investment in the first three years of the revolution tended to concentrate upon building new or reconstructing war-ravaged service infrastructure. Major capital investments went into school, hospital, housing, and urban services construction and into agricultural production.

After 1982 the government stopped publishing detailed budget information for security reasons, so that from then on investment patterns must be inferred from policy and program shifts and public comments by government officials. It is quite clear, however, that the Sandinista government's priorities progressively changed from the promotion of new programs to ensuring the survival of the revolution, thus markedly shifting investment patterns.

The rapid escalation of counterrevolutionary attacks after 1982 caused a major increase in defense spending, which may well have doubled over 1981 levels to a publicly admitted 25 percent of the budget in 1983 and 1984. Military investments included a massive acquisition of matériel to provision an army and a militia that had more than doubled in size over 1981 levels. Investment in the production of basic building materials rose. Also increased after 1982 was capital investment in agriculture, which was increasingly perceived as the key to national economic survival. The regime began a broad program of producer price increases for basic grains to stimulate their production, yet sold these and other commodities to the public at prices below their purchase and distribution costs, a subsidy of popular consumption that may have amounted to another 10 percent of the budget. Additional investments in agriculture were directed into extensive, modern production of basic grains on state farms, irrigation systems, production of nontraditional export crops, and critically needed grain storage facilities.

The government also began to curtail some types of investment after 1982. Housing and urban development investment declined, and programs became more reliant upon community self-help housing improvement strategies. Very successful, popular, and inexpensive efforts to expand popular participation in public health and preventive health care were accompanied by quite unpopular reductions in spending for very expensive hospitals and health facilities and curative medicine. Investment in school construction and education capital spending, which had added about three thousand classrooms to the national stock and raised literacy levels by 75 percent between 1980 and 1983, declined in 1983–1984. Industrial investment by the public (and private) sectors also declined. These shifts reveal clearly both of the paradoxical development strategies forced upon the government by increasingly harsh economic and political realities—that in order to survive economically Nicaragua must rely upon and promote agro-export production rather than by diversifying production and by industrializing and that it must defend the revolution itself at the cost of sacrificing many of its social welfare gains for the poor.

Fiscal Policy[45]

The new government's fiscal policy sought to mobilize resources for economic recovery and to improve the living standard of the Nicaraguan people—a major expansion of the role of the state—without accelerating inflation or increasing external economic dependency. In 1980, despite increased tax revenues, the government could finance only 56 percent of its $577-million expenditures through taxation, requiring foreign borrowing of $223 million and domestic borrowing of $31 million. In 1981 some 37 percent of the $800-million budget was debt-financed. The government justified such large deficits as emergency measures necessary for the recovery and investment programs. About half the taxes collected in 1980 came from direct levies on income and wealth. In mid-1981 new progressive taxes on income and property were added to make the system still less regressive than under the Somozas; in early 1982 additional taxes were levied on alcohol and tobacco sales. And again, in April 1982, an "extraordinary contribution" (a 10 percent surtax on income and real property) was established to help finance the additional military expenditures necessitated by the national emergency. Tax increases after 1982 were on such luxuries as tobacco, soft drinks, and alcoholic beverages; such indirect consumption taxes raised about 40 percent of the revenue in 1984. Another third of the tax revenue came from income taxes—a flat 40 percent (after a large deductible) on individuals and 40 percent across the board on larger businesses. Most additional tax revenue came from import duties. In 1984 an experiment with the sale of surplus price-controlled items at parallel market prices in seven Managua-area supermarkets began to raise substantial new revenue.

The contra war's impact on fiscal policy was extremely negative. The rapid escalation of defense spending, plus continued consumer and producer subsidies, raised public spending rapidly after 1982. The state's ability to raise revenue from foreign commerce and taxes was insufficient to cover expenditures, so the government began to finance part of its fiscal deficit by inflating the currency—by 1984 up to about 10 percent of the value of the gross domestic product. Vice-Minister of Internal Commerce Ramón Cabrales admitted that "the government has begun to operate the money-printing machines"[46] in order to underwrite a portion of the estimated $800-million deficit out of a budget for 1984 of $1.9 billion. The extra currency in circulation accelerated inflation in 1984 as consumers competed for scarce goods with abundant córdobas. Ironically, after five years, the 1984 budget deficit was 42 percent, about the same as in 1980.

Aid and External Financing[47]

External financing of the budget deficit presented the government with several difficulties. The FSLN initially expressed great reluctance to assume the Somoza regime's debt but decided to do so because its entire recovery program depended upon still further external financing. The junta eventually recognized all extant obligations, except for those funds used for arms or those for which illegal contracts had been made, and renegotiated its public and private foreign debts on much more favorable terms. By thus preventing default, Nicaragua enhanced the creditworthiness of the revolutionary government. New outside financing was then obtained, amounting to $490 million for 1980 alone. This came mainly from other nations—U.S. AID lent $80 million—and intergovernment lenders—the Inter-American Development Bank lent $141 million; the World Bank, $60 million. In 1981, however, Nicaragua began to encounter several difficulties that required that the Sandinista regime continue high levels of external

Table 10.2
Selected New Commitments of Multilateral and Bilateral Assistance to Nicaragua
by Source, 1979-1983 (in millions of U.S. $)[a]

		1979	1980	1981	1982	1983	1979-1983
Total Aid	($)	272	528	687	541	415	2443
Multilateral	($)	213	171	86	94	65	629
Organizations	(%)	78	32	13	17	16	26
Official Bi-	($)	59	357	601	448	350	1815
lateral (total)	(%)	22	68	88	83	84	74
United States	($)	0	73	0	0	0	73
	(%)	0	14	0	0	0	3
Western Europe	($)	15	63	60	39	87	263
	(%)	6	12	9	7	20	11
Africa and Asia	($)	0	0	103	3	34	140
	(%)	0	0	15	1	8	6
Latin America	($)	44	119	333	154	84	733
	(%)	16	23	48	28	20	30
Socialist bloc	($)	0	102	105	253	146	607
(COMECON)	(%)	0	19	15	47	35	25

Source: Fondo Internacional para la Reconstrucción (FIR), May 1984, adapted
from data presented in Michael E. Conroy, "External Dependence, External
Assistance, and 'Economic Aggression' Against Nicaragua," unpublished
manuscript, June 1984, Table 7.

[a] Some rounding error may be present in totals.

financing yet made external aid and credit from traditional sources much more difficult to obtain.

The advent of the Reagan administration in the United States led to a suspension of U.S. assistance to Nicaragua and to concerted U.S. pressure on multilateral lenders to curtail loans. As Table 10.2 reveals, the $73 million in U.S. assistance in 1980 constituted some 14 percent of Nicaragua's aid for that year (U.S. aid to the Somoza regime had averaged $20 million per year from 1976 to 1979). Multilateral assistance to Nicaragua in 1979–1980 had made up 48 percent of the country's new aid commitments, but under U.S. pressure multinational lenders cut back sharply so that for 1981–1983 they provided just below 15 percent of Nicaragua's aid. As an example of the new, hard-nosed policy of the multinational lenders, the World Bank's case stands out: It had lent the Somoza regime $56 million during the final stages of the 1979 war yet forced the Sandinista government to *repay* a total of $29 million between 1980 and 1982. Nicaragua began to replace shrinking U.S. and multilateral assistance with loans from three main sources. Latin American nations—mainly Mexico and Venezuela—helped fill the breach in 1981 with about half of that year's $687 million in new aid commitments. Assistance from socialist countries jumped from an average of 17 percent of Nicaragua's total in 1980–1981 to 42 percent of its total in 1982–1983. Finally, aid from Western European nations rose in 1983 to 20 percent of new assistance commitments to Nicaragua for that year—more than double the level of previous years.[48]

In summary, Nicaragua's early progress in curbing imports, raising grain production, and other reform and austerity measures were undermined badly by new needs for foreign borrowing imposed by the burgeoning defense burden of 1982–1984. Foreign borrowing continued at a high rate, and as the United States succeeded in shutting down its own and multilateral credits, Nicaragua turned to new lenders in the socialist bloc and to European and Latin Americans for more aid than they had given in the past. Although the United States failed to isolate Nicaragua from Western assistance, the war and the credit crunch had both damaged Nicaragua's financial independence and converted the country into an important new client for socialist lenders.

Supplying Basic Consumer Needs[49]

Supplying basic consumer needs constituted another major aspect of economic policy. A 1979 study estimated that more than half of Nicaragua's children under five suffered from caloric and protein undernourishment and that the poorest half of the populace consumed an average of 1,571 calories per day in 1979, well below the minimum of 2,025 calories recommended for good health. The government moved immediately to improve living standards by distributing basic foodstuffs fairly. As wages determined the capacity of the poor to buy food and clothing, the government promoted more equal income distribution and moderately higher wages. Commodity hoarding, a serious problem in 1979–1980, forced up prices and enriched speculators. The government prosecuted speculators, encouraged farmers to cultivate more basic consumption items, and imported large amounts of food. By 1981 such measures had controlled the worst aspects of the food supply crisis, and the starvation of the insurrection period had been largely eliminated, malnutrition reduced, and some improvements in food supply and distribution achieved.

In general, the Sandinistas made food policy a high priority of the revolution and sought to address simultaneously two major

Figure 10.1. Three food distribution systems (1984): (above) ice for street vendors; (middle) neighborhood store that distributes price-controlled basic foods; (below) new public market in Ciudad Sandino. (Photos by the author)

problems related to food and basic commodities—inadequate popular *consumption*, owing to the legacy of poverty among a majority of Nicaraguans, and an inadequate national *production* of basic commodities for domestic use. As noted earlier, the production of food was promoted by various agrarian policies, including stimulating the cultivation of basic grains through credit, land redistribution, producer price increases, and state investment in basic grains.

Popular consumption of food was promoted by controlling food prices, subsidizing consumption, and promoting employment (to ensure a livable income for all families). As Austin and Fox point out,[50] the Ministry of Internal Commerce (Ministerio de Comercio Interior— MICOIN) established inspectors to monitor price-controlled items and enlisted popular organizations—especially the CDSs—to support the inspection effort. Success varied, but levying fines upon price gougers did not eliminate violations, nor did it control the time-honored practice of merchants to hoard commodities in order to create artificial scarcities. When hoarding escalated after the 1982 flooding, the regime actually jailed some speculators. By 1983–1984 supply of many basic commodities had increased sufficiently (though it remained erratic) so that the government tolerated a black market in order to permit people who had sufficient cash to avail themselves of additional supplies. Subsidies to consumers—MICOIN paid more to purchase and distribute basic food products than it sold them to consumers for—constituted a key redistributive mechanism to encourage farmers to produce more and to permit consumers to consume more. The cost of this subsidy program was so great that subsidies were reduced in 1982 and again in 1984, but food subsidization continued to absorb a large share of the government's budget. The regime promoted employment by expanding government and public construction jobs during 1979–1981, but after 1981 it cut back on both because of the high cost.

On the distribution side, the government sought to alter the traditional private food distribution system in order to reduce profiteering and to direct food supplies more equitably toward the poor and rural populations. The regime imported large amounts of basic grains through 1981, but bean and rice imports had dropped markedly by 1982 because of increased domestic production. The government formed the Nicaraguan Basic Food Enterprise (Empresa Nicaragüense de Alimentos Básicos—ENABAS) to purchase and distribute basic grains. ENABAS performed badly as a purchaser at first, but altered its strategy (to cooperate with honest private middlemen) and beefed up its grain storage facilities so that it was capturing over 60 percent of the supply by 1983. The severity of speculation led ENABAS to take over entirely the wholesale distribution of sugar, cooking oil, and flour in 1982. For retail sales to the urban public, ENABAS distributed through some four thousand private merchants in neighborhoods, urban supermarkets that were partially owned by the state, and over five hundred workers' commissaries in factories and other institutions (mainly in Managua). In rural areas ENABAS had set up over three hundred special commodity distribution centers by 1982. But rural operations were vulnerable to problems caused by the war, poor transportation, and the sheer physical isolation of much of the rural populace, and the government was still struggling to improve its rural food distribution system in 1984. To reach especially needy groups, the government donated food to some sixty thousand poor preschool children and pregnant and nursing mothers.

These massive efforts to reshape the food distribution system to improve the accessibility of food stumbled as the result of several persistent problems. First, the regime's very success in increasing employment and wages to make poor people more able to purchase food so increased demand that supplies became scarcer in relation to the expanded demand. Second, from 1981 on the war disrupted distribution of some products, especially to the Atlantic zone. Third, seasonal shortages and bad weather caused periodic interruptions of supplies. Fourth, errors and inefficiencies within the bureaucracies of ENABAS and MICOIN—both struggling to develop complex new systems with few experienced personnel—caused bottlenecks and blunders such as overexporting sugar in 1982 and thus creating a shortage. The major result of these problems was recurrent, intermittent shortages of basic commodities including sugar, cooking oil, beans, rice, toilet paper, and soap. In 1982 a rationing system, administered by local CDSs, was instituted for sugar and later expanded to include the other items listed above. Although ENABAS saved on administrative costs by making community administration of the system the responsibility of the CDSs, reports of political manipulation of rationing became rather common, providing the government with yet another headache and adverse propaganda.

Evidence concerning the success of the basic consumption policies remains mixed. The worst signs of hunger disappeared, but middle- and upper-class urban Nicaraguans undoubtedly had less variety of food products (especially luxury imports) than previously. All Nicaraguans experienced frustrating intermittent shortages, a source of immense vexation. The most improved aspect of food consumption probably was among the rural people who had access to land, now far more numerous than before the revolution. Overall it appeared that per capita [food] consumption increased, not a small feat given Nicaragua's annual population growth rate of 3.3 pecent. The consumption pattern varied considerably by product. Per capita rice intake was more than 60 percent above 1977 levels, the best economic year under Somoza. In contrast, maize consumption was no better than 1977 and beans improved only slightly. Poultry was up 80 percent, cooking oil 30 percent, eggs 21 percent, while beef was down 10 percent and milk 4 percent.[51]

Employment, Salary, and Social Service Policies[52]

The revolutionary government's employment, salary, and social service policies sought to improve the standard of living of the poor and to redistribute income, goods, and services more toward workers. In 1977 the poorest half of the Nicaraguan populace earned only 15 percent of national income, a figure that is believed to have shrunk even further in 1979–1980 because of increased unemployment. However, as Sandinista policies began to bear fruit in the mid-1980s, income and wealth inequalities in Nicaragua began to diminish.

The first goal of the income policy was to get Nicaraguans back to work by increasing industrial and agricultural production as well as public-sector construction. This policy succeeded fairly well for two years, but its cost became too great to sustain beyond 1981. Public-sector jobs and construction were decreased, and various problems gradually reduced industrial employment. However, after 1981 land redistribution and increases in the size of the armed forces took up much of the slack in employment so that unemployment did not rise precipitously, remaining around 14 percent. Indeed, after 1980 seasonal shortages of agricultural workers developed for the cotton and coffee harvests, prompting the government to promote volunteer harvesting by city dwellers.

A second goal was to raise real wages for the poor without promoting inflation, and this aim led to caution in raising wages. The government did enforce the payment of minimum wages (variable by economic sector) and also required employers to meet health and safety regulations. In agriculture, land redistribution and increased producer prices boosted the income of hundreds of thousands of peasants, and many state farm workers gained access to garden plots. Wages were increased only moderately to prevent inflation, a policy that frustrated many workers and their unions. Food price subsidies somewhat placated workers' concerns about wages, but subsidy reductions in 1981 and 1983 and the expanding currency supply fueled inflation, which eroded real wages more than 35 percent between 1981 and

1983. Labor pressure for higher wages thus built steadily. In 1983 the government negotiated a new national wage-scale policy with the Nicaraguan Trade Union Coordinating Committee (Consejo Sindical Nicaragüense—CSN), which included gradually phasing in cost-of-living raises. However, the CSN-regime accord did not prevent a wave of strikes for higher wages when the state of emergency's provision against job actions was lifted in mid-1984.

In addition to the policy of subsidizing food costs and controlling housing rental costs in order to protect working-class salaries, the government sought to raise what it called the "social salary," a wide array of public services to improve the living standard of the people. Among these services were the 1980–1981 literacy crusade and a fourfold increase in education spending; the construction of parks and recreation facilities in poor neighborhoods; programs of aid and rehabilitation for the handicapped, war veterans, orphans, juvenile delinquents, and refugees; and cultural and athletic programs. Social security programs, pillaged and left bankrupt by the old regime, were revamped, modernized, and expanded under 1982 laws to provide old age pensions and to operate a universal national health care system that provided workers and families with medical and maternity care.

Another part of the social salary was a vast national primary health care program, based—as the literacy crusade had been—on voluntary community and citizen participation, which included vital neighborhood cleanup campaigns to reduce vector-borne diseases; health, nutrition, and hygiene workshops among the poor; oral re-hydration clinics; and extensive vaccination campaigns against major communicable diseases. The results were impressive as infant mortality, malaria, and polio rates dropped markedly throughout Nicaragua. The government undertook a vigorous housing construction program, which contributed over ten thousand new units in four years. Some twenty-one thousand families in squatter settlements had received titles to their lots by 1983, and service development and neighborhood improvement programs for poor urban neighborhoods had improved living conditions for an estimated two hundred and fifty thousand people. This was but a fraction of the new housing and services needed, yet the counterrevolutionary war reduced government resources rapidly after 1981. As a result, housing development moved progressively toward the low cost provision of basic housing sites and services while leaving dwelling construction and improvement up to the occupant.

In summary, wage increases, ground rent controls, food and producer price subsidies, new social service programs, nationalization

Figure 10.2. Housing and service development in Managua squatter neighborhoods (1984): (above) rickety new shanties with new water system and
streetlights; (below) older squatter barrio houses have electricity and physical
improvements. (Photos by the author)

of businesses and farms, and land redistribution had shifted important amounts of ownership and control of wealth away from the Somocistas in particular and from the bourgeoisie in general. Despite the inevitable disruptions of production caused by economic reorganization, as well as bureaucratic inexpertise and inefficiency, war, economic harassment, and disinvestment, by 1984 the Sandinistas had progressed toward their goal of shifting wealth, income, and benefits toward the poor majority. Economic austerity and the insecurity brought about by the new economic rules lowered both the sense of security and the living standards of the upper and middle classes. But revolutionary policies had increased the power and resources of the state and had also raised the share of national wealth, income, and services available to the workers. Although none of the poor had become wealthy as a result of the revolution, a majority of Nicaraguans were healthier, had better services, and had more control over vital economic resources than under the old regime.

Defense and Military Policy

The last weeks of the insurrection brought thousands of untrained volunteers into FSLN ranks. During the first year of the revolution the Front took several steps to equalize these new self-recruits with the tough and disciplined veteran cadres trained up through early 1979: (1) Many were mustered out of the armed forces, especially for lack of discipline and abuse of authority; (2) the new Sandinista Popular Army (EPS) instituted rigorous military, political, and ideological training; and (3) the FSLN restricted access to weapons for troops not on duty to reduce problems of violence. By mid-1980 the EPS had changed from a guerrilla army into a regular armed force for the external defense of the Sandinista revolution.[53]

The perceived defense needs of the Nicaraguan revolution evolved substantially after 19 July 1979. After the victory there followed a three-month period of mopping up several Somocista underground bands. The Front then reorganized its military arm into the more specialized EPS and Sandinista Police. A new threat came from ex–National Guard elements, exiled Liberal Nationalists, and some expatriate bourgeois who promised to invade to oust the Sandinistas from power. Reports in 1981 revealed that such groups were training anti-Sandinista guerrilla forces in Honduras and in Florida. Periodic attacks on literacy volunteers and other targets in northern Nicaragua convinced the EPS of the seriousness of this threat. Third, the election of Ronald Reagan as U.S. president in November 1980 worried the Sandinistas because of Reagan's frequently expressed dislike for the

Sandinistas and their revolution, U.S. military and economic aid to El Salvador's rightist military regime (and talk of sending troops to that country), increased U.S. aid to both Guatemala and Honduras, and the U.S. record of covert intervention in Guatemala (1954), Cuba (1961), and Chile (1973) and overt military intervention in the Dominican Republic (1965). In early 1982 a well-financed CIA program to "destabilize" Nicaragua was revealed. Nicaraguan exile groups used U.S. assistance and training to stage sabotage missions and armed incursions into Nicaragua, at first mainly from Honduras but in 1982 from Costa Rica as well.

This destabilization effort by the United States—financed, supplied, and at least partly directed by the CIA—was the beginning of the so-called covert war against the Sandinista regime. The Reagan administration justified it as an effort to interdict Nicaraguan arms smuggling to the Salvadorean guerrillas rather than an effort to topple the Sandinistas from power, but this rationale appeared constructed solely to avoid the appearance of violating legislation and treaties barring such attacks. Nicaraguan defense planners' early fears that the U.S. policy would become more aggressive proved accurate. The rapid escalation of the counterrevolutionary war (especially after 1983 when large numbers of the ten thousand to fifteen thousand contras invaded Nicaragua and operated with material and logistical support including helicopters, air transports, and armed light aircraft) deepened the Nicaraguan military planners' fears of a full-scale, direct U.S. military intervention on Nicaraguan soil.[54] Other anticipated attacks included U.S. support for a Honduran or Guatemalan attack on Nicaragua, or to the regionalization of a U.S. occupation of El Salvador.

The Sandinistas, therefore, began in 1980 to enlarge the armed forces to counter these threats. The EPS was reorganized (under the leadership of Defense Minister Humberto Ortega Saavedra and Vice-Minister Luís Carrión Cruz, both members of the FSLN's DN) into regular service branches with a traditional rank structure. From the victory onward the Sandinista armed forces sought military equipment from abroad to standardize and refurbish their own arms hodgepodge and the (mostly U.S.) matériel captured from the Guard. The U.S. refusal to supply arms without U.S. training led the EPS to seek military hardware and training elsewhere, including from Panama and France and from Cuba and other Eastern bloc nations. In an accelerated buildup in 1981–1982 the EPS had grown to some twenty-two thousand troops by mid-1982, the largest army in Central America. As contra attacks escalated in 1983 the government passed a military draft law and began drafting males as young as sixteen in order to build the EPS to over forty thousand troops.

Another defensive resource was the Sandinista Popular Militia. First established in 1980, then permitted to languish somewhat in 1981, the militia received renewed government attention because of international threats to Nicaragua. More than a hundred thousand strong, it supplemented the EPS by training volunteers from every walk of life in basic military skills and in Sandinista ideology. The militia, commanded until mid-1981 by Edén Pastora, was viewed as critical to Nicaragua's external defense. Militia units helped provide security for the literacy crusade and saw action against Somocista raiders from Honduras. When the national emergency was declared in March 1982, seventy thousand militia were mobilized to build defensive fortifications and step up their training, and they saw considerable action against the contras after the step-up of combat in 1983. Estimates of the size of the militia in 1984 ranged from sixty thousand to one hundred thousand.

Among the more controversial military decisions of the government were those involving equipment, military training, and advisers. The Sandinistas had no intention of accepting any U.S. military advisers or training, which they viewed as having been responsible for the character of the National Guard and the old regime. The early presence of Cuban military and security advisers in the Sandinista forces expanded rapidly to include "key military and intelligence positions"[55] and a Cuban complement that totaled around two thousand by 1983. East German advisers (estimated to total thirty-five) were brought in to counsel the State Security Directorate, and some fifty Soviets were in Nicaragua on security-related missions in 1983. The Soviet Union and other Eastern bloc countries also supplied Nicaragua with military equipment, especially after the United States refused to supply the EPS and pressured Western nations to also make such a refusal. By 1984 Nicaragua had acquired about one hundred Soviet T-54/T-55 medium tanks, twenty light amphibious tanks, and some one hundred twenty other armored vehicles. Other equipment acquired included several hundred jeeps, over a thousand military trucks, heavy ferries for armor and artillery, some fifty pieces of Soviet artillery (152-mm/122-mm howitzers) and two dozen 122-mm multiple rocket launchers. The Nicaraguan armed forces also acquired over a hundred anti-aircraft guns and some seven hundred surface-to-air missiles as well as ten Soviet Mi-8 helicopters and six light and two heavy Soviet-built transport aircraft. The EPS had trained fighter pilots in Eastern Europe, but because of U.S. warnings, had no fighter aircraft of any sort.[56] The net effect of this matériel and manpower buildup was to leave Nicaragua with the largest active armed forces in Central America by 1984. However, the absence of a tactical air capability (in comparison to Honduras's large, U.S.-assisted air force), real fears of U.S. intervention, and the growing war against the contras suggested to many experts, including U.S. intelligence officials, that the Nicaraguan armed forces were primarily defensive in character.[57] Nicaragua's armed forces in 1984 roughly equaled the combined total of the military forces of Costa Rica, Honduras, El Salvador, and Guatemala, plus U.S. forces on maneuvers in Honduras. This substantial military effort absorbed at least a quarter of the national budget in 1984 and undermined or postponed key social programs. These effects, plus the economic and human costs of the contra war ($550 million between 1981 and 1984 in war damage and lost production, over eight thousand military and civilian deaths) and the controversy surrounding the draft and defense policies deeply strained the Sandinista revolution from within.[58]

Foreign Policy and Foreign Relations

Nicaragua's experience with U.S. direct intervention (1909–1933), U.S. support for the Somozas, and the efforts of the Carter administration to bar the Sandinistas from power profoundly influenced the revolutionaries.[59] The FSLN always viewed its struggle as one against the United States and its intervention almost as much as against Somocismo. Two factors predisposed the new government to act as independently from the United States as possible: (1) Historically, U.S. desires for Nicaragua repeatedly harmed Nicaraguan interests and narrowed its developmental and policy alternatives, and (2) the Nicaraguans' sense of national dignity had suffered from the Somozas' collaboration with U.S. intervention. After the victory, the new regime's foreign policy and relations evolved through two distinct phases, with the shift from the first to the second coinciding with the beginning of the Reagan administration in the United States in 1981.

1979–1981

The Sandinista policymakers strove to maximize Nicaragua's independence in the international environment, recognizing the vulnerability of their nation's tiny export-dependent economy within the zone of preponderant economic influence of the United States. On the one hand, the objective of increasing independence, tempered by realism about the larger economic environment, led Nicaragua to seek continued healthy economic ties with the United States and to welcome U.S. aid (like any other) if unencumbered by conditions that would limit independence. On the other hand, Nicaragua sought to open nontraditional markets and accepted recovery aid from socialist and nonaligned nations. In diplomatic terms, these objectives led to surprisingly good working relations between the junta-DN and U.S. Ambassador Lawrence Pezzullo (1979–1981) and to Nicaragua's willingness to treat the United States like any other nation (but not as privileged). But Nicaragua also opened diplomatic relations with many nations from the socialist bloc and resisted certain U.S. pressures. For example, Nicaragua abstained on two U.S.-engineered United Nations votes to condemn the Soviet invasion of Afghanistan, sent a delegation to the Moscow Olympics, and joined the Movement of Non-Aligned Countries. However, Nicaragua accepted Ambassador Pezzullo's advocacy of the role of Nicaraguan entrepreneurs in a dispute with the government in early 1980 and in general responded pragmatically and flexibly to U.S. concerns until early 1981.

Nicaraguan relations with Latin American nations were generally good in the 1979–1981 period; many nations in the region had supported the insurgents against Somoza. Nicaragua had particularly close ties with Mexico, Venezuela, and Panama, which had all backed the rebels during the insurrection. Each of the three was anticommunist and highly security conscious, and each hoped through friendly aid to shape the Sandinista revolution so as to minimize Central American instability and to enhance regional security. Relations with Costa Rica, once the rebels' most ardent supporter, soon cooled because of rising Costa Rican concern about the ideology of the revolution. The Nicaraguan–Costa Rican tradition of squabbling reemerged as President Rodrigo Carazo Odio of Costa Rica sought to distance himself greatly from the Sandinistas he had helped put in power. Conservative Brazil supported the Nicaraguans with economic aid. Nicaragua's relations with Cuba were very warm. Cuban assistance after the insurrection was substantial, including health and technical advisers numbering well over a thousand. Cuban President Fidel Castro, however, counseled Nicaragua to keep some distance from Cuba lest excessively cordial ties should brand Nicaragua as a Cuban or Soviet client.

Latin American nations with which Nicaragua had problematic relations included Honduras because of the camps of ex–National Guardsmen and border problems that developed almost immediately after Somoza's ouster in 1979. Honduran-Nicaraguan hostility grew in 1981 as the U.S.- and Honduran-backed anti-Sandinista raiders increased their activity. Relations were also poor with Guatemala and El Salvador, which accused Nicaragua of aiding insurgents in their countries. Nicaragua did permit weapons shipments to pass through from Costa Rica to the Salvadoran guerrillas for a time, but it claimed to have stopped when admonished by the Reagan administration. Nicaragua also had spats with Colombia over some disputed islands and with Bolivia for criticizing the 1980 military coup there. There were also tensions with Paraguay because of Nicaragua's efforts to extradite Anastasio Somoza Debayle from his Paraguayan exile to stand trial for war crimes. (Somoza's assassination in 1980, allegedly by Paraguayan and Argentine leftists, rendered this issue moot.)

1981–1984[60]

U.S. policy toward Nicaragua took a decisively hostile turn with the advent of the Reagan administration. Reagan's tendency to view the international scene in terms of bipolar confrontation between the Soviet Union and its clients (including Cuba) and the United States and its clients led him to regard the reformism and anti-U.S. rhetoric of the Nicaraguan revolution as indicative of Nicaragua's "loss" to the socialist bloc. Moreover, the administration's tough position against the insurgency in El Salvador brought direct pressure on Nicaragua to stop alleged arms transshipments to the Salvadoran guerrillas. In 1981 the United States suspended delivery of the rest of the 1980 U.S. aid package and other credits totaling $81 million and cut off wheat shipments to the grain-starved nation. Also in 1981 a threatened U.S. veto of an Inter-American Development Bank economic infrastructure development loan led Nicaragua to withdraw its loan application.

Nicaragua's responses to these U.S. actions were critical, yet at first quite moderate in tone. As a sign of concern about the nature of policy to be made by the Reagan administration, the junta sent one of its own members—Arturo Cruz, a former banker and skilled diplomat—to Washington as ambassador. His efforts proved futile, however, as U.S.-Nicaraguan relations steadily worsened. Nicaragua privately admitted its gunrunning and apparently ended it in 1981, although it did continue to provide a headquarters and a communications facility to the Salvadoran Farabundo Marti National Liberation Front (FMLN) guerrilla organization after 1981. To reassure the United States, spokesmen for Nicaragua reiterated that that country would not promote or support directly the Guatemalan or Salvadoran insurrections, whatever its sympathies for the parties involved. In July 1981, for example, Tomás Borge said: "Nicaragua will not export revolution. Our best support for change in Latin America and the world will be to advance our revolution. Our neighbors can rest assured of this."[61] Despite heavy-handed U.S. accusations of massive Nicaraguan aid to El Salvador's insurgents, no compelling evidence had been produced by mid-1984 that such aid went much beyond sympathy for the Salvadoran rebels, pre-1981 arms transshipment, and harboring rebel leaders.

As the U.S. campaign against Nicaragua escalated on the economic, military, diplomatic, and propaganda fronts from 1982 on, Nicaragua continued to offer to negotiate its differences with the United States but simultaneously increased its military preparedness, arms purchases, and diplomatic countermeasures. Nicaragua took its complaints about U.S.-sponsored aggression to the United Nations on various occasions between 1982 and 1984 and in early 1984 sued the United States in the International Court of Justice for treaty violations involved in contra attacks on Nicaraguan facilities and citizens and in the CIA's intimate participation in the 1983 mining of Nicaragua's harbors. After rulings on procedural matters went against the United States, the Department of State in early 1985 announced the administration's decision to withdraw from the jurisdiction of the International Court of Justice in matters concerning Central America. Nicaragua also continued to curry support from European social and democratic movements and governments and sought new bilateral sources of foreign assistance and new outlets for its exports.

Nicaragua's relations with its Central American neighbors and other Latin American states deteriorated after 1981. Serious difficulties arose in early 1982 when Costa Rica, Honduras, and El Salvador formed the Central American Democratic Community (Comunidad Democrática Centro Americana—CDCA), in which Nicaragua was not invited to take part. The CDCA's avowed goal was to promote democracy, in particular to stabilize the three regimes, and it involved a mutual defense commitment. Nicaragua's relations with Venezuela also deteriorated somewhat in 1981–1982 as evidence developed of Venezuelan support for certain counterrevolutionary activities within Nicaragua. Venezuelan oil sales to Nicaragua were suspended after 1982 (the harbor mining of 1983 reduced Mexican oil shipments as well). Counterrevolutionary organizations such as the ARDE in Costa Rica and other Nicaraguan opposition elements in Venezuela became publicly active in 1983. Most observers linked the growing Costa Rican–Nicaraguan and Venezuelan-Nicaraguan tensions to U.S. pressure upon the governments of Costa Rica and Venezuela to support U.S. efforts to isolate the Nicaraguan regime.

In late 1982 Mexico, Panama, Venezuela, and Colombia, fearful of escalating regional violence and possible direct U.S. military intervention in the region, joined forces to seek a peaceful resolution to Central America's various conflicts, including those between Nicaragua and its neighbors and the Sandinistas and their external enemies. Nicaragua's early position on the Contadora process, as this diplomatic effort was called, was to participate fully while seeking bilateral accords with its neighbors so as to speed up the resolution of particular conflicts. The other Central American states and the United States (not directly involved but exerting considerable pressure upon both Honduras and Costa Rica) pressed for a global, multilateral accord. Nicaragua became progressively more flexible as early points of agreement developed and eventually accepted the multilateral framework. The United States paid lip service to the Contadora process, and sent occasional missions to Managua, but continued to finance and manage the counterrevolutionary war, tighten economic pressures, execrate the Sandinistas in a fierce propaganda barrage, and so stiffen its demands upon Nicaragua that only if the FSLN left power could the U.S. administration be pleased. Indeed, the Reagan administration seemed to fire its harshest rhetorical and policy salvos, not at the Soviet "evil empire" or the very communist People's Republic of China, but at Nicaragua.[62]

In August 1984 Nicaragua, with national elections scheduled for November, agreed to sign the draft Contadora treaty. After two years of publicly endorsing Contadora, however, the United States suddenly reversed field, strongly criticized the draft accord, and immediately pressured other Central American states not to sign and to introduce new conditions. Many observers concluded that this tactic proved that U.S. policy was less to promote regional peace than to destroy the Sandinista regime. Other people believed that the administration's "sudden" reluctance concerning the accord portended a U.S. invasion of Nicaragua should President Reagan be reelected. The U.S. administration fueled such speculation into a crisis on 7 November 1984 by announcing it suspected MiG fighter planes were being unloaded in Nicaragua and threatening military retaliation before admitting that no such planes existed.[63]

In the first four years of the Reagan administration, the consistent antagonism and aggression of the United States toward the Sandinista revolution had foreclosed many economic, diplomatic, and political options for the government in Managua. Although not ostracized by moderate Latin American states or Western Europe, Nicaragua had turned increasingly toward Soviet bloc military and economic assistance. The Sandinistas did not establish formal military ties with the Soviet bloc or even hint that Nicaragua would ever provide bases for Soviet troops or strategic weapons, for to so so would undoubtedly invoke a swift and massive preemptive attack by the United States. However, the Sandinistas' worst expectations of the United States had proved true in their own eyes, and future U.S.-Nicaraguan relations had been poisoned still further. Rather than weakening the FSLN's grasp on power and strengthening Nicaraguan private enterprise and non-Marxist opposition, the U.S. aggression led to press censorship and to a weakening of domestic opposition, human rights, and private business. U.S. hostility also broadened and deepened the agrarian reform program and vastly increased the Sandinistas' military strength.

Across a Frontier of History: The Revolution and Its Future

We press onward toward the sunrise of liberty.
—Augusto César Sandino

As a great debate rages abroad about the Nicaraguan revolution's significance,[1] the people and the leaders of Nicaragua worry much less about meaning than about managing to persevere and to recover. Perhaps they may excuse us the final scholarly luxury of taking stock and summing up, something history relentlessly denies both the agent and the object of change.

Nicaragua and the Theory of Revolution

The Nicaraguan revolution challenges little of the theory introduced in Chapter 1. However, some of the theoretical issues and generalities about revolutions bear brief review for the Nicaraguan case.

General Attributes

Leaders and followers. As has been observed in other revolutions, Nicaragua's insurrectionary and revolutionary leadership shared predominantly middle- and upper-class origins. Many key figures came from Liberal or Conservative backgrounds (or from their dissident factions) and were either socialized from birth into opposition to the Somozas or radicalized by frustrated efforts at moderate reform. Peasants and proletarians, although represented, were relatively scarce among the insurrectionary leadership in comparison to upper- and middle-class leaders. Secondary school and university students (typically of upper- and middle-class backgrounds) contributed a major share of both the rebel leaders and most active followers in the insurrection, especially within the FSLN. Nicaraguans from all classes took an active part in the insurrection. The lower classes participated in anti-Somoza organizations, unions, and neighborhood and religious groups at the movement's base, and many fought alongside the Front when combat came to their neighborhoods. After the victory, the FSLN mobilized hundreds of thousands of workers and peasants to support the revolution, but it still experienced difficulty in managing lower-class economic demands in the interest of economic recovery.

Ideology. During the insurrection, the Somoza regime appealed to Nicaraguans to support its "democratic and constitutional" institutions in order to avoid the perils of "communism." The patently bogus nature of these appeals and the atrocities committed in the name of anticommunism not only failed to persuade Nicaraguans of the legitimacy of the incumbents but eventually alienated most of them from the regime and even split the PLN. In contrast, the FSLN's Sandinismo constituted a cluster of highly nationalistic and political-economic reformist symbols with deep roots in the Nicaraguan psyche. The ideology rallied thousands to support the insurgent cause. Since the FSLN victory the Sandinist ideology has expanded and evolved to encompass a broad program of reforms to redistribute income, wealth, power, and status and to alter foreign policy and the roles of external actors. It has also, with certain necessary tensions with its populist origin and framework, pursued the somewhat contradictory goals of moderating popular redistributive demands while expanding support for the FSLN and for the revolution. One useful feature of Sandinismo, however, has been its nationalism (and especially its anti-imperialism tinged with anti-Americanism), which evokes the pronounced antipathy of most Nicaraguans toward external interference and can thus rally support to the Sandinistas as heirs to Sandino's struggle against intervention. The unfriendly drift of U.S. policy toward Nicaragua that began with the Reagan administration in early 1981 at first helped the Front continue to rally popular support despite the persistence of postwar economic difficulties.

Revolutionary organization and mass participation. As late as 1978 the plethora of opposition groups remained divided. Even the oldest rebel movement, the FSLN, had become internally fragmented over strategy. However, spontaneous popular resistance to the Somozas following the January 1978 assassination of Chamorro and again in August–September 1978 ran far ahead of the expectations of the divided Sandinistas and the other opposition groups. The insurgent organizations responded to this popular lead in the rebellion by struggling to organize, to recapture the initiative, and to capitalize on the public's energetic rejection of the regime. The FSLN very quickly reunified, and most groups soon clustered into broad coalitions to coordinate the rebellion. The insurgents' success in 1978–1979 grew in proportion to each new organizational advance toward broad rebel unity and toward the internal coherence of the FSLN.

Violence. The injurious use of force was both extensive and intensive in the Nicaraguan insurrection, building in a series of ever-strengthening waves from sporadic demonstrations, strikes, and conspiracies (1950s) to guerrilla insurgency (1960s, 1970s) to a full-scale civil insurrection involving conventional battles between the National Guard and the FSLN with widespread popular participation in combat (1978, 1979). Mass involvement appears to have been quite high by the standards of most other revolutions—probably on a par with the Mexican revolution (1910–1917) and clearly higher than in Cuba (1958–1959) and Bolivia (1952). Casualties were great—some fifty thousand, or about 2 percent of the populace, dead. Popular participation in violence was widespread and included several spontaneous uprisings. There was also extensive popular aid to conspiratorial efforts against the regime, as well as widespread participation in protests, in spite of the highly repressive policies of the government.

Both sides employed terrorism, but the regime used it indiscriminately as opposed to the FSLN's more careful use of it to demoralize the National Guard. While the old regime's heavy use of murder and torture (especially from 1974 through 1979) undermined the legitimacy of the incumbents and alienated more and more people, the general populace suffered considerably less from FSLN terrorism. Some dramatic rebel acts even aroused popular admiration, such as the FSLN's seizure of the National Palace and nearly two thousand hostages for ransom in August 1978.

The rebels' strategy moved from terrorism to expanded guerrilla warfare and eventually to conventional field combat in 1979. This shift occurred as the organizational strength of the FSLN grew and as its allies progressively tied up the Guard with widespread civil disturbances. National Guard counterinsurgency ultimately failed (1978–1979) when the civilian opposition became so diverse and well organized that the security forces simply could not attend to all the challenges to the regime and still effectively fight the rapidly growing FSLN as well. After the insurgents' victory in July 1979, violence fell off very sharply because of the complete collapse of the Somocista security forces.

External involvement. Outside actors played an important part in the Nicaraguan insurrection. Four decades of U.S. support at critical moments, plus a constant flow of military training and weapons, kept the Somoza dynasty extraordinarily resistant to rebel challenges. However, the erosion of U.S. support for the regime of Anastasio Somoza Debayle after 1977, due mainly to shifting human rights policies, began to reduce the government's pool of allies and to encourage its enemies. Simultaneously, the FSLN began to take increasing advantage of friendly sanctuary in Costa Rica and of equally valuable, if less freely given, sanctuary along Honduras's isolated southern border reaches. By 1978 the Costa Rican government clearly supported the FSLN, permitted large arms shipments to the insurgents, and collaborated with the rebels' provisional government in San José. Other governments in Latin America (Mexico, Venezuela, Panama) provided the rebels with important diplomatic backing and opposition to the Somoza government that neutralized its potential support from neighboring conservative regimes. Without such support for the insurgents and without the erosion of foreign support for the regime, the overthrow of the Somoza dynasty would surely have taken much longer. External assistance to both sides—that which built up the National Guard and that which armed and aided the guerrillas in 1978–1979—contributed to the very high level of violence in the Nicaraguan insurrection.

Causes of the Nicaraguan Revolution

Relative deprivation. Numerous sectors of Nicaraguan society experienced change of the sorts that elsewhere have led to aggressive sociopolitical behavior. Although psychological data to demonstrate the existence and degree of relative deprivation in Nicaragua do not exist, the strains and changes affecting many Nicaraguans are consistent with the types of conditions that, it is hypothesized, can produce a frustration-induced political rebellion. The 1950s, 1960s, and especially the 1970s brought rapid and dislocating socioeconomic change to several social strata. For example, tens of thousands of peasants experienced such dislocations as proletarization, loss of land for cultivation, and unemployment due to the rapid expansion of cotton and coffee production and increased concentration of land ownership by largeholders. Other peasants fell victim to "agrarian reform" programs designed for counterinsurgency purposes, which uprooted them and transported them to unimproved zones; others lost their improved land to rapacious local officials. Urban workers, despite substantial industrial growth and some wage gains in the 1960s, experienced a marked decline in real wages in the 1970s. Residents of Managua, especially lower- and lower-middle-class commercial and petty manufacturing interests in the heart of the city, suffered the devastation of the December 1972 quake, from which many never recovered economically. For the middle classes the quake reversed a decade of economic growth and improved conditions. These economic reversals for the proletariat and middle classes led to markedly increased labor unrest, which in turn became politicized because the regime so consistently repressed labor activists. For the bourgeoisie, the 1960s brought rapid industrialization and economic growth that had greatly enhanced prosperity. However, the unsettled conditions of the 1970s—quick boom-bust cycles, massive foreign borrowing, labor and political unrest, growing encroachment on established interests by the Somoza group—clearly led capitalists to fear economic catastrophe.

Other likely sources of relative deprivation had noneconomic causes. A first source was political repression. For example, in the 1956–1957 repression after Somoza García's assassination thousands of opponents of the regime—communists, Social Christians, Independent Liberals, Conservatives, students—suffered imprisonment and torture. Later, lower- and middle-class labor union members and leaders, pursuing economic goals through organization and strikes, experienced fierce repression by the regime. This repression (which was general and affected most citizens, not just labor) occurred most intensely in 1974–1977 and 1978 under states of siege in which most constitutional rights were suspended and under which the National Guard acted virtually without restraint against opponents of the regime. A second noneconomic cause was regime policies that raised popular hopes for reform. Under intense international and internal pressure, Anastasio Somoza Debayle lifted states of siege (1977, 1978) and granted amnesty to political prisoners. On both occasions, Somoza raised public hopes for an end to the violent excesses of the National Guard and for either the moderation of the regime or its negotiated demise—but both times he quickly frustrated these hopes. Expectations rapidly increased, then, but the political conditions of repression continued, and the dictator's bad faith became clear.

A third noneconomic source of relative deprivation involved indiscriminate National Guard terror against peasants, urban youth, and religious social activists and organizations. Some from these sectors fled Nicaragua to escape the horror; many others joined the FSLN, became active in its support groups, or spontaneously fought alongside the Sandinistas. Especially for youths, joining the FSLN at least gave them arms, training, and organization to help protect themselves from an enemy that could torture or kill without provocation. Among certain clergy, both Catholic and Protestant, the regime's diabolical treatment of the poor and the working classes and its terror against religious social reform efforts led to activism against the government.

In summary, many segments of Nicaraguan society experienced in the late 1970s circumstances that one may reasonably infer to have been intensely frustrating.

Catalysts of rebellion. Different rebels experienced different events that inspired them to vent their frustrations in hostile actions toward the regime. The Sandinistas cited as keys both the assassination of Anastasio Somoza García in 1956 and the 1959 overthrows of Cuba's Batista and Venezuela's Pérez Jiménez. Somoza's assassination raised hopes for a change among those who founded the FSLN and among other anti-Somocistas, and the successful ousters of the dictators in Venezuela and Cuba showed that tyrants could be defeated. The Cuban revolution also revealed a successful revolutionary method that could be used by a small but committed nucleus. This guerrilla insurgency method was familiar to Nicaraguans because it had been tried there often. Another problem, much more recent, touched the national bourgeoisie, much of which had cooperated increasingly closely with Somoza in the 1960s. The cyclical economic crises that began in 1973, as well as ballooning labor and political unrest, prompted certain business groups to break with the regime and to move cautiously toward active opposition. The assassination of Pedro Joaquín Chamorro in January 1978, however, galvanized even many of the more reluctant of Nicaragua's capitalists to work against Somoza by demonstrating that not even wealth, influence, and international visibility could protect them from the tyrant. Somoza was no longer an ally, or an asset, or even tolerable, but rather a distinct and uncontrollable menace, not only to their vested interests but also to their lives.

The Chamorro assassination also galvanized much of the general public into active opposition. Individual revulsion and opposition organization following this crime turned fifty thousand people—10 percent of the city's populace—into Managua's streets for Chamorro's funeral and a protest. Some also vented their rage by rioting and destroying Somoza businesses. Given the National Guard's history of firing on demonstrators, those involved took considerable risks by giving such overt signs of discontent. In the wake of the FSLN seizure of the National Palace in late August 1978, residents of Matagalpa and of the Masaya Indian barrio Monimbó rebelled against the regime, erecting barricades and driving out the National Guard. The government's ferocious response of shelling and aerial bombardment of these communities prompted an outraged wave of similar rebellions in dozens of cities and towns throughout Nicaragua, some spontaneous, some with coordination by and military assistance from the FSLN. From that time forward, participation by the general public in acts of resistance, strikes, demonstration, and support for the revolutionary organizations grew steadily.

Catalysts or accelerators of the Nicaraguan revolution, therefore, appear to have varied according to the sector participating. The earliest entrants in the anti-Somoza struggle were moved by different events than were those who joined later.

The Coercive Balance

The presence of great relative deprivation, and even of catalysts of overtly aggressive political behavior, however, does not sufficiently explain the shape of events in Nicaragua in the middle and late 1970s. The coercive balance, the relative strength of regime and opposition, changed significantly from the early 1970s on.

The political and economic events following the 1972 Managua earthquake, the declining income of the working and middle classes, and the state of siege swelled the ranks of opposition to the government. Beginning in 1973 with the rising opposition of organized labor and in 1974 with the birth of the UDEL, more and more groups called for reforms or for more fundamental change, and fewer groups gave their support to the regime. Despite intense repression, the multiplication of the opposition to the dynasty continued from 1975 to 1978, although the increase in the number of opponents was not matched by an increase in their organization and collaboration until the very end of this period. In 1978 the Chamorro assassination and the September–October rebellion provided the final needed goads to rebel organization. Early in 1978 the reformist FAO was formed, only to decline and be replaced in early 1979 as the reunited FSLN emerged at the head of a revolutionary coalition of opposition groups. Moreover, after August 1978 the Front grew very rapidly in size, capability, and armament, aided by some sympathetic neighboring governments and by the people of Nicaragua. By March 1979 the Front had officially reunified under a joint command.

In contrast, the capacity of the Somoza regime to deal with disaffection began to decline during the 1970s, especially following the 1972 earthquake. This disaster undermined or began to erode the (already often limited) capability of public institutions to solve problems because of the wave of corruption and mismanagement from the bottom to the top of the regime, unprecedented in scope even in Nicaragua. The regime's legitimacy plummeted as the state proved itself not only incompetent but venal, rapacious, and viciously repressive. Nicaragua's lengthy tradition of coups, political violence, and conspiracies, together with the existence of progressively more numerous and angrier dissident groups, facilitated the rapid increase in antiregime propaganda and incitement to rebellion. Somoza had increasingly closed channels for elite reformist efforts via established institutions after 1972. As a consequence, groups formerly co-opted into collaboration or willing to share power began to abandon and even to turn against the regime. The state of siege of 1974–1977 transformed many Nicaraguans' passive antipathy toward the National Guard into a raging hatred. Despite the rapid buildup of forces to record levels in 1978 and 1979, Anastasio Somoza Debayle's National Guard began to disintegrate because of desertions and combat casualties from both enlisted and command ranks. Likewise, the Liberal Nationalist party and the state itself began to disintegrate in late 1978; by early 1979 most of those Somocistas who were able to do so fled Nicaragua to avoid the possibility of punishment for collaborating with the hated and tottering dynasty. Support from the United States and elsewhere began to decline in 1977. By 1979 the Somoza regime had many more overt opponents than friends among the nations of Latin America and Europe.

In 1978 the institutional support and military strength of both sides began to equalize, a fact that caused violence to escalate to astonishing proportions in late 1978 and 1979 as the Sandinistas began to fight to win, not just to harass. In 1979 the regime could not hold itself together, much less recover its strength or support. By March 1979 the insurgents had unified militarily and politically behind the leadership of the FSLN. In June 1979 the coercive balance shifted definitively to favor the insurgents, and their victory became inevitable, retarded only by the diplomatic delaying game played by the United States in a last effort to alter the makeup of the new government.

Possible Futures for Nicaragua

Reasonable surmises about the destiny of the Nicaraguan revolution appear to depend upon two sets of factors. One is the nature and trajectory of the revolution, in particular its leaders' perceptions of its goals and accomplishments. The other factors are external and involve especially the policies of the United States vis-à-vis the Sandinista revolution. Emerging evidence in late 1984 suggested that the Sandinista revolution had attained some of its fundamental goals and was shifting from radical change to consolidation of its accomplishments. Evidence as to U.S. intentions, however, remained unclear.

The Trajectory of the Revolution

In the words of an Argentine social scientist working in Nicaragua, "The enemy of this revolution, apart from its own errors, is backwardness. . . . Nicaragua is the kingdom of practical thinking."[2] The Nicaraguan revolution under Sandinista leadership had clearly defined its pragmatic character by 1984 with programs to address the nation's most critical problems—widespread poverty, great inequality, and underdevelopment—in realistic if not always successful ways. Moderate economic reforms had redistributed services and some wealth, but a substantial private sector had been maintained. Unlike other revolutions, the Sandinistas had gambled on permitting Nicaraguans to criticize and oppose their rule and policies and had even institutionalized that opposition through the November 1984 National Assembly election. As this book went to press in 1985, the election had apparently helped legitimize the Sandinistas' rule and to institutionalize the revolution. The regime's revolutionary rhetoric, support for Salvadoran rebels, reliance upon socialist bloc arms and advisers, and support for the USSR on certain votes in the United Nations provided ideological ammunition for the regime's conservative enemies and undercut some of its support by moderates in the United States and Europe. Nevertheless, the Sandinista government had distanced itself from the United States but without becoming isolated from the rest of Latin America or Western Europe, despite a concerted U.S. effort to cut Nicaragua off from the West.

Sandinista leaders gave signs in late-1984 interviews that the Nicaraguan revolution had almost completed key elements of its policy, economic, and political foundations. For example, Jaime Wheelock Román, minister of agrarian development and reform and a member of the FSLN National Directorate, said:

We have carried out our original program: mixed economy, religious liberty, political pluralism, and elections. After two and a half years we completed our reconstruction project and shifted to policies to promote development. The year 1985 will mark the end of the first phase of the revolution, which concentrated on promoting agrarian reform. It is more and more difficult to expropriate property now—not just because of resistance within society, but within the FSLN and the National Directorate. [A consensus is emerging that] we have to consolidate, a proposition with which I agree. The second phase of the revolution will involve the return of the private sector . . . and economic aperture.[3]

In a similar vein, E.V.K. Fitzgerald, senior economic adviser to the junta, argued that the elections themselves were held to initiate the writing of a new constitution in order to clarify the economic and political rules of the game for the private sector—in essence, to provide the security that the private economy desired in order to begin to invest again. An ongoing national dialogue, involving all the parties, private-sector organizations, and the church, was convened to open access to the constitution-drafting process for those groups that had lost access by refusing to take part in the elections or in the transition from corporate representation in the Council of State to geographical representation in the National Assembly. Sergio Ramírez, vice-president elect and JGRN member, concurred with Fitzgerald and elaborated on the FSLN's view of the private sector.

> We are not hostile to private property. Witness to that is the agrarian reform system that has created 60,000 new private property owners. We can also accept joint ventures between public and private capital. The problem is to direct the creation of new means of production, rather than control those that already exist. . . . This isn't a socialist economy; it's a market economy. The law of the market prevails here, in part because of our external economic connections.[4]

Ramírez emphasized, however, that the private sector would not have economic control of Nicaragua: "In the mixed economy there is a hegemony of the state that cannot be abandoned."

Pragmatism appeared to predominate in the political realm as well. The Sandinistas had incorporated such features of "participatory democracy" as popular participation in decision making and administration through workers' management on APP farms and in factories and program implementation in education, health, and defense by CDSs and other mass organizations, as well as through the representation of popular organizations on policy and planning commissions. "In the model of the Sandinista Popular Revolution, . . . participation by workers is the fundamental guarantee of democracy."[5] However, formal national elections were integrated into the system "as one more mechanism which the workers have at their disposal to control the direction of the revolutionary state."[6] Some radicals argued that such national electoral structures and institutionalized opposition would be superfluous, if not actual barriers to "true popular democracy," in a participatory system. The Sandinistas preserved their opposition and held elections, however, in part because they believed those two factors might hold the key to the very survival of the revolution. The FSLN hoped that establishing opposition and elections in Nicaragua might help retain Western European and Latin American support for the revolution, and might make it more difficult for U.S. military intervention to overthrow the regime on the grounds that it was not democratically elected.

The regime thus took steps to assure minority party survival, full electoral participation, and pluralistic representation in the constitution drafting in 1985–1987. According to Sergio Ramírez, "We couldn't manufacture [a false partisan] equality that did not exist— a two-party system. Our great fear was that our tiny opposition parties might not even win any seats in the assembly, so we chose a system [of proportional representation and a guaranteed seat for small parties] in order to permit them to survive and develop for the future."[7] Moreover, the national dialogue was established to provide "a bridge for the participation of all social and economic sectors outside the election and National Assembly, so that they might influence the new constitution."[8] In the words of Sergio Ramírez, the national dialogue represented

> a mechanism that the Front has adopted to deal with political disparity. It is not new in the history of the revolution—the national dialogue merely continues the debates that went on in the Council of State. . . . It represents the entire political spectrum, including antirevolutionary and pro-U.S. groups. . . . We don't want to exclude even these groups from influence on the new constitution. The dialogue is a mechanism to give them a voice. It involves the defense of national sovereignty by reaching a national consensus [that can block] a foreign military intervention. Whether it will succeed we cannot say . . . that depends both on the reactionaries and the government of the United States.[9]

U.S. Intentions

The intentions of the United States toward Nicaragua at the beginning of Ronald Reagan's second presidential term remained obscure because of three possible constraints on the administration. U.S. public opinion had consistently run against the administration's arming and support of the contras in 1983 and 1984 by a margin averaging well over two to one. Opinion polls also revealed consistently strong public disapproval of the administration's handling of the situation in Central America and a moderate but consistent opposition to using U.S. forces in Central America to overthrow "unfriendly" or "communist-controlled" Caribbean or Central American regimes (such as in Grenada).[10] Second, the Democratic-controlled House of Representatives had voted twice in 1984 to cut off aid to the contras, so congressional backing for increased hostility was questionable. Finally, there apparently also existed a division among the president's closest advisers on Central America—almost from the beginning of Reagan's administration in 1981—between advocates of a hard line against Nicaragua and administration moderates. Hardliners pressed for covert action (the contra war) and overt economic, diplomatic, and military pressures intended to weaken and topple the Sandinista regime. The moderates advocated combining some of these pressures with negotiations with Nicaragua in order to alter the composition of the regime (to include U.S.-backed anti-Sandinista exiles) and to temper its policies.

Many observers expected that the advent of a second, lame-duck Reagan term might render politically insignificant whatever barrier public opinion represented to escalated military pressure against Nicaragua by the United States. U.S. objections to a tentative Central American agreement on the September 1984 Contadora treaty had angered the Contadora nations and suggested that the United States opposed *any* peace agreement with Sandinista Nicaragua.[11] U.S. criticism of the Nicaraguan elections and embassy pressures upon the PPSC, PLI, and PCD to drop out of the elections sought to deny the FSLN the international and domestic legitimacy it hoped to win by holding a clean election with meaningful opposition.[12] To some observers this pressure also portended an impending escalation of U.S. hostility. Ultimately, the administration failed to undermine the election, although the range of opposition was affected. U.S. antielection propaganda certainly damaged the credibility of the results in the United States but appeared to have had less impact in Europe and Latin America. Indeed, the similarity of the popular vote for Reagan (59 percent) and Ortega (62 percent) and a higher Nicaraguan turnout (75 percent versus about 60 percent) invited such uncomfortable comparisons for the U.S. administration that it momentarily reduced its public denunciations of the absence of any meaningful opposition in Nicaragua.

A more ominous event, however, was the "MiG scare" that began on 6 November 1984—election day in the United States. In addition to diverting media attention from positive news about the Nicaraguan election, the leak about a suspected shipment of Soviet fighters to Nicaragua caused many Nicaraguans and Americans alike to fear that bombing of Nicaraguan military targets or even a U.S. invasion was imminent. In fact, there was no MiG shipment and no likelihood of a U.S. attack upon Nicaragua at that time.

In effect, the administration's hardliners used the MiG scare to manipulate the press. In the words of a congressional aide, "the [administration's] conservatives will not accept any solution with Nicaragua that entails the continued existence of the Sandinista government."[13] Thus they sought first to gain ground in their struggle for policy influence by portraying Nicaragua as rapidly increasing its threat to its neighbors; they believed this tactic would strengthen their hand in jockeying to influence the president. Second, the MiG scare was intended "to push Congress into restoring U.S. aid to the anti-Sandinista contra rebels,"[14] a key part of the hardliners' program to bring down the regime and one that had been cut off in mid-1984. Finally, the hardliners' projected image of an expansionist, pro-Soviet Nicaragua sought to arouse domestic fears that might rally public opinion in favor of a tougher U.S. stance. The ploy appears to have succeeded, at least with the conservative *Wall Street Journal,* as during the scare its editorial page fulminated about a "confused response to a bold and dangerous Soviet thrust [that] gives the U.S. all the appearance of a befuddled giant, prone to inaction."[15]

After roughly a week, the United States admitted that no MiGs had been delivered to Nicaragua, but the incident had left the distinct impression, especially within Nicaragua, that an invasion was imminent.[16] As the details of the intra-administration dispute emerged, it appeared unlikely that such an invasion would take place in 1985. Rather, as one administration official reported to the *Christian Science Monitor,* the hardliners believed "that the Sandinistas are weak and growing weaker, and that it will eventually be possible to overthrow them using greatly strengthened contra forces."[17] The hardliners reportedly favored toughening U.S. policy "for the moment" by five major means.

[1] Encouragement of the contras with greatly expanded U.S. aid; . . . [2] An end to all negotiations, including breaking off the U.S.-Nicaraguan talks. The Contadora peace talks . . . would be left to drag on inconclusively; [3] A reduction in the status of the U.S. Embassy in Managua; . . . [4] An escalation of military pressure of all kinds on Nicaragua, using what the U.S. official referred to as "overflights, various naval interdictions, and lots more military exercises"; [5] More economic pressures, such as cutting off U.S. purchase of bananas . . . and meat, the stopping of Aeronica flights [the national airline] into Miami; and the blocking of commercial banking credits to Nicaragua.[18]

Four Scenarios

Against this background of uncertainty one can project alternative scenarios for the evolution of the Nicaraguan revolution, conditioned mainly by U.S. policies. Should U.S. policy remain much as in late

284 Across a Frontier of History

1984—diplomatically and economically unfriendly and covertly hostile through the contra war—the domestic policies and institutions of the Nicaraguan revolution would likely continue much as they were in 1984. Nicaragua's economic and human costs from the war would continue to rise; social programs, economic production, and productivity would steadily erode under the defense burden and economic sabotage. The regime would continue its overtures to U.S. Western allies in order to prevent isolation, but it would also continue to arm and train itself with Eastern bloc weapons and could either maintain current ties with the Soviet Union and Cuba or slowly strengthen them.

An escalation of U.S. hostility short of invasion could force the Sandinistas to increase conscription for the EPS and would worsen Nicaragua's economy and further disrupt production and distribution. Such problems would generate more domestic opposition and could provoke a crackdown on opposition and a deterioration of human rights conditions. Increasing defense burdens could also lead to more state encroachment on the private sector in order to finance and carry out the war. Nicaragua would probably seek closer ties to the Soviet Union and its allies in direct relation to its increasing isolation from the West and its burgeoning military burden.

An invasion of Nicaragua by the United States, alone or with help from other Central American nations, might well destroy the Sandinista revolution if sufficient forces were committed to the invasion. With a hundred times Nicaragua's population and even greater relative economic capacity, the United States undoubtedly possesses sufficient strength to occupy the country, destroy or drive out the Sandinistas, and install a regime more to its liking (probably headed by Arturo Cruz). Such an enterprise, however, would require an immense investment of U.S. lives and resources and would again scourge a Nicaragua that is still suffering from a dozen calamitous years of war and natural disaster. Nicaragua would be no Grenada. Although some Nicaraguans would hail U.S. forces as liberators, many thousands—many of them well armed, trained, and with combat experience—would fiercely resist. An airborne invasion to capture the major cities and ports, for instance, would meet with weeks of intense resistance from Sandinistas and many other Nicaraguans with military training who would follow preestablished defense plans. Once the cities were taken, there would be months of heavy resistance to the occupying forces from Sandinista forces in the countryside until munitions and supplies were depleted, and there would then follow years of guerrilla warfare and terrorism. The costs of an invasion to the United States would be measured in thousands of dead and tens of thousands of wounded, domestic unrest, deteriorated relations with Latin America and other allies, and the possible spread of war to neighboring nations. The human costs to Nicaragua's society could exceed those of the 1977–1979 insurrection.

A fourth possibility would be for relations between Nicaragua and the United States to improve. This process could begin should administration moderates in Washington win the policy debate over Nicaragua with the hardliners. It could well mean the eventual realization of a Contadora accord and a decline of contra pressure against the revolutionary regime. Should such a situation come to pass, Nicaragua would probably cut military spending, reduce the size of its armed forces, and ask some of its Eastern bloc military advisers to leave. Nicaraguan relations with the United States and Honduras could gradually improve (although one should not expect miracles of reconciliation). Economic recovery and development could accelerate, with both the state and the private sectors benefiting from new foreign investment. Social welfare, health, education, and development programs would gain impetus, and living standards would probably improve. The revolution would probably become institutionalized along lines somewhat resembling the political system of Mexico. Minor opposition parties could exist (and perhaps grow) in a system of relative political liberty alongside a dominant FSLN under the continuing leadership of the National Directorate.

Conclusions

The Nicaraguan insurrection and Sandinista revolution took their form from forces operating in Nicaragua as long ago as the early nineteenth century—violent internecine conflict, external intervention, dictatorial rule, and the confusion of public and private purpose. The Somoza dynasty was a creature, captive, and cultivator of such forces. Its founder, Anastasio Somoza García, and his oldest son, Luis Somoza Debayle, from 1936 until 1967 successfully manipulated corruption and employed espionage, co-optation, and repression to defuse or to defeat numerous conspiracies and challenges by their opponents. Under their tutelage Nicaraguan society became more industrialized and more integrated into the world economy in often unstable markets. As these changes occurred, certain internal contradictions grew, especially after 1960: overall economic growth accompanied by the reduced well-being, first of the peasantry, then later of the proletariat and even the middle classes; corrupt and dictatorial political institutions that papered over repression with proclamations of democracy and national interest; an army and a ruling political party alienated from the populace they had to exploit and to control yet corrupted and weakened by the very techniques that kept them manageable for the Somozas; and an addictive dependency upon the United States for the extra military and political power needed to rule an increasingly unwilling citizenry.

The accession to power of the founder's youngest son, Anastasio Somoza Debayle, knocked the system out of kilter, as he had less political skill and was both more repressive and greedier than either his father or his brother Luis. Under Anastasio Somoza Debayle the contradictions that had developed earlier in the dynasty became uncontrollable. The cataclysmic earthquake that smashed six hundred blocks in the heart of Managua in December 1972 also set in motion events that heightened the great strains present in Nicaraguan society: The regime and National Guard became objects of much greater hatred; labor and political unrest intensified; the economy began to gyrate between recession and overheated growth; foreign debt escalated; and the bourgeoisie began to reject the regime because of its bad management of the economy. Moreover, Nicaragua experienced a rapid escalation of energy costs and inflation in the early 1970s, as well as a notable resurgence of FSLN activity. Somoza responded to these strains with intense repression that soon increased rather than decreased the hostility of Nicaraguans toward his government; it also alienated the incoming Carter administration by the violations of human rights it entailed. But Somoza's influence on both the National Guard and public institutions had diminished the government's ability to contain the spreading opposition or to cope with the nation's critical structural problems. By late 1977 the country was like a powder keg, awaiting only a spark to set off the explosion of popular anger against the dynasty.

The great insurrection of 1977–1979 smashed the Somoza dynasty and its principal instruments, the Liberal Nationalist party and the National Guard. The large but divided opposition, caught unawares in 1978 by the scope and intensity of popular repudiation of the hated dictatorship, began to pull together. The first great political coalition, the FAO, came to the fore in late 1978 partly because of U.S. efforts to replace Somoza with moderate reformists rather than revolutionaries. When this effort failed because of the dictator's bad faith and internal dissension within the FAO, the FSLN emerged as the undisputed head of the struggle and leader of two new broad front organizations committed to much greater change in Nicaraguan society than either the FAO or the United States had sought. The Sandinistas quickly converted their leadership in the victorious coalition into a dominant role in the governance of revolutionary Nicaragua.

Several features of the Nicaraguan revolution stand out in bold relief. By any reasonable standard the Sandinistas and their collaborators have engineered a truly revolutionary transformation of Nicaraguan society. Although at this writing in early 1985 much remained to be seen as to its eventual success or failure, the revolution's goals, political structures, and programs represented a major restructuring of the social, political, and economic systems: The Somoza dynasty was gone, and the rules of the political game had changed completely. A new legitimizing myth, centered around the populist anti-imperialism of Sandino, had been established. Most political and government institutions had undergone major alterations; most of the key features of the Somocista system had been eliminated. A new political force, the FSLN, had assumed ruling power and direction of the revolution. The Sandinistas and the broader coalition that they led had restructured the economy, greatly enhancing the role of the state while retaining private ownership in many areas. Class relations had altered markedly, with public policy heavily reorienting services and infrastructure development in order to improve life for the poor. Foreign policy became purposefully independent of the once-influential United States in pursuit of developmental opportunities and relationships beneficial to and set by Nicaragua. This assertion of independence was accompanied by Nicaragua's drawing closer to Cuba and to the Soviet Union for aid and solidarity as well as material military assistance— policies that accelerated as the U.S. reaction became progressively hostile.

Perhaps the most remarkable change of all was the renunciation of the Nicaraguan political tradition of violent repression of opposition. The Sandinistas established a collaborative model of rule that gave other political forces representation in the legislative and executive councils and in the execution of public policy. But more important still was the great extent to which the Sandinistas renounced the use of torture and other abuses against their opponents. Even to the several thousand National Guard troops and regime agents who had rained death upon their fellow citizens during the insurrection the Sandinistas responded with what seemed to many observers an astonishing policy of humane treatment. This major break with Nicaragua's lengthy tradition of violent and repressive political discourse contrasts remarkably with the Iranian revolutionaries' extremely violent treatment of their opponents.

As the Sandinistas guide Nicaragua on through the late 1980s, three great problems stand out for the revolution—economic recovery, foreign relations, and the survival of the revolution itself. The great destruction of the physical, human, organizational, and economic capital of Nicaragua by the war and by the looting of the departing Somocistas has proved very difficult to repair, especially because of the rising disruption and cost of the contra war. After five and a half years of strenuous efforts and massive international borrowing, some real gains had been made, but the economy still lagged and certain areas of production remained below prewar levels. The FSLN's strategy for economic recovery was to include the "patriotic" capitalists of Nicaragua as a major factor in economic recovery, but entrepreneurs—politically outflanked, anxious about the ultimate economic goals of the Sandinista leadership, and short of capital and managers—were in part unable and in part reluctant to commit themselves heavily to rebuilding and expanding their firms in an environment of uncertainty. In short, many Nicaraguan capitalists doubted the commitment of the predominantly socialist FSLN to a mixed economy. Many others had become actively involved in the struggle to topple the Sandinistas from power, a strategy that led to disinvestment and deliberately restrained production.

In contrast the Sandinistas believed, probably correctly, that the reestablishment and maintenance of a vigorous private sector was essential to their success and to the success of the revolution, given the nation's economic problems and the preeminence of the United States in the regional economy. Ironically, then, the socialist Sandinistas earnestly sought a mixed public-private economy as the fastest route to economic recovery and to their political security, while the capitalists themselves doubted the FSLN's sincerity and held back in their participation in economic rebuilding. Unfortunately, the government's receptiveness to labor organization in field and factory and the very slow pace of recovery itself caused labor unrest and reduced the fiscal strength of the government, aggravating investor anxiety and restraining the state's capacity to promote private-sector economic recovery. A world recession, declining terms of trade, increasingly scarce credit sources, and the war—all factors beyond Nicaragua's control—added additional barriers to economic recovery.

A problem of similar magnitude was Nicaragua's foreign policy and its interaction with other states. The support of the international social democratic movement and of many European and Latin American nations helped keep the Nicaraguan regime from becoming isolated from the West as Cuba had, despite the increasingly unfriendly posture of the Reagan administration after 1981 and despite a deterioration of Nicaragua's relations with other Central American states. The Sandinistas' policies of identification with national liberation movements in general and with Cuba in particular, and certain Nicaraguan support for the Salvadoran insurgents, constituted what other Central American governments viewed as a threat to their security. By 1980 El Salvador and Guatemala were beset by many of the same strains that had toppled the Somoza regime, and in the early 1980s Honduras and Costa Rica began to experience severe economic difficulties as well as intense political pressure from the United States to cooperate with its anti-Sandinista policies. These problems and pressures led to a rising tide of accusations by Central American governments that Nicaragua was following an expansionist policy, exporting its revolution, and engaged in the subversion of their security. Nicaragua's worst relations were with Honduras, whose leaders vigorously denounced the Sandinista regime, harbored and supported the Nicaraguan exile–CIA contra war effort, and began a military buildup and collaboration with the United States that included the building of several bases and airstrips in Honduras and the continuous presence of U.S. troops there. Relations with Costa Rica also eroded as counterrevolutionary activity from there grew.

Because the Nicaraguan insurrection was the first such movement to succeed in Central America, Nicaragua was illogically held responsible for the woes and instability of its neighbors. Nevertheless, this fallacious assumption was promoted vigorously by the Reagan administration. The United States thus increased military and economic assistance to El Salvador and to Honduras and helped promote the Central American Democratic Community, whose members (Costa Rica, Honduras, and El Salvador) literally surround Nicaragua on the isthmus. The U.S. attitude and the growing tension with Nicaragua's neighbors soon led the Sandinistas to fear foreign military hostility and thus to spend more than they wished on defense and less on economic recovery and social programs. As a result, Nicaragua's increasing isolation from other Central American states and from the United States from the outset narrowed the country's development options, increased its perceived need for military preparation, and retarded economic development, which in turn reinforced the very fears that had led to the deterioration of relations within the isthmus to begin with.

By late 1984, however, not all signs were so negative as they had been in the previous couple of years—owing in part to the Contadora peace effort, which had promoted a tentative intraregional accord to reduce tensions, the regional arms race, and the number of foreign advisers in the region. As Nicaragua became increasingly convinced that the survival of the revolution was at stake, it gradually conceded on some elements of the Contadora discussions. Costa Rica and

Nicaragua engaged in continuous negotiations over border incidents and other differences. Guatemala had resisted the reactivation of the Central American Defense Command, had indicated its willingness to sign the 1984 draft Contadora treaty, and then declined to voice further objections to the accord despite U.S. pressure. The advent of the Duarte government in El Salvador brought some signs that Salvadoran-Nicaraguan relations could improve. Nevertheless, the active resistance to the Contadora accord by the United States in late 1984 succeeded in blocking any agreement and portended further lengthy and difficult negotiations in order to salvage a regional accord and détente.

The third great problem involved the prospects for the very survival of the revolution itself. Domestically, the Sandinistas appeared to have established a strong political base that was sufficiently well organized and supported to maintain control and to continue the revolutionary transformations while tolerating overt domestic criticism and opposition. Albeit at a high cost to the revolutionary programs, the FSLN had also successfully met the armed challenge by the counterrevolutionary forces supported by the United States and Nicaraguan exile groups, and it did not appear likely that such forces, even with renewed U.S. financial assistance and higher force levels, could topple the FSLN from power. The biggest threat to the revolution, then, would probably come from the United States. The question remained whether escalated U.S. pressures short of a full-scale invasion could undermine the Sandinistas' support and bring them down. Rarely, if ever, have two widespread popular insurrections against successive regimes occurred within such a short time span, so that another popular revolt seemed improbable. Nicaragua thus continued to pursue means of reaching an agreement with the United States in order to prevent the invasion that the regime believed to be the only obstacle to the survival of the revolution.

In conclusion, Nicaragua's revolution faced in the mid-1980s paradoxes that presented the revolution with enormous obstacles—internal and international fears about the nature of the regime and its program that could possibly force the Sandinistas to become what they did not wish to be—more socialist, less politically open, more repressive, more militaristic, and more reliant upon the socialist bloc and isolated from the West. The Sandinistas had destroyed the Somoza dynasty and had begun to build a new Nicaraguan society, but their path was still strewn—perhaps more critically than at any point since 1979—with obstacles that might force them to face critical choices about the future of the revolution, or even destroy it and plunge Nicaragua into another national catastrophe.

Notes

Key to Newspaper Abbreviations

Several newspapers with extensive coverage of Nicaraguan events were relied upon heavily in the preparation of this book. For the sake of space, they will be referred to in the notes by the following abbreviations:

Barricada (Managua)	B
Barricada Internacional (Managua)	BI
Excelsior (Mexico City)	EM
Excelsior (San José, Costa Rica)	ECR
La Nación (San José, Costa Rica)	N
La Nación Internacional (San José, Costa Rica)	LNI
La Prensa (Managua)	P
La Prensa Libre (San José, Costa Rica)	PL
La República (San José, Costa Rica)	R
Mesoamérica (San José, Costa Rica)	M
New York Times	NYT

Chapter 1. Revolutionary Theory and Nicaragua's Sandinista Revolution

1. H. L. Nieburg, *Political Violence: The Behavioral Process* (New York: St. Martin's, 1969), p. 9.

2. Peter Calvert, *Revolution* (New York: Praeger Publishers, 1970).

3. For useful reviews or compendia of the literature on violence and revolution, see Carl Leiden and Karl M. Schmitt, *The Politics of Violence: Revolution in the Modern World* (Englewood Cliffs, N.J.: Prentice-Hall, 1968); Thomas H. Greene, *Comparative Revolutionary Movements* (Englewood Cliffs, N.J.: Prentice-Hall, 1974); Mustafa Rejai, *The Comparative Study of Revolutionary Strategy* (New York: David McKay, 1977); Ted Robert Gurr, *Why Men Rebel* (Princeton, N.J.: Princeton University Press, 1971); Charles Tilly, *From Mobilization to Revolution* (Reading, Mass.: Addison-Wesley, 1978); Claude E. Welch, Jr., and Mavis Bunker Taintor, eds., *Revolution and Political Change* (North Scituate, Mass.: Duxbury, 1972); James C. Davies, ed., *When Men Revolt and Why* (New York: Free Press, 1971); Nieburg, *Political Violence;* and Calvert, *Revolution.*

4. See Nieburg, *Political Violence,* pp. 1–9; and Leiden and Schmitt, *Politics of Violence,* p. 3.

5. Calvert, *Revolution,* especially pp. 132–144.

6. Leiden and Schmitt, *Politics of Violence,* pp. 3–4; Greene, *Comparative Revolutionary Movements,* pp. 6–8.

7. Greene, *Comparative Revolutionary Movements,* p. 8.

8. Crane Brinton's *The Anatomy of Revolution* (New York: Vintage Books, 1965), is the most famous stage theory. He included phases of the decline of the old regime, the rule of the moderates, the accession of extremists, the reign of terror and virtue, and thermidor. Greene (*Comparative Revolutionary Movements,* p. 11) and Leiden and Schmitt (*Politics of Violence,* p. 132) had difficulty applying these to other revolutions. Leiden and Schmitt identified phases of revolutions (pp. 55–74), but they are very fluid — birth, revolutionary turmoil, and postrevolution.

9. For example, one elaborate such effort, undertaken by Samuel Huntington, typifies revolutions as "Eastern" or "Western" according to the sequence of the seizure of power and the mobilization of mass participation. Ironically, the Egyptian revolution of 1952 appears to fall within the Western type, while the Nicaraguan revolution is of the Eastern variant (mass mobilization preceding and forcing the collapse of the old regime). Whether the phenomena distinguished by Huntington have value or not, the labels mislead. See Huntington's *Political Order in Changing Societies* (New Haven, Conn.: Yale University Press, 1968), pp. 264–274. On the Egyptian revolution see Leiden and Schmitt, *Politics of Violence,* pp. 157–182.

10. For other examples of problematic typologies of revolution, see Chalmers Johnson, *Revolution and the Social System* (Stanford, Calif.: Hoover Institution, 1964), pp. 26–68. Johnson identified six types — the jacquerie, the millenarian rebellion, the anarchistic rebellion, the Jacobin communist revolution, the conspiratorial coup d'etat, and the militarized mass insurrection. His four criteria for typifying (pp. 27–28), however, generate forty-eight possible types, forty-two of which remain undiscussed. Rejai, on the other hand, reviewed several typologies (*Comparative Study of Revolutionary Strategy,* pp. 15–19) and rejected them all for his own, which is based on the target and on the success. He thus suggested three types: national (against a foreign enemy), civil (against a domestic enemy), and abortive (or failed). He then decided to include a fourth, provisional category — counterrevolution (pp. 19–23).

11. Leiden and Schmitt, *Politics of Violence,* pp. 3–112; Green, *Comparative Revolutionary Movements,* passim; Welch and Taintor, *Revolution and Political Change,* passim; Rejai, *Comparative Study of Revolutionary Strategy,* pp. 31–36.

12. This generalization should not be read to suggest that revolutionaries never have peasant or working-class origins. Indeed, they have frequently come from such backgrounds and achieved considerable mobility via education. Peasant leaders Zapata and Villa in Mexico had purely lower-class origins. Indeed, Nicaraguan revolutionaries Augusto César Sandino and Carlos Fonseca Amador both came from working-class backgrounds.

13. Greene, *Comparative Revolutionary Movements,* pp. 16–32; Leiden and Schmitt, *Politics of Violence,* pp. 75–89; Brinton, *Anatomy of Revolution,* pp. 92–120; Welch and Taintor, *Revolution and Political Change,* pp. 197–249.

14. Greene, *Comparative Revolutionary Movements,* pp. 34–49; Leiden and

Schmitt, *Politics of Violence,* pp. 90–95; Welch and Taintor, *Revolution and Political Change,* pp. 197–249.

15. Rejai, *Comparative Study of Revolutionary Strategy,* pp. 36–38; Greene, *Comparative Revolutionary Movements,* pp. 51–58; Leiden and Schmitt, *Politics of Violence,* pp. 97–112.

16. Greene, *Comparative Revolutionary Movements,* pp. 60–73; Rejai, *Comparative Study of Revolutionary Strategy,* pp. 38–41; Nieburg, *Political Violence,* pp. 99–131. For classical revolutionists' views, see V. I. Lenin, "What Is to Be Done? Burning Questions of Our Movement," in William Lutz and Harry Brent, eds., *On Revolution* (Cambridge, Mass.: Winthrop, 1971), pp. 244–263; Mikhail Bakunin, "Methods of the Preparatory Period," in G. P. Maximoff, ed., *The Political Philosophy of Bakunin* (New York: Free Press, 1964), pp. 379–389; and Regis Debray, *Revolution in the Revolution? Armed Struggle in Latin America* (New York: Grove, 1967).

17. Leiden and Schmitt, *Politics of Violence,* pp. 19–35; Rejai, *Comparative Study of Revolutionary Strategy,* pp. 41–43; Greene, *Comparative Revolutionary Movements,* pp. 75–93; Tilly, *From Mobilization to Revolution,* pp. 143–188; Brinton, *Anatomy of Revolution,* pp. 67–91, 148–204; and Gerard Chaliand, *Revolution in the Third World* (New York: Penguin, 1978), pp. 33–98.

18. Greene, *Comparative Revolutionary Movements,* pp. 95–100; Rejai, *Comparative Study of Revolutionary Strategy,* pp. 43–45; Richard J. Barnet, *Intervention and Revolution* (New York: World Publishing, 1968).

19. Greene, *Comparative Revolutionary Movements,* pp. 104–118; Leiden and Schmitt, *Politics of Violence,* pp. 37–38; Johnson, *Revolution and the Social System,* pp. 12–14; and Harry Eckstein, "On the Etiology of Internal Wars," in Welch and Taintor, *Revolution and Political Change,* pp. 60–90.

20. A typical structural approach is Johnson's functionalist notion of the society as a system that strives for equilibrium. For him, disequilibrium entails dysfunctions, and multiple dysfunctions can cause violence to promote a needed restoration of equilibrium *(Revolution and the Social System,* pp. 5–12). Other important structural treatments are Barrington Moore, Jr.'s *Structural Origins of Dictatorship and Democracy* (Boston: Beacon, 1966) and Huntington's *Political Order in Changing Societies.* For an excellent critique of structural approaches, see Eckstein, "Etiology of Internal Wars," pp. 76–78. See also pp. 70–75 for Eckstein's summary of explanations for revolution based on social structure, especially economic factors, and those based on elites, relations between elites and masses, class divisions, and social change. See also Rejai, *Comparative Study of Revolutionary Strategy,* pp. 26–29; and Greene, *Comparative Revolutionary Movements,* pp. 120–144.

21. The seminal piece in the frustration-aggression school is by John Dollard et al., *Frustration and Aggression* (New Haven, Conn.: Yale University Press, 1967), first published in 1939. James C. Davies's "Toward a Theory of Revolution," *American Sociological Review* 27 (February 1962):5–19, links this theory to social structural characteristics capable of frustrating expectations. Davies identified what he called the "J-curve" of suddenly declining need satisfaction as a generator of frustration-induced aggression. See also Davies's "Revolution and

the J-Curve," in Welch and Taintor, *Revolution and Political Change*, pp. 122–153. Other psychological theories stress alienation, anomie, etc. See, for example, David Schwartz, *A Theory of Revolutionary Behavior* (New York: Free Press, 1970); Eckstein, "Etiology of Internal Wars," pp. 76–79; and Nieburg, *Political Violence*, pp. 18–45, for further observations about psychological theories. See also Rejai, *Comparative Study of Revolutionary Strategy*, pp. 26–29.

22. In addition to *Why Men Rebel*, see also Gurr's "A Causal Model of Civil Strife: A Comparative Analysis Using New Indices," *American Political Science Review* 62 (December 1968):1104–1124; "The Revolution–Social Change Nexus; Some Old Theories and New Hypotheses," *Comparative Politics* 5 (April 1973): 359–392; and "Psychological Factors in Civil Violence," *World Politics* 20 (January 1968):245–278. Tilly's approach rests on a "rational choice model," but it clearly integrates structural and psychological features. See also Wilbur A. Chaffee, "A Theoretical Look at Revolutions with Case Studies from Latin America," Ph.D. dissertation, University of Texas at Austin, 1975.

23. Gurr, *Why Men Rebel*, pp. 92–154; Mancur Olson, Jr., "Rapid Growth as a Destabilizing Force," *Journal of Economic History* 23 (December 1963): 529–552; Greene, *Comparative Revolutionary Movements*, pp. 128–135; Leiden and Schmitt, *Politics of Violence*, pp. 41–44. For Marxist perspectives on the links of economic change to revolution, see Robert C. Tucker, *The Marxian Revolutionary Idea* (New York: W. W. Norton, 1970); and Chaliand, *Revolution in the Third World*.

24. Gurr, *Why Men Rebel*, pp. 22–91, 324–325. Because of the absence of psychological data on Nicaragua, other than in impressionistic forms, one must *assume* but cannot prove the existence of relative deprivation. Gurr's analysis of structural aspects linked to his integrated theory have found empirical confirmation for this model, despite his own lack of psychological data. His data do perform as predicted based on the integrated theory, lending credence to his similar assumptions. See his "Psychological Factors in Civil Violence" for evidence in this respect. Just as physicists have successfully based models of the atom upon assumed (deductively suggested) but unobserved particles, so can we proceed with assumed RD until data become available.

25. Ivo K. Feierabend and Rosalind L. Feierabend, "Aggressive Behaviors Within Polities: 1948–1962," *Journal of Conflict Resolution* 10(1966): 249–271; and Ivo K. Feierabend, Rosalind L. Feierabend, and Betty A. Nesvold, "The Comparative Study of Revolutions and Violence," *Comparative Politics* 5 (April 1973):393–424; Greene, *Comparative Revolutionary Movements*, pp. 120–144; Leiden and Schmitt, *Politics of Violence*, pp. 37–53; Brinton, *Anatomy of Revolution*, pp. 27–66; Tilly, *From Mobilization to Revolution*, pp. 189–222; Gurr, *Why Men Rebel*, pp. 92–231; Chaliand, *Revolution in the Third World*, pp. 1–33; Eckstein, "Etiology of Internal Wars," pp. 72–86; Chaffee, "Theoretical Look at Revolutions"; and Bruce M. Russett, "Inequality and Instability: The Relation of Land Tenure to Politics," *World Politics* 16 (April 1964):442–454.

26. Gurr, *Why Men Rebel*, pp. 331–333.

27. Ibid., pp. 332–333; Greene; *Comparative Revolutionary Movements*, pp. 120–124, 134–139.

28. Gurr, *Why Men Rebel,* pp. 338-347, and "A Causal Model." See also Douglas Bwy, "Dimensions of Social Conflict in Latin America," in Davies, *When Men Revolt and Why,* pp. 274-291.

Chapter 2. Factional Strife and Manifest Destiny

1. José Coronel Urtecho, *Reflexiones sobre la historia de Nicaragua (de Gaínza a Somoza), Tomo I: Alrededor de la independencia* (León, Nicaragua: Editorial Hospicio, 1962), p. 7.

2. See Edelberto Torres Rivas, *Interpretación del desarrollo social centroamericano* (San José, Costa Rica: Editorial Universitaria Centroamericana, 1971), pp. 37-53; Ciro F. S. Cardoso and Hector Pérez Brignoli, *Centroamérica y la economía occidental (1520-1930)* (San José, Costa Rica: Editorial de la Universidad de Costa Rica, 1977), pp. 53-85, 113-132; Ralph Lee Woodward, Jr., *Central America: A Nation Divided* (New York: Oxford University Press, 1976), pp. 25-89; and Coronel Urtecho, *Reflexiones, Tomo I* and *Tomo II: La guerra civil de 1824* (León, Nicaragua: Editorial Hospicio, 1962).

3. Edelberto Torres, "La intervención de los E.E.U.U. y la violación de los derechos humanos en Nicaragua," Comité Costarricense de Solidaridad con Nicaragua, San José, Costa Rica, 15 June 1976 (mimeo), pp. 4-5; Coronel Urtecho, *Reflexiones, Tomo II,* and *Tomo IIB: Explicaciones y revisiones* (León, Nicaragua: Editorial Hospicio, 1967); Woodward, *Central America,* pp. 89-119; and Torres Rivas, *Interpretación del desarrollo,* pp. 37-53.

4. For material on early republican Nicaragua and its society, see Woodward, *Central America,* pp. 61-119; and Cardoso and Pérez Brignoli, *Centroamerica,* pp. 149-179.

5. Woodward, *Central America,* pp. 120-123; Ricardo Jinesta, *El canal de Nicaragua y los intereses de Costa Rica en la magna obra* (San José, Costa Rica: Ministerio de Relaciones Exteriores, 1964).

6. Woodward, *Central America,* pp. 122-136; William E. Simmons, *The Nicaraguan Canal* (New York: Harper and Brothers Publishers, 1900), pp. 48-49; Torres Rivas, *Interpretación del desarrollo,* pp. 44-46; Samuel Flagg Bemis, *The Latin American Policy of the United States* (New York: W. W. Norton, 1971), p. 103.

7. Woodward, *Central America,* pp. 120-123; Bemis, *Latin American Policy,* pp. 103-105; Torres, "La intervención de los E.E.U.U.," pp. 2-3; Miguel d'Escoto Brockman, "Introducción," in Richard Millett's *Guardianes de la dinastía* (San José, Costa Rica: Editorial Universitaria Centromericana, 1979), pp. 13-14 (Millett's book is available in English: *Guardians of the Dynasty* [Maryknoll, N.Y.: Orbis Books, 1978]).

8. Frank Donovan, *Historia de la doctrina Monroe* (Mexico City: Editorial Diana, 1966); Federico Gil, *Latin American-United States Relations* (New York: Harcourt Brace Jovanovich, 1971), p. 64; Bemis, *Latin American Policy,* pp. 73-93; Woodward, *Central America,* pp. 136-139; Thomas G. Paterson et al., *American Foreign Policy: A History* (New York: D. C. Heath, 1977), pp. 121-150.

9. Bemis, *Latin American Policy,* pp. 103–108; Harold E. Davis et al., *Latin American Diplomatic History: An Introduction* (Baton Rouge: Louisiana State University Press, 1977), pp. 99–101; Paterson et al., *American Foreign Policy,* pp. 135–138; Woodward, *Central America,* p. 134. See also Andrés Vega Bolaños, ed., *1854: Bombardeo y destrucción del Puerto de San Juan del Norte de Nicaragua* (Managua, 1970).

10. See Woodward, *Central America,* pp. 138–139, and pp. 301–302 for a bibliography. For more on Walker, see Noel B. Gerson's *Sad Swashbuckler: The Life of William Walker* (New York: Thomas Nelson, 1976).

11. Woodward, *Central America,* p. 139.

12. Ibid., pp. 139–140.

13. Ibid., p. 144.

14. Torres, "La intervención de los E.E.U.U.," p. 4.

15. Woodward, *Central America,* pp. 141–145; Paterson et al., *American Foreign Policy,* pp. 131–132.

16. Woodward, *Central America,* p. 145–147.

17. Amaru Barahona Portocarrero, "Estudio sobre la historia contemporánea de Nicaragua," Avances de Investigación, No. 24 (San José, Costa Rica: Instituto de Investigaciones Sociales, Universidad de Costa Rica, 1977), pp. 1–6; Woodward, *Central America,* pp. 150–151; and Cardoso and Pérez Brignoli, *Centroamérica,* pp. 263–268.

The techniques employed to expand capitalist agriculture—the "liberal reforms"—in Nicaragua largely resemble those practiced in Mexico and Guatemala following the definitive accession to power of Liberals, even though in Nicaragua they were first implemented by Conservative regimes.

Note that some disagreement exists as to when coffee became Nicaragua's principal export. Barahona and Woodward date it around 1890, but Cardoso and Pérez Brignoli place it somewhat later. These sources concur, however, that from the 1870s on coffee production grew rather steadily, although not so fast as elsewhere in Central America, so that it began to affect national economic and political life by the end of the nineteenth century.

18. Barahona Portocarrero, "La historia contemporánea de Nicaragua," pp. 5–6.

19. Ibid., pp. 4–5; Jaime Wheelock Román, *Raices indígenas de la lucha anticolonialista en Nicaragua* (Mexico City: Siglo Veintiuno Editores, 1974), pp. 105–113.

20. Wheelock, *Raices indígenas,* pp. 105–113.

21. Woodward, *Central America,* pp. 151–155; Carlos Cuadra Pasos, *Historia de medio siglo* (Managua: Ediciones el Pez y la Serpiente, 1964), p. 13; and Barahona, "La historia contemporánea de Nicaragua," pp. 1–2.

22. Cardoso and Pérez Brignoli, *Centroamérica,* pp. 263–274.

23. Barahona Portocarrero, "La historia contemporánea de Nicaragua," p. 1.

24. Charles L. Stansifer, "José Santos Zelaya: A New Look at Nicaragua's 'Liberal' Dictator," *Revista/Review Interamericana* 7 (Fall 1977), reviews the historiography on Zelaya and reassesses his image; see especially pp. 472–480. See also Woodward, *Central America,* pp. 154–155; Cuadra Pasos, *Historia de medio*

siglo, pp., 23–24; Millett, *Guardianes de la dinastía,* pp. 33–36; Barahona Portocarrero, "La historia contemporaneo de Nicaragua," p. 7; Benjamin I. Teplitz, "The Political and Economic Foundations of Modernization in Nicaragua: The Administration of José Santos Zelaya, 1893–1909," Ph.D. dissertation, Howard University, 1973, pp. 416–417; and Carlos Selva, *Un poco de historia* (Guatemala City: Government of Guatemala, 1948).

25. Teplitz, "Modernization in Nicaragua," pp. 416–422; Barahona Portocarrero, "La historia contemporánea de Nicaragua," pp. 7–8; and Stansifer, "José Santos Zelaya," pp. 472, 478.

26. Stansifer argued convincingly, based on the comments of Zelaya's enemies, that such charges constituted myth rahter than fact ("José Santos Zelaya," pp. 474–475.)

27. Ibid.; Cuadra Pasos, *Historie de medio siglo,* pp. 18–20.

28. Woodward, *Central America,* pp. 195–196; Stansifer, "José Santos Zelaya," pp. 482–484.

29. See Paterson et al., *American Foreign Policy,* pp. 217–233; Jinesta, *El Canal de Nicaragua,* passim; Woodward, *Central America,* pp. 194–196; Bemis, *Latin American Policy,* pp. 142–167; and Stansifer, "José Santos Zelaya," pp. 483–485.

30. Teplitz, "Modernization in Nicaragua," p. 419.

31. Ibid., p. 425.

32. Stansifer emphasized this point unequivocally ("José Santos Zelaya, p. 479): "Obviously the era of construction and economic expansion ended with the fall of Zelaya."

Chapter 3. From Dollar Diplomacy to Sandino

1. Quote in Stansifer, "José Santos Zelaya," p. 468.

2. *Washington Post,* 2 June 1898, cited in Paterson et al., *American Foreign Policy,* p. 213.

3. All quotes in this paragraph are from ibid., p. 225.

4. Quoted in ibid., p. 226.

5. See ibid., pp. 212–213, 226, 229; Bemis, *Latin American Policy,* pp. 142–143, 161, 168–169, 185–187; Gil, *Latin American–United States Relations,* pp. 88–89; Torres Rivas, *Interpretación del desarrollo,* pp. 130–134.

6. Quoted in Paterson et al., *American Foreign Policy,* p. 223.

7. Ibid., pp. 218–226; Bemis, *Latin American Policy,* pp. 142–145.

8. Quoted in Paterson et al., *American Foreign Policy,* p. 221.

9. Quoted in ibid., p. 222.

10. Material on the canal question has been drawn mainly from ibid., pp. 217–223; and Bemis, *Latin American Policy,* pp. 148–151.

11. Philander C. Knox, cited in Millett, *Guardianes de la dinastía,* p. 40.

12. The discussion of the 1909–1925 period is based upon ibid., pp. 40–44; Woodward, *Central America,* pp. 196–197; Stansifer, "José Santos Zelaya," pp. 483–485; Bemis, *Latin American Policy,* pp. 162–163; Barahona Portocarrero, "La historia contemporánea de Nicaragua," pp. 7–13; Gil, *Latin American–United States Relations,* pp. 102–105; and Sergio Ramírez, "El

muchacho de Niquinohomo," introduction to Sandino's correspondence in *El pensamiento vivo de Sandino* (San José, Costa Rica: Editorial Universitaria Centroamericana, 1979), p. xviii.

13. Woodward, *Central America*, p. 197.

14. On U.S. financial involvement in Nicaragua, see Roscoe R. Hill, *Fiscal Intervention in Nicaragua* (New York: Paul Maisel, 1933); F. Taylor Peck, "Latin America Enters the World Scene, 1900-1930," in Davis et al., *Latin American Diplomatic History*, p. 162; Mayo Antonio Sánchez, *Nicaragua, año cero: La caída de la dinastia Somoza* (Mexico City: Editorial Diana, 1979), pp. 34-35; Torres, "La intervención de los E.E.U.U.," pp. 5-11; Barahona Portocarrero, "La historia contemporánea de Nicaragua," pp. 13-15; Gil, *Latin American-United States Relations*, pp. 103-104; Bemis, *Latin American Policy*, pp. 163-188; and Dana Munro, *The United States and the Caribbean Republics 1921-1933* (Princeton, N.J.: Princeton University Press, 1974), passim.

15. Ramírez, *El pensamiento vivo de Sandino*, pp. xviii. See also Sánchez, *Nicaragua*, pp. 34-35, on the related point of the nepotistic trend of the period.

16. Barahona Portocarrero, "La historia contemporánea de Nicaragua," pp. 13-14.

17. Gil, *Latin American-United States Relations*, p. 105; Woodward, *Central America*, p. 198.

18. Quoted in Jinesta, *El canal de Nicaragua*, p. 62.

19. Ibid., p. 63.

20. On the consequences of the Chamorro-Bryan treaty, see Gil, *Latin American-United States Relations*, p. 105; Woodward, *Central America*, pp. 189, 198; Bemis, *Latin American Policy*, pp. 187-189; Munro, *United States and the Caribbean Republics*, pp. 118-119; Ramírez, *El pensamiento vivo de Sandino*, p. xix; and U.S. Department of State, *A Brief History of the Relations Between the United States and Nicaragua, 1909-1928* (Washington, D.C.: Government Printing Office, 1928), passim.

21. Munro, *United States and the Caribbean Republics*, p. 10.

22. On the change in U.S. policy in this period, see ibid., pp. 3-16, 161-163, 371-383; Bryce Wood, *The Making of the Good Neighbor Policy* (New York: W. W. Norton, 1967), pp. 3-47; Bemis, *Latin American Policy*, pp. 202-225; Gil, *Latin American-United States Relations*, pp. 76-80; and Peck, "Latin America Enters the World Scene," pp. 184-190.

23. Munro, *United States and the Caribbean Republics*, p. 157.

24. Ibid.; and Barahona Portocarrero, "La historia contemporánea de Nicaragua," pp. 14-16.

25. Those interested in a more detailed account (based mainly upon U.S. Department of State records) of the political maneuverings from 1923 to 1933 should consult Munro, *United States and the Caribbean Republics;* Millett, *Guardianes de la dinastía*, pp. 51-79; and Gregorio U. Gilbert, *Junto a Sandino* (Santo Domingo Republic: Editora de la Universidad Autónoma de Santo Domingo, 1979), pp. 81-82 and passim.

26. On Sandino's life and ideas, see Ramírez, *El pensamiento vivo de Sandino*, pp. xxvi-lxix; Sánchez, *Nicaragua*, pp. 47-72; Neill Macaulay, *The Sandino Affair* (Chicago: Quadrangle Books, 1971), especially pp. 48-61; Gregorio Selser,

Sandino, general de hombres libres (San José, Costa Rica: Editorial Universitaria Centroamericana, 1979), pp. 115–302; Carlos Fonseca, ed., *Ideario político de Augusto César Sandino* (Managua: Secretaría de Propaganda y Educación Política, Frente Sandinista de Liberación Nacional, 1980); and Humberto Ortega Saavedra, *50 años de lucha sandinista* (Merida: Comité de Solidaridad con el Pueblo de Nicaragua, 1978), pp. 12–74.

Students of Sandino's writings and career (Ramírez, Selser, Macaulay, Fonseca) generally concur that Sandino's unique ideology combined an antiimperialist element with a populist sympathy for the poor and working classes. The antiimperialism was aimed primarily at the occupying forces of the United States, rather than constituting antagonism toward the United States as a whole or toward its citizens, for whom Sandino apparently held a certain admiration. Sandino's economic thinking favored reformist policies to assist the working classes but did not contain any consistent ideological thread. Although Sandino's movements ultimately attracted a variety of programmatic theoreticians and ideologists such as Dr. Arturo Vega and Salvadoran communist leader Augustín Farabundo Martí, the guerrilla leader suffered with ill will their attempts to generate support among his troops. Indeed, Sandino so resented Vega's stirring up dissent in the ranks that he had the ideologue executed. Nor did Sandino's effort represent a coherent political movement. Barahona Portocarrero ("La historia contemporánea de Nicaragua," pp. 20–23) has described Sandino's liberation struggle as informed by a precapitalist ideology lacking a clear definition of class interests or economic program, lacking a coherent political program, and caudillo-like in leadership. For a position generally similar but finding somewhat more coherence in Sandino's thought, see Humberto Ortega Saavedra, *50 años de lucha sandinista*, pp. 26–32.

27. Ramírez, *El pensamiento vivo de Sandino*, pp. xxvii–xxxv. On this period of Sandino's life more generally, see also Selser, *Sandino*, pp. 115–123; and Macaulay, *Sandino Affair*, pp. 50–55.

28. Millett, *Guardianes de la dinastía*, pp. 87–142; and Munro, *United States and the Caribbean Republics*, p. 227.

29. Augusto César Sandino, letter to General Moncada, in Ramírez, *El pensamiento vivo de Sandino*, p. 85. See also Moncada's letter to Sandino, ibid., pp. 84–85.

30. Millett, *Guardianes de la dinastía*, p. 92; and Ramírez, *El pensamiento vivo de Sandino*, pp. xxxviii–xl, and Sandino, letter of 27 June, pp. 92–93. Concerning Sandino's change in tactics, see ibid., pp. xl–xliii; and Munro, *United States and the Caribbean Republics*, pp. 235–236. A systematic analysis of Sandino's military knowledge, strategy, and tactics appears in Humberto Ortega Saavedra, *50 años de lucha sandinista*, pp. 25–68. Other material on the campaigns, makeup of the army, organization, and so forth appears in Gilbert, *Junto a Sandino*, passim; Selser, *Sandino*, pp. 139–230; Macaulay, *Sandino Affair*, pp. 62–218; Carleton Beals, *Banana Gold* (Philadelphia: Lippincott, 1932); and Abelardo Cuadra, *Hombre del Caribe*, Sergio Ramírez, ed. (San José, Costa Rica: Editorial Universitaria Centroamericana, 1979), pp. 49–115.

31. Millett appeared to discount some of the atrocities reportedly committed by Guard Company M under U.S. Marine Captain Lewis B. ("Chesty") Puller

and Lieutenant William Lee, but a substantial number of such accounts appeared throughout the occupation. For example, see Macaulay, *Sandino Affair*, pp. 111-117, 220; and Domingo Ibarra Grijalva, *The Last Night of General Augusto César Sandino* (New York: Vantage, 1973). Atrocities were also committed with frequency by the Sandinistas, according to Macaulay (pp. 111-117); Cuadra, *Hombre del Caribe*, pp. 49-115; and Anastasio Somoza García, *El verdadero Sandino, o el Calvario de las Segovias* (Managua: Tipografía Robelo, 1936), passim. Aerial bombing of towns and guerrilla positions by the National Guard and U.S. Marines caused numerous civilian casualties; see Gilbert, *Junto a Sandino*, p. 4; and Torres, "La intervención de los E.E.U.U.," p. 13.

32. Millett, *Guardianes de la dinastía*, pp. 118-164; Munro, *United States and the Caribbean Republics*, pp. 255-266.

33. Sandino, "Relato," 4 August 1932, in Ramírez, *El pensamiento vivo de Sandino*, p. 225; see also pp. 256-261.

34. Paterson et al., *American Foreign Policy*, p. 355.

35. Ibid., pp. 355-357; Millett, *Guardianes de la dinastía*, pp. 160-165; Munro, *United States and the Caribbean Republics*, pp. 267-269; Bemis, *Latin American Policy*, pp. 212-213; Wood, *Making of the Good Neighbor Policy*, pp. 13-47; Gil, *Latin American-United States Relations*, pp. 150-155; Peck, "Latin America Enters the World Scene," pp. 184-189; Sofonías Salvatierra, *Sandino, o la tragedia de un pueblo* (Managua: Máltez Representaciones, 1980; originally published in Madrid, 1934), pp. 8-126; and John J. Finan, "Foreign Relations in the 1930s: Effects of the Great Depression," in Davis et al., *Latin American Diplomatic History*, pp. 198-199.

36. For material on the period of the U.S. withdrawal, see Millett, *Guardianes de la dinastía*, pp. 78, 198-219; Munro, *United States and the Caribbean Republics*, pp. 276-278; Wood, *Making of the Good Neighbor Policy*, pp. 138-144; Salvatierra, *Sandino, o la tragedia*, pp. 80-256; Sánchez, *Nicaragua*, pp. 73-81; Cuadra, *Hombre del Caribe*, pp. 115-138; Macaulay, *Sandino Affair*, pp. 242-256; Selser, *Sandino*, pp. 281-302; and Ramírez, *El pensamiento vivo de Sandino*, pp. xlix-lxii.

37. Barahona Portocarrero, "La historia contemporánea de Nicaragua," pp. 23-25; Munro, *United States and the Caribbean Republics*, pp. 265-266; and Torres Rivas, *Interpretación del desarrollo*, pp. 154-155, 286-295.

38. Ramírez, *El Pensamiento vivo de Sandino*, pp. lxviii-lxix; and Salvatierra, *Sandino, o la tragedia*, pp. 243-250.

Chapter 4. The Foundation of the Dynasty

1. Anastasio Somoza García, *Mensaje que el Presidente de la República dirige al Hon. Congreso Nacional . . .* (Managua: Talleres Nacionales, 19 April 1952).

2. Selser, *Sandino*, p. 297.

3. Sandino's assassination has been described by several participants or witnesses: Abelardo Cuadra, in *Bohemia* (Havana), No. 7 (13 February 1949), and in "Formé parte de la conjura para asesinar a Sandino," *Universidad* (San José, Costa Rica), 25 July 1977; in Cuadra's memoirs, *Hombre del Caribe*, pp. 115-138; Salvatierra, *Sandino;* José N. Castro, in *Sábado* (Havana), No. 132

(1946). See also William Krehm, *Democracia y tiranías en la Caribe* (Mexico City: Editorial Unión Democrática Centroamericana, 1949); Ibarra Grijalva, *Last Night of Sandino;* Salvador Calderón Ramírez, *Los últimos días de Sandino* (Mexico City: Ediciones Bota, 1934); Millett, *Guardianes de la dinastía,* pp. 198–227; and Selser, *Sandino,* pp. 281–302. Anastasio Somoza García's personal version may be found in *El Verdadero Sandino.*

4. Selser, *Sandino,* pp. 303–306; Krehm, *Democracia y tiraniás,* pp. 13–15.

5. Somoza García's early months as director of the Guard are described in Millett, *Guardianes de la dinastía,* pp. 198–229; Selser, *Sandino,* pp. 283–301; Ibarra Grijalva, *Last Night of Sandino,* pp. 212–213; Wood, *Making of the Good Neighbor Policy,* pp. 140–141; and Cuadra, *Hombre del Caribe,* and "Formé parte de la conjura."

6. Material on Somoza's final assumption of power is drawn from Millet, *Guardianes de la dinastía,* pp. 228–246.

7. Ibid., pp. 198–233; and Jesús Miguel Blandón, *Entre Sandino y Fonseca Amador* (n.p., c. 1979).

8. Benjamin I. Teplitz reported them for José Santos Zelaya, in "Modernization in Nicaragua," pp. 416–425. Joaquín Ibarra Narvaez cited similar acts by nineteenth-century Conservative Fruto Chamorro, in *Estudio sobre la ubicación histórica, sociológica e ideológica de los partidos políticos de Nicaragua* (León, Nicaragua: Editorial Centroamericana, 1961), pp. 11–23.

9. Material on Somoza García and the evolution of the National Guard has been drawn primarily from Millett, *Guardianes de la dinastía,* pp. 259–297; Pedro Joaquín Chamorro C., *Los Somoza: Una estirpe sangrienta* (Buenos Aires: El Cid Editores, 1979), pp. 17–28 and passim; and Blandón, *Entre Sandino y Fonseca Amador,* pp. 26–56.

10. Millett, *Guardianes de la dinastía,* p. 261.

11. Wood, *Making of the Good Neighbor Policy,* pp. 118–140; Bemis, *Latin American Policy,* pp. 202–225, 256–294; and Munro, *United States and the Caribbean Republics,* pp. 371–383.

12. Wood, *Making of the Good Neighbor Policy,* pp. 140–151; Millett, *Guardianes de la dinastía,* pp. 233–237; Jaime Wheelock Román, *Imperialismo y dictadura* (Mexico City: Siglo Veintiuno Editores, 1979), pp. 124–126.

13. Material on Somoza García and U.S. foreign policy is drawn from Millett, *Guardianes de la dinastía,* pp. 266–285; John J. Finan, "Latin America and World War II," in Davis et al., *Latin American Diplomatic History,* pp. 222–224; G. Pope Atkins, *Latin America in the International Political System* (New York: Free Press, 1977), pp. 99–101, 251, 311–336; Gil, *Latin American–United States Relations,* pp. 168–184, 189–220; Selser, *Sandino,* pp. 327–330; Finan, "Latin America and the Cold War," pp. 342–348; Robert A. Packenham, *Liberal America and the Third World: Political Development Ideas in Foreign Aid and Social Service* (Princeton, N.J.: Princeton University Press, 1973), pp. 27–31; and Sánchez, *Nicaragua,* p. 95. See also Anastasio Somoza García," *Mensaje que el Presidente de la República, General de División Anastasio Somoza García, dirige al Hon. Congreso Nacional . . .* (Managua: Talleres Nacionales, 15 April 1951), p. 14.

14. Quote from Chamorro C., *Los Somoza,* p. 17.

15. Ibid., pp. 45–51; Pedro Hurtado Cárdenas, *Las torturas como sistema* (Managua: Editorial Asel, 1946); María Haydée Traña Paguaya, "El caso político de Nicaragua ante la faz mundial," Licenciatura thesis, Universidad Nacional Autónoma de Nicaragua, 1964, pp. 143–153; Blandón, *Entre Sandino y Fonseca Amador,* pp. 36–50; and Millett, *Guardianes de la dinastía,* p. 56.

16. Hurtado Cárdenas, *Las torturas como sistema,* pp. 8–19.

17. Teodoro Picado Michalski, father of Anastasio Somoza Debayle's fellow torturer, was president of Costa Rica from 1944 to 1948. Picado Michalski sought refuge in Nicaragua in 1948 (during the revolution led by José Figueres) and became an adviser and speech writer for Anastasio Somoza García. His son Teodoro Picado Lara became an intimate of Anastasio Somoza Debayle and led a Somoza-sponsored attempt to overthrow Figueres in 1955, in retaliation for Figueres's backing of the 1954 invasion in which Pedro Chamorro had participated. See Harold H. Bonilla, *Los presidentes, Tomo II* (San José: Editorial Universidad Nacional Estatal a Distancia–Editorial Costa Rica, 1979), pp. 525–567; Miguel Acuña, *El 55* (San José, Costa Rica: Librería Lehman, 1977); and Millett, *Guardianes de la dinastía,* pp. 283–284.

18. Chamorro C., *Los Somoza,* p. 51.

19. See ibid., passim; Blandón, *Entre Sandino y Fonseca Amador,* pp. 10–51; Millett, *Guardianes de la dinastía,* passim; José Fajardo et al., *Los sandinistas* (Bogotá: Editorial La Oveja Negra, 1979), pp. 259–269; and Sánchez, *Nicaragua,* pp. 73–97.

20. Chamorro C., *Los Somoza,* p. 129.

21. Quote from ibid., p. 124; see also pp. 45–50, 128–129; and Pedro Joaquín Chamorro C., *5 p.m.,* Rolando Steiner, ed. (Managua: personal publication, 1967), pp. 27–29, 143–145; Traña Paguaya, "El caso político de Nicaragua," p. 152b; Millett, *Guardianes de la dinastía,* p. 268; Blandón, *Entre Sandino y Fonseca Amador,* pp. 114–118; Selser, *Sandino,* pp. 333–334; and Barahona Portocarrero, "La historia contemporánea de Nicaragua," pp. 40–42.

22. Enrique Alvarado Martínez, *El pensamiento político nicaragüense de los últimos aõs* (Managua: Artes Gráficas, 1968), pp. 9–11, 31; Ibarra Narvaez, *La ubicación de los partidos,* pp. 14–31; Chamorro C., *Los Somoza,* p. 48; and Millet, *Guardianes de la dinastía,* pp. 228–269.

23. Wheelock Román, *Imperialismo y dictadura,* p. 122.

24. Ibid., pp. 80–207; Chamorro C., *Los Somoza,* pp. 47–48; Alvarado Martínez, *El pensamiento politico nicaragüense,* pp. 7–54; Millet, *Guardianes de la dinastía,* pp. 238–344; Barahona Portocarrero, "La historia contemporánea de Nicaragua," pp. 26–30; Humberto Ortega Saavedra, *50 años de lucha sandinista,* pp. 80–82; Ibarra Narvaez, *La ubicación de los partidos,* pp. 14–31.

25. Wheelock Román, *Imperialismo y dictadura,* pp. 71–127, 156–157, 202–207; Torres Rivas, *Interpretación de desarrollo,* pp. 119–230; Barahona Portocarrero, "La historia contemporánea de Nicaragua," pp. 23–25; Selser, *Sandino,* pp. 315–331; Krehm, *Democracia y tiranías,* p. 177; and Mario A. De Franco and Carlos F. Chamorro, "Nicaragua: Crecimiento industrial y empleo," in Daniel Camacho et al., *El fracaso social de la integración centroamericana: Capital, tecnología, empleo* (San José, Costa Rica: Editorial Universitaria Centroamericana, 1979), pp. 95–100.

26. For example, see Murray C. Havens, Carl Leiden, and Karl M. Schmitt, *Assassination and Terrorism* (Manchaca, Tex.: Sterling Swift, 1975), pp. 54–61. Havens et al. also take as evidence of Somoza's working-class popularity and populism that his death occurred in a union hall in León. The crowd at the union hall on 21 September 1956 was not of workers, but of the local Liberal Nationalist elite.

27. Barahona Portocarrero, "La historia contemporánea de Nicaragua," pp. 35–38; Torres Rivas, *Interpretación del desarrollo*, pp. 176–218; and Wheelock Román, *Imperialismo y dictadura*, pp. 82–83, 126–127.

28. Barahona Portocarrero, "La historia contemporánea de Nicaragua," pp. 43–45; Wheelock Román, *Imperialismo y dictadura*, pp. 141–174. Wheelock Román also identified three smaller groups that stand apart from these main three. The Calley-Dagnall banking group, centered in the coffee–growing North, primarily financed coffee-related investments (pp. 142–148). The much younger CAPSA (Centroamericana de Ahorro y Préstamo, S.A.) group financed housing construction and urban developments, as did FRANCOFIN (Corporación Francoamericana de Finanzas).

29. Wheelock Román, *Imperialismo y dictadura*, p. 193.

30. The material on the Somoza García fortune and economic activities comes from several sources, including ibid., pp. 163–176; Krehm, *Democracia y tiranías*, pp. 20–24, 164–177; Millett, *Guardianes de la dinastía*, pp. 264–265; Selser, *Sandino*, pp. 309–335; Barahona Portocarrero, "La historia contemporánea de Nicaragua," pp. 31–32; and Manuel Cordero Reyes et al., *Nicaragua bajo el régimen de Somoza* (San Salvador, 1944), pp. 8–135. The material presented here is not exhaustive, merely representative of Somoza García's investment methods and holdings, both legitimate and illegitimate.

31. Wheelock Román, *Imperialismo y dictadura*, pp. 197–198.

32. Selser, *Sandino*, p. 327. Barahona Portocarrero, "La historia contemporánea de Nicaragua," pp. 36–37.

33. Chamorro C., *Los Somoza*, p. 165.

34. Ibid., pp. 176–177; Havens et al., *Assassinations and Terrorism*, pp. 54–61; and Clemente Guido, *Noches de tortura* (Managua: Ediciones Nicarao, 1980), pp. 81–147.

35. Quote from Chamorro C., *Los Somoza*, p. 126. See also pp. 125–126; and Frente Sandinista de Liberación Nacional, *Iremos hacia el sol de la libertad* (Managua, 1979), p. 55; Millett, *Guardianes de la dinastía*, p. 285; Sánchez, *Nicaragua*, pp. 94–97.

Chapter 5: Like Father Like Sons

1. Quoted in Armando Luna Silva, *Filosofía social del gobierno del General Anastasio Somoza, Presidente de la República de Nicaragua* (Managua: Secretaría de Información y Prensa de la República, 1976), no pagination.

2. Chamorro C., *Los Somoza*, passim; Millett, *Guardianes de la dinastía*, pp. 297–298; Julio López C., Orlando Núñez S., Carlos Fernando Chamorro Barrios, and Pascual Serres, *La caída del somocismo y la lucha sandinista en*

Nicaragua (San José, Costa Rica: Editorial Universitaria Centroamericana, 1979), p. 24.

3. Chamorro C., *Los Somoza*, p. 60.

4. Ibid., p. 63.

5. Ibid., p. 77.

6. Ibid., pp. 62–63, 231–233; Millett, *Guardianes de la dinastía*, p. 297; interview with Ernesto Cardenal, *Proceso* (Mexico City), 28 August 1978, p. 41; Sánchez, *Nicaragua*, pp. 98–100.

7. Quote from Chamorro C., *Los Somoza*, p. 232.

8. Millett, *Guardianes de la dinastía*, pp. 297–322; Edelberto Torres, letter to Dr. Carlos Agüero, *PL*, 3 January 1979, p. 7; López C. et al., *La caída del somocismo*, pp. 23–33.

9. Packenham, *Liberal America and the Third World*, pp. 4–5, 109–160.

10. Ibid., p. 110.

11. Data from Agency for International Development, "U.S. Overseas Loans and Assistance from International Organizations," workpapers as of April 1976, cited in Atkins, *Latin America in the International Political System*, pp. 166–169, 183. See also Table 7.1 for details.

12. Material for this section is drawn from Atkins, *Latin America in the International Political System*, 180–184; J. A. Robleto Siles, *Yo deserté de la Guardia Nacional de Nicaragua* (San José, Costa Rica: Editorial Universitaria Centroamericana, 1979), pp. 11–18; Wheelock Román, *Imperialismo y dictadura*, pp. 131–138, 173–174; López C. et al., *La caída del somocismo*, pp. 240–247; Millett, *Guardianes de la dinastía*, pp. 300–318; Humberto Ortega Saavedra, *50 años de lucha sandinista*, pp. 116–118; Torres, letter to Agüero; Fernando Cardenal, "El gobierno de USA y el régimen de Somoza," *ECR* 9 July 1976, p. 8; and Jack R. Binns, U.S. Department of State, personal conversation with the author, San José, Costa Rica, 2 March 1980.

13. Laura Richardson, "Wilson and the Dictator: The Congressman from Nicaragua," *Texas Observer*, 23 September 1977, pp. 6–8; López C. et al., *La caída del somocismo*, pp. 245–247; *EM*, 11 July 1979, pp. 1, 13; *Foreign Assistance Legislation for Fiscal Year 1979 (Part 4)*, Hearings Before the Subcommittee on International Organizations of the Committee on International Relations, U.S. House of Representatives, 95th Congress, 15, 16, and 28 February 1978 (Washington, D.C.: Government Printing Office, 1978), pp. 82–92, 559–570.

14. Wheelock Román, *Imperialismo y dictadura*, pp. 127–140, Tables 1, 8; Torres Rivas, *Interpretación del desarrollo*, pp. 231–249; Barahona Portocarrero, "La historia contemporánea de Nicaragua," pp. 38–41; López C. et al., *La caída del somocismo*, pp. 42–54; and De Franco and Chamorro, "Nicaragua," pp. 95–110, Table 1.

15. De Franco and Chamorro, "Nicaragua," p. 103.

16. Ibid., p. 110; Woodward, *Central America*, p. 325.

17. López C. et al., *La caída del somocismo*, pp. 54–61, 274–286; quote from p. 57.

18. Ibid., pp. 68–98; Wheelock Román, *Imperialismo y dictadura*, pp.

148-162; and Barahona Portocarrero, "La historia contemporánea de Nicaragua," pp. 43-44, all divide the upper classes into a bourgeoisie (foreign, grand local, and middle local) and a nonproductive *"rentista"* sector (property owners, real estate speculators, and speculators in government services)—mostly connected with the Somoza faction.

19. Wheelock Román, *Imperialismo y dictadura,* pp. 171-172.

20. Ibid., pp. 171-176; Chamorro C., *5 p.m.,* pp. 17-18, 27-29, 117-119, 143-145; Harry Wallace Strachan, "The Role of Business Groups in Economic Development: The Case of Nicaragua," D.B.A. dissertation, Harvard University, 1972; and Leonel Poveda S., vice-director of Fondo Internacional para la Reconstrucción, interview with the author, Managua, 18 December 1979.

21. Wheelock Román, *Imperialismo y dictadura,* p. 174.

22. Ibid., p. 176. Another estimate is a half billion dollars as of 1978 (López C. et al., *La caída del somocismo,* pp. 343-349).

23. Wheelock Román, *Imperialismo y dictadura,* pp. 180-188; Barahona Portocarrero, "La historia contemporánea de Nicaragua," pp. 39-47; Torres Rivas, *Interpretación del desarrollo,* Table 19; Woodward, *Central America,* pp. 250-258, Table 6: López C. et al., *La caída del somocismo,* pp. 78-92; and De Franco and Chamorro, "Nicaragua," pp. 110-114, Tables 9-11.

24. De Franco and Chamorro, "Nicaragua," p. 105.

25. Ibid., pp. 105-106. See also López C. et al., *La caída del somocismo,* pp. 72-78; and Susanne Jonas Bodenheimer, "El Mercomún y la ayuda norteamericana," in Rafael Menjívar, ed., *La inversión extranjera en Centroamérica* (San José, Costa Rica: Editorial Universitaria Centroamericana, 1974), pp. 23-166.

26. Olson, "Rapid Growth as a Destabilizing Force," pp. 529-552; Gurr, *Why Men Rebel;* Davies, "Toward a Theory of Revolution," pp. 5-19; and Ivo K. Feierabend, Rosalind Feierabend, and Betty A. Nesvold, "Social Change and Political Violence," in H. D. Graham and T. R. Gurr, eds., *Violence in America,* (Washington, D.C.: National Commission on the Causes and Prevention of Violence, 1969).

27. Woodward, *Central America,* Table 2, p. 323; Torres Rivas, *Interpretación del desarrollo,* Table 16, p. 307; Ministerio de Planificación, *Programa de emergencia y reactivación en beneficio del pueblo, 1980-1981* (Managua, 1980), p. 111; and De Franco and Chamorro, "Nicaragua," Table 2, pp. 103-104, 120.

28. Wheelock Román, *Imperialismo y dictadura,* pp. 84-103, 128-219; Barahona Portocarrero, "La historia contemporánea de Nicaragua," pp. 41-47; De Franco y Chamorro, "Nicaragua," passim; López C. et al., *La caída del somocismo,* pp. 54-61; 78-139; Ministerio de Planificación, *Programa de emergencia,* pp. 81, 111; Woodward, *Central America,* Table 4; and Note 26 above.

29. Data from sources in Table 5.2 or cited in López C. et al., *La caída del somocismo,* pp. 333-334; and Millett, *Guardianes de la dinastía,* p. 334.

30. Quoted in Luna Silva, *Filosofía social,* n.p.

31. Barahona Portocarrero, "La historia contemporánea de Nicaragua," pp.

40-42; López C. et al., *La caída del somocismo*, pp. 24-75.

32. Millett, *Guardianes de la dinastía*, p. 334, 307-308; Chamorro C., *5 p.m.*, pp. 17-18, 27-29, 33-34, 117-119, 120-122, 143-145; López C., *La caída del somocismo*, pp. 24-26, 93-98; Cardenal, "El gobierno de USA," p. 8.

33. Chamorro C., *5 p.m.*, p. 118.

34. Torres, letter to Agüero, p. 7.

35. Material on the political parties during this period has been drawn from Alvarado Martínez, *El pensamiento político nicaragüense*, pp. 7-56; López C. et al., *La caída del somocismo*, pp. 95-135; Millett, *Guardianes de la dinastía*, pp. 299-333; Lafitte Fernández, "Pedro J. Chamorro: Gobierno de Somoza está agotado; no puede existir," *ECR*, 5 September 1975, p. 4; Torres, letter to Agüero; Chamorro C., *5 p.m.*, pp. 43-46, 220-222; Chamorro C., *Los Somoza*, pp. 83-160; Blandón, *Entre Sandino y Fonseca Amador*, pp. 52-99; Ibarra Narvaez, *La ubicación de los partidos*, pp. 24-31; and Humberto Ortega Saavedra, *50 años de lucha sandinista*, p. 93.

36. Material on the National Guard in this period is drawn from Woodward, *Central America*, p. 238; Steve C. Ropp and Neale J. Pearson, "Attitudes of Honduran and Nicaraguan Junior Officers Toward the Role of the Military in Latin America," paper presented to the Southwestern Political Science Association meeting, San Antonio, Tex., March 1974, p. 21; Steve C. Ropp, "Goal Orientations of Nicaraguan Cadets," *Journal of Comparative Administration* 4 (May 1973); Wheelock Román, *Imperialismo y dictadura*, p. 136; Millett, *Guardianes de la dinastía*, pp. 302-339; Robleto Siles, *Yo deserté de la Guardia Nacional*, pp. 187-191 and passim; Blandón, *Entre Sandino y Fonseca Amador*, pp. 6-7, 52-66, 100-113, and passim; and Atkins, *Latin America in the International Political System*, p. 183.

37. *Declaración americana de los derechos y deberes del hombre* (1948), Documentos de Estudio, Serie Derechos del Hombre No. 2 (Heredia, Costa Rica: Escuela de Relaciones Internacionales, Universidad Nacional, 1980), pp. 7-11; see also in the same publication, "Convención americana sobre derechos humanos," pp. 13-35. Of most immediate relevance here are the rights to life and security, freedom of opinion and press, protection from arbitrary treatment by government, free association, free elections, due process of law, speedy civil trial, and humane incarceration and punishment.

38. Amnesty International, *República de Nicaragua: Informe incluyendo las recomendaciones de una misión enviada a Nicaragua entre el 10 y el 15 de mayo de 1976* (London: Amnesty International Publications, 1978), pp. 50-51.

39. For evidence of political repression see ibid., passim; and Inter-American Commission on Human Rights (hereafter IACHR), *Report on the Situation of Human Rights in Nicaragua: Findings of the 'On-Site' Observation in the Republic of Nicaragua, October 3-12, 1978* (Washington, D.C.: Organization of American States, 1978), passim. U.S. Department of State, "Human Rights Report on Nicaragua," in *Foreign Assistance Legislation 1979 (Part 4)*, pp. 85-91 and passim; Robleto Siles, *Yo deserté de la Guardia Nacional*, passim; Chamorro C., *Los Somoza*, passim; Wheelock Román, *Imperialismo y dictadura*, p. 128; Chamorro C., *5 p.m.*, pp. 220-222, Fernández, "Pedro J. Chamorro," p. 4;

López C. et al., *La caída del somocismo*, pp. 23-31, 99-105, 268-269; Cardenal, "El gobierno de USA," p. 8; Millett, *Guardianes de la dinastía*, pp. 298-322; Torres, "La intervención de los E.E.U.U.," pp. 17-19; and material from the following newspapers: *N*:11 May 1977, 11 November 1977, 4 September 1978.

40. Luna Silva, *Filosofía social*, n.p.

41. *Foreign Assistance Legislation 1979 (Part 4)*, p. 92.

Chapter 6. Social Class and Opposition

1. Roger Mendieta Alfaro, *El último marine, La caída de Somoza* (Managua: Editorial Unión, 1979), p. 1.

2. Quoted in *R.*, 2 June 1978.

3. Foreign capitalists somewhat complicate the analysis of Nicaraguan politics since the 1950s. No longer intervening in politics so openly as before 1940 (see Chapters 2 and 3), foreign investors have acted through Nicaraguan agents who were often members of the bourgeoisie by virture of their own wealth.

4. Material on the Conservatives is drawn from López C. et al., *La caída del somocismo*, pp. 35, 381-383; Barahona Portocarrero, "La historia contemporánea de Nicaragua," pp. 32-34; Torres, letter to Agüero, p. 7; Torres, "La intervención de los E.E.U.U.," pp. 16-17; José Coronel Urtecho, "Sobre la universalidad nicaragüense," in Pablo Antonio Cuadra, *El nicaragüense* (San José, Costa Rica: Editorial Universitaria Centroamericana, 1976), pp. 273-274; Blandón, *Entre Sandino y Fonseca Amador*, pp. 22-98; Millett, *Guardianes de la dinastía*, pp. 275-302; Chamorro C., *5 p.m.*, pp. 43-46, 220-222; Traña Paguaya, "El caso política de Nicaragua," pp. 160-162; Thomas W. Walker, *The Christian Democratic Movement in Nicaragua*, (Tucson: University of Arizona Press, 1970), pp. 26-42; Ibarra Narvaez, *La ubicación de los partidos*, pp. 24-26; *N*, 30 August 1977; Franciso Urcuyo Maliaño, *Sólos: Las últimas 43 horas en el bunker de Somoza* (Guatemala City: Editorial Académica Centro Americana, 1979), pp. 199-200 n.12; 202 n. 14.

5. Ibarra Narvaez, *La ubicación de los partidos*, pp. 23-25.

6. Of the Conservative party, FSLN Directorate member Daniel Ortega Saavedra (in an interview with the author, Managua, 22 January 1980), said, "The Conservative Party is buried . . . it is the past." Violeta Barrios de Chamorro, then a member of the Governing Junta of National Reconstruction (author's interview, 23 January 1980) opined that "the Conservative Party is dead. . . . Who wants to be in the Conservative Party of Agüero? Nobody."

7. On dissident Liberals, see Ibarra Narvaez, *La ubicación de los partidos*, pp. 24-31; Millett, *Guardianes de la dinastía*, pp. 220-280, 318-319; Blandón, *Entre Sandino y Fonseca Amador*, pp. 21-24; Urcuyo Maliaño, *Sólos*, pp. 159-171, 202 n.15; Traña Paguaya, "El caso político de Nicaragua," p. 147-148; Walker, *Christian Democratic Movement*, pp. 16-17; *N*, 1 August 1978.

For a list of the principles of the Liberal Nationalist party see Urcuyo Maliaño, *Sólos*, pp. 163-171. The party called itself "democratic and republican," advocated "liberty and social justice," and described suffrage as "the genuine expression of the popular will." The PLN also pledged itself to "alternation in the

Presidency of the Republic" and to the propositions that "human life is inviolable," that "no one should be deprived of liberty except by the law," and that "the army should be professional and apolitical."

8. Material on upper-class groups is drawn from the following sources: author's interview with Alfonso Robelo Callejas, then a member of the Governing Junta of National Reconstruction, Managua, 25 January 1980; author's interview with Violeta Barrios de Chamorro; López C. et al., *La caída del somocismo,* pp. 88–90, 154–355; Wheelock Román, *Imperialismo y dictadura,* pp. 151–152, 183–184; Humberto Ortega Saavedra, *50 años de lucha sandinista,* pp. 99–102; Enrique Dreyfus, "Un nuevo marco socioeconómico dentro de la revolución: Informe anual del presidente del INDE," Colección la Iniciativa Privada en la Revolución, No. 2 (Managua: INDE, 1980); Fernández, "Pedro J. Chamorro," p. 4; FUNDE, *Desarrollo institucional: Crecimiento cooperativo promovido 1973/1979* (Managua: Fundación Nicaragüense de Desarrollo, 1979), Figure 2; INDE, *Informe Anual: INDE y sus programas FUNDE y EDUCREDITO, 1976* (Managua: Instituto Nicaragüense de Desarrollo, 1976); Urcuyo Maliaño, *Sólos,* pp. 42–43; *ECR:* 9 October 1977; 20 October 1977; 20 October 1978; *R:* 17 August 1978; 5 September 1978; 16 November 1978; and *N:* 6 June 1978; 16 June 1978, p. 47A; 18 June 1978; 5 July 1978, p. 4A; 27 August 1978, p. 19A; 4 September 1978, p. 18A; 12 October 1978.

9. Material on the repression of the press has been drawn from the author's interviews with Violeta Barrios de Chamorro and with Alfonso Robelo Callejas, as well as from Blandón, *Entre Sandino y Fonseca Amador,* pp. 114–120, 183–189; Chamorro C., *5 p.m.,* pp. 120–122; IACHR, *Report on Human Rights in Nicaragua,* pp. 65–68; Amnesty International, *Republica de Nicaragua,* pp. 45–46; Jacinto Vélez Bárcenas, *Dr. P. J. Chamorro C., ¡Asesinado!* (San José, Costa Rica: Trejos Hermanos Sucesores, 1979), pp. 371–443; Dreyfus, "Un nuevo marco socioeconómico"; *R:* 12 January 1978; 25 January 1978, p. 1; 29 April 1979, p. 4; *N:* 20 September 1977; 15 January 1978; 2 March 1978, p. 12A; 22 April 1978; 26 April 1978; 10 June 1978; 23 June 1978, p. 4A; 13 July 1978; 12 June 1979, p. 19A; *ECR,* 24 January 1978, p. 1.

10. Vélez Bárcenas, *Chamorro, ¡Asesinado!* passim; *ECR,* 11 January 1978; *N,* 11 October 1979, p. 19A; and *P,* 23 January 1980, pp. 1, 4.

11. Quoted in *N,* 29 June 1978.

12. Material on the Independent Liberals is drawn from Millett, *Guardianes de la dinastía,* pp. 276–283; Urcuyo Maliaño, p. 202; Torres, "La intervención de los E.E.U.U.," pp. 16–17; Fernández, "Pedro J. Chamorro," p. 4; and Chamorro C., *Los Somoza,* passim.

Speaking of his own torture after the 1956 assassination of Anastasio Somoza García, Clemente Guido affirmed: "That was the whiplash on my conscience . . . that committed me to struggle against the hereditary dictatorship of the Somozas. It was them, the Somozas, who with a cruel and unjust act, changed me from a passive opponent into a highly active opponent." Quoted from his *Noches de Tortura* (Managua: Ediciones Nicarao, 1980), p. 28.

13. Ibarra Narvaez, *La ubicación de los partidos,* pp. 28–30.

14. Quoted in Blandón, *Entre Sandino y Fonseca Amador,* p. 183.

15. This discussion of the Christian Democratic–social Christian movements up to 1970 has been drawn mainly from Walker, *Christian Democratic Movement,* pp. 18–56; Michael Dodson and Tommie Sue Montgomery, "The Churches in the Nicaraguan Revolution," paper presented to the Latin American Studies Association meeting, Bloomington, Ind., 16–19 October 1980, pp. 2–8; and "El movimiento obrero," in José Fajardo et al., *Los sandinistas* (Bogotá: Editorial la Oveja Negra, 1979), p. 268. See also Dreyfus, "Un nuevo marco socioeconómico"; Blandón, *Entre Sandino y Fonseca Amador,* pp. 213–215; Fernández, "Pedro J. Chamorro"; López C. et al., *La caída del somocismo,* pp. 353–355; and *N,* 26 September 1977. Also consulted was the author's interview with Robelo Callejas.

16. Material on students is drawn from Blandón, *Entre Sandino y Fonseca Amador,* pp. 14–51, 100–175, 183–184; Humberto Ortega Saavedra, *50 años de lucha sandinista,* pp. 92–134; Humberto Ortega Saavedra, "La insurrección nacional victoriosa," interview in *Nicaráuac* 1 (May–June 1980), pp. 31–33; Torres, "La intervención de los E.E.U.U.," pp. 16–17; Walker, *Christian Democratic Movement,* pp. 24–42; Henry Ruíz, "La montaña era como un crisol donde se forjaban los mejores cuadros," interview in *Nicaráuac* 1 (May–June 1980), pp. 17–18; Dodson and Montgomery, "Churches," pp. 12–23; author's interviews with Daniel Ortega Saavedra and with Germán Ruiz, of the FSLN's July 19th Sandinista Youth, Managua, 24 January 1980; and FSLN, *Pedro Arauz Palacios: Datos biográficos,* Colección Juan de Diós Muñoz, Série Biografías Populares, No. 8 (Managua: Secretaría Nacional de Propaganda y Educación Política, FSLN, 1980), pp. 7–10.

17. The Arbenz government in Guatemala permitted the left a degree of political freedom and participation in political affairs previously unknown anywhere in Central America. A friend of Fonseca and former classmate of Borge, Gutiérrez Castro, lived from 1950 to 1953 in Guatemala, where he became familiar with Marxist writings. He returned and introduced Fonseca to these works. "Marxism," Gutiérrez Castro later related, "fit him like a suit he had been awaiting for a long time" (quoted in Blandón, *Entre Sandino y Fonseca Amador,* pp. 184–185).

18. This remarkable periodical attracted national recognition for its poetry, art, and political commentary. Even more remarkable, however, is the degree to which the three friends from Matagalpa—Borge, Fonseca, and Mayorga—would later shape national events. See ibid., pp. 185–190, and Chapter 7 of this book.

19. The FER was led by such people as Sócrates Flores, Michel Najlís, Doris Tijerino, Daniel Ortega Saavedra, and Bayardo Arce, all important Sandinista leaders. For a description of FER activism, see FSLN, *Francisco Meza Rojas: Datos biográficos,* Colección Juan de Diós Muñoz, Série Biografías Populares, No. 9 (Managua: Secretaría Nacional de Propaganda y Educación Política, FSLN, 1980), pp. 5–10; or Urcuyo M., *Sólos,* pp. 49–50.

20. One example is Edgar Lang Sacasa, scion of a wealthy family with major commercial interests, who fought and died with the FSLN's Guerra Popular Prolongada wing (see Chapter 7 of this book). See *N:* 30 November 1977; 22 April 1979, p. 19A; and Mendieta Alfaro, *El último marine,* p. 73.

21. Quote from IACHR, *Report on Human Rights in Nicaragua,* p. 77. See also ibid., pp. 50–54; Medieta Alfaro, *El último marine,* pp. 77–78; and *R,* 16 February 1979, p. 3.

22. Material on university professors and the insurrection is drawn from an interview by the author with Carlos Tunnerman Bernheim, minister of education, Managua, 23 January 1980; and from *N:* 18 June 1978, p. 2A; 3 February 1979, p. 18A; 20 April 1979, p. 19A; and 26 April 1979, p. 21A. A hostile, but often accurate, account of the university's role is that of Urcuyo Maliaño, *Sólos,* pp. 44–51.

23. Author's interview with Tunnerman Bernheim.

24. This material based on López C. et al., *La caída del somocismo,* pp. 112–114, 353–356; "El movimiento obrero," pp. 261–276; author's interviews with Paul Oquist, Department of Government Information and Promotion (Departamiento de Información y Gestión Estatal—DIGE), General Secretariat of the Governing Junta, Managua, 27 May 1980 and 16 July 1980; and *N:* 1 May 1978; 10 August 1978; 26 April 1979, pp. 19A, 21A.

25. López C. et al., *La caída del somocismo,* pp. 110–112; and author's conversations with hotel keepers, taxi drivers, and small-business people from January to July 1980.

26. Material on the Socialists is drawn from Humberto Ortega Saavedra, *50 años de lucha sandinista,* pp. 82–83; Barahona Portocarrero, "La historia contemporánea de Nicaragua," pp. 48–51; Blandón, *Entre Sandino y Fonseca Amador,* pp. 185–206; Luis Favré, "Revolución proletaria en Nicaragua," in Carlos Vig, ed., *Nicaragua: ¿Reforma o revolución?* Vol. 2 (Bogotá: Partido Socialista de los Trabajadores de Colombia, 1980), pp. 563–564; Fausto Amador, "La creciente oposición al régimen de Somoza," in ibid., Vol. 1, pp. 80–84.

27. Jaime Wheelock Román, *Diciembre victorioso* (Managua: Secretaría Nacional de Propaganda y Educación Política, FSLN, n.d., c. 1979), pp. 50–52; Humberto Ortega Saavedra, *50 años de lucha sandinista,* pp. 111–112, 129; Blandón, *Entre Sandino y Fonseca Amador,* pp. 36–81, 213–214; and author's interview with Daniel Ortega Saavedra.

28. López apparently stayed with the FSLN for some time, although his role is not clear. He is seldom mentioned prominently in FSLN leaders' accounts, but he is mentioned as an active *comandante* (commander) during a wave of FSLN bank robberies in 1963; see Humberto Ortega Saavedra's *50 años de lucha sandinista,* p. 129.

29. This and subsequent discussions of changes in the agrarian economy are drawn from CSUCA/Programa Centroamericana de Ciencias Sociales, *Estructura agrária, dinámica de población, y desarrollo capitalista en Centroamérica* (San José, Costa Rica: Editorial Universitaria Centroamericana, 1978), pp. 204–254; Wheelock Román, *Imperialismo y dictadura,* pp. 32–103; Wheelock Román, *Diciembre victorioso,* pp. 72–73; and author's interview with Ariel Granera, DIGE, Managua, 16 July 1980.

30. On the radicalization of the peasantry see Dodson and Montgomery, "Churches," pp. 15–19; López C. et al., *La caída del somocismo,* pp. 98–105; and Amnesty International, *República de Nicaragua,* pp. 30–40, 69–79; FSLN, *Com-*

andante Germán Pomares Ordoñez: Datos biográficos, Colección Juan de Diós Muñoz, Série Biografías Populares, No.5 (Managua: Secretaría Nacional de Propaganda y Educación Política, FSLN, 1980), pp. 7-8; IACHR, *Report on Human Rights in Nicaragua,* pp. 12-20. Robleto Siles, *Yo deserté de la Guardia Nacional,* pp. 153-154, estimated conservatively that *at least* three thousand peasants were executed by the Guard, based on his own diary, access to National Guard records, and projections over time to other regions from those for which he obtained data. For details see pp. 10-157.

31. *P,* 24 February 1980, pp. 1, 9. Other examples of such testimony in the Nicaraguan press during this period are too numerous to cite.

32. Robleto Siles, *Yo deserté de la Guardia Nacional,* p. 61.

33. Ibid., p. 77.

34. Ibid., p. 143.

35. Some observers have regarded Somoza García as a populist because of his ties to organized labor. However, the actual record of his treatment of the labor movement should dispel such an interpretation (see Chapter 5).

For this material on organized labor the following sources were consulted: "El movimiento obrero," pp. 261-274; Humberto Ortega Saavedra, *50 años de lucha sandinista,* pp. 82-83; Walker, *Christian Democratic Movement,* pp. 43-45; Thomas W. Walker, "The Somoza Family Regime," in Howard J. Wiarda and Harvey F. Kline, *Latin American Politics and Development* (Boston: Houghton Mifflin, 1979), pp. 328-329; Chamorro C., *5 p.m.,* pp. 74-76, 93-95; Favré, "Revolución proletaria," pp. 563-565; IACHR, *Report on Human Rights in Nicaragua,* pp. 73-74; and the author's interview with Robelo Callejas. Material on the general strikes was drawn from *ECR,* 24 January 1978, p. 1; *R:* 25, 26 January 1978; 28 August 1978; *PL,* 31 May 1979, p. 17; *N:* 8 February 1978, p. 10A; 10 August 1978; 18 September 1978, p. 10A.

36. See Chapter 5 of this volume for more details on economic conditions affecting the urban proletariat.

37. IACHR, *Report on Human Rights in Nicaragua,* p. 74.

38. Material on the urban poor is based upon Dodson and Montgomery, "Churches," pp. 5-23; Humberto Ortega Saavedra, *50 años de lucha sandinista,* pp. 103-114, and "La insurrección nacional victoriosa," pp. 27-28, 40-44; Ignacio Briones Torres, "Monimbó rebelde," in Fajardo et al., *Los sandinistas,* pp. 51-59; "Testimonios de la insurrección," in ibid., pp. 63-97; Mendieta Alfaro, *El último marine,* pp. 46-52; Oquist interview; and Pedro Miranda M., *El pueblo que asombra al mundo: Nicaragua* (Panama City: Ediciones Punto Rojo, 1979), p. 89; *N:* 2 March 1978; 2 September 1978, p. 18A; 12 September 1978, p. 4A; 11 June 1979, p. 19A; *R,* 28 February 1978; *PL,* 25 February 1978.

Chapter 7. Foreign and Domestic Opposition

1. Anastasio Somoza as told to Jack Cox, *Nicaragua Betrayed* (Boston: Western Islands, 1980), pp. 397, 91 respectively.

2. *PL,* 15 June 1979, p. 10; *EM:* 4 July 1979, p. 1; 9 July 1979, p. 1; *N:* 18 November 1978; 13 June 1979, p. 21A.

3. Material on the United States and the Somoza regime is drawn largely from the following sources: *N:* 5 August 1978; 10 August 1978; 2 September 1978; 4 September 1978, p. 18A; 14 September 1978; 17 September 1978, p. 12A; 23 September 1978, p. 12A; 24 September 1978, p. 18A; 3 November 1978, p. 18A; 10 November 1978, p. 18A; 9 February 1979, p. 18A; 10 February 1979, p. 18A; *R,* 16 September 1978, p. 4; *PL:* 22 December 1978; 14 June 1979, p. 6; 5 July 1979, p. 4; and 7 July 1979, p. 6.

4. Urcuyo Maliaño, *Sólos,* pp. xiii–xv.

5. Quoted in *N,* 2 September 1978.

6. Sandinista leaders are most emphatic about this point, as I discovered in my interview with FSLN Directorate and junta member Daniel Ortega Saavedra.

7. For a more detailed discussion of Costa Rican–Nicaraguan relations, see William J. Carroll III and Mitchell A. Seligson, "The Costa Rican Connection in the Downfall of Somoza," paper presented to the Conference on Central America in the 1980s: Options for U.S. Policy, El Paso, Tex., 16–17 November 1979, pp. 1–9.

8. Conversations with a former national security adviser to President Oduber (Mr. B.), San José, March–June 1980; and *R,* 16 September 1978, p. 3; *N:* 7 September 1978, p. 18A; 13 September 1978, p. 10A; 30 September 1978.

9. Interview with an official (Mr. A.) of the Costa Rican Ministry of Public Security, San José, August 1979. Subsequent details of the arms smuggling through Costa Rica were revealed in a Costa Rican scandal; see Lafitte Fernández and Edgar Fonseca, "El enigma de las armas," *N,* 20–26 July 1980; and *N:* 22 July 1980, p. 12A; 23 July 1980, p. 12A; 30 July 1980, p. 12A.

10. *N,* 15 September 1978, p. 10A.

11. Material on the Somoza regime's relations with other Latin American nations was drawn from *ECR,* 18 October 1977; *R:* 16 October 1977; 24 May 1979, p. 2; *N:* 23 June 1978; 29 June 1978; 3 September 1978, p. 18A; 30 September 1978; 2 February 1979, p. 3A; 23 May 1979; *EM:* 10 July 1979, 11 July 1979, p. 1; 13 July 1979, p. 1.

12. Material on the activity of the OAS with regard to the Somoza regime was drawn mainly from IACHR, *Report on Human Rights in Nicaragua;* "Marx and Nicaragua," *Newsweek* (international ed.), 23 July 1979, p. 16; *EM:* 11 July 1979, p. 1; 13 July 1979, p. 1; 15 July 1979, p. 1; *R:* 11 November 1978; 31 December 1978, p. 3; *N:* 14 September 1978, p. 3; 26 September 1978; 19 November 1978, p. 18A; 20 November 1978; 24 November 1978; 31 December 1978, p. 84A; and 16 February 1979, p. 16A.

13. Material on Cuban involvement in the Nicaraguan insurrection was drawn from Blandón, *Entre Sandino y Fonseca Amador,* pp. 82–90, 199–205; Ruiz, "La montaña," p. 20; "Who's Behind the Rebels," *Newsweek* (international ed.), 9 July 1979, p. 7; *PL,* 22 July 1978. Evidence of the FSLN's sources of aid includes Cuba to a minor degree but clearly reveals that Panama, Costa Rica, and possibly Venezuela were much more important.

14. Ruiz, "La montaña," p. 20.

15. "Who's Behind the Rebels," p. 7.

16. Material on the Catholic Church is drawn from Walker, *Christian*

Democratic Movement, p. 17; Walker, "Nicaragua," pp. 327–338; Traña Paguaya, "El caso político de Nicaragua," pp. 160–162; Dodson and Montgomery, "Churches"; Urcuyo Maliaño, *Sólos,* pp. 37–41; "Carta Pastoral de los obispos de Nicaragua sobre los principios de la actividad política de la Iglesia," Managua, 1972; Somoza and Cox, *Nicaragua Betrayed,* pp. 55–56; *R,* 13 December 1978, p. 21; *ECR,* 26 November 1977; *PL,* 7 January 1978.

17. *Pueblo* (San José, Costa Rica), 18–25 December 1978, p. 7.

18. Dodson and Montgomery, "Churches," pp. 10–12, 21–23.

19. Blandón, *Entre Sandino y Fonseca Amador,* pp. 14–28, 100–114, 176–224; Mendieta Alfaro, *El último marine,* pp. 93–104; Wheelock Román, *Diciembre victorioso,* passim; Humberto Ortega Saavedra, *50 años de lucha sandinista,* pp. 92–97, and "La insurrección nacional victoriosa," p. 34; Tomás Borge, "Extracto del discurso del Comandante de la Revolución Tómas Borge, en La Gruta Javier, Diciembre 12, 1979," in *La revolución a través de nuestra Dirección Nacional* (Managua: Secretaría Nacional de Propaganda y Educación Política, FSLN, 1980), pp. 27–36; and Oleg Ignatiev and Guenrij Borovik, *La agonía de una dictadura* (Moscow: Editorial Progreso, 1980).

20. Author's interview with Daniel Ortega Saavedra; and interview with Daniel Ortega Saavedra, in Fajardo et al., *Los sandinistas,* pp. 229–233; Humberto Ortega Saavedra, "La insurrección nacional victoriosa," pp. 32–34, and *50 años de lucha sandinista,* pp. 85–133; Ruíz, "La montaña," pp. 10–22; Borge, "Extracto," pp. 27–34; Wheelock Román, *Diciembre victorioso,* passim; and Blandón, *Entre Sandino y Fonseca Amador,* pp. 14–28, 100–114, 202–219.

21. Humberto Ortega Saavedra, *50 años de lucha sandinista,* p. 112.

22. Ibid., p. 119.

23. Ruíz, "La montaña," p. 14.

24. Ibid., pp. 14–16.

25. Material on the FSLN in this period is drawn mainly from Ruíz, "La montaña," pp. 10–24; Humberto Ortega Saavedra, "La insurrección nacional victoriosa," pp. 10–57; López C. et al., *La caída del somocismo,* pp. 173–191, 272–273; Daniel Ortega Saavedra, interview with the author, and interview in Fajardo et al., *Los sandinistas,* pp. 171–195; and ibid., pp. 196–241.

26. Ruíz, "La montaña," p. 17.

27. For example, Daniel Ortega Saavedra, of the Terceristas, in 1978 said of the Proletario tendency: "They really don't represent the traditions and the content that have characterized the FSLN . . . they have attacked us continuously for our insurrectional strategy. . . . The [Proletario tendency] doesn't transcend propagandism. . . ." Of the GPP Ortega said, "They have gone along proposing the accumulation of forces, [but] they go into the jungle and isolate themselves from the daily struggle of the masses" (Fajardo et al., *Los sandinistas,* p. 227). See also the comments by Henry Ruíz in ibid., pp. 234–241; for a detailed accounting of the differences among the tendencies, see David Nolan, *The Ideology of the Sandinistas and the Nicaraguan Revolution* (Coral Gables, Fla.: Institute of Interamerican Studies–Graduate School of International Studies, University of Miami, 1984), pp. 32–84.

28. Edén Pastora's nom de guerre, Commandante Cero (Commander Zero), originated in and refers to his rank in the famous assault on the National Palace in 1978. The principal commander in a squad was always designated Zero, the second in command was One, and so forth. This name stuck with Pastora after the National Palace incident. The Sandinistas also employed a system of code names to help preserve anonymity. These code names will be presented in the text in parentheses following the real name: e.g., Germán Pomares (El Danto), Henry Ruíz (Modesto), and Pedro Aráuz Palacios (Federico).

29. Humberto Ortega Saavedra, "La insurrección nacional victoriosa," p. 44.

30. Ibid.

31. Ibid.

32. Carlos Fonseca Amador, ed., *Ideario político de Augusto César Sandino,* (Managua: Secretaría Nacional de Propaganda y Educación Política, FSLN, 1980); Fajardo et al., *Los sandinistas,* pp. 243–257; Humberto Ortega Saavedra, *50 años de lucha sandinista,* pp. 102–105, 141–152, and "La lucha de Sandino, base de la revolución sandinista," in *La revolución a través de nuestra Dirección Nacional,* pp. 9–13; Victor Tirado López, "El pensamiento político de Carlos Fonseca Amador," in ibid., pp. 17–24; Henry Ruíz, "Extracto del discurso pronunciado en el acto de clausura de la asamblea nacional constitutiva del la A.T.C.," in ibid., pp. 75–83; Jaime Wheelock Román, "No hay dos reformas agrarias iguales," interview in *Nicaráuac* 1 (May-June 1980), pp. 60–75; Orlando Núñez S., Centro de Investigación, Instituto Nacional de Reforma Agraria, and member of the Comisión Política of the Secretaría Nacional de Propaganda y Educación Política, FSLN, interview with the author, Managua, 27 May 1980; Nolan, *Ideology of the Sandinistas,* passim. Material on post-1979 ideology drawn from an interview with Jaime Wheelock Román, member of the FSLN National Directorate, Managua, 3 November 1984; and FSLN, *Political Platform of the FSLN* (Managua: FSLN National Campaign Committee, 17 July 1984), pp. 11–20.

33. In his book *The Cuban Revolution* (New York: Harper & Row, 1977), pp. 300–301 and passim, Hugh Thomas argued that Castro was not a committed Marxist at the moment of taking power. Fonseca, in contrast, had been a Marxist for years before Castro, having been introduced to Marx in the early 1950s (see above).

34. "La reunificación del FSLN con las tendencias Guerra Popular Prolongada y Tendencia Proletaria" (July 1978), in Fajardo et al., *Los sandinistas,* p. 215 (see pp. 210–218 for entire text).

35. Fajardo et al., *Los sandinistas,* p. 253.

36. For the organization of the FSLN see Ruíz, "La montaña," pp. 14–18; Humberto Ortega Saavedra, "La insurrección nacional victoriosa"; FSLN, *Francisco Meza Rojas, Datos biográficos,* Colección Juan de Diós Muñoz, Série Biografías Populares, No. 9 (Managua: Secretaría Nacional de Propaganda y Educación Política, FSLN, 1980); and *Pedro Aráuz Palacios, Datos biográficos,* Colección Juan de Diós Muñoz, Série Biografías Populares, No. 8

(Managua: Secretaría Nacional de Propaganda y Educación Política, FSLN, 1980); Miranda M., *El Pueblo que asombra,* pp. 39–96; Borge, "Extracto"; "Dos mil soldados desfilaron ante Edén Pastora," *Respuesta* (Costa Rica), No. 2 (December 1978):25–27; "Una nueva Nicaragua, no una nueva Cuba," interview with Sérgio Ramírez and Alfonso Robelo, in *Proceso* (Mexico City), 140 (9 July 1979):41–42; *N,* 10 June 1979, p. 19A; *EM,* 12 July 1979, p. 1; *PL,* 18 June 1979, p. 15.

37. Ruíz, "La montaña," p. 19.

38. Ibid., p. 20.

39. Humberto Ortega Saavedra, *50 años de lucha sandinista,* pp. 85–130, and "La insurrección nacional victoriosa," pp. 27–29; Ruíz, "La montaña," pp. 17–22; Miranda M., *El pueblo que asombra,* pp. 71–75; and Dodson and Montgomery, "Churches."

40. Humberto Ortega Saavedra, "La insurrección nacional victoriosa," p. 57. See also Miranda M., *El pueblo que asombra,* pp. 71–75; and Mendieta Alfaro, *El último marine,* pp. 41–52.

41. Ruíz, "La montaña," pp. 17–21; Humberto Ortega Saavedra, "La insurrección nacional victoriosa," pp. 29, 43–44.

42. The price for such collaboration by the security officials of Panama and Costa Rica was a share of the arms purchased by the FSLN. According to reports that have surfaced since, public officials in each country kept one-fourth of the arms in payment for their services. Some of these arms have since been sold by Costa Rican security officials to the rebels in El Salvador. Sources on Costa Rican and Panamanian arms aid to the FSLN include the following: an interview by the author with an official of Costa Rica's Ministry of Public Security (Mr. A.), San José, August 1979; and *Tico Times* (San José, Costa Rica), 27 March 1981, pp. 1, 4.

43. "On one occasion, the pilots testified, Sandinista commander Victor Tirado López watched the distribution of arms with tears in his eyes, as the Costa Rican security officials claimed the lion's share of the shipment," *Tico Times,* 27 March 1981, p. 4. The Nicaraguan government's accusations about Cuban arms ferried through Costa Rica and Panama were substantially accurate as to the connections.

44. The organizations in UDEL were Conservative National Action (Acción Nacional Conservadora), PLI, Liberal Constitutionalist Movement (Movimiento Liberal ˙Constitucionalista), PSCN, PSN, CTN, and CGT.

45. The organizations in the FAO were UDEL and its groups, MDN, Group of Twelve (los Doce), Partido Conservador Oficialista (the official wing of the Conservative party, sitting in Congress), Authentic Conservative party (Partido Auténtico Conservador), Partido Conservador Agüerista (Agüero faction of the Conservative party), and PSCN. Information on the FAO is also drawn from López et al., *La caída del somocismo,* pp. 220–226, 354–372; Sánchez, *Nicaragua,* pp. 137–146; Miranda M., *El pueblo que asombra,* pp. 35–37; Ignatiev and Borovik, *La agonía de una dictadura,* pp. 89–102; Somoza and Cox, *Nicaragua Betrayed,* 209–229; author's interview with Robelo Callejas; *N:* 22 August 1978, p. 19A; 20 December 1978, p. 18A, *PL:* 19 December 1978, p. 1; 22 December 1978, p. 2.

46. The organizations making up the MPU were the PC, PSN, CAUS, CGT, Workers Struggle Committee (Comité de Lucha de los Trabajadores), Revolutionary Worker Movement (Movimiento del Obrero Revolucionario), ATC, UNE, ANDEN, AMPRONAC, FER, FER-Marxista Leninista, Private University Student Association (Centro Estudiantil de la Universidad Privada—CEUPA), Secondary Students Association (Asociación de Estudiantes de Secundaria—AES), JRN, Nicaraguan Sandinista Youth (Juventud Sandinista Nicaragüense—JSN), and Federation of Youth Movements of Managua (Federación de Movimientos Juveniles de Managua).

47. The groups making up the FPN were the MPU and its member organizations, PLI, PPSC, Workers' Front, Group of Twelve, CTN, and Union of Radio-Journalists (Sindicato de Radio-Periodistas). Other material on the FPN was taken from López et al., *La caída del somocismo,* pp. 306–319, 372–378; *N,* 25 April 1979, p. 19A; and the Robelo Callejas interview.

Chapter 8. The Insurrection of 1977–1979

1. Quoted in *N,* 12 June 1979, p. 21A.

2. Quoted in *N,* 16 June 1979, p. 19A.

3. The accounts of political events of 1977 reported in this section are based upon Somoza and Cox, *Nicaragua Betrayed,* pp. 57–108; Sánchez, *Nicaragua,* pp. 123–134; Humberto Ortega Saavedra, "La insurrección nacional victoriosa," pp. 33–39; Thomas W. Walker, *Nicaragua: The Land of Sandino* (Boulder, Colo.: Westview Press, 1981), Chapter 3; López C. et al., *La caída del somocismo,* pp. 117–163, 383–384; Ruíz, "La montaña," pp. 20–23; *ECR,* 15 October 1977; U.S. Arms Control and Disarmament Agency, *World Military Expenditures and Arms Transfers, 1968–1977* (Washington, D.C.: Government Printing Office, 1979); *N,* 3 December 1977, p. 18A; *R:* 14 October 1977, pp. 2–3; 15 October 1977, p. 2.

4. Vélez Bárcenas, *Chamorro: ¡Asesinado!* contains a wealth of information about the Chamorro assassination. Vélez Bárcenas defended the accused assassin, Silvio José Peña Rivas. For the regime's version of the story see Somoza and Cox, *Nicaragua Betrayed,* pp. 109–122. Also consulted here were the author's interviews with Violeta Barrios de Chamorro, the victim's widow, and with Robelo Callejas; *R:* 25 January 1978; 26 January 1978; 6 February 1978; and *ECR:* 26 January 1978, p. 3; 6 February 1978; 9 July 1978, p. 8.

5. On the Monimbó uprising, see Ignacio Briones Torres, "Monimbó Rebelde," in Fajardo et al., *Los sandinistas,* pp. 51–59; Humberto Ortega Saavedra, "La insurrección nacional victoriosa," pp. 39–41; López C. et al., *La caída del somocismo,* p. 384; *PL,* 25 February 1978; *R,* 28 February 1978; *ECR:* 2 March 1978; 6 March 1978.

6. López C. et al., *La caída del somocismo,* pp. 384–386; Somoza and Cox, *Nicaragua Betrayed,* pp. 137–149; *N:* 9 April 1978; 17 April 1978; 20 April 1978; 22 April 1978; 26 April 1978; 6 June 1978; 7 June 1978; 16 June 1978, p. 47A; 17 June 1978; 20 June 1978, p. 2A; 24 June 1978.

7. *N:* 9 April 1978; 17 June 1978; 28 June 1978; and Somoza and Cox, *Nicaragua Betrayed,* pp. 123–136.

8. From a 23 July 1978 *Washington Post* story, cited in Somoza and Cox, p. 412.

9. Text of Carter's letter to Somoza is reproduced in facsimile in ibid., p. 412.

10. For material on Operación Chanchera see Gabriel García Márquez, "Crónica del asalto a la 'Casa de los Chanchos,'" in Fajardo et al., *Los sandinistas,* pp. 29–48; Roger Mendieta Alfaro, *Cero y van dos* (n.p., Editorial Tiposa, 1979); Manuel Eugarrios, *Dos . . . uno . . . Cero Comandante* (San José, Costa Rica: Editorial Lehman, 1979); Humberto Ortega Saavedra, "La insurrección nacional victoriosa," pp. 41–46; López C. et al., *La caída del somocismo,* pp. 191–192; *N,* 27 August 1978, p. 12A.

11. Humberto Ortega Saavedra, "La insurrección nacional victoriosa," pp. 44–45.

12. This material is drawn from López C. et al., *La caída del somocismo,* pp. 192–214, 384; author's interview with Daniel Ortega Saavedra; Somoza and Cox, *Nicaragua Betrayed,* pp. 150–168, 181–229; and numerous press sources, including the following: *R:* 17 August 1978; 29 August 1978; 16 September 1978, pp. 3–4; 29 September 1978.

13. This section is drawn from the author's interview with Robelo Callejas; "Somoza: la quiebra," *Respuesta* (San José, Costa Rica), December 1978, pp. 9–10; and dozens of newspaper articles from the following: *N:* 1 October 1978, p. 18A; 10 October 1978; 12 October 1978; 20 October 1978; 27 October 1978, p. 18A; 30 October 1978; 11 November 1978; 18 November 1978; 22 November 1978; 27 November 1978; 1 December 1978, p. 18A; 8 December 1978, p. 18A.

14. Torres, letter to Agüero.

15. Somoza and Cox, *Nicaragua Betrayed,* p. 191.

16. This section is drawn mainly from Pedro Miranda, "Dos mil soldados desfilaron ante Edén Pastora," *Respuesta,* December 1978, pp. 25–27; Urcuyo Maliaño, *Sólos,* pp. 58–67; Somoza and Cox, *Nicaragua Betrayed,* pp. 216–229; López C. et al., *La caída del somocismo,* pp. 233–262; Sánchez, *Nicaragua,* pp. 140–147. Newspaper accounts were also consulted extensively, including the following: *N:* 2 October 1978, p. 20A; 9 October 1978; 10 November 1978, p. 18A; 19 November 1978, p. 18A; 24 November 1978; 9 December 1978, p. 60A; *R:* 16 December 1978, p. 4; 31 December 1978, p. 3.

17. *N:* 12 August 1978; 26 November 1978; December 30, 1978, p. 4A; "Dramática situación de refugiados en Honduras," *Respuesta,* December 1978, p. 28.

18. Material for this section is based, among others, on the following sources: *N:* 2 February 1979, p. 18A; 10 February 1979, p. 18A; 1 March 1979, p. 21A; 4 April 1979, p. 20A; 6 April 1979, p. 10A; 17 April 1979, p. 19A; 23 April 1979, p. 21A; 25 April 1979, p. 19A; 27 April 1979, p. 29A; 2 May 1979, p. 19A; 26 May 1979, p. 30A; 27 May 1979, p. 19A; *PL:* 25 January 1979, p. 10; 2 January 1979, p. 4; 5 January 1979, p. 13; 20

March 1979, p. 6; 3 April 1979, p. 7; 21 May 1979, p. 30; 25 May 1979, p. 15; *R:* 17 March 1979, p. 6; 8 April 1979, p. 6; 10 May 1979, p. 3; 11 May 1979, p. 4; 24 May 1979, p. 2; 27 May 1979, p. 6; 29 May 1979, p. 4; López C. et al., *La caída del somocismo,* pp. 274–293; and author's interview with Robelo Callejas.

19. Quote from *N,* 6 April 1979, p. 19A.

20. López C. et al., *La caída del somocismo,* pp. 263–273, 302–319; Humberto Ortega Saavedra, "La insurrección nacional victoriosa," pp. 46–56; Urcuyo Maliaño, *Sólos,* pp. 68–72; Sánchez, *Nicaragua,* pp. 149–153; author's interviews with Robelo Callejas and with Paul Oquist.

21. This material is drawn from Urcuyo Maliaño, *Sólos,* pp. 72–90; Mendieta Alfaro, *El último marine,* pp. 211–262 and passim; Humberto Ortega Saavedra, "La insurección nacional victoriosa," pp. 46–56; Somoza and Cox, *Nicaragua Betrayed,* pp. 230–261; César Sánchez, *Comandante el Sobrino presente!! FSLN* (Managua: Editorial Flórez, 1979), passim; "The Final Days," *Newsweek* (international ed.), 16 July 1979, p. 4; and from numerous newspaper citations, including the following: *N:* 1 June 1979, p. 19A; 2 June 1979, 18A; 11 June 1979, p. 19A; 16 June 1979, p. 16A; 2 July 1979, p. 19A; 7 July 1979, p. 19A; 24 June 1979, p. 21A; *PL:* 16 June 1979; 18 June 1979, p. 8; 29 June 1979, p. 24; 25 June 1979, p. 31; 4 July 1979, p. 14; *R:* 18 June 1979, p. 2; 26 June 1979, p. 4; *EM:* 12 July 1979, p. 1A; 13 July 1979, p. 1A.

For evidence on FSLN executions of Somocistas, see *N:* 15 April 1979, p. 8A; 24 June 1979, 21A; 2 June 1979, p. 18A; Urcuyo Maliaño, *Sólos,* pp. 75–76; and Somoza and Cox, *Nicaragua Betrayed,* pp. 238–293.

22. Sergio Ramírez Mercado and Alfonso Robelo Callejas, "Una nueva Nicaragua, no una nueva Cuba," interview in *Proceso* (Mexico City), 9 July 1979, pp. 41–42; Viktor Morales Henríquez, *Los últimos momentos de la dictadura somocista* (Managua: Editorial Union, 1979), passim; Miguel Escotto [d'Escoto], "Estados Unidos busca una intervención política en Nicaragua," interview in *Proceso,* 9 July 1979, pp. 43–44; and "Downfall of a Dictator," *Time* (international ed.), 30 July 1979, pp. 20–22.

Useful chronicles of events in the final offensive may be found in Mendieta Alfaro, *El último marine,* passim; Vig, *Nicaragua: ¿Reforma o revolución?* pp. 173–233; Ignatiev and Borovik, *La agonía de la dictadura somocista,* pp. 129–144. See also Urcuyo, *Sólos,* pp. 72–113; and Somoza and Cox, *Nicaragua Betrayed,* pp. 230–284.

23. *N:* 29 June 1979, p. 19A; 30 June 1979, p. 18A; "The Final Days," pp. 18–20; Somoza and Cox, *Nicaragua Betrayed,* pp. 230–284, 311–381; and "Downfall of a Dictator," pp. 20–22.

24. Somoza and Cox, *Nicaragua Betrayed,* p. 267.

25. Urcuyo Maliaño, *Sólos,* pp. 108–144; *EM:* 17 July 1979, p. 1A; 19 July 1979, p. 1A; 20 July 1979, p. 1A.

26. For data on the impact of the war overall, see *EM:* 12 July 1979, p. 1A; 21 July 1979, pp. 1A, 10A; 24 July 1979, pp. 1A, 10A, 16A; López C. et al., *La caída del somocismo,* pp. 78–79, 274–286; Juan Javané and Roger

Vásquez, assistants to the minister of planning, interview with the author, Managua, 22 January 1980; and Leonel Poveda S., interview with the author.

Chapter 9. The Beginning

1. Somoza and Cox, *Nicaragua Betrayed,* pp. 395–396.
2. Tomás Borge Martínez, "Tomás Borge speaks on Human Rights in Nicaragua," *Intercontinental Press,* 16 March 1981, p. 250.
3. Ibid., pp. 248–255; Walker, *Nicaragua,* Chapter 3; James Petras, "Nicaragua: The Transition to a New Society," *Latin American Perspectives* 8 (Spring 1981):74–94; "Sergio Ramírez: 'Nos encaminamos hacia un proceso democrático,'" *N,* 13 April 1980, p. 22A; Orlando Núñez, "Crisis y revolución en Nicaragua," paper presented at the II Seminario Centroamérica y el Caribe: En busca de una Alternativa Regional, Managua, Nicaragua, 9–12 February 1983.
4. First quote from David Nolan, *Ideology of the Sandinistas,* p. 107; second quote from the FSLN National Directorate, *Nicaragua: On the General Political-Military Platform of Struggle of the Sandinista Front for National Liberation for the Triumph of the Sandinista Popular Revolution* (Oakland, Calif.: Resistance Publications, ca. 1977), quoted in Nolan, p. 188.
5. "Estatuto fundamental de la república, Articles 3 and 4, in Consejo de Estado, *Leyes relacionados con el Consejo de Estado* (Managua, 1981), p. 7.
6. Ibid., Article 11, p. 8.
7. Material on the junta and the quotes in this section are drawn from interviews by the author with three members of the Governing Junta: Daniel Ortega Saavedra, Alfonso Robelo Callejas, and Violeta Barrios de Chamorro. See also Matilde Zimmermann, "Nicaragua: New Governing Junta Named," *Intercontinental Press,* 16 March 1981, p. 255; Walker, *Nicaragua,* Chapter 6; Stephen M. Gorman, "Sandinista Chess: How the Left Took Control," *Caribbean Review* 10 (Winter 1981):15–17, 55; and idem, "Power and Consolidation in the Nicaraguan Revolution," paper presented at the Southwestern Conference of Latin American Studies, Arlington, Tex., 5–6 March 1981; Violeta Barrios de Chamorro, letter of resignation from the junta, in "Cansada, pero firme," *P,* 20 April 1980, pp. 1, 12.
8. Material on the cabinet and bureaucracy is drawn from interviews by the author with Alfonso Robelo Callejas; Carlos Tunnermann Bernheim; Paul Oquist; Paul Oquist, Manuel Cordero, and Ariel Granera, DIGE, Managua, 16 July 1980; Javané and Vásquez; Teresa Núñez, Press Division, Ministry of Finance, Managua, 16 July 1980; Guillermo Genie Espinoza, Director de Política Exterior, Ministry of Interior, Managua, 25 January 1980; and Iván García M., Planning Division, Ministry of Agricultural Development and Reform, Managua, 11 August 1983. See also Walker, *Nicaragua,* Chapter 6; Gorman, "Power and Consolidation"; Ministerio de Planificación, *Programa de emergencia,* passim; and *P,* 28 December 1979, pp. 1, 9.

9. See, for example, Carlos Tunnermann Bernheim, *Hacia una nueva educación en Nicaragua* (Managua: Ediciones Distribuidora Cultural, 1983), pp. 269–290; *B,* 12 August 1983, p. 1; *BI,* 5 March 1984, p. 9.

10. Consejo de Estado, *Leyes relacionados con el Consejo de Estado,* pp. 87–103.

11. John A. Booth, "National Government," in Thomas W. Walker, ed., *Nicaragua: The First Five Years* (forthcoming), Chapter 1.

12. Charles Downs, "Local and Regional Government," in Walker, ed., *Nicaragua: The First Five Years,* Chapter 2; and *Envío monográfico* (Instituto Histórico Centroamericano, Managua) 9 (June 1983), p. 25.

13. Interview by the author with Orlando Núñez S., Centro de Investigación de Reforma Agraria, Instituto Nacional de Reforma Agraria (INRA), and member of the Policy Commission of the FSLN's National Propaganda Secretariat, Managua, 27 May 1980.

14. Information from internationalists working in Nicaraguan bureaucracies, 1982 and 1983.

15. Interview with Oquist, Cordero, and Granera.

16. *NYT,* 19 July 1984, p. 7.

17. Material on the Council of State is drawn from Consejo de Estado, "Saludo al primer aniversario de nuestra revolución popular sandinista," Boletín de Prensa No. 1, Organo Informativo del Consejo de Estado, Managua, July 1980; Gorman, "Sandinista Chess," and "Power and Consolidation," pp. 10–12; Walker, *Nicaragua,* Chapter 6; Auxiliadora de Figueroa, Public Relations, Council of State, interview with the author, Managua, 16 July 1980; Alvaro Jeréz, national secretary of the Nicaraguan Democratic Movement (MDN), interview with the author, Managua, 26 May 1980; Carmen Diana Deere and Peter Marchetti, "The Worker-Peasant Alliance in the First Year of the Nicaraguan Agrarian Reform," *Latin American Perspectives* 8 (Spring 1981):66–67; Consejo de Estado, *Leyes relacionados con el Consejo de Estado; Monexico* (journal of the Council of State) 1 (November 1982); *Monexico* 2 (April 1983); and author's interview with Rafael Solís, secretary of the Council of State and subcommander of the Sandinista Popular Army (EPS), 14 August 1983, Managua.

18. Hugo Torres Jiménez, in Consejo de Estado, "Saludo al primer aniversario."

19. Decree no. 338, "Estatuto general de Consejo del Estado," in Consejo de Estado, *Leyes relacionados con el Consejo de Estado,* pp. 25–29.

20. Booth, "National Government."

21. The leadership of the Council of State also included three vice-presidents and three secretaries.

22. Inteview with Luis Rivas Leiva, president of the Social Democratic party (PSD), *LNI,* 8–14 March 1984, p. 8.

23. *BI:* 5 March 1984, p. 3; 27 February 1984, pp. 3–7; *LNI,* 1–7 March 1984, p. 7.

24. Material on the courts is drawn from Borge, "Tomás Borge Speaks," passim; Guillermo Genie Espinoza, interview; Daniel Ortega Saavedra, in

press conference of the Governing Junta, Managua, 26 May 1980; and *P:* 13 March 1980, p. 1; 18 March 1980, pp. 1, 12; 29 March 1980, p. 1.

25. Material on the special tribunals is drawn from *B,* 30 November 1979, p. 1; *P:* 29 January 1980, p. 1; 9 February 1980, p. 1; from personal observation by the author in Managua, December 1979–May 1980; and from the author's interview with Boris Vega, prosecutor of the Fourth Special Tribunal, Managua, 18 December 1979.

26. Americas Watch, *On Human Rights in Nicaragua* (New York, May 1982), pp. 27–30.

27. *Monexico* 1 (November 1982):51–67; *Monexico* 2 (April 1983):36–41; Consejo de Estado, *Leyes relacionados con el Consejo de Estado,* p. 83.

28. Material on the FSLN is drawn from the author's interviews with Germán Ruíz, July 19th Sandinista Youth, Managua, 24 January 1980; Daniel Ortega Saavedra; Alfonso Robelo Callejas; Alvaro Jeréz; Violeta Barrios de Chamorro; Guillermo Genie Espinoza; Orlando Núñez S.; Charles Brayshaw, first secretary, U.S. Embassy in Managua, Managua, 17 December 1979; Mayer Nudel, political officer, U.S. Embassy in Managua, and Charles Brayshaw, Managua, 27 May 1980; Carlos Zamora, FSLN regional director for Matagalpa-Jinotega (Zone VI), Matagalpa, Nicaragua, 31 October 1984; and Sergio Ramírez Mercado, JGRN member and FSLN vice-presidential candidate, Managua, 3 November 1984. See also Gorman, "Sandinista Chess," and "Power and Consolidation"; Petras, "Nicaragua"; *P:* 22 February 1980, p. 1; 27 June 1980, p. 1; Walker, *Nicaragua,* Chapter 6; Adolfo Gilly, *La nueva Nicaragua: Antimperialismo y lucha de clases* (Mexico City: Editorial Nueva Imagen, 1980), pp. 1–78; Consejo de Estado, "Saludo al primer aniversario"; Tomás Borge Martínez, press conference, Managua, 25 January 1980.

29. "Estatuto Fundamental de la República," Article 11, p. 8.

30. Ibid., Articles 24 and 26, p. 11.

31. Ibid., Articles 11 and 16, pp. 10–11.

32. Material on the MDN is drawn from Jeréz interview and from MDN, *Ideario político del Movimiento Democrático Nicaragüense* (Managua, January 1980); Alfonso Robelo Callejas, letter to Daniel Ortega Saavedra, Moisés Hassán Morales, and Sergio Ramírez Mercado of the Governing Junta of National Reconstruction, resigning from that body, Managua, 22 April 1980; Consejo de Estado, "Saludo al primer aniversario"; *N:* 21 March 1980, p. 18A; 13 May 1980, p. 4A; 29 June 1980, p. 8A.

33. For material on the unions, see Petras, "Nicaragua"; Deere and Marchetti, "Worker-Peasant Alliance"; Gorman, "Power and Consolidation"; *B,* 31 January 1980, p. 1; Carlos Núñez Tellez, "La revolución y las organizaciones de los trabajadores," in Humberto Ortega Saavedra et al., *La revolución a través de nuestra Dirección Nacional* (Managua: Secretaría Nacional de Propaganda y Educación Política—FSLN, 1980), pp. 61–72; and Henry Ruíz, address to the ATC, in ibid., pp. 73–83.

34. Data drawn from Petras, "Nicaragua," pp. 83–96.

35. Comisión Permanente de Derechos Humanos de Nicaragua (CPDH), "Informe de junio 1984," Managua, June 1984 (mimeo), pp. 2–4; CPDH,

"Informe de junio," Managua, June 1983 (mimeo), pp. 5–6; *LNI:* 30 August–5 September 1984, pp. 4–5; 23–29 August 1984, p. 13.

36. Material on the private sector is drawn from author's interviews with Brayshaw; Nudel and Brayshaw; Javané and Vásquez; Orlando Núñez S.; and William Baez, president of the Nicaraguan Development Institute (INDE), Managua, 17 July 1980. See also *N,* 12 May 1980, p. 4A; Dreyfus, "Un nuevo marco socioeconómico"; Lars Palmgren, "Nicaraguan Capitalists Fearful of FSLN's Political Course," *Intercontinental Press,* 8 September 1980, pp. 913–914; COSEP, communiqué, published as "Protesta y llamado de COSEP," *P,* 3 March 1980, p. 1; U.S. Agency for International Development, "The $70,000,000 Program Loan," Managua, July 1980 (photocopy); Petras, "Nicaragua," pp. 78–80, 91–93; Deere and Marchetti, "Worker-Peasant Alliance," pp. 65–68; "Nicaragua's Birthday Party," *Newsweek* (international ed.), 28 July 1980, pp. 8–12; Borge, 25 January 1980, press conference; Daniel Ortega Saavedra, press conference, Managua, 26 May 1980; interview with Enrique Bolaños Geyer, president of COSEP, Managua, 16 August 1983; interview with Gilbert Calloway, public affairs officer, U.S. Embassy, Managua, 16 August 1983; interview with senior U.S. diplomatic official, Managua, 16 August 1983; Dennis Gilbert, "The Bourgeoisie," and John Weeks, "The Industrial Sector," both in Walker, ed., *Nicaragua: The First Five Years,* Chapters 7 and 13, respectively.

37. Orlando Núñez interview.

38. On the business-government clashes, see Deere and Marchetti, "Worker-Peasant Alliance," pp. 65–68; Gorman, "Power and Consolidation"; "Nicaragua's Birthday Party," pp. 9–10; Daniel Ortega Saavedra, 26 May 1980, press conference; *N:* 15 May 1980, p. 20A; 18 May 1980, p. 10A; 3 October 1980, pp. 1, 14; *P,* 6 May 1980, pp. 1, 12; information also drawn from Calloway and Bolaños interviews; interview with E.V.K. Fitzgerald, economic adviser to the JGRN, Managua, 3 November 1984; interview with Jaime Wheelock Román, minister of agrarian reform and development and DN member, Managua, 3 November 1984; interview with Gladys Bolt, coffee farmer, Matagalpa, 31 October 1984.

39. *EM,* 10 September 1981, pp. 2A, 26A; "The Junta Decrees an Emergency," *Newsweek,* 21 September 1981, p. 67.

40. See *M:* August 1983, pp. 8–12; April 1984, pp. 6–7; *LNI,* 26 April–2 May 1984, p. 5.

41. *NYT:* 24 May 1984, p. 8; 1 June 1984, p. 1; 14 June 1984, p. 6; 25 July 1984, p. 1; *LNI,* 31 May–5 June 1984, pp. 6–7; interviews with former Sandinista commanders Sebastián González, 28 June–4 July 1984, pp. 6–7; Leonel Poveda Sediles, 5–11 July 1984, pp. 6–7; and Alejandro Martínez, 12–18 July 1984, pp. 12–13; also *LNI:* 2–9 August 1984, p. 9; 30 August–5 September 1984, p. 8; Carlos Zamora interview.

42. Julio Ramos, chief of intelligence, Ministry of Defense, military briefing, Managua, 2 November 1984; *NYT,* 30 November 1984, p. 8.

43. Ibid.; Zamora interview; Alex Zeledón, president of Regional Electoral Council VI (Matagalpa-Jinotega), Matagalpa, 31 October 1984, interview; Bolt interview; *Washington Post Weekly,* 24 December 1984, p. 17.

44. Ramírez interview; Wheelock Román interview; decree of the JGRN, 6 August 1984.

45. "Estatuto fundamental de la república," Articles 11 and 16, respectively, pp. 10–11.

46. Booth, "National Government."

47. *BI:* 5 March 1984, p. 3; 27 February 1984, pp. 3–7; *LNI,* 1–7 March 1984, p. 7.

48. *N,* 23 June 1980, p. 6A; Council of Bishops of Nicaragua, pastoral letter of 17 November 1979, published as "Pastoral de los obispos nicaragüenses," *Respuesta,* 1–15 December 1979, pp. 23–26; *P,* 28 June 1980, p. 1; Dodson and Montgomery, "Churches," pp. 23–32; *EM,* 10 September 1981, pp. 1A, 12A, 28A; "Cristianismo en Revolución," *Ya Veremos* (Managua), June 1980, pp. 39–48; interview with Juan Hernández Pico, S.J., Managua, 31 October 1984; Phillip Berryman, *The Religious Roots of Rebellion: Christians in Central American Revolutions* (Maryknoll, N.Y.: Orbis Books, 1984), pp. 227–267.

49. Council of Bishops, pastoral letter of 17 November 1979, pp. 24–25.

50. Ibid., p. 25.

51. *EM,* 10 September 1981, p. 12A.

52. Quoted by Steven Kinzer, *NYT,* 22 May 1984, p. 5.

53. Quoted in *M,* September 1983.

54. *M,* March 1984; see also the bishops' pastoral letter in *LNI,* 17–23 May 1984, p. 15.

55. Quoted by Steven Kinzer, *NYT,* 22 May 1984, p. 5.

56. Quoted in *Amanecer* (March–April 1984):4.

57. *LNI,* 12–18 July 1984, p. 4; *NYT,* 11 December 1984, p. 3.

58. Pablo Antonio Vega, press conference, Managua, 29 October 1984, quoted in *El Nuevo Diario,* 4 November 1984, p. 1.

59. *P:* 13 August 1983, p. 1; 15 August 1983, p. 1; *M:* September 1983, pp. 9–10; February 1984, p. 7; author's observations during August 1983 and November 1984 visits to Managua; and John Spicer Nichols, "The Media," in Walker, ed., *Nicaragua: The First Five Years,* Chapter 8. See also *Rumbo Centroamericano* (formerly *LNI*): 3–9 January 1985, p. 14; 20–26 December 1984, p. 4.

60. Consejo de Estado, *Ley de partidos políticos* (Managua, 17 August 1983); interview with Luís Rivas Leiva, president of the Social Democratic party (PSD), in *LNI,* 1–7 March 1984, p. 8.

61. Consejo de Estado, *Ley de partidos políticos,* Article 2.

62. *M,* February 1984 and March 1984; *BI:* 27 February 1984, p. 1; 9 April 1984, p. 1; *LNI:* 15–21 December 1983, p. 6; 15–21 March 1984, p. 5.

63. "Estatuto fundamental de la república," Article 28, p. 11.

64. Consejo de Estado, *Ley electoral* (Managua, 15 March 1984); *BI:* 27 February 1984, p. 3; 26 March 1984, pp. 6–7.

65. Interview with Adán Fletes, president of the PPSC and vice-presidential candidate of the Democratic Coordinating Committee, Managua, 30 October

1984; interview with a self-styled "senior U.S. diplomatic official in Central America," Managua, 29 October 1984; interview with Guillermo Mejía, vice-presidential candidate, and Luis Humberto Guzmán, director of international relations, PPSC, Managua, 30 October 1984.

66. Interview with Mejía and Guzmán; interview with Virgilio Godoy Reyes, presidential candidate of the PLI, Managua, 3 November 1984; *The Electoral Process in Nicaragua—Domestic and International Influences: The Report of the Latin American Studies Association Delegation to Observe the Nicaraguan General Election of November 4, 1984* (Austin, Texas: Latin American Studies Association, 19 November 1984), pp. 29–31.

67. *Amanecer* (March-April 1984):5–7.

68. *LNI:* 2–9 August 1984, pp. 4, 8; 23–29 August 1984, p. 8; 30 August–5 September 1984, pp. 6–7; interview with Mariano Fiallos Oyanguren, president of the CSE, Managua, 29 October 1984; interview with Rosa Marina Zeleya, secretary of the CSE, Managua, 2 November 1984; for details on the review of CSE complaint files, see *The Electoral Process in Nicaragua,* pp. 23–26 and passim.

69. Interview with Mejía and Guzmán; press conference with Elí Altamirano Pérez, secretary general of the Communist party of Nicaragua, Managua, 29 October 1984; interview with Steven Kinzer, *NYT* correspondent in Managua, 1 November 1984.

70. *LNI,* 2–9 August 1984, pp. 4, 8; 23–29 August 1984, p. 8; 30 August–5 September 1984, pp. 6–7.

71. The author observed the election as a member of the Latin American Studies Association observer team 28 October–5 November 1984. For further details on the election and the team's findings, see *The Electoral Process in Nicaragua,* passim; provisional regional data drawn from *El Nuevo Diario,* 5 November 1984, pp. 1, 7.

72. E.g., *NYT:* 5 November 1984, p. 4; 6 November 1984, p. 4; Richard Beene, *Dallas Times Herald,* 6 November 1984, pp. 1, 10; Juan Tamayo, *Miami Herald,* 5 November 1984, pp. 1, 10. See also *NYT,* 15 November 1984, p. 8; and *The Electoral Process in Nicaragua,* passim.

73. Material on the new cabinet, inaugural, and National Assembly drawn from *BI,* 17 January 1985, pp. 3–7.

74. Ibid., pp. 4, 7; interviews with Sergio Ramírez Mercado and with Jaime Wheelock Román.

Chapter 10. Policies and Performance of the Revolutionary Government

1. "This Time We Know What's Happening," *Reader's Digest,* July 1983, also in Mark Falcoff and Robert Royal, eds., *Crisis and Opportunity: U.S. Policy in Central America and the Caribbean* (Washington, D.C.: Ethics and Public Policy Center, 1984), pp. 165–172, quote from pp. 167–168.

2. *M,* December 1982, p. 7.

3. Material on the police system and the restoration of public order is drawn from Borge, "Tomás Borge Speaks"; author's inteviews with Guillermo

Genie Espinoza and with Javané and Vásquez; *B,* 20 September 1979, p. 1; *P:* 29 January 1980, p. 1; 17 February 1980, p. 1; 12 March 1980, p. 1; 17 April 1980, p. 1.

4. Stephen M. Gorman and Thomas W. Walker, "The Armed Forces," in Walker, ed., *Nicaragua: The First Five Years,* Chapter 4; and author's observations in Nicaragua on various trips from 1979 to late 1984.

5. This useful distinction is from Gorman and Walker, "The Armed Forces."

6. Material on human rights is drawn from various sources: for the 1982–1983 deterioration, the Permanent Commission on Human Rights monthly *Informes* for 1982–1983; Americas Watch, *On Human Rights in Nicaragua;* Americas Watch, *Human Rights in Nicaragua, November 1982 Update* (New York, November 1982); interview with Mary Hartman, member of the Nicaraguan Commission on Human Rights, Managua, 16 August 1983. For earlier material, see Borge, "Tomás Borge Speaks"; Guillermo Genie Espinoza, interview; *Estatuto fundamental y estatuto sobre derechos y garantías de los Nicaragüenses,* Ediciones Patria Libre, No. 1 (Managua: Dirección de Divulgación y Prensa, Junta de Gobierno de Reconstrucción Nacional, 1979); "Slanderer Retracts Charges of Torture by FSLN," *Intercontinental Press,* 16 March 1981, p. 249; *N,* 6 February 1980, p. 20A; Tomás Borge Martínez, *Conferencia de prensa,* 14 November 1979 (Managua: Oficino de Divulgación y Prensa, Ministerio del Interior).

7. Interview with Francisco Solano and Agustin Sambola, Catholic priests, in *BI: Archives* 11 (January 1984):3–5; author's conversation with Galio Gurdian, official of the Atlantic Coast Development Commission, 7 September 1982, Manchester, England.

8. Quoted in *NYT,* 6 June 1984, p. 5.

9. Quote from decree in *BI,* 12 December 1983, p. 3, see also pp. 1–5; *BI,* 8 February 1984, p. 4; and *M,* June 1984, p. 9.

10. For evidence on human rights violations in Honduras and elsewhere in Central America for comparison with those in Nicaragua, see Americas Watch, *On Human Rights in Nicaragua* and *Human Rights in Nicaragua, November 1982 Update,* p. 6. These findings were confirmed by the author's interview with a senior U.S. diplomatic official in the U.S. Embassy in Managua, 16 August 1983.

11. On press and information freedom, see *B:* 3 February 1980, p. 1; 4 February 1980, p. 1; 11 February 1980, p. 1; *N:* 25 August 1979, p. 2B; 18 March 1980, p. 4A; 1 July 1980, p. 8A; 10 October 1980, p. 10A. On the 1982 emergency and its effect on press freedom, see *Uno Más Uno* (Mexico City), 17 March 1982, pp. 1, 13; and *LNI,* 19–25 March 1982, p. 1. See also John Spicer Nichols, "The Media," in Walker, ed., *Nicaragua: The First Five Years,* Chapter 8.

12. *M,* June 1984, p. 9; *BI,* 12 March 1984, pp. 3–4.

13. Nichols, "The Media," cites a late 1983 personal interview with Lt. Nelba Blandón, Directorate of Communication Media, Ministry of Interior, the office that exercised censorship.

14. *NYT,* 14 June 1984, p. 6; *BI,* 26 March 1984, p. 7.

15. Quote from Nichols, "The Media"; see also Americas Watch, *Human Rights in Nicaragua, November 1982 Update,* pp. 20–25.

16. Walker, *Nicaragua,* Chapter 5; Aaron Segal, "Poetry and Politics in Nicaragua," *Caribbean Review* 10 (Winter 1981):26–28; Richard N. Adams, "The Sandinistas and the Indians: The 'Problem' of the Indian in Nicaragua," *Caribbean Review* 10 (Winter 1981):23–25, 55–56; Ejército Popular Sandinista, *Avances y logros de la revolución popular sandinista* (Managua: Sección de Formación Política y Cultural del EPS, 1980); Ministerio de Educación, *Situación del sistema educativo después de 45 años de dictadura militar somocista y perspectivas que plantea la revolución sandinista* (Managua, December 1979), pp. 161–187; Sergio Ramírez Mercado, "Mensaje de la Junta de Gobierno de Reconstrucción Nacional, 4 May 1980," pp. 1–7; Ernesto Cardenal, "Cultura revolucionaria, popular, nacionalista, antimperialista," *Nicaráuac* 1 (May-June, 1980):163–168. See also Nolan, *Ideology of the Sandinistas,* pp. 106–126.

17. *Cruzada Nacional de Alfabetización* (Managua: Ministerio de Educación, Sistema Estadístico Nacional, and Instituto Nacional de Estadística y Censos, December 1979); *Encuentro* 16 (1980), special issue on the literacy crusade; Ministerio de Educación, *Situación del sistema educativo; N,* 13 March 1980, p. 4A; Leonor Blum, "The Literacy Campaign, Nicaraguan Style," *Caribbean Review* 10 (Winter 1981):18–21.

18. Among such critics was Enrique Bolaños, president of COSEP, author's interview, Managua, 16 August 1983.

19. Elizabeth Dore, "Culture," in Walker, ed., *Nicaragua: The First Five Years,* Chapter 20; author's observations in Nicaragua, 1979–1984; Ernesto Cardenal, *La democratización de la cultura* (Managua: Ministerio de Cultura, 1982), pp. 16–27.

20. Adams, "Sandinistas and Indians"; Philippe Bourgois, "Class, Ethnicity, and the State Among the Miskitu Amerindians of Northeastern Nicaragua," *Latin American Perspectives* 8 (Spring 1981):22–36; Tani Marilena Adams, "Life Giving, Life Threatening: Gold Mining in Atlantic Nicaragua, Mine Work in Siuna and the Response to Nationalization by the Sandinista Regime," M.A. thesis, University of Chicago, 1981; and Philippe Bourgois and Jorge Grunberg, *La Mosquitía y la revolución: Informe de una investigación rural en la Costa Atlántica Norte (1980)* (Managua: Instituto Histórico Cultural de la Costa Atlántica, May 1980); Walker, *Nicaragua,* Chapter 5; *B,* 3 October 1980, pp. 1, 5, 14.

21. Walker, *Nicaragua,* Chapter 5; Violeta Barrios de Chamorro, interview; Susan Ramírez-Horton, "The Role of Women in the Nicaraguan Revolution," in Walker, *Nicaragua in Revolution,* Chapter 17. The press code explicitly prohibits exploitation of females in advertising (see "Ley general provisional"). See also Margaret Randall, ed., *Sandino's Daughters* (London: Zed Press, 1981).

22. This section is drawn mainly from Maxine Molyneux, "Women," in Walker, ed., *Nicaragua: The First Five Years,* Chapter 6.

23. Ibid.

24. Data from Michael E. Conroy, "External Dependence, External Assistance, and 'Economic Aggression' Against Nicaragua," unpublished manuscript, 1 June 1984, Tables 1 and 3.

25. Ministerio de Planificación, *Programa de emergencia,* passim; Sergio Ramírez Mercado, "Mensaje de la Junta"; and Jaime Wheelock Román, "No hay 2 reformas agrarias iguales," *Nicaráuac* 1 (May-June 1980):58–75; Deere and Marchetti, "Worker-Peasant Alliance," pp. 51–59; and Humberto Ortega Saavedra et al., *La revolución,* passim; Walker, *Nicaragua,* Chapter 4; and Petras, "Nicaragua."

26. Material on the economic policy of the regime comes mainly from Ministerio de Planificación, *Programa de emergencia,* passim; Walker, *Nicaragua,* Chapter 4; Arnold Weissberg, "Nicaraguans Discuss 1981 Economic Plan," *Intercontinental Press,* 2 February 1981, pp. 63–64; *EM:* 8 September 1981, p. 1A; 10 September 1981, p. 2A; Ramírez Mercado, "Mensaje de la Junta," pp. 7–17, 38–54; E.V.K. Fitzgerald, "The Economics of the Revolution" (Chapter 6), and David Chaimowitz and Joseph Thome, "Nicaragua's Agrarian Reform: The First Year" (Chapter 7), in Walker, *Nicaragua in Revolution;* and *LNI,* 9–15 April 1982, p. 3.

27. Based on Petras, "Nicaragua"; Deere and Marchetti, "Worker-Peasant Alliance"; and author's interviews with Orlando Núñez S.; Oquist, Cordero, and Granera; Javané and Vásquez; Tunnermann; Genie Espinoza; and Teresa Núñez. Material on developments since 1982 are drawn from author's interviews with Jaime Wheelock Román, minister of agrarian reform and development, Managua, 3 November 1984; and E.V.K. Fitzgerald, economic adviser to the JGRN, Managua, 3 November 1984.

28. Quote and other data from Conroy, "External Dependence," pp. 15–20.

29. Quote and other data from Daniel Ortega, address to the Council of State, 4 May 1984, excerpted in *BI,* 14 May 1984, p. 7; see also *LNI,* 19–25 April 1984, pp. 18–19.

30. Data on agriculture drawn from Joseph R. Thome and David Kaimowitz, "Agrarian Reform," in Walker, ed., *Nicaragua: The First Five Years,* Chapter 14; and Carmen Diana Deere, Peter Marchetti, and Nola Reinhardt, "From State Farms to Peasant Property: The Development of Sandinista Agrarian Policy, 1979–1984," *Latin American Research Review* (forthcoming).

31. See also Deere and Marchetti, "Worker-Peasant Alliance," pp. 55–56; Petras, "Nicaragua," pp. 77–80; Wheelock, Román, "No hay 2"; Bourgois and Grunberg, "La Mosquitía," pp. 21–75; Chaimowitz and Thome, "Nicaragua's Agrarian Reform"; Laura Enríquez, "The Dilemmas of Agro-Export Planning," in Walker, ed., *Nicaragua: The First Five Years,* Chapter 12; and Wheelock Román interview.

32. Quote from Thome and Kaimowitz, "Agrarian Reform."

33. Jaime Wheelock Román, quoted in ibid.

34. Ibid.; Joseph Collins, *What Difference Could A Revolution Make?* (San Francisco: Institute for Food and Development Policy, 1982), pp. 141–144; Deere, Marchetti, and Reinhardt, "From State Farms to Peasant Property"; Wheelock Román interview.

35. JGRN, Decree no. 782 (August 1981). See also *Producción y orga-nización en el agro Nicaragüense* (Managua: Centro de Investigaciones y Estudios de la Reforma Agraria—Asociación de Trabajadores del Campo—Unión Nicaragüense de Agricultores y Ganaderos, 1982).

36. Thome and Kaimowitz, "Agrarian Reform."

37. Petras, "Nicaragua"; William Baez, interview; "Los convenios de Producción," *Poder Sandinista*, 30 May 1980, p. 8; John Weeks, "The Industrial Sector," in Walker, ed., *Nicaragua: The First Five Years*, Chapter 13.

38. Data drawn from Weeks, "The Industrial Sector."

39. Ibid.

40. See *P*, 30 March 1980, p. 1; Conroy, "External Dependence"; and Sylvia Maxfield and Richard Stahler Sholk, "External Constraints," in Walker, ed., *Nicaragua: The First Five Years*, Chapter 11.

41. Maxfield and Sholk, "External Constraints."

42. Ibid.

43. Conroy, "External Dependence," pp. 10–14; and *LNI*, 19–25 April 1984, p. 18.

44. Petras, "Nicaragua," pp. 78–80; James E. Austin and Jonathan Fox, "Food Policy" (Chapter 19), Thomas John Bossert, "Health Policy: The Dilemma of Success" (Chapter 16), Maxfield and Sholk, "External Con-straints," and Weeks, "The Industrial Sector," all in Walker, ed., *Nicaragua: The First Five Years;* John M. Donahue, "The Politics of Health Care in Nicaragua Before and After the Revolution of 1979," *Human Organization* 42 (Fall 1983):264–272.

45. Interviews with Teresa Núñez, Javané and Vásquez, and Fitzgerald.

46. Quote from *LNI*, 11–17 October 1984, p. 16. Other data from ibid. and Fitzgerald interview.

47. Author's interviews with Javané and Vásquez, and with Leonel Poveda Sediles.

48. Conroy, "External Dependence," Table 6.

49. On distribution problems and speculation, see, for example, *B*, 29 January 1980, p. 1; *P:* 29 January 1980, p. 1; 31 January 1980, p. 1; 19 February 1980, p. 1; 10 March 1980, p. 1; *NYT*, 22 October 1984, p. 1.

50. Austin and Fox, "Food Policy," contains a good overview of the system.

51. Ibid.

52. See Petras, "Nicaragua," pp. 85–90; Mark B. Rosenberg, "Social Reform in the New Nicaragua," unpublished manuscript, Miami, July 1980; Thomas Bossert, "Public Health in Revolutionary Nicaragua" (Chapter 9), Harvey Williams, "Housing Policy in Sandinist Nicaragua" (Chapter 10), and Eric Wagner, "Sports and Revolution in Nicaragua" (Chapter 11), all in Walker, *Nicaragua in Revolution; BI*, 5 March 1984, p. 5; Bossert, "Health Policy"; Donahue, "The Politics of Health Care"; and Harvey Williams, "Housing Policy," in Walker, ed., *Nicaragua: The First Five Years*, Chapter 18.

53. For material on defense policy, see Walker, *Nicaragua*, Chapter 6; *LNI:* 19–25 March 1982, p. 1; 9–15 April 1982, p. 3; *Uno Más Uno*, 17

March 1982, pp. 1, 13; Ramírez Mercado, "Mensaje de la Junta," pp. 60–61; Ejército Popular Sandinista, *Avances y logros;* interviews with Brayshaw, Orlando Núñez S., and Javané and Vásquez; Gorman, "Power and Consolidation," pp. 12–20, and "Sandinista Chess," pp. 16–17; *EM:* 20 July 1981, pp. 20–21A; 3 September 1981, pp. 1A, 10–11A; 8 September 1981, pp. 1A, 10A; 3 February 1982, pp. 1A, 14A; 26 March 1982, pp. 1A, 18A; *P:* 5 February 1981, p. 1; 13 February 1980, p. 1; 18 March 1980, pp. 1, 9; Stephen M. Gorman, "The Role of the Revolutionary Armed Forces," in Walker, *Nicaragua in Revolution,* Chapter 15.

54. Gorman and Walker, "The Armed Forces"; *NYT,* 3 October 1984, p. 1; *BI,* 11 October 1984, pp. 1–4. Also Daniel Ortega, FSLN presidential candidate, address to the closing rally of the FSLN's Managua campaign, 1 November 1984; *NYT,* 10 November 1984, p. 4; *BI,* 11 October 1984, p. 1.

55. Robert S. Leiken, "Soviet and Cuban Policy in the Caribbean Basin," in Donald E. Schulz and Douglas H. Graham, eds., *Revolution and Counterrevolution in Central America and the Caribbean* (Boulder, Colo.: Westview Press, 1984), p. 459.

56. Ibid., pp. 458–460; U.S. Department of State and Department of Defense; *Background Paper: Nicaragua's Military Build-Up and Support for Central American Subversion* (Washington, D.C., 18 July 1984), pp. 8–11.

57. Lt. Col. John H. Buchanan, USMC (Ret.), testimony before the Subcommittee on Interamerican Affairs, Committee on Foreign Affairs, U.S. House of Representatives, "U.S. Military Aid to Honduras," 21 September 1982, Washington, D.C. (mimeo); and Gorman and Walker, "The Armed Forces."

58. *NYT,* 23 October 1984, pp. 1, 6; Brigade Commander Julio Ramos, chief of intelligence, Ministry of Defense of Nicaragua, military briefing, 2 November 1984, Managua; Wheelock Román interview; Fitzgerald interview.

59. Material on foreign policy comes from Ramírez Mercado, "Mensaje de la Junta," pp. 54–59; *EM:* 20 July 1981, pp. 20–21A; 3 September 1981, pp. 10–11A; 3 February 1982, pp. 1A, 14A; 26 March 1982, p. 1A; Walker, *Nicaragua,* Chapter 6; Tomás Borge, "Revolutions Are Not Exported," interview in *Newsweek* (international ed.), 24 September 1979, p. 52; "Quién ayuda más a Nicaragua," *Respuesta,* December 1979, pp. 29–31; "Nicaragua's Birthday Party"; *N:* 9 November 1979, p. 21A; 12 November 1979, p. 19A; 22 November 1979, p. 3C; 22 May 1980, pp. 22A; Edén Pastora Gómez, *Intervención del Comandante Guerrillero Edén Pastora Gómez referente a su viaje a Europa, la ayuda obtenida, y sus pláticas con la Internacional Socialista* (Managua: Oficina de Divulgación, Ministerio del Interior, 12 November 1979); Daniel Ortega Saavedra, "El imperialismo: Enemigo fundamental de la revolución sandinista," in Humberto Ortega Saavedra et al., *La revolución,* pp. 47–59; author's interviews with Daniel Ortega, Poveda, Robelo, Brayshaw, and Nudel and Brayshaw; and Tomás Borge, Humberto Ortega, and Alfonso Robelo, press conference, Managua, 25 January 1980. See also Alejandro Bendaña, "The Foreign Policy of the Nicaraguan Revolution" (Chapter 18), William LeoGrande, "The U.S. Reaction to the Sandinist

Revolution" (Chapter 3), Susanne Jonas, "The Nicaraguan Revolution and the Re-emerging Cold War" (Chapter 21), and Max Azicri, "A Cuban Perspective on the Nicaraguan Revolution" (Chapter 20), in Walker, *Nicaragua in Revolution.*

60. William M. LeoGrande, "Through the Looking Glass: The Kissinger Report on Central America," *World Policy Journal* 1 (Winter 1984):251–284; William M. LeoGrande, "The United States and Nicaragua" (Chapter 21), Theodore Schwab and Harold Sims, "Relations with Communist States" (Chapter 22), Waltraud Queiser Morales and Harry Vanden, "Relations with the Non Aligned Movement" (Chapter 23), Nadia Malley, "Relations with Western Europe and the Socialist International" (Chapter 24), and Max Azicri, "Relations with Latin America" (Chapter 25), all in Walker, ed., *Nicaragua: The First Five Years;* Dennis M. Hanratty, "Mexican Policy Toward Central America and the Caribbean" (Chapter 12), Leiken, "Soviet and Cuban Policy" (Chapter 13), and Wayne S. Smith, "Reagan's Central American Policy: Disaster in the Making" (Chapter 14), all in Schulz and Graham, eds., *Revolution and Counterrevolution;* author's interviews with Sergio Ramírez Mercado, FSLN candidate for vice-president and member of the JGRN, Managua, 2 November 1984; author's interview with Nora Astorga, vice-minister of exterior, Managua, 2 November 1984; and author's interviews with senior U.S. diplomats in Managua, August 1983 and November 1984.

61. Quoted in *EM,* 20 July 1981, p. 21A.

62. See, for example, excerpts from articles, speeches, and reports by Ronald Reagan, U.S. Ambassador to the UN Jeanne Kirkpatrick, and the Bipartisan National Commission on Central America in Falcoff and Royal, eds., *Crisis and Opportunity;* see also *NYT,* 20 July 1984, p. 1.

63. Azicri, "Relations with Latin America"; *NYT:* 24 July 1984, p. 3; 23 September 1984, p. 1; 24 September 1984, p. 1; 28 September 1984, p. 3. For material on the MiG scare of early November 1984, see *NYT:* 8 November 1984, p. 1; 9 November 1984, p. 1; 10 November 1984, pp. 1, 4.

Chapter 11. Across a Frontier of History:
The Revolution and Its Future

1. See, for instance, John A. Booth, "Celebrating the Demise of *Somocismo:* Fifty Spanish Sources on the Nicaraguan Revolution," *Latin American Research Review* 17, No. 1 (1982):173–189, for a discussion of some of this debate.

2. Interview with Carlos Vilas, Atlantic Coast Development Agency, Managua, 29 October 1984.

3. Wheelock Román interview.

4. This and the following quote are from the Ramírez interview.

5. Centro de Investigaciones y Estudios de la Reforma Agraria, *Participatory Democracy in Nicaragua* (Managua: CIERA, 1984), p. 7 and passim.

6. Ibid., p. 7.

7. Ramírez interview; similar views were expressed by Xavier Gorostiaga, director of the Nicaraguan Institute of Social and Economic Research, Managua, 3 November 1984.

8. Wheelock Román interview.

9. Ramírez interview; see also *The Electoral Process in Nicaragua,* pp. 32–34.

10. William M. LeoGrande, *Central America and the Polls,* Special report of the Washington Office on Latin America (Washington, D.C., May 1984), Tables 21, 31, 32.

11. *NYT,* 14 November 1984, p. 7.

12. *The Electoral Process in Nicaragua,* pp. 28–32.

13. Quote from the *Christian Science Monitor,* 15 November 1984, p. 40.

14. Ibid., p. 1; see also *NYT:* 14 November 1984, p. 6; 12 November 1984, p. 1; *Washington Report on the Hemisphere,* 27 November 1984, p. 3.

15. *Wall Street Journal,* 15 November 1984, p. 34.

16. *BI,* 8 November 1984, p. 3.

17. *Christian Science Monitor,* 15 November 1984, p. 40.

18. Ibid.

Abbreviations

ACLEN	National Association of Clergy
AES	Secondary Students' Association
AID	Agency for International Development
AMNLAE	Luisa Amanda Espinosa Nicaraguan Women's Association
AMPRONAC	Association of Women Confronting National Problems
ANC	Conservative National Action
ANDEN	National Association of Educators of Nicaragua
APP	People's Property Area
ARDE	Revolutionary Democratic Alliance
ASTC	Sandinista Cultural Workers' Association
ATC	Association of Rural Workers
BAN-AMERICA	Banco de América
BANIC	Banco Nicaragüense
BECAT	Special Antiterrorist Activity Brigade
CACM	Central American Common Market
CADIN	Nicaraguan Chamber of Industries
CAUS	Center for Union Action and Unity
CCCN	Confederation of Chambers of Commerce
CD	Democratic Coordinating Committee
CDCA	Central American Democratic Community
CDS	Sandinista Defense Committee
CE	Council of State
CEB	Christian base community
CEPA	Evangelistic Committee for Agrarian Promotion
CEPAD	Christian Committee for the Promotion of Development
CGT	General Confederation of Workers
CGTI	Independent General Workers' Confederation
CIA	Central Intelligence Agency

CNC	Nicaraguan Chamber of Construction
CNES	National Council of Higher Education
COIP	People's Industrial Corporation
CONDECA	Central American Defense Council
COSEP	Superior Council of Private Enterprise
COSIP	Superior Council of Private Initiative
CSE	Supreme Electoral Council
CSN	Nicaraguan Trade Union Coordinating Committee
CST	Sandinista Workers' Central
CTN	Nicaraguan Workers' Confederation
CUS	Council for Union Unity
DIGE	Department of Government Information and Promotion
DN	Joint National Directorate (FSLN)
EAP	economically active population
EDU-CREDITO	Educational Credit Program
EEBI	Basic Infantry Training School
ENABAS	Nicaraguan Basic Food Enterprise
EPS	Sandinista Popular Army
FAD	Democratic Action Front
FAN	National Air Force
FAO	Broad Opposition Front
FARN	Nicaraguan Revolutionary Armed Forces
FDC	Christian Democratic Front
FDN	Nicaraguan Democratic Forces
FER	Student Revolutionary Front
FETSALUD	Federation of Health Workers
FJD	Democratic Youth Front
FMLN	Farabundo Marti National Liberation Front (El Salvador)
FMN	Federation of Nicaraguan Teachers
FPN	National Patriotic Front
FRS	Sandinista Revolutionary Front
FSLN	Sandinista National Liberation Front
FUNDE	Nicaraguan Development Foundation
GNP	gross national product
GPP	Prolonged People's War
IACHR	Inter-American Commission on Human Rights
IAPA	Inter-American Press Association
IMF	International Monetary Fund
INCAE	Central American Business Administration Institute

INDE	Nicaraguan Development Institute
INFONAC	National Development Institute
INRA	National Agrarian Reform Institute
INVI	National Housing Institute
JDC	Christian Democratic Youth
JGRN	Governing Junta of National Reconstruction
JPN	Nicaraguan Patriotic Youth
JRN	Nicaraguan Revolutionary Youth
JSN	Nicaraguan Sandinista Youth
JS-19	July 19th Sandinista Youth
LANICA	Líneas Aéras de Nicaragua
MAP-ML	Marxist-Leninist Popular Action Movement
MDN	Nicaraguan Democratic Movement
MEC-CELADEC	Ecumenical Axis
MICOIN	Ministry of Internal Commerce
MIDINRA	Ministry of Agricultural Development and Agrarian Reform
MILPAS	Popular Anti-Somocista Militia
MISURA	Miskitu, Sumu, Rama organization
MISURA-SATA	Unity of the Miskitu, Sumu, Rama, and Sandinistas
MOSAN	Nicaraguan Autonomous Union Movement
MPDC	Popular Christian Democratic Movement
MPU	United People's Movement
OAS	Organization of American States
ORIT	Interamerican Regional Workers' Organization
OSN	Office of National Security
PC	Communist party of Nicaragua
PCD	Democratic Conservative party
PLC	Constitutionalist Liberal party
PLI	Independent Liberal Party
PLN	Liberal Nationalist party
PPSC	People's Social Christian party
PS	Sandinista Police
PSCN	Nicaraguan Social Christian party
PSD	Social Democratic party
PSN	Nicaraguan Socialist party
PTN	Nicaraguan Worker party
RD	relative deprivation
UCA	Central American University
UDEL	Democratic Liberation Union
UNAG	National Union of Farmers and Cattlemen

UNAN	National Autonomous University of Nicaragua
UNAP	National Union of Popular Action
UNE	National Employees Union
UNO	National Opposition Union
UPANIC	Union of Nicaraguan Agricultural Producers
UPN	Nicaraguan Journalists' Union

Index

Abortion, 238
Accessory Transit Company
    (U.S.), 14(fig.), 18, 19, 20
Acción Nacional Conservadora.
    See Conservative National
    Action
ACLEN. *See* National Association
    of Clergy
Aeronica airline, 283
AES. *See* Secondary Students'
    Association
Afghanistan, 265
AFL-CIO (American Federation of
    Labor and Congress of
    Industrial Organizations), 122
African palm, 249
Aggression, 5, 6
Agrarian Institute, 88
Agrarian reform, 241–245, 269
Agrarian Reform Law (1984), 243
Agrarian squatters, 64
Agricultural Development,
    Ministry of, 188, 189(table),
    199, 222(table), 241
Agricultural Development and
    Agrarian Reform, Ministry of
    (MIDINRA), 242, 243–244,
    245
Agricultural proletariat, 64, 66,
    114, 119
Agricultural regions, 117–121
Aguado, Enoc, 99, 100, 105
Agüero, Fernando, 75, 76–77, 83,
    89, 90, 99, 100, 107

Agüero-Somoza pact (1971), 111
AID. *See* United States, Agency
    for International Development
Algeria. *See under* Nicaragua
Alineados, 191
Alliance for Progress (1962), 75,
    78, 81, 88, 101, 110
Altamirano, Marcos, 139
American Declaration of the
    Rights and Duties of Man
    (1948), 93
Amnesty International, 94, 120,
    227
AMNLAE. *See* Luisa Amanda
    Espinosa Nicaraguan
    Women's Association
Amparo, 195, 196
AMPRONAC. *See* Association of
    Women Confronting National
    Problems
ANC. *See* Conservative National
    Action
Andean Group (1969), 132, 172,
    182
ANDEN. *See* National
    Association of Educators of
    Nicaragua
Anduray, Plutarcho, 189(table)
Añil. See Dyes
Anti-Sandinista guerrillas. *See*
    Sandinista National
    Liberation Front, opposition
    to
APP. *See* People's Property Area

Deneken Die, Alfonso, 142
Dennis, Lawrence, 38, 39
Denver, U.S.S., 39
Depistolization campaign, 226
D'Escoto Brockman, Miguel, 136,
179, 189(table), 212, 222(table)
Díaz, Adolfo, 31, 32, 34, 39, 40,
41
Díaz, Mauricio, 222(table)
Díaz y Sotelo, Manuel, 106
DIGE. *See* Government
Information and Promotion,
Department of
Dirección General de Sanidad.
See Nicaragua, National
Health Service
Directorio Nacional Conjunto. *See*
Joint National Directorate
Diriamba (Nicaragua) uprising
(1978), 161
DN. *See* Joint National
Directorate
"Doce, los." *See* Group of Twelve
Domestic Commerce, Ministry of,
222(table)
Dominican Republic, 167. *See
also* United States, and
Dominican Republic
Dos. *See* Téllez, Dora María
Dreyfus, Enrique, 102
Dyes, 15, 20

EAP. *See* Economically active
population
Earthquake. *See* Managua,
earthquake
Economically active poulation
(EAP), 237
Economic liberalism, 11–12, 21,
98, 105
Ecuador, 132, 172
Ecumenical Axis, 192, 193(table)
Education, Ministry of, 189(table),
222(table), 232
Educational Credit Program
(EDUCREDITO), 102

EDUCREDITO. *See* Educational
Credit Program
EEBI. *See* Basic Infantry Training
School
Eisenhower, Dwight D., 59
Ejército Defensor de la Soberania
Nacional de Nicaragua. *See*
Army for the Defense of
Nicaraguan National
Sovereignty
Ejército Popular Sandinista. *See*
Sandinista Popular Army
Ejido lands, 20
El Chaparral (Nicaragua), 138–139
El Chipote, 44
Election (1984), 215–223, 279
Electoral Law (1984), 195, 215,
216, 231
Elites. *See* Nicaragua, politico-
economic elite; Nicaragua,
socioeconomic elite; Political
elite
El Naranjo (Nicaragua), 176
El Salvador, 13, 15, 22, 59, 76,
86–87(table), 289. *See also*
Nicaragua, and El Salvador;
United States, and El
Salvador
ENABAS. *See* Nicaraguan Basic
Food Enterprise
EPS. *See* Sandinista Popular
Army
Escuela de Entrenamiento Básico
de Infantéria. *See* Basic
Infantry Training School
Espino Negro Pact (1927), 41, 42
Estelí (Nicaragua), 117(fig.), 119,
125, 135, 145, 148, 149(fig.),
165, 166, 170, 173, 174,
175(fig.)
Estrada, Juan, 30, 31, 51
Ethiopia, 198, 212
Evangelistic Committee for
Agrarian Promotion (CEPA),
118, 119, 135, 136

income, 69, 78, 79(table), 80,
83, 85, 258–259. *See also*
Wages
independence (1823), 9, 12
industrialization, 78, 80, 81, 82,
88, 275, 285. *See also*
Industry
industrial proletariat, 64, 69, 84
infant and child mortality, 85,
86–87(table)
inflation, 79–80, 83, 122, 141,
170, 241, 252
infrastructure, 20, 22, 58, 68,
78, 88, 250
and Iran, 248
and Israel, 127, 169
and Japan, 30, 35, 82, 247,
248(table)
junta (1972–1974), 100. *See also*
Governing Junta of National
Reconstruction
labor draft, 22, 23
labor unions, 23, 65, 78, 84,
104, 107, 113–114, 121–124,
126, 155, 161, 259, 277. *See
also* Sandinista National
Liberation Front, and unions
language, 19
Liberals, 9, 11, 12–13, 14, 17,
18, 19, 20, 21–22, 24, 25, 26,
30, 31, 32, 37, 38, 44, 45, 50,
52, 59, 62, 67, 80, 100–101,
111, 115, 124. *See also*
Independent Liberal party;
Liberal Nationalist party;
National Liberty Party
Liberals uprisings (1926), 38–40
life expectancy, 85, 86–87(table)
maps, 14, 117, 150, 175
and Mexico, 39, 132–133, 172,
182, 247, 248(table), 254, 265,
267, 274
militarism, 9
Military Academy, 56, 58, 92
murder rate, 85
National Guard, 37, 38, 39, 40,
43, 44, 45, 46, 48, 50, 69, 71,

75, 89, 91–93, 102, 105, 110,
111, 112, 119, 125, 126, 129,
135, 153, 160–161, 166, 168,
171, 180, 181, 182, 275
National Health Service, 55
navy, 55, 58
1912 insurrections, 31–32
and OAS, 76, 131, 132, 133,
137, 154, 167, 168, 169, 172,
179
and outside interference, 9, 15,
17, 25–26, 132, 266–269
Pacific region, 234
and Panama, 132, 265, 267, 274
and Paraguay, 266
petty bourgeoisie, 114
political factionalism, 8–9,
14–15, 17–19, 22, 24, 25, 31,
38–40, 62, 83, 90
politico-economic elite, 9, 22,
24, 52
population, 13, 14, 22, 36, 69,
82, 83, 258
and Portugal, 127
poverty, 78, 85
Price and Commerce Control
Board, 59
race, 13. *See also* Creoles;
Indians; Ladinos
rail and steamship lines, 33
rebellion (1881), 21
recession, 63, 65, 78, 83
reform, 22, 78, 84, 102, 110
refugees, 183
revolution. *See* Nicaraguan
revolution
rural labor, 21, 64, 66, 84,
117–121
social indicators, 86–87(table)
socioeconomic elite, 9, 24, 25,
37, 62, 64, 66, 69, 78, 98,
141
and Soviet Union, 114, 121,
247, 263, 265, 279
and Spain, 127
as Spanish colony, 9, 11–13